PORTRAIT OF A FLYING LADY

THE STORIES OF THOSE
SHE FLEW WITH IN BATTLE

by George H. Menzel

TURNER PUBLISHING COMPANY

B-17G, Serial Number 44-6508 nicknamed "Maiden U.S.A." painted by R.G. Smith. The painting is one of four by Mr. Smith called the "Silver Wings Collection" commissioned by the MPB Corporation of Keene, New Hampshire. The original is displayed at the Air Force Museum at the Wright-Patterson Air Force Base in Ohio. Courtesy of the MPB Corporation.

TURNER PUBLISHING COMPANY

Author: George H. Menzel
Cover Design: James Asher

Library of Congress
Catalog Card No. 94-60145
ISBN: 978-1-68162-352-8

Limited Edition

Front Endsheet: "Purple Heart Corner" by A. Ric Druet

Rear Endsheet: 613th Squadron at "Bombs Away"

TABLE OF CONTENTS

DEDICATION

To my comrades of the 401st Bombardment Group (H)
who, by their deeds, wrote this book; and to my wife
Joyce, without whom the story would not have been told.

LIST OF ILLUSTRATIONS AND PHOTOGRAPHS

ACKNOWLEDGEMENTS

George H. Menzel — 1993

I am greatly indebted to so many who have contributed to this book, those who guided me in the right direction and the many others who kindly expressed their interest and provided me the motivation I needed. All of these have made the labors of the last three years a joy. I sincerely hope that in recognition of the following I have not neglected anyone; if so, such an oversight is regretted. Naturally, I am indebted to R.G. Smith for his painting of "Maiden U.S.A." which provided me with the inspiration for this story. My wife Joyce was a most patient and understanding counsel; she also pitched in to help review musty old records and files at the USAF Historical Research Center and at the National Archives. Norm Sisson provided much of his own memorabilia as did his bombardier, Nathan Picker. Their records helped to piece together their love for the "Maiden." Myron King overcame his initial reluctance to tell the story of his unfortunate experiences and his own records speak for his courage and patriotism.

There are so many others who by their letters, their very old newspaper clippings and their memories contributed greatly and provided me the material to tell a story aside from the rather bland historical facts on which that story is based. They include: Frederick H. Babcock, Allen H. Crawford, Ralph W. Trout, Brig. Gen. Harold W. Bowman USAF (Ret), Brig. Gen. William T. Seawell USAF (Ret), Lt. Gen. Bryan M. Shotts USAF (Ret), Roger A. Freeman, Col. Harold M. Kennard USAF (Ret), Col. I. Wayne Eveland USAFR (Ret), Donald V. Kirkhuff, Alvah H. Chapman, Jr., Dr. Peter J. Carter, Edward H. Daves, Charles W. Utter, Stephen A. Zaborsky, John Hope, John F. Collins, Jack Healy, Paul M. Andrews, Brig. Gen. Jack Pink USA (Ret), C. Richard Rostrom, Col. Leslie E. Gaskins USAF (Ret), Theodore F. Klefisch, Arthur R. Seder, Jr., Harry L. Thompson, Sherman Oatman, Richard Mettlen, John Seider, William F. Schiefer, Dr. David H. Stauffer, Robert M. Stehman, Edwin R. Cranz, Russell Aufrance, Dr. William J. Sweeney III, Richard I. Lowe, Philip A. Reinoehl, K. Hampton Speelman, George E. Atkinson, Frank G. Mendez, Mrs. Rosemary DeVito, Carolyn C. (Mrs. Vincent) Browne, Robert L. Stelzer, Donald S. Anderson, V.R. "Ron" Sismey, Graham D. Bratley, Ray

Corby, Leon Dolin, Mary B. Dennis, Deputy Clerk of Court, U.S. Army Legal Services Agency, Captain George W. Cully, USAF Historical Research Center, Gen. Bryce Poe III USAF (Ret), Major John F. Kreis USAF (Ret), John R. Althoff, Elliott F. Cameron, Robert L. Davidson, Dr. Ward J. Fellows, Chester H. Smith, Miriam Fox, Virgil F. Thompson, Edward G. Dana, Kenneth D. Schlessinger and Richard L. Boylan, National Archives.

I am grateful to Melissa Keiser, Dan Hagedorn and Tim Cronin of the National Air and Space Museum and David Burgervin of the Smithsonian Institute for their assistance. I am appreciative for the permission of A. Ric Druet which made possible the reproduction of his painting "Purple Heart Corner" and the help and appreciation of Bob Chartier and Tom Rudziensky of the MPB Corporation which permitted the reproduction of R. G. Smith's painting of the "Maiden U.S.A."

Also, I appreciate the advice of my former colleagues at Armstrong State College, Dean William L. Megathlin, Dr. Robert Magnus, and Professor Byung Moo Lee. Col. Francis E. Rundell USAF (Ret) contributed materially to two chapters and lent his 30 years of Air Force expertise in reviewing the entire manuscript. His wife, Nancy T. Rundell, an author, former newspaper reporter and editor deserves my special appreciation; she took on what she thought was a "polishing job" on the manuscript and ended up redrafting it. I consider her efforts praiseworthy.

Lastly, I would be remiss if I didn't thank Dave Turner, my Publisher, for his blind faith in my story and Pamela Wood, my Editor, for putting it together for me.

George H. Menzel, Savannah, GA
June, 1993

PREFACE

George H. Menzel — 1945

Have you ever been so fascinated by something that you couldn't put it aside, no matter how hard you tried, until curiosity was satisfied?

Such was the reason for the quest I undertook in 1986 which led down a crooked path with many surprising turns along the way to the story behind a painting of a particular World War II B-17 Flying Fortress. The story of necessity evolved to include the tales of the crews that flew her in battle and comrades who shared her combat missions in other B-17s.

The painting, which so fascinated me, was painted by R.G. Smith, one of the world's masters of aviation art. The original of that painting, with three others which made up Mr. Smith's series called the "Silver Wings Collection" is prominently displayed at the Air Force Museum at the Wright- Patterson Air Force Base in Dayton, Ohio. The MPB Corporation of Keene, New Hampshire commissioned these paintings and was responsible for prints which were made from them.

My curiosity concerning this painting relates to my personal involvement and love affair with the B-17 which carried me to battle over Europe and brought me back safely 35 times.

My own war began when I left my home near Baltimore, Maryland on my nineteenth birthday, interrupting my college education, to begin my training in the U.S. Army Aviation Cadet Program. Almost 18 months later I won my Silver Wings as a bombardier and my Gold Bar as a second lieutenant; I was finally on my way.

My crew, led by our pilot Fred Babcock of Michigan, picked up a brand new B-17 at Hunter Army Air Field in Savannah, Georgia and we flew to the United Kingdom (UK) by way of New Hampshire, Labrador and Iceland arriving in Wales on October 2, 1944. There we became a part of the 8th Air Force, and after several days we arrived at our new base, officially designated Station 128. The base was the home of the 401st Bombardment Group (H). Located near the English villages of Weldon, Upper Benefield and Deenethorpe, the base took the latter name from its previous occupant, the Royal Air Force (RAF),

Deenethorpe.[1] The 401st became Deenethorpe's new tenant in October 1943, and flew its first combat mission to Bremen, Germany November 25, 1943.[2] In the year prior to the arrival of the Babcock crew the 401st had distinguished itself in battle on more than 150 missions over Europe.

On our arrival at Deenethorpe we were assigned to the 614th Squadron. My combat tour began on October 25, 1944 with a mission to Hamburg, Germany. The great and bloody air battles over Europe with the horrendous losses suffered by the Eighth were mostly behind us, but we too had our moments over targets such as Berlin, Merseburg and others of repute. I finished my combat tour of 35 missions, flying 22 as a bombardier and 13 as a navigator, in five months and six days. VE Day found me in the mid-Atlantic on an Army troop ship on my way home. It was a short war in terms of days but it was packed full with danger but exciting experiences, fond friendships and fabulous memories which have lasted a lifetime. (See Appendix 1)

Like many of my vintage who served our country in war, I was anxious to get out of uniform in the Fall of 1945 after the war abruptly ended following the dropping of atomic bombs on the Japanese cities, Hiroshima and Nagasaki. Like so many others I had a sense of urgency to get on with my life, to catch up after those years spent in the service of my country. In my own experience I raced pell mell to finish college, get married, go to law school, embark on a career in the FBI and raise a family of two lovely daughters. During those very busy years I only infrequently reminisced about those war years and even more infrequently chatted with others about our mutual experiences in the military. We were just too busy. The pressures of life, such as career and family were so great that there was little opportunity, or point then, to look back as the years rushed by.

Now in the twilight of my life the media regularly reports of military veterans getting together for reunions with their wartime buddies. One old friend and fellow warrior once said that as he had grown older he had more time to reflect on his life experiences. I honestly believe that is why these reunions have continually grown in popularity. It reminds me of a "Peanuts" cartoon by Schulz: In the first frame Charlie Brown's friend says "My Grandpa went to his high school's 40th reunion last night". In the second frame he tells Charlie Brown, "He's also been to a college reunion and an Army reunion...." In the final frame he opines, "He has a new career ... He goes back to things." Many of us are like his Grandpa. We also have a new career, and thoroughly enjoy going back to things.

In the early 1970s the late Leon Stewart of Holly Hill, Florida, a member of our crew, let me know that the 401st was having its first reunion at Harlingen, Texas and had formed an association of its World War II members. From that start it has grown and is a viable organization under the watchful eye of its primary founder and "ringmaster," Ralph "Rainbow" Trout of Tampa, Florida. I attended my first reunion in 1978 at St. Louis and each of the biennial reunions since 1984.

In 1986 my wife and I hosted the reunion in Savannah, Georgia, our hometown. We also attended two off-year mini-reunions in England hosted by some very special English friends who treated us royally.

So much for background, for delightful memories and for friendships rekindled. The centerpiece of this saga is the beautiful painting of a B-17; the story begins with how "Rainbow" Trout and the Savannah reunion were responsible for my obsession to learn all I could about the aircraft it depicted.

George H. Menzel, Savannah, Georgia
February, 1993

Notes to Preface
1. Bowman, Harold W. & Selwyn V. Maslen Bowman's Bombers p.4   2. Ibid. p.5

FOREWORD

George Menzel has an investigative mind, as one might expect of a man whose main career was with the FBI and subsequent connections with private security and law enforcement. As he reveals in the following pages, it was the detective in him that would not rest until he had traced the reason for an artist's choice of subject in a print that fascinated. The subject was a B-17 Fortress bomber bearing the markings of the squadron with which, as a young man, George Menzel had served during the trouble with Adolf Hitler and his supporters. One thing led to another and soon the detective discovered that the individual Flying Fortress portrayed by the artist had been involved in a remarkable adventure. And, like all good detectives, George Menzel did not rest until he had gathered and sifted all the evidence; not an easy task after nearly half a century since his **Flying Lady** existed. The resulting dossier reveals international intrigue and political expediency which involved one of the bomber's crews in a somewhat fraught sojourn in the domain of the Soviets. But, in presenting the dossier in book form, the detective turned author has rounded out an account of a unique wartime episode with cover of this B-17s record and its crews' experiences during the day-by-day slogging match with the defences of the Third Reich in missions to destroy war industry. While George Menzel's principal intent is to present the history of one individual aircraft of that long-gone conflict, in so doing he has also given a valuable insight into the life and times of the young men who flew those lengthy, uncomfortable and, above all, dangerous missions with the famous Eighth Air Force.

Roger A. Freeman

*Roger Freeman, a prominent English historian and author, is renowned as the authority on the air war in Europe during World War II. He is the preeminent historian on the Eighth Air Force during that conflict. He authored **The Mighty Eighth** and two companion volumes, **The Mighty Eighth War Diary** and **The Mighty Eighth War Manual** which were essential in the research by the author of this book. He has almost two dozen other books to his credit in his field of expertise and more to come. He makes his home in Essex, England and is sought after as a most entertaining speaker and panel member for seminars by veteran groups of the Mighty Eighth.*

CHAPTER 1 —
THE PICTURE...A LOVELY BIRD

In early 1986 "Rainbow" Trout and his wife Mary Jane visited my wife Joyce and me in Savannah to review our plans for the 401st reunion scheduled for that Fall. During that visit he presented me with a print of an R.G. Smith painting. He said he thought that I would particularly like to have it since the aircraft portrayed was not just one of our 401st B-17s but one from my own 614th Squadron. I remembered that years ago Allen Crawford, one of our crew, had told me about his visit to the Air Force Museum and how surprised he was to see the original of that painting. I had totally forgotten that conversation, had never seen the original or even a print of the painting. I wasn't just thrilled to have it, I was ecstatic!

To appreciate this, one needs to be aware of how the details of the painting so definitely establishes it as a 614th B-17. The B-17 was portrayed so as to provide an unobstructed view of the vertical tail fin and the fuselage to the rear of the wing. The aircraft itself was left in its natural silver finish, those built prior to January 1944 left the manufacturer finished in a rather unattractive olive drab camouflage paint.[1] The most striking feature of the picture is the very prominent large vertical tail fin. It has a very distinctive bright yellow diagonal stripe bordered in black. Superimposed over the stripe at the top of the tail fin is a black triangle and inside that triangle is a large block letter S painted white. Below the triangle and across the diagonal stripe is the serial number of the aircraft, 46508. Below the serial number is a large letter A, painted black. On the fuselage, forward of the tail in the following order are: another large letter A, in black, the blue and white star and bar National symbol and forward of the waist window in black paint the large block letters IW. The letters IW are the code letters for the 614th Squadron and the letter A, the code letter for that particular B-17 of that squadron.

The 8th Air Force by 1944 included three divisions. A triangle on the vertical fin represented the 1st Division and the letter S the 401st Bomb Group. The "Triangle First," as it became known, had under its command four combat wings (CBWs) and a diagonal stripe on the tail fin indicated that aircraft was a part of the 94th CBW. The three groups making up the 94th CBW each had a different color diagonal stripe, the 401st being yellow, and the other two, blue and red.[2] The bottom of the print has the following unobtrusive notation, "Commissioned by the MPB Corporation, manufacturer of precision aircraft bearings." I learned that the company was located in Keene, New Hampshire and I contacted them for information about the painting and its artist.

I have had several conversations with Mr. Bob Chartier, the company Distribution Sales Manager. He said the company has been in business for many years but was not widely known by its corporate name. As a public relations effort to increase public awareness of the MPB name, they began an art program and commissioned R.G. Smith to do a number of aircraft paintings. Four of these are known as the "Silver Wings Collection," were presented to the Air Force Museum by MPB.

He said these four depict four different World War II U.S. Army aircraft: the P-51 Mustang, known with fondness as "little friend" to bomber crews they protected; the C-47 Dakota, a workhorse cargo/transport; the B-25 Mitchell, the medium bomber famous for the bombing of Japan by General James H. Doolittle; and last but not least, the B-17 Flying Fortress.

Mr. Chartier said the company has discontinued its art program. He added that all of the prints of the B-17 had been disposed of and a reprinting is not contemplated by the company. He also said they did not realize that the painting represented a specific aircraft of the 401st. They would therefore not be familiar with the history of that B-17 or the experiences of those who flew her in combat. However, he was instrumental in my being able to locate the artist, R.G. Smith who then resided near Los Angeles at Rolling Hills Estates.

I had several telephone conversations with him and found him to be a likeable person who seems somewhat surprised that he is considered a master of his particular art form. His given name is Robert G. Smith. He signs his works of art R.G. Smith, but he is better known

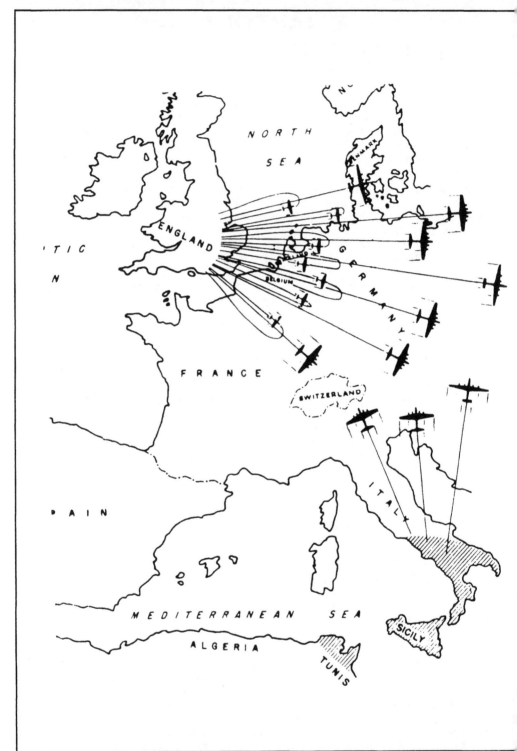

Chart which displays the organization structure of the European Theater of Operations (ETO) with particular detail on the United States Strategic Air Forces (USSTAF) and the Eighth Air Force. Note the 401st Bombardment

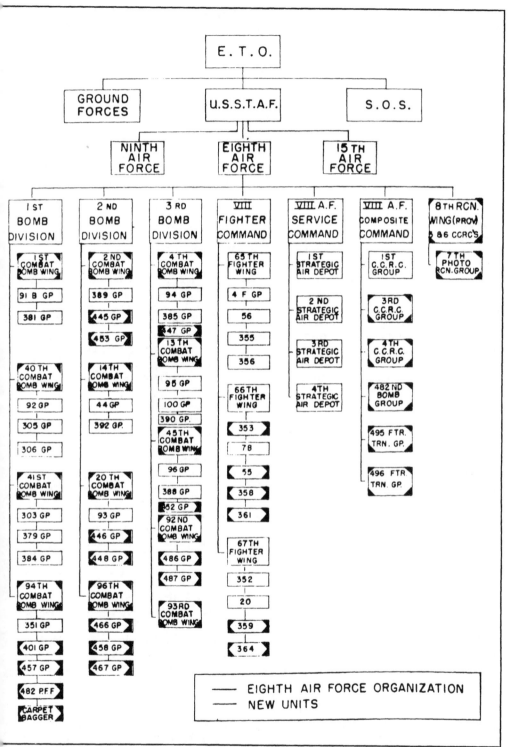

Group (H) is listed in the 94th Combat Bomb Wing (CBW) of the 1st Bomb Division. Source is the Eighth Air Force Tactical Development August 1942 - May 1945. Prepared by Eighth Air Force and AAF Evaluation Board (ETO).

simply as "R.G.". He grew up in Oakland, California where the solo flight of Charles Lindbergh to Europe in 1927 influenced him to become an aircraft designer. In 1934 R.G. graduated from Polytechnic College of Engineering with a degree in aeronautical engineering. Since 1936 he has been associated with the Douglas Aircraft Company, now known as McDonnell Douglas. By 1939 he was working as a configuration engineer in a design room with an aerodynamicist, and from that time on he was involved with the design of every tactical aircraft produced by that company. R.G. describes himself as having worn two hats during those years. He explained that when it was time to present a new aircraft design back in Washington it was important to have a picture of the aircraft to exhibit because people have difficulty visualizing in three dimensions. In the creation of such pictures he became an aviation artist. His success in the latter aspect of his career is obvious from the number of his paintings that appear in the National Air and Space Museum, the Naval Aviation Museum, the Air Force Museum, the Pentagon, Congressional offices, military installations and aerospace industrial facilities.

I asked R.G. how, out of all the 26 B-17 bombardment groups in the 1st and 3rd Air Divisions of the 8th Air Force (the 2nd Air Division flew B-24s), did he happen to choose a 401st aircraft for his model, and of all of the B-17s in the 401st, how did he choose the paint work, serial number and other markings which distinguish 46508 IW-A.

R.G. replied that accuracy is important to an aviation artist because any slight deviation is sure to be recognized and called to his attention by someone. He said that for this reason he referred to the book, *The Mighty Eighth*, by the noted British historian, Roger A. Freeman. In this famous history of the 8th Air Force there are pages devoted to drawings of fighter and bomber aircraft representing every 8th Air Force unit. R.G. said that he studied each of the drawings of B-17 groups and found himself drawn aesthetically to the bright yellow diagonal stripe bordered in black and the black triangle S which appeared on the vertical portion of the tail of the 401st drawing. He said that since Mr. Freeman's book is the recognized authority on the 8th Air Force he merely copied all of that paint work as well as the serial number 46508 and fuselage markings as they appeared in that book.[3]

With an apology to R.G. I have noticed a little artistic license taken by him in his painting of IW-A which I merely mention before one of my comrades takes me to task for my lack of observation and memory. He was not completely steadfast in reproducing the drawing which appears in Mr. Freeman's book since he painted a machine gun protruding from the radio room hatch. This does not appear on the drawing because the gun had been removed from that position in the B-17G which is the model depicted by Freeman's artist. I hope that the above is not taken as criticism in any way of Mr. Smith's painting of IW-A because I love her nonetheless.

The information from R.G. left me with another question: how did Freeman or his artist, John Rabbets, happen to choose the paint work and markings for the drawing that appears in *The Mighty Eighth*? I later learned from Mr. Freeman that he had provided Mr. Rabbets with a photograph of this B-17 which appeared in another of his books titled *The Mighty Eighth War Manual*. He said that he chose the photograph because it was a side view and the paint work and markings were clearly visible.[4]

The words I have thus far used do not make for a word picture which would do justice to the painting done by Mr. Smith. On his canvas R.G. painted a B-17 aloft with a background of layered cumulus clouds above the aircraft and a darkened sky below. It is quite unusual and I believe it illustrates what R.G. said in an interview in the summer 1988 edition of a magazine, *AeroArt:* "The one fault I find with many of today's aviation artists is that they are so conscious of the 'center of interest' that they forget its only a **part** of the total picture. The background is just as important as the subject matter."

Nor did he neglect the subject matter. In the same interview he said, "Some airplanes are basically good-looking in some views and very awkward in others" and the answer is to pick a flattering one if possible.[5] I would describe the painting of IW-A to present what I understand R.G. Smith to mean when he refers to a three-quarter frontal view. I admit to prejudice but I think it to be a flattering view of the B-17. The clouds and the darkened sky cogently enhance the total picture and call attention to the silver fuselage and the bright yellow and black paint work.

It is easy to understand his decision to choose a 401st B-17 as his model. She is a truly lovely bird who once flew with a flock of many with like plumage. The IW-A print elegantly framed graces the wall of my study. During the summer of 1986 I found myself being drawn to it more and more. My imagination began to take hold, and as I daydreamed I began to wonder whether the paint work and markings copied by R.G. from Freeman's book represented an actual B-17 from the 614th Squadron of the 401st Bombardment Group. If so I wondered, what crew or crews flew her in combat? Further, what missions did she fly and what were the experiences of her crews? So began the search founded to satisfy curiosity.

Notes to Chapter 1

1. Freeman, _The Mighty Eighth,_ p. 283
2. Rust, _Eighth Air Force Story,_ p. 58
3. Personal telephone interviews of R.G. Smith, 1990
4. Personal letter from Roger A. Freeman, September 24, 1990
5. _AeroArt_ magazine, Vol. I, No.1, Summer 1988 p. 4-8

CHAPTER 2 — THE SEVENTH GENERATION

The B-17 bloodline began in a hangar at Boeing Field, sired by the aircraft manufacturer of that name, several miles southeast of Seattle, Washington. She made her first public appearance on July 16, 1935 as a prototype of an advanced bomber, a four engine aircraft, and the first of its generation of 13 sisters, acquired by the Army Air Corps. That event in 1935 was covered by press representatives of the *Seattle Daily Times* one of whom wrote, "Ropes kept a throng of spectators from closely inspecting the 15-ton flying fortress, which made its first public appearance yesterday afternoon when it was rolled out of its hangar and its motors tested." With those words a legend was born.[1]

The Army Air Corps designated her the B-17; the B for bomber and the number 17 which identified her as the seventeenth bomber design to have been accepted by the Corps. The next generation, the B-17B, was the first production model with 39 such aircraft produced, beginning shortly after the war in Europe began in 1939.[2] It is interesting to note that the 1935 model which gave the B-17 the name "Fortress" had only five machine guns, all of which were hand-held; in other words there were no power turrets. This generation was followed by the B-17C and 20 of the 38 built went to the British. This model was followed by 42 of the B-17D. Among the many modifications made to the C and D models was an increase in the armament to provide six .50 caliber and one .30 caliber machine guns. The increase in fire power was without question influenced by the British war experience with the B-17C which they determined not only lacked adequate armament but was otherwise unable to defend against Luftwaffe attacks. The B-17E was virtually a new bird in appearance, as well as in its ability to defend itself through a notable increase in fire power. First, her new appearance made her a direct ancestor of the B-17G painted by R.G. Smith. She had a much enlarged tail assembly, but it was the vertical fin that made her look so different. The vertical fin, in addition to being much larger, swept forward on the top of the fuselage to mid-ship, ending about even with the trailing edge of the wing. It was this prominent vertical fin which resulted in another appellation for this and subsequent models of the B-17. Airmen, with affection, often referred to her as the "Big Ass Bird."[3]

The large tail assembly also improved on the aircraft's performance at high altitude and her ability to resist attack by providing room for a tail gun position. Further, there were added two power turrets: one on the top of the fuselage just to the rear of the flight deck, and a ball turret on the underside of the fuselage to the rear of the radio room. Both of these turrets, combined with the tail guns and enlarged waist gun windows on each side, provided the B-17 with a much broadened field of fire in its own defense. Lastly, the armament was increased to enhance the fire power providing a total of 10 machine guns: two in the tail, two in the waist positions, two in each of the two turrets, one in the radio room which was .50 caliber, and one .30 caliber machine gun in the nose.[4]

In May 1942 the B-17F began rolling off the line not just at Boeing but at Douglas, in Tulsa, Oklahoma and Lockheed-Vega in Burbank, California. Very minor changes were made in the exterior appearance of the new bird with most of the modifications directed to improving her performance aloft. The B-17F was able to operate at 25,000 feet, but she was no longer immune from fighter attack and anti-aircraft fire as she was when the first generation took to the air in the 1930s.[5] There had been 512 B-17E models produced and more than 3,000 of the B-17F version with war making an impact on production. The B-17F was the model that became the major heavy bombardment vehicle for the 8th Air Force from late 1942 into 1944.[6]

Even as she distinguished herself in battle, a seventh generation of the B-17 was on the way. The notable change was the addition of a remote controlled power turret with two more .50 caliber guns under the bombardier's feet, a "chin" turret made by Bendix. There were 8,680 of them, one of which was R.G. Smith's model.[7]

The B-17G weighed in at 36,135 pounds, over three tons more than the prototype model in 1935. Her normal fuel capacity was 2,810 gallons, her range with a bomb load of 5,000 pounds was 2,000 miles. She had four Wright Cyclone engines which provided a total of 4,000 horsepower for take-off and a maximum speed of 287 miles per hour at operating altitude. Her maximum service ceiling of 35,000 feet remained her biggest asset. No other comparable heavy bomber of that time could come close to that.[8]

Notes to Chapter 2

1. Freeman, Roger A., B-17 Fortress at War   p. 8
2. Freeman, Roger A., B-17 Flying Fortress in World War II   p.5
3. Freeman, see 1 above p. 32
4. Ibid.
5. Ibid. p. 33
6. Freeman, see 2 above p. 5
7. Ibid.
8. Ibid. p. 44

CHAPTER 3 —
"VIC MASLEN - THE HISTORIAN"

The story of this B-17 could not have been told had it not been for Selwyn "Vic" Maslen. Vic resided at Corby, England, just west of our base at Deenethorpe. He compiled an overall book on the history of the 401st Bomb Group, a separate one on each of its four squadrons and other volumes on topics, all related to the 401st.

Four of these books were of great value in providing factual information for this story; they were: (1) *Bowman'sBombers*, (2) *614th Bombardment Squadron (H) - Squadron History*, (3) *614th Squadron: Crews - Missions - Aircraft*, and (4) *401st B.G.(H) Casualties in W.W.II*. The first and fourth of these works Vic coauthored with Brigadier General Harold W. Bowman, USAF Retired, the 401st Commanding Officer who took the Group to England and led it to greatness. The other volumes, all of which have provided many veterans of the 401st with satisfaction, were written by Vic himself. The four volumes mentioned were within my reach, on my own shelves, and provided me with the basis for this story. Most important, they answered my most pressing question - was the B-17 portrayed in the painting an authentic aircraft of the 401st Bomb Group's 614th Squadron? Not only did those volumes provide an affirmative answer, they also contain a significant number of other references to that lovely bird.

In addition Vic, by personal letter, provided me with the following data concerning the main subject of this story: her full serial number was 44-6508; the first two digits reveal that she was produced under a government contract for 1944. That number was abbreviated, for convenience, dropping the first digit and carried on her tail as 46508. Later that serial number was further shortened for operational purposes to 6508 or 508, particularly when used with her squadron letters IW-A, such as on mission formation and loading lists. Vic also determined that this lady was built by the Douglas Aircraft Company which gave birth to 2395 B-17s.

As a replacement aircraft this B-17 was delivered from the United States to Deenethorpe on September 23, 1944 and assigned to the 614th Squadron.[1] Vic's volumes reveal much more. She was the fourth in a line of distinguished B-17s which were to bear the 614th code letters IW-A.

The first was "Flak Rat," 42-37770, which went down south of Bordeaux on December 31, 1943 with the crew of Lt. Homer E. McDanal, along with Major Wayne Eveland, the 614th Squadron Commander. Major Eveland, McDanal, Lt. D.H. Goetsch, the bombardier, and S/Sgt. J.L. Kirker, the radio operator, all evaded capture and walked out over the Pyrenees into Spain, eventually returning to Deenethorpe. Unfortunately, S/Sgt. D.L. Jerue, the engineer, and Sgt. H.W. Sanders, a waist gunner, were killed in action (KIA). The others became prisoners of war (POWs).[2]

Next with the code letters IW-A was "Flak Rat II," 42-97440. That aircraft, with the crew of Lt. C.L. Wilson on a mission to Oschersleben on May 30, 1944 was shot down near the target by German FW 190s. The waist gunners; S/Sgts. J.F. McMahon and G.R. Smith were KIA and the rest were POWs.[3]

The third IW-A was "Rosie's Sweat Box" which crashed on take-off at Deenethorpe on September 17, 1944, killing the entire crew of Lt. F.E. Cook, on what was to have been their second combat mission. Vic quoted from 401st microfilm as follows: "The aircraft failed to clear the hedge at the end of the main east-west runway and crashed onto the main Weldon to Oundle road. The explosion was instant – and devastating – as was to be expected with 6,000 pounds of fragmentation bombs and 2,400 gallons of aviation fuel. It seemed miraculous to those who rushed to the scene to find someone still alive, sitting by the side of the road. Sadly, he proved to be fatally injured, and died later that day. This was the tail gunner, Cpl. W.J. Ambrogetti, who was buried at the American Cemetery at Maddingley, Cambridge."[4]

The fourth IW-A, the model for R. G. Smith's painting, began her operational life with a mission to Cologne, Germany on September 27, 1944. Her pilot on that occasion was Lt.

The second memorial to the 401st dedicated at Deenethorpe September 16, 1989; the wreaths are in memory of Selwyn "Vic" Maslen. Photograph courtesy of Ralph W. Trout.

Norman L. Sisson. Sisson's crew rightly claims that aircraft as their own since they flew her on 19 of her 35 combat missions.[5] His crew gave her the nickname "Maiden U.S.A."; and I consider it a fitting name for such a lovely lady bird.[6]

Vic Maslen's volume on the history of the 614th Squadron made it possible to put together the "Maiden's" mission record including the identity of the crews who manned her on each of her missions over Europe. I am grateful to the members of those crews and the many others who flew with her in battle for their assistance in this effort. It is their story! To do special honor to the crews that actually took the "Maiden" to war I will list them here:

- ✈ N.L. Sisson and crew
- ✈ H.J. Ochsenhirt and crew
- ✈ A.R. Seder and crew
- ✈ G.H. St. Aubyn and crew
- ✈ R.B. Richardson and crew
- ✈ P.F. Wittman and crew

- ✈ J.E. Fondren and crew
- ✈ M.L. King and crew
- ✈ W.K. White and crew
- ✈ K.J. Hartsock and crew
- ✈ W.L. Morton and crew

I was saddened when I learned of Vic's terminal illness shortly before he passed away on October 2, 1991. He had been a continuing source of valued assistance to me, and it was particularly distressing that I had not told him that this chapter was dedicated to his work and to his friendship that did honor to all who served as members of the 401st Bombardment Group.

Over the years Vic was also responsible for the association with others who had an interest in the 8th Air Force, and in particular, an interest in our Bomb Group. Two of such organizations deserve to be mentioned here: The 401st Historical Society and The Friends of the 401st. Members of our 401st Bombardment Group (H) Association have come to know these organizations well. In addition to Vic other members are: V.R. "Ron" Sismey, Graham Bratley and Ray Corby. This unique quartet of Englishmen came to be fondly known to us all as "The Four Aces."

Under Vic's leadership they have welcomed hundreds of our comrades who have returned to their neighborhood to remember those days between 1943 and 1945. They hosted two "mini reunions" in 1983 and 1989. In 1983 we attended the dedication of a stained glass window from the 401st Chapel in the Church of St. Mary the Virgin at Weldon and in 1989 the dedication of the memorial monument within sight of the crumbling Flying Control Tower on what had been our airdrome. Both were magnificently organized and well directed events that those who attended will never forget. Over those same years these Englishmen have attended many of our biennial reunions in the United States where they are always honored guests.

At Vic Maslen's funeral service at the church in Weldon Ron Sismey delivered the eulogy. He said that he and Vic had been friends for some 25 years having met through their mutual employment at the steelworks at Corby. He said they began their research of the 401st Bombardment Group in 1971 as the result of a fortuitous contact they had with the late Joe Cromer and his former co-pilot, Ralph "Rainbow" Trout.[7]

Vic's interest in the history of the 401st led to other areas of research. Most prominently was his work with Alan Crouchman, the spade work for Roger A. Freeman's book, *The Mighty Eighth War Diary*, published in 1981. Freeman, the preeminent historian of the 8th Air Force, said, "The daily statistics required a prodigious research effort, and the basic work of putting this into acceptable form was the contribution of these two persons, requiring very many hours of toil on this formidable undertaking." That book was another valued source to me.[8]

At Vic's funeral service Ron also said his devotion to history is such that "no other Group of that era has had such a detailed record published as the 401st." He also provided an insight into the other historical interests of this scholar who was our good friend. Vic Maslen has published material on church brass rubbing and translation of early church records from old English.[9]

Through the tireless labor of Vic Maslen we have a written history of the 401st Bombardment Group (H) which is a testament to what we stood for. In addition, his leadership of our other English friends, their hospitality and their never flagging dedication to the 401st have been a source of strength to our own organization. We miss him so very much!

Notes to Chapter 3

1. Bowman, Harold W. & Selwyn V. Maslen Bowman's Bombers p. 141
2. Bowman, Harold W. & Selwyn V. Maslen 401st B.G. Casualties in WW II p. 5
3. Ibid. p. 34
4. Ibid. p. 53
5. Maslen, Selwyn V. 614th Squadron: Crews - Missions - Aircraft p. 78
6. Bowman & Maslen, see 1 above p. 142
7. Sismey, Ron "A Tribute To Vic Maslen", Poop From Group, December 1991, The 401st Bombardment Group (H) Association. Inc.
8. Freeman, Roger A. The Mighty Eighth War Diary, Acknowledgments
9. See 7 above.

CHAPTER 4 —
BOWMAN'S BOMBERS

When the "Maiden" flew into Deenethorpe on September 23, 1944 she found herself in not just excellent company but surrounded by the finest of American youth, all male. What more could a lady wish for?

How those young men happened to be there is now a part of military aviation history. Much of that story was not then known to most of those who served, in whatever capacity. In retrospect, that history and the part played by the 401st Bomb Group is part of the "Maiden's" story.

In 1940 the Army's Air Corps was reorganized with General Henry H. Arnold as its chief. The reorganization permitted a degree of autonomy which had until then been stifled. After this reorganization a group of young officers drew up a plan called AWPD-1 which stood for Air War Plans Division-1. This plan forecast the strategy and requirements for a successfully waged war against Germany and Japan months before war became a reality to the American people. It has been said that "AWPD-1 became a book of air prophecy."[1] One of this group of planners, then a Major, was Haywood S. Hansell, known as "Possum" because of his "scoop nose and wily mind."[2] Hansell, after a distinguished career retired as a Major General to his native Georgia. For some years prior to his death he resided at Hilton Head, South Carolina. I knew him briefly and found him to be a most interesting person, quite humble, and above all a real gentleman.

When operation TORCH (the invasion of North Africa) was being planned General Eisenhower picked Hansell to be his air planner for TORCH and operations out of the UK. It has been said that these concerns made the objectives of AWPD-1 obsolete.[3] The result was AWPD-42 which turned out to be a reaffirmation of AWPD-1 reflecting the "Europe first" priority adopted formally in March, 1941.[4]

AWPD-42 was not a complex concept; rather it was a practical plan for a country that found itself not ready for a war in progress. The priority for fighting Germany and Italy first over Japan was a practical decision. It was obvious at the time that strong offensives in both theaters could not be mounted because we lacked the resources, both material and personnel. The choice of placing priority on the enemies in Europe was based on the fact that a fight could be initiated in the immediate future from an allied base of operations in England. An all out war in the Pacific, on the other hand, would require time to amass material and to train thousands of troops, not to mention the numerous invasions necessary to provide bases from which to operate.

The plan proposed the fight in Europe would begin with an aerial war from England as the allies prepared for the cross-channel invasion of the European continent itself. The aerial war from England envisioned by AWPD-42 had as its objective the destruction of the German war machine, and most particularly the destruction of that nation's industrial means to wage war.[5] AWPD-42 established 177 specific military targets, both military and industrial, all of which were within seven categories chosen to bring about the stated objective of the plan. These categories, listed in the order of their importance to the success of AWPD-42, were:

1. German aircraft plants
2. Submarine yards
3. Transportation facilities
4. Electric power

5. Oil
6. Aluminum
7. Rubber

AWPD-42 also dealt with the air power the USAAF would require to carry out its mission. In doing so the plan called for unheard of production of aircraft beginning with that year, 1942. The United States Navy opposed the plan in its entirety, not just because of the emphasis given to the war in Europe but also because the plan would deprive the Navy of aircraft it needed in other theaters of the war. The War Department approved the plan and it was adopted by President Roosevelt. However, the timetable would have to be stretched because the President ordered the aircraft production requirements downward to be within the reach of the nation's industrial capacity to deliver on schedule. [7]

The 8th Air Force was born on January 28, 1942 at Savannah, Georgia. It was headquartered in an Army National Guard Armory at 1108 Bull Street which is now the home of Post 135 of the American Legion. The creation of the 8th Air Force involved several interesting historical facts and quick changes of direction for the newly activated organization.

Shortly after the United States entered the war President Roosevelt and Prime Minister Winston Churchill met for a series of conferences in Washington, D.C. between December 23, 1941 and January 14, 1942. These meetings became known as the ARCADIA Conference. The purpose of the ARCADIA Conference was to establish priorities and to set a plan for carrying out the war. One of the key decisions was to adopt the "Europe first" philosophy. Appropriate to this decision was another to move an American air force to England as soon as possible. Also included was the plan to invade North Africa under an operational code name of SUPER GYMNAST, later to be referred to as GYMNAST. Originally, a 5th Air Force was conceived for the purpose of providing the necessary air power for GYMNAST, but this was soon changed and the 8th Air Force was created for that purpose. Five weeks later this new outfit was without a mission when GYMNAST was relegated to a "study." They didn't have to wait very long for a new assignment because on April 8, 1942 it was selected to be the American Air Force to be rushed to England.[8]

In February, 1942 a small group of USAAF officers arrived in England as a forerunner of the Air Force which was to come. The head of this group was Major General Ira C. Eaker who would become the commander of the VIII Bomber Command and later the 8th Air Force.[9] Meanwhile, the 8th began to assemble units within its command which included three heavy bombardment groups flying B-17Es, a light bomb squadron flying A-20 Havocs and two pursuit groups, flying P-38 Lightnings and P-39 Airacobras. These latter two outfits would soon be called fighter groups. By April 28 one of the B-17 groups and the two fighter groups were ordered to be prepared for overseas shipment by June 1.[10]

The first all-American mission over Europe on August 17, 1942 was led by Eaker. The force consisted of 12 B-17s of the 97th Bombardment Group, their target was a railroad marshalling yard at Rouen, France.[11] It was the beginning of what would become the "Mighty Eighth" with its 1,000 bomber raids on Germany, supported by the fighter aircraft of its fighter command and the fighters of the 9th Air Force.

The British theory of heavy bombardment was diametrically opposed to the American concept of daylight precision bombing advocated by these "Johnny Come-lately" chaps from the States. It is best to remember that the RAF had been fighting this war since 1939 and from experience thought their doctrine of area bombing at night would provide heavier destruction and minimize losses of valued aircraft and aircrews. They also theorized their method would not only destroy the German industrial might but would also destroy the homes and occupants in the areas they saturated with bombs. They reasoned that this would not only harm the targeted facility but would so lower the morale of the German people that they would lose their will to fight and would weaken their support of the Nazi regime. This disagreement became a policy conflict between the two new allies all the way up to the highest levels of each government. The mindset of the American military leaders was their commitment to comply with the aims of AWPD-42 which they believed they could do with precision bombing by their heavy bombers with the Norden Bombsight on daylight missions.

The differences were settled, at least as far as the two nations were concerned, by the Casablanca Conference in January, 1943. Eaker was selected to present the American position on bombing strategy, one on one, to Churchill who had been doubtful that daylight bombing was practical. Eaker sold the Prime Minister on the U.S. view. It was agreed that the British would continue their night raids with saturation bombing of targeted areas. The RAF flyers remained unconvinced that the Americans would be able to withstand the prohibitive losses from flak (anti-aircraft fire) and the very effective Luftwaffe (German Air Force).[12]

At the outset the British prophecy came close to being fulfilled. During the month of

February, 1943 the 8th lost 22 of less than 100 effective bombers in six missions. Although newly arrived aircraft and crews bolstered the force, the losses climbed to 132 lost aircraft in June and July on eight missions into Germany where they claimed they could survive without tremendous losses.[13]

The Casablanca Directive handed down at that Conference said the primary objectives of the Combined Bomber Offensive (CBO) would include objectives with the following priority:

(a) German submarine yards   (d) Oil Plants
(b) German aircraft industry   (e) Other targets in enemy war industry[14]
(c) Transportation

The losses suffered by the 8th Air Force in the months which followed the Casablanca Directive brought on a change which modified the above priorities to bring them in line with the top order of AWPD-42. By another directive known as POINTBLANK on June 10, 1943 the Casablanca Directive was amended to give top priority to the destruction of the Luftwaffe and the German aircraft industry.[15]

It was becoming quite obvious that the Americans lacked a long-range fighter which could provide escort for the bomber formations deep into Germany to hit the AWPD-42 targets.[16] The losses of the 8th Air Force established that a small group of unescorted bombers could not defend themselves against the experienced Luftwaffe fighters attacking in overwhelming numbers. There were those who believed that the aircrews had been rushed into combat with minimal training and were just too inexperienced to cope with the situation. The truth was that they were being quashed by a force much greater than their own. Further, the concept that a bomber could go it alone was incorrect.

To deal with this problem both American and British ingenuity went to work to create an auxiliary fuel tank for the fighters which could be carried on the exterior of their aircraft and jettisoned when empty or when the enemy was engaged. There were a number of different tanks developed and modifications made on different models which came to be called "drop tanks" because of their expendable nature. They were first introduced on P-47 Thunderbolts in July, 1943. This innovation helped but was not the complete answer to the problem.[17]

On August 17, 1943 the VIII Bomber Command put up a strike aimed at the Schweinfurt ball bearing works, so essential to aircraft and other military industry, and the Me-109 assembly plant at Regensburg. The fighters escorted the bombers as far as they could go before turning back due to the lack of fuel. The Regensburg force was under attack along a 150 mile route unprotected by fighters during which they were hit by German FW-190s and Me-109s singly, and in bunches, losing 16 aircraft to the enemy before reaching the target. Their bombing accuracy was excellent. After leaving the target they surprised the defenders by not turning back for England. As briefed, they continued to Italy, then crossed the Mediterranean Sea to North Africa. Five more B-17s ran out of fuel and were forced to ditch in the Mediterranean. Counting one other which crash landed in Italy and two which were required to go to neutral Switzerland, the force lost a total of 24 aircraft.[18] The Schweinfurt force was greeted by an even more vicious Luftwaffe attack which was initiated in the vicinity of Antwerp, Belgium. The German fighters blasted away at the bombers all the way to the target and back until they crossed the North Sea. Although their bombing was also accurate it was at a terrible cost of 36 aircraft lost.[19] The total loss of 60 bombers and their crews made believers out of many who now realized that the concentrated fire from the B-17 Fortresses was not enough to ward off the Luftwaffe; gaining air superiority over Europe was another matter. Those who lived through Regensburg and Schweinfurt witnessed hell in the skies on that August 17.

As the VIII Bomber Command grew its organizational structure became strained. It had three bomb wings which were called Combat Bombardment Wings (CBWs). Under each of these CBWs were the operational bombardment group commands. On September 13 this was changed to create three bomb divisions, later called air divisions. Under each of the divisions were either two or three CBWs. The wings managed the two or three bombardment groups assigned to them. This was the basic structure which lasted for the rest of the war in Europe.[20] Although the growth of the bomber force in England continued to outdistance the combat losses, they were still being brutalized by the Luftwaffe. The following month, October, 1943 was an absolute disaster! The week from October 8 to October 14 has come to be known as "Black Week" as the Eighth lost 148 bombers in four missions:

| October 8 – Bremen/Vegesack – 30 | October 10 – Munster – 30 |
| October 9 – Anklam et al – 28 | October 14 – Schweinfurt – 60 |

Again the bombing of Schweinfurt was accurate and was the kind of a blow that AWPD-42 had in mind, although no one would have ever considered those two strikes on that target worth the loss of 96 bombers and the more than nine hundred airmen on board. At the end of "Black Week" the Americans were seriously hurt but they came back fighting.[21] After the October experience General Arnold convinced the Joint Chiefs that the 8th Air Force would not be able to destroy all 177 targets set forth in AWPD-42. He gained their support to again modify the plan and go all out to destroy the number one priority on that list, the German air force and aircraft industry. To provide another base from which to accomplish this they also approved the creation of a new 15th Air Force to be based in Italy.[22] Again the structure had to be altered to accommodate such growth of air power. In early 1944 they established the United States Strategic and Tactical Air Forces in Europe (USSTAF) under the command of General Carl Spaatz. It would be the role of the USSTAF to coordinate the operations of the 8th and 15th Air Forces. Eaker was moved to head up the Mediterranean Allied Air Forces (MAAF) and General James H. Doolittle, then commanding the 15th Air Force, became Eaker's replacement as commander of the 8th Air Force. [23] With these changes the VIII Bomber Command, having served its purpose, was disbanded.[24]

Also, more help was on the way...replacement crews and new bombardment groups were filling out the new organizational chart. Out of Montana came one new bomb group, the 401st Bombardment Group (H). If there was one thing about this new outfit, which in retrospect was responsible for the greatness it achieved, it was its leadership at the top. The first Commanding Officer (C.O.) was Colonel Neil Harding. Wayne Eveland, the original 614th Squadron Commander said, "Colonel Harding proved to be a most popular C.O. He was an old-timer and seemed to know his business. He also had a good sense of humor and in that month or six weeks he was with us we all became fond of him. When you are expecting to go to war, it helps to believe your C.O. is a real professional and a good guy to boot!"[25]

After only one month with the 401st Colonel Harding was called to combat on June 9, 1943 taking over command of the 100th Bomb Group in the 8th Air Force. Joining the 401st as its new C.O. was Colonel Harold W. Bowman. Eveland said that when they learned Colonel Harding had been transferred "our morale dropped 99 points. Next, we heard a colonel from Headquarters, Washington, D.C. (a staff officer and desk pilot) had been selected to take over the 401st. Our morale dropped some more. Whoever heard of drawing two good commanding colonels in succession, especially when the second was reputed to be a paper pushing specialist?" He then said, "He won us over, and in short order. I think he used the same technique on all his squadron commanders and staff. He took me to lunch, privately. He ... knew how we felt about Colonel Harding ... and he volunteered he had gone from Captain to Colonel as a staff officer largely in public relations work.

His only command, years ago, was as a flight commander. On the other hand he thought his young squadron commanders had been well trained and had a lot of the field experience he had not received in staff. He said he needed lots of help. He would rely on me – and others – to assist him whenever his experience was short. He promised to learn fast as he could and with luck, in a month or two, he would have mastered enough detail knowledge to **help me and the other commanders with our problems**."

"Remember, this guy was a full colonel and I was only a very junior captain. He talked in a frank, modest, and sincere manner. And he **asked me** for suggestions - and **help**! It caught me completely by surprise ... his sincerity was amazing. My reaction was immediate. This guy was not just another headquarters colonel. His modesty and sincerity was really special; I knew I could work for this guy. In fact, if this man's actions measured up to his words, I knew I'd work my butt off for him! And I did! I now believe his 'down- playing' his experience was exaggerated, to say the least ... combined with modesty and a man-to-man appeal for help - that's **salesmanship** - and plenty sharp!"[26]

In Chapter 3 reference was made to the fact that Wayne Eveland was shot down on New Year's Eve, 1943. The story of his adventures and return to England in March, 1944 is told in Chapter 5. When Eveland later got back to Deenethorpe he said he had every intention of "calling on Colonel Bowman first, as a matter of courtesy, then returning to my squadron area to visit with the lads of my own outfit. However, I made a strategic mistake. The route to Colonel Bowman's quarters led past the 614th area. I lost my resolve and had the driver turn in! In no time at all I was clinking glasses with my friends and I found it necessary to phone Colonel Bowman. I apologized for making this impulsive stop at the 614th, and

Colonel Harold W. Bowman, USAAF — 1945 (Retired Brigadier General, USAF). USAF Photo Collection neg. #65694AC courtesy of the National Air and Space Museum (NASM), Smithsonian Institution.

after the alcoholic greeting I received, I thought it best to delay my visit to his quarters until the next evening. He laughed, understood, and agreed!"

Eveland told another story concerning Colonel Bowman which illustrates that he was a caring leader. He said that in 1945 he was called to the office of the base commander at Minter Field in California. The commander had a telegram from General Arnold which authorized the promotion of anyone who had been recommended for such but had not received it because of being lost due to enemy action. He said the telegram specifically named himself as falling within that provision and instructed the commander to respond as to his intention.

Eveland said he was soon promoted to Lieutenant Colonel and commented "... only one man would take the trouble to search me out and would have the `loyalty downward to a subordinate' to initiate that telegram." He referred of course to Colonel Bowman who was back on General Arnold's staff.[27]

This man who took the 401st to war was born in Waverly, Nebraska February 12, 1903, to school teacher parents who later settled in Vallejo, California the year he finished high school. After a stint as a school teacher at Vacaville, California he entered the University of California at Berkeley, joined the ROTC, and graduated in 1928 with a Bachelor of Science degree in Business Administration. That same year he became a Flying Cadet at March Field, California and won his wings in bombardment aviation at Kelly Field, Texas, in June, 1929.

During his first assignment at Rockwell Field, San Diego (now the Navy's North Island) he met and married Etta Buchanan, a drama student at San Diego State College. In the early

1930s he was the public relations officer for then Lt. Col. Henry H. Arnold and then Major Carl Spaatz. In the mid-1930s he was a pursuit pilot at Clark Field in the Philippines. From there he went to Langley Field, Virginia where he was involved in training and operations. His next stop was Wright Field (now Wright-Patterson Air Force Base) where he was in charge of photography, the museum, public relations and intelligence.

In 1939 the Bowmans' were moved to Air Corps headquarters in Washington for an assignment in Plans and Administration. There he remained until he joined the 401st.[28]

After Colonel Bowman established the 401st as "The Best Damned Outfit In The USAAF" he was taken from us when General Arnold told General Carl Spaatz that he needed at USSTAF a Deputy Chief of Staff for Public Relations. Recalling that he had once served in such a capacity Bowman said, "my fate was sealed. I flew to France and tried to beg off. General Doolittle and General Travis, Commander of the 1st Division, both said "not available". The answer was, "No hurry, Next Monday is soon enuf'."[29]

In 1945 the Hal Bowman was back in the Capitol where he served as Deputy and as Chief of USAF Public Relations. In 1948 he graduated from the National War College and became Chief of Staff for the 9th Air Force and thereafter Deputy Chief of Staff for Personnel to the Tactical Air Command, both at Langley.

In 1951 our Colonel became a Brigadier General and Commander of the 62nd Troop Carrier Wing at McChord and Larson AF Bases in Washington. He returned to Paris in 1954 as Deputy J-3 for Operations and Strategic Planning, U.S. European Command. Returning to the States in 1957 the General became Air Deputy Commandant at the Armed Forces Staff College, Norfolk, Virginia. In 1959 General Bowman retired to Jupiter, Florida. His awards and decorations include the Silver Star, Legion of Merit, Distinguished Flying Cross with oak leaf cluster, Bronze Star, Air Medal with oak leaf cluster, Distinguished Unit Citation with oak leaf cluster and Citation A L'Ordre L'Arme (France).[30]

Into Colonel Bowman's shoes stepped William Thomas Seawell who was born in 1918 at Pine Bluff, Arkansas. He attended the Marion Military Institute in Alabama and the University of Arkansas before West Point where he received a Bachelor of Science Degree in 1941. In March of that year he won his wings at Ellington Field, Texas. On June 12, 1941 he married the former Judith Alexander, a hometown girl, who graduated from Wellesley College.

Seawell served as Chief of Staff A-3 for the 2nd Air Force, Fort George Wright, Washington and was also assigned to the 88th Bomb Group at Walla Walla, Washington. On April 1, 1943 he joined the 401st and was the original C.O. of the 615th Squadron.[31] By then he was a Captain and in September of 1943 was promoted to Major. In the Spring of 1944 he was again promoted, to Lieutenant Colonel, and on June 15 became the 401st Air Executive. He finished his first tour of combat and returned to the States for a leave which was interrupted when he was recalled to assume command of the 401st as the replacement for Bowman. He was then 26 years of age and the youngest group commander in the 8th Air Force. He became a full Colonel in May, 1945 [32] and remained the C.O. of the 401st until its deactivation in late 1945.

After World War II Colonel Seawell obtained a Doctor of Jurisprudence degree from Harvard University's Law School. His post war assignments included the following: Member of the Advisory Council of the Commanding General, USAAF and on the Military Staff Committee of the United Nations. He also commanded the 11th Bomb Wing of the Strategic Air Command at Fort Worth, Texas. Along the way he was promoted to Brigadier General and served as Military Assistant to the Secretary of the USAF and to the Deputy Secretary of Defense. From 1961 until his retirement from the military in 1963 General Seawell was the Commandant of Cadets at the Air Force Academy, Colorado Springs, Colorado. His military career brought General Seawell many awards and decorations which include the following: the Silver Star, the Distinguished Flying Cross with three oak leaf clusters, the Distinguished Unit Citation with an oak leaf cluster and the French Croix de Guerre with palms.

There followed a distinguished career in business. General Seawell served as Vice President-Operations and Engineering with the Air Transport Association of America.

Thereafter he was a Senior Vice President for American Airlines. He also was President of Rolls-Royce Aero Engines, Inc. and held the posts of Chairman of the Board of Rolls- Royce (Canada) Limited, and President of Rolls-Royce Holdings North America Limited. General Seawell joined Pan American World Airways in 1971 as President and Chief Operating Officer and in 1972 he was elected Chairman and Chief Executive Officer.[33] General Seawell has since retired but remains active in business affairs. He and Judy resided at Vero Beach for some years before going home to Pine Bluff, Arkansas.

To me, both of our Colonels were real honest-to-God leaders in combat and on the ground. Having then been only a "first John" I was in awe of them both, but I vividly recall one thing about Col. Seawell which was the way he constantly harangued us about the need for close formation and getting our aircraft down at Deenethorpe in an orderly and prompt way. As to the former, it was probably the close formation as much as anything else that gained the 401st the record for the lowest loss rates in the 8th Air Force. For things like that we have been forever thankful, even if Fred Babcock scared me half to death as he would close in on our neighboring B-17 until I could tell him whether the bar on the shoulder of the neighboring pilot or co-pilot was gold or silver.

It should be obvious that our top leadership was first class, but there were others that had real ability and proven leadership. In this chapter the story of Allison Brooks leading the mission to Oschersleben is told. He was our Group Operations Officer who later left us ultimately to become the Commander of the 1st Air Division Scouting Force in P-51 Mustangs. He also had a great military career and at the time of his retirement was a Major General.[34]

Also at Group Headquarters was William C. Garland, later a Major General, about whom I will brag in the next Chapter dealing with the 614th Squadron.

We had one other leader, Bryan M. Shotts, who was a lead crew pilot and a member of the 613th Squadron from its inception. He was wounded over Berlin and sent home to recuperate. He rose to the rank of Lieutenant General before retiring to live at Ocean Springs, Mississippi. General Shotts achieved the highest Air Force rank of all those who served in the 401st.[35]

Along with these we had a host of comrades who made Colonel after the war and we are proud of them all.

The group was activated on April 1, 1943 at Spokane, Washington. They set up temporary headquarters at the Ephrata, Washington Army Air Field (AAF) and Colonel Bowman took command in June. They moved briefly to Geiger Field at Spokane and then to Great Falls, Montana and three other satellite bases in Montana for their combat training. On October 18 the air crews departed in their B-17s en route overseas. The next day the ground personnel left by train for Camp Shanks, New York, a staging base for overseas shipment. They left from New York on board the Queen Mary for a five day crossing arriving off Glasgow, Scotland November 2, 1943.

The following day they

Lt. Col. William T. Seawell, USAAF — 1944 (Retired Brigadier General USAF). USAF Photo Collection neg. #65684AC courtesy of the NASM, Smithsonian Institution.

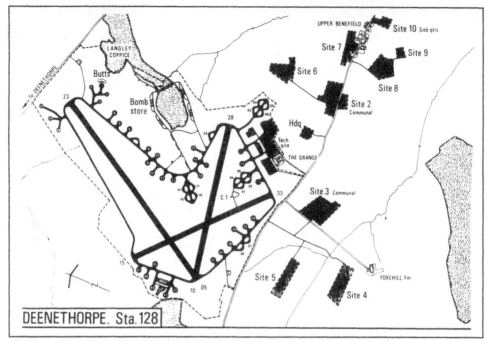

Illustration of Station 128, the airfield and its facilities at Deenethorpe, Northamptonshire, England. The home of the 401st Bombardment Group (H) from November 1943 to May 1945. (Courtesy of Roger A. Freeman from **The Mighty Eighth War Manual***)*

disembarked and by train and truck made their way south to England and Northamptonshire. There they found their new home, an airfield near the village of Deenethorpe, or as it became known to their loved ones, Station 128, APO 557, NY, NY – and as it was referred to by the wartime media, "somewhere in England."

The air crews arrived at Prestwick, Scotland between November 13 and 15th. After several days training at Bassingbourn they landed at Deenethorpe on November 19.[36] They wasted no time getting settled; there was real work to be done, the work they had been trained for and sent there to do. On November 26th they flew their first mission to Bremen with Colonel Bowman leading the group.[37] It was the largest force assembled by the 8th Air Force up to that time, with 633 bombers. Their target was the port area of the city but en route they found themselves under attack by 100 German fighters.[38] During the mission they had their first combat fatality. A B-17 from another group below the 401st went out of control and climbed up colliding with the underside of "Fancy Nancy" flown by Lt. Scribner C. Dailey of the 612th Squadron. The crash sheared off the ball turret of "Fancy Nancy" with the gunner, Sgt. L. Baranik inside.[39] Sgt. Baranik was interred at the American Cemetery at Ardennes, Belgium.[40] "Fancy Nancy" made it back to England that day but was so badly damaged it had to be scrapped.[41] Over the target on November 26 the 401st ran into heavy flak and the target was covered by clouds so that the bombing results could not be observed.[42] A total of 60 enemy planes were shot down, 24 of them claimed by aerial gunners on the bomber crews. Unfortunately, the 8th Air Force lost 29 of its 633 bombers and four of its 381 fighters.[43]

The modification of AWPD-42 by POINTBLANK, which gave the highest priority to attacks on the Luftwaffe and the German aircraft industry was not designed merely to help reduce losses suffered by the 8th Air Force. The real purpose was OVERLORD, the code name for the cross-channel invasion of Europe planned for Spring, 1944. It was imperative that the allies hit those targets with a degree of success that would gain for them air superiority if that invasion was to succeed. Arnold in a message to Doolittle on December 27 said in closing, "It is a conceded fact that OVERLORD will not be possible unless the German Air Force is destroyed. Therefore, my personal message to you ... this is a must... is to destroy the enemy air force wherever you find them, in the air, on the ground and in the factories."[44] They were given a deadline of Spring, 1944 to accomplish this almost impossible task. Doolittle was not one to back away from a challenge; he mounted a constant bombing attack on the German aircraft industry. P-38 Lightning fighters joined the P-47 Thunderbolts in the effort to protect the B-17 and B-24 formations over the Reich.[45]

Then came the answer to the prayers of all; from Doolittle on down to the overworked crew chiefs and the dispirited aircrews. It was the arrival of the P-51 Mustang fighter. As of February 1, 1944 the 357th Fighter Group was the first 8th Air Force outfit to be equipped with this new aircraft.[46] It was originally designed for the British by North American Aviation which had received earlier models as far back as 1941. With many modifications along the way and with a more powerful engine the new Mustang was really needed by the USAAF which ordered 2,200 of them in 1942. By directive all of the P-51s produced during the last four months of 1943 were to go to the European Theater of Operations (ETO). However, they were specifically earmarked for the 9th Air Force to be used as tactical support for OVERLORD. The VIII Fighter Command solved the problem by "borrowing" the 9th Air Force P-51s for bomber escort since the invasion was some months away.[47]

During 1944 and 1945 8th Air Force bomber crews came to know this versatile fighter as "Little Friend" and her addition to the war in the European skies made a great difference. She began her duties as an escort on a mission to Paris on December 5, 1943.[48] After a variety of "drop tanks" were tested, they settled on a 108 gallon paper tank slung under the belly of the Mustang.[49] This auxiliary fuel gave the P-51 the ability to provide a protective umbrella over the heavies wherever they went in Europe. The 8th was again ready to penetrate into the deepest areas of Germany to hit those vital priority targets.

On January 11, 1944 a maximum effort (ME) was mounted with all groups of each of the three Divisions participating to bomb aircraft factories at Waggum, Halberstadt and Oschersleben in the Brunswick area, where flak and fighter opposition was famous. The FW-190 plant at Marienburg was destroyed in October, 1943 and the one at Oschersleben had replaced it as the principal producer of that formidable aircraft. Weather over England was very bad resulting in a number of escort fighters aborting the mission. The Luftwaffe pilots in eastern Germany did not have that problem and were ready to take-off and make a mass

Deene Park the ancestral home of the Brudenells' from the 15th Century. One of that family was the 7th Earl of Cardigan who led the Charge of the Light Brigade in 1854. The Manor House is located near Station 128.

attack on the bomber stream as it came their way. Both the Second and Third Divisions were recalled due to the lack of sufficient escort; the Triangle First, by then only 100 miles from Brunswick, was allowed to continue. The task force commander was Brigadier General Robert Travis, of Savannah, flying with the lead crew on "Hell's Angels" of the 303rd Bomb Group based at Molesworth. The bombers found themselves under attack by some 100 fighters, the like of which had not been seen since the air battles of the previous October. Travis later told newsmen: "... the fighters ... in spite of our escort, came at us in bunches. Our first attack was by four FW-190s, the next from 30 Me-109s, then 12 and they just kept coming..."[50] On that day the 401st was leading the 94th CBW, with Major Allison Brooks as the air commander in what was later described as the "greatest air battle of WW II". After bombs away the escort protection, getting low on fuel, was forced to head for home; the German pilots then pressed their advantage.[51] The force at Oschersleben lost 34 B-17s, of which four were 401st aircraft. It was conceded that the losses that day would have been much greater had it not been for the one lone P-51 that stayed behind to protect the 401st and the 351st Bomb Group from Polebrook. The 351st lost six crews that day.[52] That one fighter pilot took on a swarm of 30 Luftwaffe fighters by diving right into the midst of them and, with raw courage, fighting them for 20 minutes in an exhibition the aircrews of those B-17s had never before witnessed.[53] The pilot, then Major John H. Howard, was a Squadron Commander, with the 354th Fighter Group of the 9th Air Force. Allison Brooks, Operations Officer for the 401st, said of Howard's daring: "It was a case of one lone American against what seemed to be the entire Luftwaffe."[54]

Howard, had been a Navy pilot who resigned his commission to join Claire Chennault's "Flying Tigers" in China where he distinguished himself. He came home with dengue fever and after his recovery was commissioned in the USAAF. His P-51, nicknamed "Ding Hao" (a Chinese expression meaning "very good") was credited with three confirmed enemy aircraft destroyed over Oschersleben. Howard later said, "I scared some of the enemy away

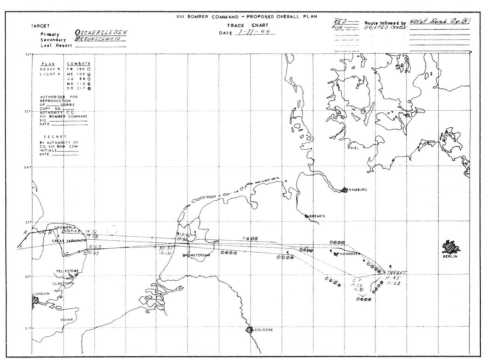

Track Chart for mission to Oschersleben January 11, 1944 called the greatest air battle of World War II. Note symbols along route which identify combat attacks by various German aircraft and the presence of light or heavy flak. Courtesy of the National Archives.

by 'stooging' up to them suddenly. Others, I gave a 'squirt' which caused them to break away ... On the first encounter which turned into a melee, my flight lost me. I regained bomber altitude and then discovered that I was alone. I spent half an hour chasing and scaring away attacking enemy aircraft from 21,000 to 15,000 feet. I had five encounters during this time. For the first two encounters and combat all four guns fired. On the third I had two guns, and on the fourth and fifth only one gun." Howard, released from active duty after the war retired from the USAF Reserves as a Brigadier General. For his exploits over Oschersleben he received the Medal of Honor and the unending appreciation from those who flew with the 401st.[55] Following the mission the Group Operations Officer's memorandum described the mission as "good." He commented that the 401st underwent heavy air attacks by the enemy for two hours when they were without friendly protection. He said that the great percentage of the German attacks by Me-110s, Me-210s, Ju-88s and FW-190s were from the rear and such attacks included the use of rockets. The Commanding Officer's memorandum agreed that the results were good from the 240 500 pound GP (General Purpose demolition) bombs that had been dropped on the target.[56] For their valiant performance the 401st and the other bomb groups of the First Division who participated in the January 11 mission to Oschersleben received the Presidential Unit Citation.[57]

After January 11 it was plain the Eighth was again prepared to lay it on the line! The deadline for OVERLORD approached and at hand was ARGUMENT, the code word for the all out campaign against the German aircraft industry. ARGUMENT was to take the form of a series of joint attacks by the 8th Air Force, the 15th Air Force and the RAF.[58] It required good weather to assure visual daylight bombing by the Americans, but such weather was hard to come by during the winter months. On February 8th Arnold ordered Spaatz to begin the air offensive and to complete it by March 1st.[59] For ARGUMENT to be a real success the heavies needed three straight days of good weather. In mid February wind, rain and snow swept down off the North Sea and across the face of East Anglia. The airfields of the 8th Air Force sparkled and glistened under the snow and all operations came to a halt. Then the weather warmed and the men cleared the runways. Storms still persisted over the continent but by February 19 it began to break up. Three or four days of good weather were predicted and ARGUMENT was on.[60] On the night of February 19/20 the RAF opened what came to be called "Big Week" with a heavy raid on Leipzig, an aircraft manufacturing center.[61] On the morning of February 20, 1944 the Eighth put up its largest combat mission to date as it dispatched 964 heavies and 835 fighters assisted by two squadrons of RAF Mustangs and 14 squadrons of Spitfires.[62] This was another ME, with all bomb groups participating, and most CBWs providing two wing formations.

Brig. Gen. (then Major) James Howard on the wing of his plane "Ding Hoa." He was awarded the Medal of Honor for attacking 30 German planes single handed in order to protect the 401st Bomb Group formations over Oshersleben, Germany on January 11, 1944.

The Third Division was briefed for Focke-Wulf factories at Tutlow, Germany and Posen and Kreising, Poland. Clouds would not permit visual bombing so they bombed the Marienehe Heinkel plant and a shipyard at Rostock with excellent results.

The Second Division was targeted at two Messerschmidt factories in the Brunswick area, a Ju-88 plant at Halberstadt and a Me-110 assembly plant at Gotha. Their results overall were poor except for good bombing results on a secondary target at Helmstedt.[63]

The main First Division force, with the 401st leading the way and Colonel Bowman calling the shots was briefed for Me-109 factories at Leipzig, a Junkers assembly plant at Bernburg and a Ju-88 component factory at Aschersleben. Colonel Bowman's wingmen were Donald V. Kirkhuff and Delwyn E. Silver. The 401st fielded 20 aircraft plus spares and PFF (Pathfinder force radar) aircraft as its contribution to a six wing formation[64] which had to fight its way to battle through very foul weather.[65] Over England clouds began to move in, and snow clouds were encountered during takeoff.[66] However, they were able to maintain takeoff and assembly on schedule. As they entered Europe they set a course hoping that it would give the impression that they were headed for Berlin. The ruse did not fool the Luftwaffe which played a waiting game by holding back much of its force, rather than scrambling prematurely which would waste fuel and valued air time.[67]

In the meantime, before the First Division was committed to a course toward Leipzig they were hit by a variety of Luftwaffe aircraft: Ju-87s, He-111s, Do-17s and FW-190s. The attacks were bold and fierce with passes made singly and four abreast diving right through their formations.[68] The Forts flew on, finally making their move, turning south away from Berlin. When the Me-109s in the Berlin area learned the force was headed for central Germany they took off in pursuit. As Bowman's Bombers reached the IP (Initial Point or the start of the bomb run) the Germans were ready. They dove toward the 401st formation with the lead aircraft their choice on the first pass.

Watching from above was the 357th Fighter Group. When they saw the Germans make their move, they dove at them and the fight was on.[69] In addition to P-51s, P-38s and P-47s were participating, and they shot down 61 enemy aircraft while losing four of their own. Despite heavy flak on the bomb run which did major damage to Colonel Bowman's B-17, the bombing results were excellent. Colonel Bowman recalled, "Because the weather was uncertain we were provided with a PFF crew especially trained for instrument bombing. The weather en route was indeed bad and preparations were made for aiming by instrument means but as we approached the target area, the clouds opened up to 'scattered' and a visual sighting was made. The result was, for our group, 100 percent of our bombs were within 1,000 feet of the aiming point. Hits were made on the principal assembly shop of the Erla Messerschmidt production factory, and its other large assembly building was observed to be on fire as the bombers left the target area."[70] With respect to his own contribution that day Colonel Bowman was predictably modest. He said: "So if every person performs perfectly, 'as briefed,' the aircraft behaves, the weather cooperates, and the enemy doesn't mess things up in this very complicated operation, the Air Commander has little to do. He rides in the co-pilot's seat, performing co-pilot duties as required by the pilot ... The Air Commander can direct the units he is leading to abort the mission if, for example, the weather makes that necessary. He can decide on alternative targets if the primary assignment is not bombed. He can 'crack the whip', via radio, for sloppy formation or useless radio chatter. Or warn of enemy fighters. But mostly, he sits and observes, taking too much credit for success and too much blame for failure, as all leaders do."[71] As he sat and observed, though he did not mention it, I am sure he was very mindful of the burden he bore as the leader, responsible for those 417 precious B-17s and their even more precious crews, more than 4,100 young men.

Also typical of the 401st leadership during its combat experience was the team spirit which was so evident in later remarks by Colonel Bowman concerning that February 20 mission. He said, "In my case, on the Leipzig mission, Captain William Riegler and his highly professional lead crew performed faultlessly, resulting in the high praise we shared proudly."[72]

Colonel Bowman also later recalled that after "Big Week" he attended a conference called by Major General Robert B. Williams, who commanded the First Division. He said the conference was "the time for appraisals" which was attended by the Division's Wing, Group and Mission commanders to critique each mission of "Big Week" with each leader called on for his comments. Colonel Bowman recalled that there were the usual comments about loose formations, timing, etc. and when it came his turn to report on the Leipzig mission he said he had no complaints and reported: "Sir, nothing unusual to report. The mission was accomplished as briefed." He said General Williams replied: "Nothing unusual except it was the most successful mission ever run by the 8th Air Force." He said the General then left the stage, walked down the aisle and pinned a Silver Star on him.[73] The 401st received its second Presidential Unit Citation for the Leipzig mission.[74]

February 21 marked the second mission of "Big Week". The primary targets for the First Division were airfields and air depots at Gutersloh, Lippstadt and Werl.[75] Bombing was to have been visual but the Eighth continued to be plagued by bad weather. Undercast over the North Sea continued well into Germany clearing at the IP. However, clouds at flying altitude on the bomb run bothered the low box of the 94th CBW and necessitated the 401st seek a target of opportunity. The lead group bombed a railroad and warehouse at Emlichheim near the Dutch border while the low box bombed an airdrome near the Rhine, with excellent results.[76] They reported that fighter attacks were not effective and the flak was meager and inaccurate.[77] Actually, only one German fighter made an attack on the low box of the 94th CBW probably due to the excellent fighter cover.[78]

The next "Big Week" target for the Triangle First was the Junkers works at Oschersleben on February 22 with Major Seawell, C.O. of the 615th, leading the 401st Bomb Group. After their visit to that city on January 11 there had to be a fair amount of apprehension about a return visit. Due to solid cloud cover over the primary target, they skirted the area for a target of opportunity. A large city later identified as Misburg was selected and the bombing of warehouses was rated fair.[79] Another source agreed that the bombing results were fair,[80] but a third account called the bombing a "notable success".[81] Whatever the results, the First Division encountered violent fighter attacks by the Luftwaffe, losing forty-one bombers and eleven fighters. But it was costly for the Germans also with 34 aircraft destroyed, 18 probably destroyed and 17 damaged.[82] The 401st lost two aircraft on February 22. The first was that of V.A. Arenson of the 614th Squadron. The bombardier, G.J. Gilmore, and the waist gunner, A.L. Shutes, were KIA and the rest of the crew became POWs. Amazing is the story of the tail gunner, R.G. Schmidt. As Schmidt tried to put on his parachute he found it had been riddled by machine gun fire. Unable to use it, he went forward to the cockpit to find that all the other crew members had bailed out. Although the controls of the B-17 had been shot out, the Fortress landed itself and Schmidt survived the crash landing without injuries. The other loss was the aircraft of L.M. Shanks of the 613th Squadron. The engineer, W.H. Jarret was KIA but the rest of the crew became POWs. The ball turret gunner, H.A. Gibson, had suffered a bad ankle wound during the fight. His fellow crew members gave him a shot of morphine, dressed the wound and bailed him out. He was picked up by the Germans and was taken to a small hospital where a German lady doctor operated on him and saved the leg from amputation. It was also reported that the pilot, Shanks, had accidently pulled the rip cord on his parachute while inside the aircraft. Jarret gave Shanks his parachute and went back to the

The first memorial to the 401st Bomb Group at Memorial Park adjacent to the Air Force Museum at Wright-Patterson AFB Dayton, Ohio. It was dedicated September 14, 1988. Photograph courtesy of Ralph W. Trout.

waist for a spare. For some reason Jarret's spare parachute never opened when he bailed out and he fell to his death.[83]

An unusual feature of the mission on February 22 was the fact that it was the first joint operation executed by both the 15th Air Force in Italy and the Mighty Eighth in England.[84] Due to the continued rotten weather the crews of the 8th Air Force did not fly on February 23; they got a much deserved rest while the ground crews worked around the clock getting aircraft repaired and ready to fly again.[85]

On February 24 the 8th Air Force was sent to targets throughout Germany. The First Division, including the 401st Bombardment Group, drew Schweinfurt as their target.[86] It was reported that the famous ball bearing factory was back in operation; Captain William C. Garland led the 401st; bombing was done visually and photographs indicated it was a very successful mission.[87] Flak over the target was described as moderate with scattered barrage fire; there were also a few ground rockets fired near the IP. The formation experienced several enemy fighter attacks which were made singly or in pairs. Captain Garland said the lead navigator, Charles M. Smith, did an excellent job of avoiding all flak area along the route. Smith became the 614th Squadron Navigator and after a career in the USAF he retired as a Colonel.[88] Although all the 401st birds came back to Deenethorpe the First Division lost eleven aircraft. They still fared better than the Second Division which lost 33 at Gotha and Eisenach.[89]

The culmination of "Big Week" came with the mission on February 25. This was to be the deepest penetration into Germany up to this point. The First Division was assigned to bomb the Messerschmidt experimental and assembly plants at Augsburg and the VLK ball bearing plant at Stuttgart. The Second Division had an aircraft industry target at Furth and the Third Division was assigned to a similar target at Regensburg.[90]

Major William T. Seawell, Commander of the 615th Squadron, was the Air Commander leading the 401st, flying with Ralph Dempsey. They encountered overcast over England, broken clouds over the Channel and clear skies over Europe. There was some flak over the French coast but friendly fighter support was quite protective. Near the IP the 94th CBW was forced to do a slight "S" turn to avoid interference by the following CBW which was flying abreast of them. Flak on the bomb run was accurate but Julius Pickoff, the Group Bombardier, later said the results were excellent. He said the lead bombardier, Arnold C. Kuenning, had scored "squarely on machine shops of the MPI."[91] (The MPI refers to the Mean Point of Impact, the center of the target). The overall results by the First Division were likewise excellent at Augsburg and fair at Stuttgart although 13 of their big birds were lost.[92] The Eighth lost a total of 31 of its bombers with the Second having lost 12 and the Third six on their missions.[93] On the night of February 25/26 the RAF closed out "Big Week" with a raid on Augsburg. Clouds and increasingly bad weather brought a premature end to operation ARGUMENT.[94]

It has been said that the bombing results during ARGUMENT were not as effective as were first reported. Such criticism ignores other facts, not the least of which was that never again, after that bloody week, would the Luftwaffe threaten the 8th Air Force in strength.[95]

In the five missions of "Big Week" 219 German aircraft were destroyed as opposed to 33 fighters of the 8th and 9th Air Forces.[96] These statistics account for the subsequent absence of Luftwaffe ferocity and their rare presence in such large numbers after "Big Week." Did the combined USAAF and RAF air offensive achieve their mission and win air superiority over Europe? Without question! From June 5 to June 8 P-38s provided cover for the OVERLORD invasions of France without the intrusion of a single enemy aircraft.[97]

After February 1944 the 8th Air Force continued to grow, and as it gathered strength the Luftwaffe and the entire Nazi war machine weakened dramatically. Bowman's Bombers had made it to the big time and after only five months were a highly respected part of the Mighty Eighth. By March, 1944 the 401st Bombardment Group (H) had only flown 28 missions in combat. They went on to fly a total of 255 missions, dropping 17,778 ton of bombs, with the second best bombing record for accuracy in the Eighth.[98]

The "Maiden" could have done worse in her choice of a nest. Deenethorpe was a place where valiant men lived (and some died) as they built a reputation for courage under fire in only a few months of combat. It is no wonder that they and those who followed them developed an esprit de corps and still, after all these years, speak of themselves, irreverently but with conviction as the "Best damned outfit in the USAAF".[99] They have since proclaimed that declaration by having it chiseled twice in granite and once had those words cast in bronze. Yes, the "Maiden" would be comfortable with "Bowman's Bombers."

Notes to Chapter 4

1. Sunderman, Col. James F. (Editor). _World War II in the Air: Europe_ p.56
2. Parton, James. _Air Force Spoken Here_ p.179
3. Ibid. p.180-181
4. Julian, Dr. Thomas A. _Operation FRANTIC_ p.12
5. Infield, Glenn B. _Big Week_ p.15-16
6. Ibid. p.16
7. Ibid. p.17-19
8. Rust, Kenn C. _Eighth Air Force Story_ p.4
9. Infield, see 5 above p.19
10. Rust, see 8 above
11. Infield, see 5 above p.19
12. Churchill, Winston S. _The Second World War_ Vol. 5 _Closing the Ring_ p. 518-519
13. Infield, see 5 above p.41-43
14. Churchill, see 12 above p.519-520
15. Ibid. p.520
16. Infield, see 5 above
17. Freeman, Roger A. _The Mighty Eighth War Manual_ p.218-221
18. Freeman, Roger A. _The Mighty Eighth_ p.68
19. Ibid. p.69
20. Rust, see 8 above p.22
21. Ibid. p.24-26
22. Infield, see 5 above p.49
23. Ibid. p.51
24. Freeman, see 18 above p.104
25. Eveland, I. Wayne _Memories and Reflections_ p.43-44
26. Ibid. p.81
27. Ibid. p.91
28. _Poop From Group_ March, 1979
29. Bowman, Harold W. & Selwyn V. Maslen _Bowman's Bombers_ Forward, 5th page
30. See 28 above
31. Ibid.
32. Bowman & Maslen, see 29 above p.2,26,29,55,74
33. See 28 above
34. _Poop From Group_ July, 1979
35. _Poop From Group_ December, 1979
36. Closway, Gordon R. _614th Squadron History_ p.15-16
37. Bowman & Maslen, see 29 above p.5
38. Bowman, Martin W. _Castles in the Air_ p.104
39. Bowman & Maslen, see 29 above p.5
40. Bowman, Harold W. & Selwyn V. Maslen _401st B.G. Casualties in W.W.II_ p.2
41. Bowman & Maslen, see 29 above p.5
42. Bowman, see 38 above p.104

43. Freeman, Roger A. *The Mighty Eighth War Diary* p.142
44. Infield, see 5 above p.55-56.
45. Ibid.
46. Freeman, see 18 above p.251
47. Infield, see 5 above p.58-59
48. Ibid. p.60
49. Freeman, see 17 above p.220-221
50. Bowman, see 38 above p.111
51. Bowman & Maslen, see 29 above p.8
52. Freeman, see 43 above p.165
53. Rust, see 8 above p.31
54. Howard, James H. *Roar of the Tiger* p.222
55. Rust, see 8 above p.31
56. National Archives, Suitland Md. Reference Branch, Record Group 18 401st Bombardment Group (H) Mission Reports
57. Freeman, see 18 above p.256
58. Rust, see 8 above p.31
59. Infield, see 5 above p.82
60. Rust, see 8 above p.31
61. Ibid.
62. Ibid.
63. Ibid.
64. National Archives, see 56 above
65. Rust, see 8 above p.31
66. Bowman, see 38 above p.112
67. Infield, see 5 above p.97-99
68. Bowman, see 38 above p.115
69. Infield, see 5 above p.105
70. Bowman, see 38 above p.115
71. Bowman & Maslen, see 29 above p.86
72. Ibid. p.87
73. Ibid. p.86
74. Freeman, see 18 above p.251
75. Rust, see 8 above p.32
76. National Archives, see 56 above
77. Maslen, Selwyn V. *614th Bombardment Squadron (H): Squadron History* p.28
78. National Archives, see 56 above
79. Ibid.
80. Maslen, see 77 above p.28
81. Bowman, see 38 above p.117
82. Freeman, see 43 above p.185-186
83. Bowman & Maslen, see 40 above p.13-14
84. Bowman & Maslen see 29 above p.17
85. Bowman, see 38 above p.117
86. Ibid.
87. Maslen, see 77 above p.28
88. National Archives, see 56 above
89. Freeman, see 43 above p.187
90. Bowman, see 38 above p.118
91. National Archives, see 56 above
92. Rust, see 8 above p.33
93. Freeman, see 43 above p.188
94. Rust, see 8 above p,33
95. Bowman, see 38 above p.119
96. Rust, see 8 above p.32
97. Ibid. p.38
98. Freeman, see 18 above p.251
99. Bowman & Maslen, see 29 above, Forward 5th page

CHAPTER 5 — THE LUCKY DEVILS

By the time the "Maiden" joined "Bowman's Bombers" in September, 1944 all four Squadrons were battlewise, and as the last chapter demonstrated, the Group had established an enviable record for itself in combat.

The "Maiden's" nest was with the 614th Squadron. Its members were, and its veterans are, a proud bunch. The four Squadron areas including their barracks were widely separated at Deenethorpe. Although flying personnel of all Squadrons shared a common mess, the airmen usually associated with their own crew members and barracks buddies and rarely with those of the other Squadrons. During my tour I do not recall visiting any of the three other Squadron areas. I suppose that because of being somewhat remote from each other, rather than any other reason I can think of, each Squadron developed its own identity and esprit de corps. From my personal experience I believe this was particularly true of the 614th Squadron. As an example, that Squadron since 1953 has celebrated its own reunions, two decades before the Group Association was formed and began its biennial get-togethers.

Each Squadron adopted its own symbolic emblem and cloth patches of those emblems were proudly sewn to their leather A-2 jackets. All four are unique. The origin of the "winged bomb" emblem of the 612th Squadron is not recorded but the "punching bomb" of the 613th Squadron was created by the cartoonist, Walt Disney, "symbolic of a squadron which was 'always right in there, punching!'" That of the 615th Squadron was drawn by the cartoonist, Milton Caniff, author of the popular comic strip "Terry and the Pirates." That emblem featured the crosshairs of a bombsight and three falling bombs with the angry faces which represented Roosevelt, Churchill and Stalin.

Naturally, I am partial to the 614th Squadron emblem, which artistically is distinctively different from the rest. The 614ths "Lucky Devils" emblem was created by Mrs. J.J. Casagrande, wife of the first Squadron Navigator. Casagrande was a member of the crew of Captain J.W. Foster, the Squadron's

The Imperial War Museum at Duxford, England devotes one of the hangars to the 8th Air Force. Along one of its walls is an illuminated display of the insignia and or coats of arms of the many units of the Mighty Eighth. For some reason the 401st Bomb Group had no Group insignia. So as not to leave Bowman's Bombers out of the display they chose one of the four squadron insignia to represent the Group. They made a wise and tasteful choice when they selected the 614th Lucky Devil for that purpose.

Operations Officer shot down on that memorable mission to Oschersleben January 11, 1944. All crew members were POWs.[1] The "Lucky Devils" emblem predates its combat experience and must have met with unusual affirmation among the members of the Squadron from the following comment found in a history of the Squadron recorded while still stateside: "Our new Squadron insignias for our flight jackets arrived ... 500 being sold within a few hours...squadron stationery with the insignia in four colors was obtained and the "Lucky Devil" insignia painted on our flyaway airplanes."[2]

To my knowledge the 614th Squadron was the only one in the 401st Bombardment Group that had its own poem but I am sorry to say that I have been unable to learn the identity of our poet laureate. I remember laboriously copying it into a letter home to my family with a great deal of pride that I was a part of that great bunch of men. During the period of researching this story I appreciated the number of copies of this poem that were sent to me, in various printed forms, some on the "Lucky Devils" stationery - all of them saved over these many years by my comrades.

LUCKY DEVILS OF THE 614TH

The Devil is their mascot
    The C.O. is their boss
And they're the wildest hellions
    That ever came across

At three A.M. is breakfast
    And briefing comes at four
At seven they are in the air
    With a thousand planes or more

At ten they are assembled
    And off across the coast
The weather's fine, they start to climb
    Each gunner at his post

At noon they reach Initial Point
    And turn onto the run
The bombardier takes over here
    To drop 'em on the hun

There's flak above the target
    And the M.P.I.'s in view
Now its Bombs Away, and hell's to pay
    With flak and fighters too

"Bandits high at six o'clock"
    Comes over the interphone
They pull in tight, prepared to fight
    Its a hell of a long way home

Come MEs' from the cloud bank
    One-nineties from the sun
The fifties start to do their part
    And now the fight's begun

Attacks are pressed to fifty yards
    They roll and dive away
A plane becomes a pyre of flame
    We lost a few today

ETR is three o'clock
    The ground crews scan the sky
They've hung about, and "sweated out"
    The boys who went to fly

They fly high in the heavens
    And find a hell up there
Hence came the name they brought to fame
    Heaven's HELLIONS of the air'

Both the 614th emblem and their poem, heavy in symbolism for those who served in that Squadron, which remain important to them today. The leadership of the 614th was without question "top drawer."

Their first C.O. was Captain I. Wayne Eveland. The first name is Ivan but I have never heard anyone call him anything but Wayne. He was born in Missoula, Montana, attended the Montana School of Mines, graduating from the University of Montana in 1938.[3] He worked for a year as a social worker before becoming a Flying Cadet on August 9, 1939. He was commissioned and won his wings May 12, 1940. Assignments in twin engine aircraft before Pearl Harbor took Lt. Eveland to Barksdale, Louisiana, Fort Benning and Savannah, Georgia and Manchester, New Hampshire.[4] In 1941 Wayne left the Army to join Pan American Airways (PAA) which was establishing a route across northern Africa. He gained considerable experience, logged many hours of flight time and had many adventures flying

The ceiling of the combat mess at Deenethope was divided into four areas, one for each of the squadrons. In the panels of each area were the nicknames of the aircraft of those squadrons and the names of the crew members. Displayed are some of the panels of the 614th Squadron aircraft.

for PAA in Africa, India and Burma. He resigned to return to the United States in July, 1942 and one month later was back on active duty in the USAAF.[5] After being initially trained in B-24s he and his crew were assigned to B-17 combat training at Geiger Field, Washington. In January, 1943 Wayne became the Squadron C.O. of the 540th Squadron of the 383rd Bombardment Group which was based at remote Ainsworth, Nebraska, population less than 2300 souls today and only 1280 in 1943.[6]

In April, 1943 Wayne was transferred to the newly formed 401st Bombardment Group (H) then at Ephrata, Washington where he was assigned as Commander of the 614th Squadron. He trained them, led them to England and into combat. It will be recalled that then Major Eveland, flying with the crew of Lt. Homer E. McDonal on "Flak Rat," the original IW-A, was shot

Lt. Col. Wayne Eveland, Original C.O., 614th Squadron.

down on New Year's Eve 1943. The briefed target that day was an enemy air base at Bordeaux, France. The presence of bad weather resulted in a change to the secondary target, another air base at Cognac. Wayne said that near the I.P. a "terrific attack was launched against our Group."[7]

Gordon Closway's history recorded: "Enemy Me-109s and FW-190s attacked McDonal's ship, two engines were shot out and the ship began to lose altitude. Five parachutes were seen to come out and when last seen the ship was steadily losing altitude, had two or more fighters on its tail and, still under control, disappeared into the undercast ... It was a dull New Year's Eve around the 614th Squadron December 31, 1943, when news spread around that our much respected and greatly liked C.O. was down."[8] Wayne recalled "Flak Rat" was in the "number four slot in the low echelon, better known as 'tail-ass-Charlie'." Before takeoff they had experienced problems with a supercharger which seemed to have corrected itself. After it was too late to abort the problem recurred and they were unable to hold a tight formation. Wayne said that after landfall near Arachon they came under fighter attack. Being a straggler the plane was singled out by the Germans and was "worked over from front to rear." He said he could "feel" the 20mm shells as they hit something going through the cockpit above the din of their 50 caliber machine guns. Their B-17 was soon out of control and he ordered the crew by interphone to bailout as McDonal hit the bailout alarm. Wayne followed McDonal out of the aircraft. As he drifted helplessly in his parachute one of the fighters made several passes firing his guns at him without success.

On the ground Wayne experienced incredible adventures as he evaded capture, adventures that make a great story of determination and perseverance by a courageous man. He was injured and quite ill before he gained help from French peasants who put him in touch with the underground "Maquis" also known as the "Resistance." Eventually, he made his way to the Pyrenees Mountains which bordered France from neutral Spain to the south. He became part of a group of allied evaders, including English, French, Americans, at least one New Zealander and six Poles. Through horrendous weather and over unbelievable terrain they walked over the mountains in three days of blizzard conditions. Wayne described the period as "probably the most perilous days of my life." He suffered frostbite and lost consciousness but was carried by his companions into Spain.

Once across the border the travail had not ended when he and his companions were held virtual hostages by the Spanish Basque guides, who themselves risked prison if apprehended by Spanish authorities. Finally, Wayne made his way to Barcelona and the British Consulate. His travels from there took him to Madrid (including a bull fight) and on to Gibraltar and back to London where he arrived in late March, 1944.

As an evader, Wayne, for security reasons would not be allowed to resume command of the 614th or fly combat in the ETO. He served briefly as Assistant Operations Officer under General J.K. Lacey, the C.O. of the 94th CBW headquartered nearby at Polebrook, the home of our friends of the 351st Bombardment Group, before he returned home on leave. He was released from active duty October 14, 1945 and soon returned to his native Montana. Wayne established himself in the insurance business but stayed active in the U.S. Air Force Reserve. He was promoted to Colonel in 1950 and was retired May 17, 1976. He is now retired from

Debriefing with Major Carl C. Hinkle left, the second C.O. of the 614th Squadron with Col. Harold W. Bowman. Photograph from the USAF Collection courtesy of the NASM of the Smithsonian.

business and resides at Helena, Montana.[9]

The loss of Eveland was a tremendous blow to a squadron which had been in combat only two months. However, I believe that they were prepared for such a loss from the way their history records that event: "But the show must go on and every member of the Squadron... more revengeful now than ever to get even with and get 'Jerry'...settled down to work."[10]

Vic Maslen dedicated his history of the 614th Squadron to its four wartime commanders and each responded with letters that are included in that volume. In his, Wayne Eveland said: "In those days, so long ago, we were all so enthusiastic - and so very young - but the sudden growth of maturity and courage was awesome. The privilege of serving with such fine men has been a rewarding and humbling experience and has touched my life deeply. The Lord has blessed me in so many ways and my 614th experience has been one of the most profound."[11]

Lt. Col. William C. Garland, the third C.O. of the 614th Lucky Devils. Photograph from the USAF Collection of the NASM of the Smithsonian.

There was no leadership vacuum. On News Year's Day 1944 Captain Carl Hinkle, also an original member of the Group, then the Operations Officer of the 613th Squadron, assumed the command of the 614th.[12] Carl Columbus Hinkle was born in 1916 at Hendersonville, Tennessee. He graduated from Vanderbilt University with a BA degree in 1938,[13] after having distinguished himself as an All-American football star.[14] He then attended the USMA at West Point where he was also an outstanding athlete graduating in 1942 with a BS degree.[15] Before joining the 401st Hinkle, like Eveland, had been a member of the 383rd Bombardment Group. He was welcomed to the 614th as its Commander - "Captain Hinkle was promised every cooperation by all members of the Squadron."[16] In April of 1944 Carl Hinkle was promoted to Major, and in July of that year he completed his combat tour and was transferred to the neighboring 351st Bombardment Group at Polebrook as the Group Operations Officer.[17] Colonel Hinkle, a Command Pilot, retired December 31, 1963 and resided in Little Rock, Arkansas for many years until his death in 1992.

Taking command of the 614th next was William C. Garland who came from Barnesville, Georgia where he was born in 1916. For rather obvious reasons his friends called him "Judy" as did his subordinates, the latter rather discreetly but with affection. He attended high school and junior college at Gordon Military College in Barnesville and served four years in the Georgia National Guard. In 1942 he graduated from the USMA,[18] where he was a varsity baseball player. He immediately entered pilot training and won his wings at Turner Field, Georgia in March, 1943. After completing B-17 transition training at Seebring, Florida he caught up with the 401st in Montana as a flight leader in the 612th Squadron.[19] On a mission to Kiel January 4, 1944 Captain Garland was flying with Major W.K. Martin, the 612th C.O. who that day was the Air Commander. They developed engine trouble over the North Sea and were forced to ditch. Their aircraft, "Carolyne," one of the 401st originals, was landed on the sea by Captain Garland between two British trawlers. It took over an hour to rescue the crew from what the British Admiralty called the coldest and roughest day of the winter. Unfortunately, two were lost; the bombardier, Floyd G. Howe, was deceased when removed from the water and the body of waist gunner, S/Sgt. R.D. Newton was not recovered. Captain Garland said, "We were lucky. We would have had lots more trouble than we

Captain Alvah H. Chapman, Jr. (left) and Lt. Elmer Mercer beside aircraft "Polar Star" (in Russian). The aircraft was a loaner PFF aircraft not assigned to the 401st Bomb Group. Loading lists indicate it was SN 43-38600 flown by Chapman and Mercer on a mission to Harburg November 6, 1944. USAF Photo Collection neg. #65466AC courtesy of NASM, Smithsonian Institution.

encountered, but every man on the crew did exactly what he was supposed to do when the time came. The enlisted men in particular did a fine job. Lt. Nolte, my navigator, stayed at his job until we were only 100 feet over the water. Lt. E.G. Owens (flying as observer in the tail gunner position) was everywhere at once. He supervised the crew when they were forced to throw things overboard to lighten the ship, he got them set up in the radio compartment when we were forced to crash, and he kept up a line of chatter and banter throughout that was unbeatable. The British did a wonderful job of recovering the bombardier and trying to revive him, but he was gone beyond all hope. They searched unceasingly for the other man but the sea was too angry and the undertow too great for anyone to survive alone that day."[20]

The following week Captain Garland joined the 614th Squadron as its Operations Officer to replace Captain James Foster who was lost at Oschersleben January 11, 1944 during the greatest air battle of World War II. Garland became the 614th C.O. when Hinkle was transferred July 15, 1944. In September, he completed a combat tour and returned to the United States on leave. During his absence the acting Squadron Commander was Captain Alvah H. Chapman, Jr. In December Garland returned to resume his command. He was promoted to Lt. Colonel and was reassigned as the Group Operations Officer.[21] During World War II Garland flew 32 combat missions.

He later enjoyed a very successful career in the military in many prestigious assignments. At the time of his retirement, August 1, 1972, as a Major General, he was the Commander of the 1st Strategic Aerospace Division at Vandenberg AFB, California. He resides at Indian Wells, California. His decorations include the Distinguished Service Medal, Legion of Merit, Distinguished Flying Cross with one oak leaf cluster, the Air Medal with three oak leaf clusters, Air Force Commendation Medal with two oak leaf clusters and the Army Commendation Medal.[22]

The last wartime C.O. of the 614th Squadron was Major Alvah H. Chapman, Jr. who took over from Garland in March, 1945.[23] He is a native of Columbus, Georgia and a 1942 graduate of the Citadel, in Charleston, South Carolina. In addition to his B.S. Degree he received a commission as a second lieutenant when he graduated. In March, 1943 he married Betty Bateman.[24] In July of that year Chapman joined the 614th Squadron at Great Falls, Montana as a flight commander.[25] In less than a year he had completed a combat tour and by then was a Captain and the Squadron Operations Officer. After home leave he returned to Deenethorpe where, as mentioned before, he was acting Squadron Commander during Garland's leave of absence.[26] Before the end of the war in Europe he had flown 37 combat missions and his decorations include: the Distinguished Flying Cross with two oak leaf clusters, the Air Medal with five oak leaf clusters and the French Croix de Guerre.[27]

During my own combat tour I saw more of Chapman than I did of Garland and came to appreciate his leadership style and his brand of quiet courage. I was always relieved on those cold dark English mornings when I learned that he was going to lead us to battle over Germany. My respect for him grew as I followed his peacetime career and must confess that I was not at all surprised at his accomplishments. He is a true leader of men with a determination for getting the job done; and with it all he has remained a true gentleman. I told him once that I always knew he had "class." After he left the military in 1945 he returned home to Columbus to become the Business Manager for the local newspaper, "The Ledger." He remained there until 1953 and his track record in business since then has been no less than phenomenal:

- Executive Vice President, St. Petersburg, Florida "Times" - 1953 to 1957
- President and Publisher, Savannah Georgia "Morning News" and "Evening Press" 1957 to 1960
- Executive, Knight Ridder Newspapers since 1960 .....
  - Executive Vice President, 1967 to 1973
  - President, 1973 to 1982
  - C.E.O., 1976 to 1988
  - Chairman, 1982 to 1989
  - Director and Chairman, Executive Committee, 1989...
- Vice President and General Manager "Miami Herald" – 1962 to 1970 and President 1970 to 1982

He has received honorary degrees from Barry University, Florida International University and the University of Miami.

His leadership and accomplishments have led to the following other awards and recognition:

- One of the Outstanding Young Men in Georgia, 1951
- Outstanding Citizen of Columbus, Georgia by Junior Chamber of Commerce, 1952
- Dade County's Outstanding Citizen, 1968-1969
- International Businessman of the Year, by Brigham Young University, 1954
- Citadel Palmetto Award, 1985
- Isaiah Thomas Award from the Rochester Technical Institute, 1986
- John Wharton Statesman Award, 1988
- Distinguished Service Award of the United Negro College Fund, 1988
- "Miami Herald" Spirit of Excellence Lifetime Achievement Award, 1989

Although he is ostensibly retired, Alvah Chapman still maintains an office at Knight Ridder, Inc., 1 Herald Plaza in Miami. He serves on various boards, and foundations remaining involved in civic endeavors. Having been Vice Chairman of the Miami Coalition for a Drug Free Community, not surprisingly in 1990 he was appointed by President George Bush to the Presidential Drug Advisory Council.[28] In 1992 the President called on him to direct reconstruction efforts in south Florida following the devastating Hurricane Andrew.

In 1986 Chapman prepared a letter for the Foreword to Vic Maslen's history of the 614th Squadron. In part he said, "The success of my missions and of the missions flown by other combat crews was a great testimonial to the dedication, commitment, professionalism, patriotism and bravery of the men of the 614th. It was one of the greatest experiences of my life to lead this outstanding group of Americans. Their contributions brought great honor and respect wherever the 614th Bomb Squadron name is recorded and wherever its history is written, not only in Vic Maslen's book, but in the hearts and minds of all who were a part of this great and noble cause. Vic has written our record, but the men of the 614th made that record become a reality."[29] It must be obvious that the "Lucky Devils" are mighty proud of Alvah Chapman!

The recollection of events of those days over Europe have grown hazy for some, but at reunions the "war stories" abound. Many of our 614th veterans can recount at least one memorable incident on a combat mission where they were truly "Lucky Devils." Several of these true tales come to mind.

* * *

One of these stories, now a virtual legend, which has been published several times,

Alvah Chapman's "Battlin' Betty" and the ground crew. Left to right: Sgt. Bill Bell, M/Sgt. Charles Barker, M/Sgt. "Doc" Sanford, and M/Sgt. "Bogey" Bogenrief. Photo from the USAF Collection courtesy of the NASM of the Smithsonian.

involves the hair-raising experiences of Alvah Chapman's crew. Lt. Chapman and crew flying "Battlin Betty" were on the famous mission to Leipzig, February 20, 1944. The reader will recall this was the first mission of "Big Week" described in Chapter 4, and led by Colonel Bowman. Chapman was deputy lead of the lead box of the 94th CBW and his co-pilot that day was Captain Delwyn C. Silver, then the Assistant Group Operations Officer. Even with drop tanks providing additional fuel the fighter escort could not go deep into the Reich. So, running low they turned for home and left the bomber task force to go it the rest of the way alone.

As soon as they lost that protective umbrella the 401st was attacked by Me-109s which made three or four passes. On the third pass one of the German fighters shot out the supercharger to Chapman's #4 engine. He called the radio operator telling him to change the amplifier to bring the supercharger back in. At that point he was still able to hold formation but ordered the bombardier, Lt. Frank M. Deville, to toggle out all but two of their bombs to lighten the load in the hope that he could still carry the remaining bombs as far as the primary target. They then suffered three more attacks by the Luftwaffe during which the waist gunner reported that the #3 engine was smoking badly. Chapman knew that he could no longer keep up with the formation. He ordered the bombardier to salvo the remaining bombs and asked his navigator, Lt. Charles M. Smith, to plot a course for home. Added to their problems was a landing gear that kept coming down. As Captain Silver worked frantically to retract the gear manually it would then come down again.

Meanwhile, the Germans recognized that they had a wounded bird, now alone deep in enemy territory, and continued to press an attack to bring her down. Captain Silver ordered the aircraft to descend in a spiral hoping that such a maneuver would deceive the enemy into thinking that they were out of control from which they would not recover. The ruse did not fool the fighters which followed them down continuing the attack from 20,000 feet to 12,000 feet. Lt. Chapman urged his crew, "You'll have to do some good shooting if we are going to make it."

The problems aboard "Battlin Betty" continued to mount – the #3 engine ran away, the control cables and the elevator trim tabs were shot out. The aircraft vibrated so badly that it was next to physically impossible to hold it under control. The intercom was inoperative and the navigator had to crawl back, under and up to the flight deck from the nose to provide a change in course as they zigzagged across Europe trying to avoid centers of known flak concentrations. One fighter continued to attack them with suicidal ferocity. Chapman told the engineer, T/Sgt. George S. Wilson, in the top turret to his rear, "If you don't get him, he is going to get us!" Chapman was still trying every kind of evasive action he could think of with the crippled vibrating bomber when Wilson yelled, "I got the son-of-a-bitch!" The German fighter was literally blown out of the sky.

Then they "hit the deck" at between 1,500 and 2,000 feet trying to stay hidden in the clouds which varied between 5/10 and 10/10 coverage. During their battle the ball turret gunner, S/Sgt. Bruno J. Spatilson, was wounded but remained at his post inside the turret until after Wilson had disposed of the last fighter. Lt. Chapman said that Lt. Smith had done "an expert job" as he navigated their B-17 for over two hours, insuring that they avoided cities such as Amsterdam and cleverly skirting small towns and known flak areas. As they were about to depart the Dutch coast an enemy fighter came at them from six o'clock but was beaten off by their now furious gunners. Lt. Chapman later said that he thought of ditching in the North Sea but discarded the idea because their radio was out and there was no way to send an S.O.S. for air-sea rescue to come and pick them up. They made it all the way!

One crew member said, "Lt. Chapman and Captain Silver saved our lives, and their landing on return was perfect." Chapman himself said, "Ten men working together as a team brought us safely home." The teamwork on the flight deck was significant and unusually physical. Because the trim tabs were shot out it required great strength to hold the aircraft in position all the way home. They accomplished this by changing off at regular intervals, giving each other a chance for a brief rest.

But "Battlin Betty" was a sorry sight! Engines #1 and #2 received hits in their induction system; engine #3 was knocked out by hits in the oil line and its dangling propeller fell off when they landed. The controls to engine #4 were shot away and its propeller was badly damaged by bullet holes. There were four direct hits by 20mm bursts in the left side of the fuselage, and machine gun bullets also raked that side of the B-17 hitting oxygen and radio equipment. Another 20mm shell hit behind the armor plate in the ball turret which was what caused the wound incurred by S/Sgt. Spatilson. Still another 20mm burst in the left wing caused fuel leaks creating a dangerous fire hazard. There were numerous flak and bullet holes in the wings and elevator; bracing in the fuselage was cut by bullet holes all along the left side. Their hydraulic system had a direct hit cutting the lines to brakes, and trim tabs on one side were also shot away. All told there were 150 holes in that B-17 and wonders of wonders, a large section of a Me-109 propeller was found lodged in one of the gun emplacements.[30]

The story demonstrates the exceptional flying skills on the fight deck and the teamwork and courage of the entire crew which served as a role model for the 614th Squadron in the year that lay ahead. That they were also "Lucky Devils" on that February 20 is a given!

Another example of outstanding flying skill with a great deal of luck thrown in was the experience of Lt. Russell B. Thompson and his crew on January 10, 1945. Their target that day was the marshalling yards at Euskirchen near Cologne. They lost an engine shortly after entering enemy territory but opted to continue. Two minutes before reaching the target another engine was hit by flak and its propeller began to windmill violently. Unable to hold their aircraft, "Hard Seventeen," in formation, Lt. Thompson turned out and his bombardier, Lt. W.M. Bruce, dropped his bombs on an isolated highway junction.

Lt. Thompson headed the aircraft west. A few minutes later a third engine, also damaged by flak, was lost and they began to lose altitude rapidly. They headed for allied occupied Belgium and shortly after clearing enemy lines, the navigator located a small airfield for an emergency landing. This was home to a Polish Squadron attached to the RAF. With very poor visibility of between 500 to 700 yards Lt. Thompson came in for a landing and found himself 90 degrees from the runway. He then decided to go around and land downwind, but when he turned left he found himself on a level with a grove of very tall trees. He then turned right and found two very tall industrial chimneys directly in front of him. He lacked the power to fly over them or go around them so he decided to go between them. The wingspan of "Hard

Russell B. Thompson crew. Standing left to right: Lt. H.J. Lupowitz - navigator, Lt. Russell B. Thompson - pilot, Lt. Clarence Cassidy - copilot, Lt. William B. Bruce - bombardier. Kneeling left to right: S/Sgt. James P. Christianson - ball, S/Sgt. Edward G. Dana - waist, S/Sgt. Dale Heikes - tail, T/Sgt. Robert E. Bode - radio, (missing from the photograph, T/Sgt. Rodney Wilson - engineer. USAF Photo Collection neg. #65783AC courtesy of NASM, Smithsonian Institution.

Seventeen" was 103 feet. The co-pilot claimed they cleared the chimney on the right by three feet, and the waist gunner said there was about a six foot clearance from the chimney on their left.

Having gotten past that obstacle Lt. Thompson was immediately faced with power lines that provided electricity to the industrial plant into which they had nearly crashed seconds before. He said he had no choice; he had to fly under them! Again he beat the odds, and later said that when he went under those wires he believes he was about three feet off the ground.

Directly in their path remained two houses. He managed to clear the first, a one-story structure, and had to lift his wing to get over the second, which was a two-story residence. Beyond the houses was a field, rolling terrain with slight rises and gullies so filled with snow that fence posts were barely visible. Lt. Thompson ordered his co-pilot, Lt. Clarence Cassidy, to shut off the fuel switches before he put "Hard Seventeen" down on that Belgian farm. He waited to cut off the ignition until the fuel was consumed to prevent the possibility of fire. He put her down on the crest of a hill and the entire tail section aft of the waist door broke off.

Somehow, Lt. Thompson flew what was left of the aircraft as it bounced to the next rise where it struck the ground with a thud, swerving to a sudden stop. "In ten seconds ... probably less," Lt. Thompson said, "the entire crew was out and nobody was scratched. I can't praise my co-pilot enough for the wonderful job he did and I think my entire crew should be commended for their behavior." The Belgians took the Thompson crew to a nearby home where they were wined and dined until a military truck came to take them to the nearby airfield where they waited for transportation back to England. Unfortunately, "Hard Seventeen" was left behind to be scrapped.[31]

No wonder they were called the "Lucky Devils" of the 614th!

Notes to Chapter 5

1. Closway, Gordon R. _Pictorial Record of the 401st Bomb Group_ unnumbered p. 25
2. Closway, Gordon R. _614th Squadron History_ p. 14
3. Eveland, I. Wayne _Memories and Reflections_ p. 3-4
4. Ibid. p. 5-9
5. Ibid. p. 9-30
6. Ibid. p. 38A-41
7. Ibid. p. 53
8. Closway, see 2 above p. 20-21
9. Eveland, see 3 above p. 54, 55-78, 82, 84
10. Closway, see 2 above p. 21
11. Maslen, Selwyn V. _614th Bombardment Squadron (H): Squadron History,_ Forward, unnumbered p. 3
12. Bowman, Harold W. & Selwyn V. Maslen _Bowman's Bombers_ p. 7
13. Strong, Russell A. _Biographical Directory of the Eighth Air Force, 1942-1945_ p. 111
14. Closway, see 2 above p. 21
15. Strong, see 13 above p. 111
16. Closway, see 2 above p. 21
17. Bowman & Maslen, see 12 above p. 20,32
18. _Poop From Group,_ December, 1979
19. Closway, see 2 above p. 109
20. Bowman & Maslen, see 12 above p. 8, 80 and Bowman, Harold W. & Selwyn V. Maslen _401st B.G.(H)_ _Casualties in W.W.II_ p. 6
21. Bowman & Maslen, see 12 above p. 7, 32, 41, 56, 67
22. See 18 above
23. Maslen, see 11 above p. 138
24. _Who's Who in America 1990-1991_
25. Maslen, see 11 above, Forward, unnumbered p. 5-6
26. Bowman & Maslen, see 12 above p. 36, 41
27. See 24 above
28. Ibid.
29. Maslen, see 11 above, Forward, unnumbnered p. 5-6
30. Closway, see 2 above p. 88B-88F
31. Ibid. see Summary of Events for January, 1945

CHAPTER 6 — NORM SISSON AND CREW

As the post war years passed I could only recall Norm Sisson as one of our pilots, and a contemporary in the 614th Squadron, a familiar name like those of Spuhler, Mays, Seder, St. Aubyn and others. However, try as I might, I could not recall his face until we met during a 401st reunion in the 1980s. After we met again my best image of him during the war was that he was a rather austere young man, certainly not loquacious and a loner of sorts. This impression was vindicated by his present day admission that he took his responsibilities most seriously. He was discomforted by his youth as an aircraft commander and made a conscious effort to appear mature beyond his years. We had not been friends in those days, or barracks buddies in the 614th, so I did not get to know him well, but in researching this book I learned that the "Maiden" had been his aircraft from the time she was ready for combat. Since then, through reunion meetings, letters, and telephone conversations and our mutual attraction to that lovely bird we have become friends.

In the war years of the 1940s the Topeka, Kansas newspapers, like those all over our country, faithfully reported the military exploits of its young men in the service of their country. They regularly printed news of the military career of Norman L. Sisson, a hometown product.

He was described as the son of Mr. and Mrs. Earl Sisson of 2601 Wisconsin Avenue and a graduate of the Highland Park High School of that city in 1942.

After he graduated from high school Norm was employed by North American Aviation at its Kansas City plant until he enlisted in the United States Army in October, 1942. For six months he worked on machine guns and aircraft turrets at MacDill Army Airfield at Tampa, Florida until he was accepted as an Aviation Cadet.

Norm won his wings as a pilot in January, 1944 at Freeman Army Airfield, Seymour, Indiana. He was then assigned to Hendricks Field, Seebring, Florida where he received transitional training, learning to fly the B-17 Flying Fortress. After completing this course of training Norm was ordered to Salt Lake City, Utah where he met the crew he would lead in combat.[1]

The crew, each member trained for his specific position on the aircraft, was now ready to be molded into a fighting team. These ten young men, all volunteers, were a microcosm of America. They came from such diverse places as Topeka, Kansas, Brooklyn, New York, Philadelphia, Pennsylvania, El Paso and Fort Worth, Texas. [2]

Sisson's crew members were:

Norman L. Sisson	first pilot	Andrew S. Haluck	radio operator
Eugene E. Hoemann	co-pilot	Jose M. Torres	waist gunner
Lavern Crossen	navigator	Mark M. Helf	waist gunner
Nathan Picker	bombardier	Calvin J. Stevens.	ball turret gunner
Peter J. Carter	engineer	Francis T. Ritchie	tail gunner [3]

Sisson, a product of the heart of America, was typical of so many young men of his age in the 1940s who entered the Aviation Cadet program. He was only two years out of high school, trained to fly a four-engine bomber, expected to assume a leadership role and be responsible for the lives of his crew and their very expensive aircraft. Wayne Eveland said it this way: "All over America, youngsters who should still be in school were holding down tough jobs made for mature men - and **succeeding** at it. That's how we eventually won the war!"[4]

The Sisson crew completed their combat training at Dyersburg Army Airfield, Tennessee and were then sent to a staging base at Kearney Army Airfield, Nebraska. Their time had come. Their "orders" dated July 7 directed them to proceed, by B-17 aircraft 43-38001, to Grenier Army Airfield, Manchester, New Hampshire, "or such other Air Port of Embarkation as the CG, ATC, may direct, thence to the overseas destination of shipment FP-900-BA."[5]

That destination was to become "somewhere in England." Their route was probably the same that my crew followed several months later as we left Manchester, stopping at Goose Bay, Labrador, Meeks Field at Reykjavik, Iceland and on to Valley, Wales. Leaving the aircraft they "ferried" across the ocean, they were taken to a nearby personnel replacement depot. They spent several days there before being shipped to Station 128, the 401st Bombardment Group at Deenethorpe, where they were assigned as a replacement crew to the 614th Squadron. They soon learned that combat crews were no longer using a ten-man crew, it having been determined that one waist gunner could handle both guns back to back on either side of the fuselage. According to Sisson, Mark M. Helf, was removed from the crew and was shipped back to the United States for further assignment.[6]

At last, "Uncle Sam" was ready to

Lt. Norman L. Sisson — 1944. Courtesy of Norman L. Sisson

Sisson crew. Standing left to right: Lt. Nathan Picker - bombardier, Lt. Lavern Crossen - navigator, Lt. Norman L. Sisson - pilot, Lt. Eugene Hoemann - copilot. Front row left to right: S/Sgt. Francis T. Ritchie - tail, T/Sgt. Peter Carter - engineer, S/Sgt. Jose Torres - waist, T/Sgt. Andrew S. Haluck - radio, S/Sgt. Calvin J. Stevens - ball. Courtesy of Norman L. Sisson

get a return on his investment of several years of intensive training in the crew of Norman L. Sisson. On August 16, 1944 they flew their first combat mission. Their aircraft was "Down 'N Go" [7] and their target was the main assembly plant for the German Ju-88 aircraft [8] at Schkeuditz.[9] Sisson incorrectly recorded the mission as being to Leipzig[10] and his bombardier, Nathan Picker, called it the "Leipzig-Magdeburg area."[11] Since both of their personal logs are in most instances accurate, I "chalked up" this discrepancy as being due to jitters on their first time out. Picker carried a bomb load of five 1,000 pound GPs which he salvoed on a secondary target, an airfield at Halberstadt, from 25,000 feet. Halberstadt is about 50 miles southwest of Magdeburg. He described the flak as being intense, noting there were 13 holes in the aircraft. One of those holes was of particular interest to him since it was in the nose compartment which he shared with the navigator.[12] Of the 425 aircraft of the 1st Division flying that day, ten were lost, 234 had battle damage, including all nine of the B-17s furnished by the 614th Squadron.[13]

Two days later they were up again, this time on board IW-B to bomb a railroad bridge over the Meuse River at Yvoir, Belgium. The purpose of this mission was to cut off the escape of German troops retreating from northern France.[14] Picker carried six 1,000 pound GPs which he salvoed at "bombs away."[15] The bomb strikes covered the target area and one bomb was observed to make a direct hit on the bridge. [16] Although both Picker and Sisson recorded having not seen any flak on the mission, officially, about ten bursts were reported from the area of Liege. That German gunner was pretty good since he damaged five of our aircraft.[17]

On August 25, the Sisson crew flew a 613th aircraft, IN-Q, to bomb the rocket experimental station at Peenemunde, way up on the Baltic Sea.[18] Bombing was done visually from 20,000 feet with Picker dropping five 1,000 pound GPs. Three of these failed to release at "bombs away." Malfunctions such as this were frequent usually caused by condensation freezing in the shackles. Tripping the mechanism was all that was generally needed, though at times it seemed to help to give the bomb a good kick. This necessitated Picker attaching a "walk around" bottle of oxygen, crawling back and up to the flight deck, entering the bomb bay and crossing its narrow catwalk. He then had to reach over and use a screwdriver to trip each shackle holding the bombs, manually releasing them.[19] Picture this - there he was with his electric suit unplugged so he could move around and it is well below zero at that altitude. He was standing in the open bomb bay almost four miles above the earth. Because he was carrying his own oxygen supply, he was unable to wear his chest pack parachute or his heavy flak suit (body armor). It was not a very easy or a very safe chore and I recall the crew always being relieved when the radio operator who checked the bomb bay reported it to be clear after "bombs away."

Bombing results at Peenemunde were excellent with 80 percent of the bombs hitting within a 1,000 foot circle.[20] Picker reported "some flak very accurate" with three holes in their aircraft.[21] Two 401st aircraft suffered major flak damage and 23 others had minor damage.[22] It was a very long ride - Sisson recorded nine hours flight time. [23]

Long missions remind me of a true story recorded by the aviation historian, Roger A. Freeman, who described how our Colonel Bowman overcame one of the "more personal crew problems, but nonetheless crucial in the matter of comfort." Colonel Bowman said:

"Those who designed the B-17 were aware that on long missions some modern conveniences must be provided. So at each station small funnels were attached to outlet tubes. What the designers, sitting in their comfortable offices, failed to realize was that at 50 degrees below zero it wasn't long before the ball turret gunner's plastic bubble was covered with human frost and the relief tubes were frozen solid. So, of course, we had to shut them off. But we were unable to shut off people. We tried everything. Personally, I hung a one quart canteen on the control wheel, but with heavy flying clothing, flak vests, parachutes, lap straps, and temperatures, there were some problems in meeting the little container. Some of the boys took off their `tin hats' for the purpose. Of course that relieved them of the protection but it had one advantage, at the end of the mission it was easy to knock the ice off on the ground and be ready for the next mission. But we had far to many in the hospital with frostbite. The problem caused much concern. So the two problems finally met.

"I woke up one night with the solution: prophylactic rubber condoms. Over-zealous

planners had supplied us with enough rubber safes to last thru' World War Ten. I jumped out of bed and phoned the Group Bombardier, Major Julius Pickoff, and said: 'Pick you are hereby appointed Group Pee Officer. Before today's mission I want 2,000 rubbers distributed!' He said: 'Oh boss; at 0200 hrs you call me out of my much needed sleep just for a funny?' I finally persuaded him I was serious and he then phoned the Group Supply Officer, who answered in a very sleepy voice out of the sack. Pick demanded: 'The Old Man wants 2,000 safes and he wants them right now.' The irate Supply Officer said 'That old Son of a Bitch!' Pick had to go over and pull him out of bed to get the job done. The system may not have been equal to the Savoy Hotel facilities - but it worked," [24]

Wayne Eveland recalled the following concerning Colonel Bowman's brilliant solution to this major personal personnel problem. He said, "Once a condom was used for relief it would be set on the floor and in minutes would be frozen and over Germany the crewmen sometimes threw them overboard as frozen missiles."[25]

Their next time out was on August 27 with the Sisson crew on "Betty's Revenge." The target was Berlin with the 401st leading the 94th CBW. Over the Danish peninsula they encountered some German flak, but worse than that the weather turned so bad that they were recalled and returned to England with their bombs. The crews on that mission were credited with a combat mission because they had been shot at over enemy territory.[26] I think it is important to say that the Eighth Air Force may have been recalled from time to time because of the volatile weather over Europe but they were never turned back because of enemy flak or fighter opposition!

That recall may have been fortuitous for the Sisson crew if one believes in dreams. Sisson told me that the abortive mission to Berlin was special to him. He explained that during the night his navigator, Lavern Crossen, had a dream that they were going to be shot down on

Capt. Walter E. Haberer, navigator looks on as Col. Harold W. Bowman gives the OK sign congratulating Maj. Julius Pickoff, the Group Bombardier on his bombing accuracy on the mission to Paris where the target was the famous Le Bourget Airdrome on June 14, 1944. USAF Photo Collection neg. #65694AC courtesy of NASM, Smithsonian Institution.

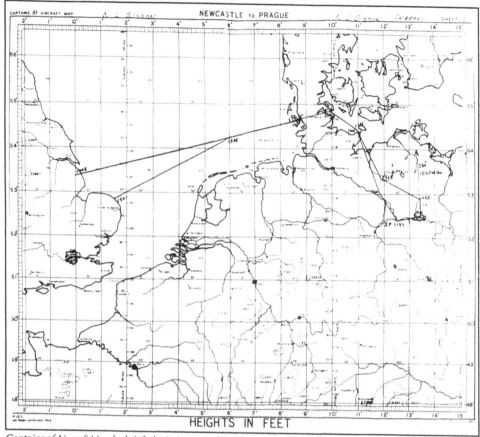

HEIGHTS IN FEET

Captains of Aircraft Map for briefed mission to Berlin on August 27, 1944 which was recalled due to impassable weather over Denmark. Sisson's superstitious navigator dreamt they would be shot down and, just in case, drew a heading 330 degrees north from Berlin toward Sweden which he gave Sisson before takeoff. Courtesy of Norman L. Sisson.

the next mission. That morning Sisson said that Crossen was so concerned that he told him of his dream, and on the "Captains of Aircraft Map" on which the navigator projected their route in and out of Germany, Crossen had added an alternative course from the target north to neutral Sweden. Sisson furnished me with a copy of that map which shows an arrow drawn north from Berlin with a compass heading of 330 degrees and a radio frequency of 1312. Sisson said that Crossen told him that if they were hit over that heavily defended target they should try to make it to Sweden where they would be interned by that neutral country.[27] As it turned out Sisson did not have to heed Crossen's advice. But it is also interesting that the Sisson crew was never again briefed for a mission to Berlin.

Their fifth mission on August 30 aboard IW-O was to a rocket site at Coubronne, France.[28] Although this target is not listed in the current Atlas or on current road maps it was a launching site for V-1 missiles located in the Pas de Calais area, directly across the Channel from the white cliffs of Dover. The V-1 was a terrorist weapon popularly known to wartime Britons as the "buzz bomb," a robot device fired from the continent against England. They bombed the V-1 site using the Gee-H system.[29]

The Gee was a navigational aid developed by the British which made use of signals from established ground stations.[30] The British further developed this concept as a bombing aid and called it Gee-H or G-H. It utilized an airborne transmitter which interrogated the ground stations so as to provide a "fix" or location to bomb through the clouds.[31] Although the results that day were not observed due to clouds, Picker said that he had unloaded his twenty 250

401st formation; note the lead B-17 IY-S has a PFF radome replacing the ball turret.

pound GPs from 24,000 feet.[32] Sisson said there was no flak and of course no damage to the B-17.[33] Roger Freeman has said that V-1 and the later V-2 sites were targets when unsuitable weather prevailed over Germany, and that "NOBALL" was the code word used for these targets.[34]

On September 1 the Sisson crew was briefed for a mission to Ludwigshaven but got only as far as Paris when they were recalled due to extremely bad weather conditions over Germany.[35] Two days later with Colonel Bowman leading the 1st Division, Sisson again headed for Ludwigshaven on board IW-B. The target was the I.G. Farbenindustrie plant, the largest of its numerous facilities in that heavily defended city. Bombing on this mission was done by another development in radar called PFF, an acronym for Pathfinder Force.[36]

The British had first developed this airborne scanner as H2S which the Americans later refined and called H2X. The scanner was housed in a retractable radome. It was first installed under the nose of B-17s. The lack of space in that compartment resulted in the removal of the ball turret in PFF B-17s and replacing it with the radome, locating the operator just forward in the radio room. The device was code named "mickey mouse" which was later shortened and more commonly known as "mickey."[37]

One of the major obstacles in bombing German targets was the presence of clouds or overcast which were there more often than not. The earlier systems, such as Gee-H and later PFF, made operations possible. The plan was to assign B-17s installed with PFF and the trained "mickey" operators to a squadron for each Division, then to each CBW, and as they became more abundantly available, to each Group. At the end of hostilities there was an average of 12 PFF aircraft assigned to each Group.[38]

Picker took four 1,000 pound GPs and four 500 pound IBs (incendiary clusters) to Ludwigshaven that day which he trailed out at 250 foot intervals from 24,000 feet.[39] The bombing results were not observed due to the cloud cover but the flak was observed for sure! Twenty-five of the 39 401st B-17s were damaged, five seriously.[40] Sisson's aircraft received a hole in its wing and in the #3 engine, which, leaking oil had to be feathered.[41]

Two days later, September 5, Sisson and crew were assigned to a 613th Squadron aircraft named "Homing Pigeon," returning to the same target at Ludwigshaven. Again they bombed by PFF but results were observed through broken clouds and assessed as good.[42] Meager flak was observed at the IP (initial point or start of the bomb run) and increased in intensity down their bomb run to the target.[43] Picker agreed that it was intense[44] and Sisson recorded the mission with a "star" which in his grading system defined it as a "downright hazardous mission."[45] Their aircraft had eight flak holes including one in the navigator's astrodome, right over his head and right in front of the pilot and co-pilot's windscreen.[46] The 1st Division put up 277 Fortresses that day; they lost two, 163 were damaged and they brought home two crewmen KIA and 11 wounded.[47]

On September 9 the Sisson crew was assigned to "Shade Ruff II." Their primary target, if they could bomb visually, was the same I.G. Farbenindustrie plant at Ludwigshaven. However, clouds covered the target so they moved on to their secondary target, the large railroad complex at Mannheim. They bombed by PFF, without being able to observe the results.[48] Picker unloaded twelve 250 pound IB clusters from 24,000 feet. He said the flak was heavy and that he had observed two B-17s shot down.[49] One of those lost was the aircraft and crew of Lt. David Loughlin of the 612th Squadron whose aircraft took a direct hit in the radio room with fire spreading along the wing. The pilot pulled out of formation and at 20,000 feet the aircraft broke in half aft of the radio room. Only two survived, Lt. R.L. Burnard, the navigator, and T/Sgt. O.E. Livingston, the engineer who were POWs.[50]

On September 17 the Sisson crew flew what came to be called the "Groesbeck mission." The name was derived from the small Dutch town, Groesbeck, located just across the border from Germany and close to the German fortifications called the Siegfried Line. Picker logged the mission as Eindhoven which is a larger city about 30 miles southwest of Groesbeck, also located in the Netherlands.[51] Allied ground forces had made an urgent appeal to the Eighth Air Force to provide support in the form of a tactical mission.[52] The purpose was to support the largest airborne operation of the war under the code name "MARKET GARDEN," which was to be an attack centered in the area of Arnhem. The specific target for the 401st was a concentration of guns and tanks located in a forested area. The raid was to be made from an unusually low altitude for B-17s at 12,000 feet.[53] Lt. Colonel Seawell led the 1st Division.[54] They were assigned an area bounded by specific geographical coordinates with bombing done by elements of six aircraft. There was virtually no opposition from the ground or in the air.[55] Picker carried a load of 24 250 pound fragmentation bombs which were anti-personnel devices that exploded, scattering small metal fragments in all directions.[56]

Norm Sisson had some special recollections of the "Groesbeck Mission" which are interesting in their detail and invoke memories for those who flew combat in the Eighth. He recalled the Squadron orderly came into the barracks with his flashlight at 4:30 A.M. on September 17 to wake those who were scheduled to fly that day. He confessed to being awake, and that he always had trouble sleeping the night before his crew was to fly a mission. He heard the grumbling voices of those being roused by the orderly to fly, as well as the others whose sleep was being disturbed by activity in the barracks. Norm admitted to grave concerns about survival of his crew and ongoing thoughts about death before each mission. He was often reminded of a private promise extracted by the wives of Hoemann and Crossen before they left the States that he would bring their husbands home safe. He always thought having made this vow was somewhat strange when one considered that Hoemann and Crossen and their wives were in their mid-twenties and he had just turned 20. He said he was self-conscious of his youth and purposely hid his age from them. He considered himself mature for his age and serious with respect to his responsibilities and obligations as the first pilot. His seriousness probably had something to do with his comment that he never tolerated irresponsible conduct or horseplay.

"Shade Ruff #2" B-17 42-97478 IW-Q of the 614th Squadron.

401st formation. From top to bottom: IW-D, IW-Q, IW-X, and IW-F.

In my barracks there was a "free spirit," a pilot whose name was Paul Wittman, known to his friends as Moe. It seemed Moe frequently returned from his evening of pleasure when the wake-up ritual began. He had this old windup phonograph, vintage early 1930s. As the alerted crews began to dress quietly and the others tried to settle down to sleep, Moe would play a record, British made, of a song I never heard before or since called "American Eagles." It was a rousing song with a vocal chorus that in each verse screamed "American Eagles! American Eagles!" To those present at that moment it was the most revolting kind of militant message. All were dedicated to destroying that record but never did. The blasphemous oaths hurled in Moe's direction met with only his raucous laughter. Those moments, in the cold barracks, as we dressed were private very solemn ones; not meant to be shared with loud, boisterous, martial music of any kind. After dressing that morning the aircrews walked or rode their bicycles down the English road from their 614th Squadron area to the mess hall, about a quarter of a mile away, for breakfast. Norm recalled there was considerable fog that morning. Breakfast included the usual powdered eggs which were the subject of regular "bitching" and appreciated by very few. About an hour after being awakened, they rode trucks to the building where they pulled on their electric suits and found their seats in the briefing room. Then came that suspenseful moment when the screen covering the map was pulled, revealing a red line across the Channel into Europe, ending at their target for the day. Norm said that on this morning there were three things quite different from most other missions. First, the total bomb load consisted of 250 pound clusters of small fragmentation bombs; second, the bombing altitude was 12,000 feet whereas they hardly ever went in under 20,000 feet; and last, the bombing by six ship elements rather than by Group formation with its three Squadrons of 12 aircraft. After the general briefing the pilots, navigators and bombardiers had special briefings. The latter was short and the bombardier with the rest of the crew again boarded trucks, picking up their machine guns which they installed when they arrived at their aircraft. When they arrived they found the bombs had already been loaded by some of those dedicated guys they hardly ever saw. Some of them probably still think their efforts were not appreciated, but they were - by all who flew and depended on them. After the duties were performed there was a long wait which was usually spent in the ground crews' tent trying to stay warm.

Sisson said that when he arrived at the aircraft that morning his suspicions were confirmed that their B-17 was another "war weary." He said there were aluminum patches over patches covering flak holes. He said, and I concur, it seemed that as a newer crew, which his was, they always got the older aircraft. Norm said that he was always serious about the pre-flight of his aircraft, but that he was dead serious when it came to checking out a war weary aircraft. The time finally came to start engines which was done with the crew chief standing there with the fire extinguisher, just in case. The runup was done at 500 rpm (revolutions per minute), generators checked, turbo superchargers switched in and out, and propeller controls moved through various rpm settings. Each engine was also run at high manifold pressure to check each of two magnetos. Turbo superchargers were set for takeoff and the check list was again rechecked for all pre-takeoff requirements. Engine #4 ran rough on the generator check but smoothed out to a reassuring roar at full power. At the first sign of daylight the green flare was fired from flying control and the 144th mission of the 401st was on.

At their briefing each pilot received a taxi diagram which identified the aircraft he should follow onto the taxi perimeter strip from their own hardstand. There they paraded, one after the other, toward the runway. Takeoff for each aircraft was to be at 60 second intervals because of the fog.

Norm said: "I wheeled our bomber on the end of the runway as soon as the aircraft ahead of us disappeared in to the fog. As soon as I had completed our turn a tremendous orange flash appeared directly in front of our bomber. The ground shook from a thunderous explosion. We instantly knew that the bomber in front of us had exploded. The orange ball from the burning aircraft continued to grow. A red flare was fired from the tower. We held our position still poised for takeoff ... After about three minutes a green flare was fired. I knew we had to clear the burning wreckage with more clearance than usual. I eased the four throttles of the Wright Cyclone engines until they were roaring at 37 inches manifold pressure and 2500 rpm. I yelled to Hoemann to call out the air speed. Instrument takeoff was required for all aircraft that morning because of the fog ... the aircraft had to be held to dead center on the runway; any slight over correction could cause the bomber to swerve off the concrete runway. The aircraft shuddered under 4800 horsepower; brakes were held until maximum takeoff power was obtained, then released. The bomber leaped forward and reached 110 mph in 40 seconds." Norm felt the weight shift off the landing gear. He eased back on the wheel and the bomber slowly lifted off the runway. Norm said that his eyes never left the instruments but that when they passed over the orange flame in the fog Hoemann said: "poor bastards" as he pressed the brakes to stop the spinning gear and retracted it. When the Fortress reached 140 mph Sisson throttled back the engines to 2300 rpm and climbed away from the explosion. After they returned from the mission they learned that the crash they saw was that of "Rosie's Sweat Box" with all members of the crew of Francis E. Cook killed when they crashed on the Weldon Oundle Road. It will be recalled from Chapter 3 that "Rosie's Sweat Box" was the third B-17 to have the call letters IW-A. Six days later those call letters were adopted by the "Maiden" when she arrived at Deenethorpe.[57]

The leaders of the "Groesbeck Mission" were commended by Colonel Bowman who said: "An especially laudable feature of your achievement was the fact that the lack of target material, particularly photos, made the mission at the outside a tough one. Examining the very poor photo you were given to identify the target and then observing the splendid results as shown by the bomb strike photos, it is gratifying to note the efficiency with which you pinpointed the target. The success which greeted your effort could only have been obtained by thorough pre-mission planning and preparation, smooth teamwork and determination."[58]

In the 614th Squadron History it is recorded that during the month of September 1944 the 401st Bombardment Group was devoted mostly to PFF bombing of synthetic oil targets. In the "Summary of Events" for that month the history said the "Groesbeck Mission" was the notable exception to those strategic missions. It referred to the raid on the ground defenses around Groesbeck as a very successful operation and said that Lt. Ted Carroll and crew were to be commended. The Summary noted such performance "illustrates the achievement of the 614th Squadron."[59]

A newspaper article at the time reported the following concerning the "Groesbeck Mission": "Attacking in advance of airborne assault about 850 'Flying Fortresses' escorted by approximately 100 P-51s, yesterday blasted communications, flak positions, and other military objectives throughout a wide area of Holland."[60]

The Sisson crew flew its tenth mission on September 19 to Hamm on board "Betty's Revenge."[61] The primary target that day was the railroad yard at Soest. The purpose of the raid was to provide support for the airborne landing at Arnhem by attacking German ability to transport materials and personnel needed by their ground forces.[62] Things began to go wrong just before the bombers reached their IP when a weather aircraft at target area reported that clouds would not permit visual bombing. Soon after, on their bomb run, they ran into a weather front with clouds up to 28,000 and 30,000 feet.[63] Picker admits that due to the very bad weather which "set in rapidly" his bombs landed in an open field.[64] The lead box bombed railroad yards at Wessel, a few miles southeast of Arnhem, on the Rhine River, while the low box bombed blindly at the yards at Hamm, a few miles from Soest.[65] If all that confusion wasn't enough, the weather on their return to England was equally bad and the 401st was diverted to North Pickenham, home of the 491st Bombardment Group, as well as other bases scattered around. Nathan Picker said the weather was so bad that they were unable to return to Deenethorpe for two days.[66]

By the close of business on September 19 the Sisson crew had completed ten missions flying eight different aircraft. Norm recalled that most of those B-17s were combat- repaired 1942 models. He remembered that "Down 'N Go" that took them on their first mission went down just eight days later with the crew of Lt. P.W. Finney.[67] Lt. Finney's crew was one of five replacement crews to have arrived at Deenethorpe during July, 1944. Three of those crews were shot down[68] while Sisson's crew was building up combat experience. On their fourth and tenth missions the Sisson crew flew "Betty's Revenge" later lost over Politz on October 7 with Lt. A. Harasyn's crew. On their seventh mission, September 5 they were on "Homing Pigeon" a 1944 model with factory installed chin turret. He said the 1944 models had flying characteristics superior to the older ones. "Homing Pigeon" went down with Lt. R. J. Keck's crew at Merseburg on November 21 as described in Chapter 10.

With ten missions under their belts Norm felt his crew was coming together "as one of the finest," with each member knowing his job and performing with great efficiency and care.

Members of the Babcock crew, September 1988 at the 401st Bomb Group Reunion at Dearborn, Michigan. Left to right: John F. Bilby - radio, Frederick H. Babcock - pilot, Allen H. Crawford - navigator, John Bousfield - copilot, the author - George Menzel - bombardier, and seated Walter E. Parnham - tail.

It had become more and more apparent to him that it was less and less necessary to give anyone of them instructions as they were performing as a single combat unit. Norm has since been amazed how nine men, some mere boys, from very different social, educational and geographical backgrounds, could be thrown together and be molded into a team relying on each other in combat. He said this was impressive when one considered there was no particular selection process, since names were taken randomly from lists of individuals who had completed the necessary training to fill a spot on a crew. Norm said, "I noticed that personal friendships were developed between crew members within the Squadron in the earlier stages of our training and missions. As they came to the realization that death could come at any time, friendships took on a more businesslike relationship. As crew members began to lose friends ... a natural barrier to personal friendship came into play as a defense mechanism. I found that I became more reserved, less willing to discuss personal matters and generally isolated my feelings from other crew members. I also was reluctant to accept any attempt to enter into personal friendships and am certain that others looked upon this behavior as being aloof and standoffish."[69]

It is true that combat experience affects men in different ways. Although I had my own fears, the gravity of what I survived did not really hit me until my tour was over and I was back in the States. As far as our crew relationships were concerned I am of a different persuasion. Our crew, Fred Babcock's, grew closer together as time passed, and after I left my crew to be a navigator on another, I was consciously concerned about them.

These shared experiences we'll never forget: wake-up calls for missions in the middle of the night for the next mission; those individual and most private thoughts as one dressed in the cold barracks; the anticipation and dread when the screen was removed from the map in the briefing room to disclose the target for the day; those personal concerns while waiting for the green flare to be fired ordering takeoff; the confusing and frequently frightening experiences of assembly, often in predawn darkness. All of these were only a prelude to enemy aerial attacks or the insidious flak from the ground. One never got used to flak, but I remained fascinated by it and when it was reported, I had to see it. Nor did one get used to hearing it rain on the fuselage like hail on a tin roof or get used to the bursts so close that you could see the inside characteristic flash of fiery red.

Even as we would return to friendly skies there was the always-present threat to the bomber crews, the English weather! No matter how clear the morning, we came to expect it to be foul when we returned. The peril of midair collisions as hundreds of bombers let down through clouds, and frequently rain, was always a clear and present danger. Often unable to see anything, even the aircraft that had been on one's wing for hours, we let down through that mess and as we lost altitude, all eyes on board were straining to see something, anything! Frequently, the first thing we saw were the white caps on the cold, gray and forbidding North Sea. But at least then there was some visibility. At times it was so bad that it was necessary to make emergency landings at special bases along or near the English coast. One of these I became familiar with was Woodbridge, with its wide runways capable of handling two aircraft landing side by side and extra long for damaged aircraft. The sides of the runways were equipped with fog burners that lifted the fog several hundred feet. Once over England and headed for home the stress from such weather frequently accelerated, as we neared Deenethorpe the bombers were all doing the same thing, trying to land on those many airfields, so close together on that little island. The thought brings to mind an old comrade, who at the time said, "We go out in the morning to fight the 'Hun' and have an even greater fight with the English weather when we try to get back home."

When Sisson and crew returned to Deenethorpe from their tenth mission they had a special treat coming. Six days later they would meet their own B-17, the one they came to name "Maiden U.S.A.".

Notes to Chapter 6

1. Newspaper articles, publication and date of publication unknown furnished the author as an enclosure to a letter from Norman L. Sisson February 13, 1991.
2. Letter from Ralph W. Trout to Norman L. Sisson February 6, 1984 furnished the author by Sisson as an enclosure to his letter February 13, 1991.

3. *Movement Orders 370.5-1008(198-20) 7 July 1944 Headquarters, 271st Staging Base, Kearney AAF, Kearney, Nebraska. Furnished the author by Norman L. Sisson as an enclosure to his letter February 13, 1991.*

4. Eveland, I. Wayne <u>Memories and Reflections</u> p. 42-43

5. See 3 above

6. Letter from Norman L. Sisson to the author February 13, 1991.

7. Maslen, Selwyn V. <u>614th Squadron: Crews - Missions - Aircraft</u> p. 78.

8. Maslen, Selwyn V. <u>614 Bombardment Squadron (H): Squadron History</u> p. 80.

9. Freeman, Roger A. <u>The Mighty Eighth War Diary</u> p. 236

10. Photocopies of personal log of Norman L. Sisson and bomb fuse tags with Sisson's notations furnished the author as an enclosure to Sisson's letter February 13, 1991.

11. Photocopy of personal log of Nathan Picker furnished the author as an enclosure to a letter from Norman L. Sisson February 13, 1991.

12. Ibid.

13. Maslen, see 8 above p. 80

14. Ibid.

15. See 11 above

16. Bowman, Harold W. & Selwyn V. Maslen <u>Bowman's Bombers</u> p.38.

17. Maslen, see 8 above p. 81

18. Maslen, see 8 above p. 82

19. See 11 above

20. Maslen, see 8 above p. 82

21. See 11 above

22. Bowman & Maslen see 16 above p. 39

23. See 10 above

24. Freeman, Roger A. <u>B-17 Fortress at War</u> p. 86

25. Eveland, see 4 above p. 72A

26. Maslen, see 7 above p. 83

27. Copy of Captains of Aircraft Map furnished by Norman L. Sisson as an enclosure to his letter to the author February 13, 1991.

28. Maslen, see 8 above p.83-84

29. Freeman, see 9 above p.336

30. Freeman, Roger A. <u>The Mighty Eighth War Manual</u> p.239

31. Ibid. p.241

32. See 11 above

33. See 10 above

34. Freeman, Roger A. <u>The Mighty Eighth</u> p.174

35. See 11 above

36. Maslen, see 8 above p. 86

37. Freeman, see 34 above p. 99-100

38. Freeman, see 30 above p. 49

39. See 11 above

40. Maslen, see 8 above p. 86

41. See 11 above

42. Bowman & Maslen, see 16 above p. 42

43. Maslen, see 8 above p.86

44. See 11 above

45. See 10 above

46. See 11 above

47. Freeman, see 9 above p. 338

48. Maslen, see 8 above p. 87

49. See 11 above

50. Bowman, Harold W. & Maslen, Selwyn V. <u>401st B.G. (H) Casualties in WW II</u> p. 50

51. See 11 above

52. Bowman & Maslen, see 16 above p. 44

53. Maslen, see 8 above p.89

54. Bowman & Maslen, see 16 above p.44

55. Maslen, see 8 above p.89

56. See 11 above

57. Enclosure to letter from Norman L. Sisson to the author January 17, 1992

58. Bowman & Maslen, see 16 above p. 44

59. Closway, Gordon R. <u>614th Squadron History</u> p. 420

60. See 1 above

61. Maslen, see 7 above p. 78

62. Maslen, see 8 above p. 89

63. Ibid.

64. See 11 above

65. Bowman & Maslen, see 16 above p. 45

66. See 11 above

67. Letter, Norman L. Sisson to the author February 17, 1992

68. Maslen, see 8 above p. 74

69. See 67 above

CHAPTER 7 — A MAIDEN GOES TO WAR

The "Maiden" had only been at Deenethorpe four days before she was adopted by the Sisson crew and flew her first mission with them to Cologne on September 27, 1944.[1] And she was ready! All decked out in her new wardrobe, the bright yellow diagonal stripe bordered in black on the vertical tail fin – the stripe representative of the 94th CBW, the yellow and black 401st colors with the 401st letter "S" inside the triangle of the 1st Division. On her sides were the large letters "IW" the call letters of the 614th Squadron and the letter "A," her own letter of identification. On her sides she also proudly wore a large blue and white star and bar National Insignia. For the Sisson crew it was love at first sight and, as we say today, the beginning of a meaningful relationship.

At this point all she needed was a name. Norm Sisson said that the crew members each wanted her to be given a nickname which would be representative of their girl friends and wives.[2] The word maiden seemed appropriate and they added U.S.A. to epitomize their girls back home. Norm said they planned to have her name painted on the aircraft but never got around to it. It is also true that they never had the nickname properly recorded, although that nickname is listed as one without a related aircraft serial number.[3] However, evidence of their choice and their commitment to the lady they had her name painted on the back of their A-2 jackets. More recent documentation of her name is found in a recent publication funded by the Eighth Air Force Memorial Museum Foundation which includes a listing for a B-17 with SN 46508 of the 401st Bomb Group's 614th Squadron bearing the identifying Squadron letter "A" as having had the nickname "Maiden U.S.A.".[4]

Targets for the 8th Air Force on September 27 were industrial plants and transportation facilities in west Germany. The 1st Division's 462 Fortresses, including those of the 401st were dispatched to Cologne.[5] The specific target for Bowman's Bombers was an interesting one. It was a manufacturing plant which made portable gas producers, the gas produced resulting from burning coal or wood.[6] Picker carried 12 500 pound GPs which he trailed at intervals from 27,000 feet. Although the flak was described officially as moderate, Picker assessed it as light and inaccurate. Five of the 401st bombers suffered minor damage.[7] They were doubly fortunate in that the flak was less deadly and the 401st did not experience the German fighter opposition suffered by other bomber outfits. The Germans had developed a new attack tactic introduced that day; it was called "Sturmgruppen." The concept called for a number of fighter aircraft to make a simultaneous mass attack on a bomber formation rather than making passes singly. The tactic was called a "company front" attack by the Americans. Attacks that day involved from 8 to

Back of a leather A-2 jacket bearing the aircraft nickname "Maiden U.S.A." worn by members of the Sisson crew. Note the 35 bombs which signify the wearer completed a combat tour of duty. The "Maiden's" modest attire was probably among the most decorous in the Eighth Air Force. (Courtesy of Norman L. Sisson.)

15 Luftwaffe fighters making a single pass on the bombers in a wedge-shaped formation. One horrified airman described an attack by what he estimated were 50 German aircraft en masse. The 1st Division fared rather well that day although there were three KIA and seven wounded. It was the 2nd Division which got the brunt of the new Luftwaffe tactics. The 445th Bombardment Group of that Division lost 25 of its B-24s (250 precious crew members) out of 37 aircraft; another two crashed in France and a third crashed in England. It was the largest such loss by a single Group on any one mission of the 8th Air Force during the war. Those who made it back said that the attacks were pressed so close as to be termed suicidal. It wasn't a one-sided victory however. The 361st Fighter Group of the Eighth in their P-51s engaged the FW-190s and the Me-109s in a fierce fight ranging from 24,000 feet to the "deck," shooting down 18 and in doing so probably averted a further tragedy.[8]

The "Maiden" hardly had a chance to catch her breath when she took off with Sisson's crew for Magdeburg the following morning, September 28. Other 8th Air Force targets were oil refineries and military vehicle plants.[9] The 401st target however, was the marshalling yards at Magdeburg and the results were good.[10] Picker carried ten 500 pound GPs which he dropped at 200 foot intervals from 25,000 feet; he called the flak moderate to heavy and fairly accurate.[11]

At Magdeburg the 615th Squadron lost the crew of Lt. Edward H. Daves who was flying "Little Moe." He described the mission as fairly routine until they reached the IP. He said at that point they began to receive heavy flak and just after John C. MacDougall, his bombardier, called "bombs away" the aircraft seemed to "hump." He said smoke began to enter the flight deck through the deicer tubes and the tail gunner, John R. Rollet, reported that parts of their aircraft were flying past him. Ed said his #2 engine was on fire and his controls became mushy and unresponsive. Then the co-pilot, Clay F. Crunk, reported that one of the starboard engines was running away. He ordered the crew by intercom to bailout but received acknowledgment from only the nose compartment. The co-pilot; the navigator, Ralph J. Mezydo; and the engineer, Bill R. Mayfield left the aircraft via the nose hatch. Ed then left the controls and looked into the bomb bay where he saw a large hole in the fuselage on the port side at the base of the wing with flames shooting through the hole and up the interior wall of the bomb bay. He then returned to the controls and MacDougall asked him if he was going to "jump or fly it home?" Ed said he told him to bailout and followed him out the nose hatch. Ed recalled that he held on to the edge of the hatch as he left the aircraft and looked back at the open bomb bay doors, noting that the guns on the ball turret were pointing down. He said he lost consciousness at this point, due to anoxia, and came to in a sitting position with the sensation of a roaring in his ears and the feel of his trousers flapping as he fell. He put out one arm which caused his body to roll over so that he was facing earthward; he could see nothing below but undercast. Ed said that he made up his mind to fall through the undercast as far as possible so that when he landed he would have a chance to evade capture, or at least avoid capture by civilians who were reported to have violated the Geneva Convention, abusing and killing prisoners. Later he realized that in his stupefied state that the undercast could have been ground fog. Fortunately, it wasn't, and as he fell through that undercast he noticed the ground was coming up very fast so he pulled the rip cord to open his parachute. The jolt which followed the opening of his parachute again caused him to blackout briefly. When he came to he found himself swinging wildly from side to side. To stop the swinging he would pull on the shroud lines. This stopped the swinging, but as he emptied the air out of his parachute he would drop like a rock until he released the shroud lines; then the swinging started again. Finally, as he approached the ground he swung from the top of his arc, his feet barely brushing the grass, and he continued to swing up again. As he reached the apex with his feet pointed toward the sky, the parachute collapsed and he fell to the ground landing on the back of his head and back.

He found himself in a meadow which was surrounded by trees, and as he looked around he saw several men at the edge of the trees watching him. He tried to converse with them without success, until shortly later a motorcycle approached. The rider was a "little fat German with the longest rifle I have ever seen strapped on his back." He relieved Ed of his personal possessions and then, pushing his motorcycle with Ed's parachute strapped on the

Bomb strikes of the 401st Bomb Group at Magdeburg September 28, 1944. Bombing was done by PFF with excellent results. Note that 67% of bombs were within 1000 feet of the MPI and 97% were withing 2000 feet. The Air Commander was Capt. Locher and the lead crew included Lt. Mannix - pilot, Lt. Strong - PFF Operator, Lt. Maloney - navigator, Lt. Rostrom - bombardier. (Courtesy National Archives)

machine, he marched his prisoner down the main street of the small town nearby. Ed said that the town's citizenry came out and called him names and spit on him as he passed.

He was then locked up in what appeared to have been a chicken coop, until nightfall, when a truck arrived to take him to an air base where he was interrogated and spent several days in isolation. He was then moved by truck and train to the Dulag, a regional collecting point for prisoners and an interrogation center, near Frankfort Am Main. After several more days of interrogation and isolation he was transported by train with a group of other POWs to Stalag Luft I, which Ed, rather cynically described as "beautiful Barth on the Baltic." The town of Barth is located on a promontory very close to the Baltic Sea about 44 kilometers from Rostock. It was there Ed would spend the next seven months until the defeat of Germany. Ed recalled that the senior officer at Stalag Luft I was the famous ace Colonel Hubert Zemke, whose aircraft went down October 30, 1944. One of the Block Commanders was another well known ace, Lt. Col. Francis S. Gabreski who went down July 20, 1944. Zemke had been the C.O. of the 56th Fighter Group, and at the time he became a POW was the Commander of the 479th Fighter Group. Gabreski at the time he crash-landed in Germany was the C.O. of the 61st Fighter Squadron of the 56th Fighter Group. Ed Daves opined that some of his experiences at Barth were "hilarious" but might not be considered appropriate for the printed page. He said that when the war in Europe was coming to an end Colonel Zemke wanted to keep the POW population together as the Red Army drew near.

Ed said that he and three other Americans escaped on their own and met up with the Russian troops. He said that they walked and rode Russian trucks to Rostock and then on to Wismar about 40 kilometers west of Rostock. At Wismar they made contact with the British Army which got the RAF to fly them to England on a Lancaster bomber.

Following their escape from Stalag Luft I, until they met the British, Ed and his companions were very hungry. At one place they discovered a whole barrel of pickles on which they gorged themselves to the point of being very sick. He commented that before his experience as a POW he had never eaten potatoes without salt, wormy rutabagas, ersatz coffee, bread made from potatoes and barley flour, or bloated dead horses and cows, and he "never will again!"

The other three officers from his crew were also POWs at Stalag Luft I and all of the enlisted crew members were imprisoned elsewhere. Ed said that he was able to confirm that all of his crew made it home safely with the exception of T/Sgt. Bill R. Mayfield, his engineer. After he had returned to the States he was assigned to a base in Texas and one night he visited a dance hall off the base. There was Mayfield playing the bass fiddle in the band.[12]

There was a happier ending to the Magdeburg mission for the crew of friend Charles Utter of the 614th Squadron. Charlie's story has been told in print several times and there is no substitute for his ability to tell a story. There is no quarrel that the target that day was at Magdeburg and the specific target were the marshalling yards.[13] Maslen's history of the 614th records that the low squadron that day, apparently including Utter, hit an "aeroengine factory."[14] Utter agrees, and recalled it was a Junker engine plant.[15] On the bomb run at Magdeburg the lead bombardier peered into his bombsight at the cross hairs and the rate hair (the horizontal one) was short of the target MPI. He made the necessary adjustment and the bombs dropped. The bombs started hitting short of the MPI and "walked up to it." Smoke from other bomb strikes prevented further observation of the results.[16] The flak was described as moderate and fairly accurate and the results were later called "excellent."[17] Charlie recalled that on that bomb run he saw barrages of flak bursts from four or five guns just ahead and below the lead aircraft. Shortly after "bombs away" flak from the third or fourth volley exploded under his B-17, "Miss 'B' Haven." He said his "#4 engine was knocked out by the flak and feathered before oil pressure dropped; #3 engine started to run low on power output and #2 engine was smoking badly. Only #1 engine was holding its own out there on the wing tip." In addition Charlie said, "the hydraulic system controlling the brakes and the cowl flaps for cooling the engines had been blown out..."

Although no one on board was wounded there were many close shaves. The flak helmets of the bombardier, John Hope, and the navigator, Edwin Damp, were dented. Damp had his chart ripped out of his hands by a piece of flak, and Charlie himself had a piece of flak rip a hole in the right shoulder of his flight suit. The co-pilot, Ted Oden, was very fortunate when a piece of flak just missed his legs and imbedded itself in the control console. The engineer, "Red" La Vigne, was in his top turret when a piece of flak came through the Plexiglas and seemed to "buzz around" the turret ricochetting until it fell harmlessly to the deck below. The radio operator, Dave Fulton, was almost hit leaning into the bomb bay to check to be sure all of the bombs had dropped; a piece of flak entered the bomb bay from below and exited through the top of the fuselage. The tail gunner, Steve Zaborsky, had a hunk of flak rip the flak suit he was wearing. The ball turret gunner, "Shorty Cole," was soaked to the skin by leaking hydraulic fluid, and freezing, had to be removed from his position. Charlie said that only the waist gunner, Don St. Peter, reported "nothing out of the ordinary" at his position.[18]

Charlie recalled that during an earlier mission briefing, the crews were encouraged to leave their pistols at home based on a belief that if they were armed when captured by the Germans they might be treated more severely. However, at the briefing that morning it was suggested that they take their pistols to ward off attacks by hostile Germans armed with pitchforks. Many of us had heard that German civilians, terrorized by the allied bombings, had committed atrocities on downed airmen. Charlie said this possibility worried him as he fought to keep "Miss 'B' Haven" aloft as they headed west alone, at 15,000 feet, losing more altitude as they flew on. He elaborated on his concern that if he ordered the crew to bailout they might have to face brutal hostility of the German people. He said: "... I still believe I was correct in refusing to jump my crew ... to fall into the hands of the Nazis at a Belgium airstrip might grant us the rights of the Geneva Convention; my guess was that I could not get the plane across the North Sea."[19]

Roger Freeman wrote: "Perhaps the most feared of natural hazards was the sea, or more correctly fear of having to ditch or parachute into it. The Mediterranean and Adriatic could be warm in summer but they still took a toll of airmen's lives. The North Sea was the real dread, so cold in winter that once submerged in its icy embrace life expectancy was just a few minutes."[20]

We had all heard that it would be safer to be captured by the German military, particularly the Luftwaffe. So the Utter crew plowed on continuing to lose altitude, well below the bomber stream. For some reason they were not attacked. Charlie ordered Damp and MacDougall to look for an airfield. They found one, a fighter strip, on the edge of the city of Ghent, Belgium. He had ruled out the possibility of being able to reach England, rejecting it as he considered the "cold water and the possibility of not being found in the late afternoon...until they were frozen" if they had to ditch in the sea.[21] Charlie realized with very limited power and no brakes he would have no chance for a second pass at the field. It was a runway for fighters and not nearly as long as those for heavy bombers. Further, add to his lack of brakes that a problem was compounded further by the fact that there was a large drainage ditch at the very end of the runway. Utter took "Miss 'B' Haven" over the rooftops of the city. Except for himself, the co-pilot and the engineer all the rest of the crew had assumed the prescribed positions in the radio room for which they were trained for crash landing or ditching. Charlie said the final approach looked good. Although he had called the tower and proclaimed he was coming in for an emergency landing, he had no response or any way of knowing that he was cleared to land. But land he must! Because he was so worried about the possibility of fire if they crashed he said: "... I cut all power and dead sticked it into the field...the nose of the B-17 came to a stop over that dirty ditch."[22] Oden rose from his seat and looking toward the rear fell back laughing. Utter turned to see the reason for his mirth. Standing on the runway looking up into the open bomb bay was a corpulent British officer who said, "Jolly good landing sir." Charlie said, "Who the hell are you?" The intruder introduced himself, a Major General of the Royal Canadian Engineers. Charlie asked, "Who are those guys out there on the runway?" The General responded, "Oh, they are my 'sappers' digging up Nazi land mines; you just landed on a mined airstrip."[23] Charlie wrote to Dieter Busch in Germany in 1983 regarding this forced landing and said, "The field I landed on, a fighter strip, was yours until afternoon, but was Canadian when I landed about 3:00 P.M."[24]

They managed to hitchhike on a British army truck to Brussels where they spent some interesting days. Charlie said: "We were well fed, learned the European custom that ladies worked as attendants in restrooms for gentlemen, heard 'Lilli Marlene' sung for the last time in that city, followed by an English ditty 'We'll Hang Our Laundry on the Siegfried Line'."[25] One evening Charlie and Ted Oden were stopped on the street and taken into custody by the Belgium Underground which suspected they were German fliers. They were released by the court when the Judge determined they could not speak German. They were told to remain indoors because every German caught that night would be given an immediate trial and then shot! Charlie added: "We stayed inside and heard shots."

Another of their experiences in Brussels I am compelled to share: He and Ted shared a room on the fifth floor of the Hotel Cour St. Georges. Charlie described it as a nice room with an adjoining bath. The only problem was that the outside wall of the bath was down in the street having been put there by allied bombing. Charlie said that he and Ted tested the floor of the bath which seemed sound and were particularly surprised and pleased to find that the water pipes were intact and working. Ted held him by his belt as he leaned out to fill the tub with water. He said, "Nothing gave way! Both of us used it from then on, took tub baths and enjoyed the scenery from five flights up without a wall!"[26] They finally got a ride back to England on a C-47. John Hope recalled the aircraft was one "which made the run into Arnhem and there were a lot of British survivors of that fiasco enplaning at the time we took off."[27]

Charlie's tail gunner, Steve Zaborsky, says he has few memories of the Magdeburg mission except that, "I do remember we wanted Charlie...to head for Sweden, but you know good old Charlie! ... a true blue fighter, so we headed for home, and right now we love him for it."[28]

At the time of their return to Deenethorpe the following was attributed to a member of Charlie's crew who was not identified: "It was the slickest job we have ever seen...despite a stiff crosswind, buildings at one end of the runway and the ditch at the other, Lt. Utter brought her around with two dead engines high, hit the end of the runway and stopped just in time." Charlie himself said at the time, "I think we were the first Americans many of the Belgians had seen ... and they were grand to us. They are a happy people and you could sense their new feeling of freedom in the air."[29]

In a letter Charlie wrote some years ago he made one comment which I take exception to, and I feel sure that on reflection he would agree. He said, "That day in the sky over Germany..."Miss 'B' Haven" misbehaved." I submit that lovely lady endured a lot that afternoon over Germany but she brought them back out of harms way![30]

A newspaper account at the time described the events at Magdeburg on September 28: "... more than 1,000 Eighth Air Force Fortresses and Liberators yesterday plastered the Reich for the fourth day in a row ... 49 heavies and 12 fighters were lost...36 enemy planes were shot down. For the second consecutive day there were great air battles as the escorting fighters tangled with the Luftwaffe which concentrated their attacks on small elements of the bomber force. Between 500 and 750 Mustang, Thunderbolt and Lightning fighters escorted the heavies which bombed a synthetic oil plant and railroad yards at Magdeburg."[31] Although the 401st was not jumped by fighters at Magdeburg, the German "Sturmgruppen" attack tactic continued and 18 B-17s were shot down in one pass, including 11 from the 303rd Bomb Group at Molesworth.[32] The "Maiden" was slighty bloodied at Magdeburg with seven flak holes counted by Picker. He said the crew saw the aircraft of Lt. Daves as it went down but they did not observe any parachutes though fortunately, as Ed reported, they all made it out OK.[33]

Two days later, September 30, the "Maiden" took the Sisson bunch to Munster to bomb the marshalling yards in that city. Bombing was done visually from 27,000 feet with Picker's load of 12 500 pound GPs salvoed[34] with good results.[35] Sisson noted the temperature that day at altitude was minus 29 degrees centigrade and the rheostat on the electrically heated suits were turned to full heat. In this regard he mentioned something I had forgotten over the years.

The rheostats by many of us would be turned down on the bomb run when fear provided its own heat. During the bomb run Sisson said they experienced moderate flak which caused slight damage to the "Maiden".[36]

Fred Koger, a toggelier with the 92nd Bomb Group at Podington, wrote about that Munster mission as follows: "The last day of September was spent flying around west Germany, just south of Osnabruck, frustrated by the weather and trying to find a decent target somewhere near our briefed primary. The whole area was covered by a solid deck of cloud. We bombed PFF and unloaded over 100 tons of high explosive on Munster. The intention was to tear up some more railroad track in the central marshalling yards and switching station. The raids on Munster and Osnabruck were more strategic than tactical, but they produced a more immediate result than some strategic missions. Bombing a factory or oil refinery had a definite effect on the German war effort, but it was a long-term proposition. When we tore up a railroad yard, this could immediately disrupt the movement of troops and supplies to or from the battle front. To add to the German woes, our fighters often followed up our strike with low-level strafing runs on individual trains, blowing up engines and wrecking tank cars or boxcars."[37]

Officially, the flak that day was described as intense over the target which resulted in the loss of two of our crews, with two other B-17s receiving major damage and 24 having incurred minor flak damage. Our losses were, the crew of Lt. T.A. Davis of the 615th Squadron on "Packawalup II" and the crew of Lt. O.F. Nagel of the 612th Squadron on "I.P." All members of both crews became POWs.[38] "Packawalup II" on the previous day had the honor of ferrying actress, Marlene Dietrich, to Deenethorpe for a U.S.O. performance.[39]

On October 3 the "Maiden" went to Nurnberg so the Sisson crew could bomb a factory that produced heavy engines, trucks, other motor vehicles and tanks.[40] The 614th Squadron furnished 12 aircraft led by Capt. A.H. Chapman making up the low squadron.[41] They bombed by PFF and although they could not observe the strikes they thought they were good.[42] Picker dropped ten 500 pound IB clusters from 26,000 feet and described the flak as moderate but accurate.[43]

On October 6 the "Maiden" drew a long hop with Sisson & Company. The primary target, if they could bomb visually, was the Politz Oil Refinery, near Stettin, but as usual the weather at the target was not good. Instead, they bombed their secondary target, a Luftwaffe airfield at Stargard, Poland which was located about 20 kilometers east of Stettin. Bombing was done visually with excellent results observed through broken clouds.[44] Picker unloaded ten 500 pound GPs from 25,000 feet and the Group had all of its bombs within 2,000 feet of the MPI. They experienced meager but accurate flak from boats and barges as they crossed the Danish Peninsula but reported no flak at the target.[45]

A newspaper article described the missions of that day as follows, "Industrial objectives and airdromes over a wide area of the Reich were plastered by 1,250 Fortresses and Liberators of the Eighth Air Force. Almost 1,000 Thunderbolt and Mustang fighters escorted the heavies, which reported good to excellent bombing results in favorable weather. In addition to industrial targets in the Berlin, Hamburg and Harburg area the aircraft bombed airdromes at Stargard, New Brandenburg and Weizendorf."[46] Sisson referred to the target as a Luftwaffe Headquarters and Picker's records called it an advanced training base.[47] Norm also recalled that the German flak gunners were accurate and put some more holes in the "Maiden." He said the other uncomfortable aspects of that mission were the ten hours and a half flying time and the need to wear that tortuous oxygen mask stuck to one's face for about nine of those hours.[48]

Jack Healy was the engineer on the crew of Lt. Pete Lerwick. He and several of his fellow crew members needed a few more missions to finish their tours and go home. The rest of Lerwick's crew had finished up at Munster on September 30. Sisson needed a substitute for one of his crew that day and Healy flew with them as their waist gunner. In his diary he wrote: "...Politz, an area where I heard research is in progress, is near the Baltic Sea, and a reasonably long haul. We went out over water for awhile perhaps to avoid land based anti-aircraft batteries. At 28,500 feet I noticed tiny white caps so what I heard about the roughness of that sea is apparently true. I was hoping the engines would not become temperamental and that we would not encounter German interceptors. I'm sure the others felt the same way ... I had intestinal discomfort and was glad to get this one over ... back at the base, there has been speculative talk about a big one tomorrow..."[49]

After Stargard the "Maiden" had completed five combat missions. Sisson said she "performed beautifully" and was fine-tuned to combat. Norm said their crew chief was very proud of his new aircraft, took great care of her and was quick to correct his crew if he thought we were abusing "his" Fortress. He said he was amused when they returned from a mission and the crew chief would first inquire about the well being of the "Maiden," and after being reassured, he would then ask about the crew. The crew chief was quick to look over Sisson's

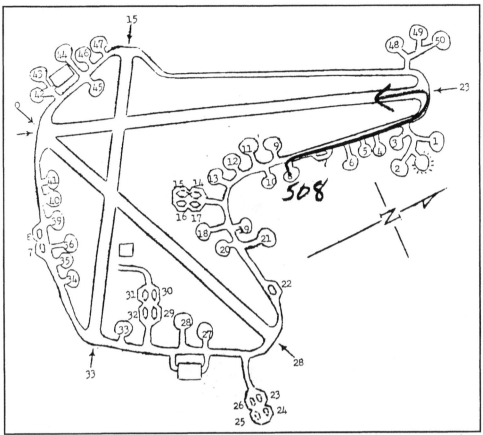

Taxi instructions at Deenethorpe for the "Maiden" with the Sisson crew aboard for the mission to Nurnberg October 3, 1944. The instructions tell Sisson in aircraft 508 (abbreviation of the "Maiden's" serial number) from its diapersal hard stand #8 to follow aircraft 628 from hard stand #15 for takeoff from runway 23. (Courtesy of Norman L. Sisson)

write-up sheet on the "Maiden's" performance, but there were few items that ever needed attention except battle damage. These were Sisson's words: "Aircraft 6508 was a flying dream, a Cadillac of the Fortresses. This bomber would fly without trim and respond instantly to any control. It was a breeze to fly in formation. This aircraft more than once saved our crew. It could maintain the Group's airspeed on three engines and would land with the touch of a feather. Our crew was proud of their aircraft, and pampered it. On two occasions when it was necessary to feather an engine it was accomplished without leaving the formation or slowing the airspeed. This Fortress would fly on three engines near the red line on the superchargers without any abnormal engine instrument indication. She was truly the Queen over the German skies."[50]

These remarks may seem over generous, but they expressed a feeling shared not just by pilots but by the other members of air crews. Roger Freeman agrees and wrote: "Few flyers were indifferent to the aircraft in which they went to war. Most had strong feelings about the worthiness of the machine to perform the task for which it was built ... a natural reaction of loyalty to the plane that had seen you through."[51]

To his credit Norm Sisson made further references to all of the ground personnel who kept us flying. He said: "Our ground crews were absolutely superior. The mechanics kept the aircraft flying under almost impossible circumstances. All of the ground personnel worked constantly in all kinds of weather, snow and freezing, out in the open to keep the aircraft flying. They changed engines on the hardstands ... would slow time the engines, whatever

A 401st Bomb Group B-17 coming home to Deenthorpe. (Photograph from the USAF Collection courtesy of the NASM of the Smithsonian)

was necessary in the time allowed to get ready for the next mission. The success in supplying aircraft for maximum effort missions had to be the result of effort by them. They cannibalized crashed Fortresses, improvised from old parts, hacked and riveted aircraft back into flying status... Men and boys from virtually every trade or profession, trained in minimal time to be experts...they performed miracles..."[52]

Their trip to Stargard was a long day for the Sisson crew and their "Maiden." It was a prelude of things to come the very next day, in the same neck of the woods... and a real test for them all.

Notes to Chapter 7

1. Maslen, Selwyn V. <u>614th Squadron: Crews - Missions - Aircraft</u> p. 78
2. Letter Norman L. Sisson to author January 17, 1992
3. Bowman, Harold W. & Selwyn V. Maslen <u>Bowman's Bombers</u> p. 142
4. Andrews, Paul M., William H. Adams, & John H. Woolnough <u>Bits and Pieces of the Mighty Eighth</u> p. 28
5. Freeman, Roger A. <u>The Mighty Eighth War Diary</u> p.354
6. Maslen, Selwyn V. <u>614th Bombardment Squadron (H): Squadron History</u> p. 91
7. Photocopy of personal log of Nathan Picker furnished author as enclosure to letter from Norman L. Sisson February 13, 1991
8. Freeman, see 5 above p. 355
9. Ibid.
10. Bowman & Maslen, see 3 above p. 46

11. *See 7 above*

12. *Letter, Edward H. Daves to author March 25, 1991*

13. *Bowman & Maslen, see 3 above p. 46*

14. *Maslen, see 6 above p. 92*

15. *Letter, Charles W. Utter to author January 25, 1991*

16. *National Archives, Record Group 18, 401st Bombardment Group (H) - Mission Reports*

17. *Maslen, see 6 above p. 92*

18. *Letter, Charles W. Utter to Cynrik De Decker; Lede, Belgium furnished author as enclosure to letter from Mr. Utter January 25, 1991*

19. *Enclosure to letter to author from Charles W. Utter January 25, 1991*

20. *Freeman, Roger A. Experiences of War: The American Airman in Europe p. 77*

21. *See 18 above*

22. *See 15 above*

23. *See 18 above*

24. *Letter, Charles W. Utter to Dieter Busch, Winterbach, West Germany December 29, 1983 furnished author as enclosure to letter from Charles W. Utter January 25, 1991*

25. *See 19 above*

26. *Ibid.*

27. *Letter, John Hope to author February 23, 1991*

28. *Letter, Stephen A. Zaborsky to author March 5, 1991*

29. *Maslen, see 6 above p. 91*

30. *See 18 above*

31. *Newspaper article, publication and date of publication in England unknown. Furnished as enclosure to letter Norman L. Sisson to author February 13, 1991*

32. *Maslen, see 6 above p. 91*

33. *See 7 above*

34. *Ibid.*

35. *Maslen, see 6 above p. 92*

36. *See 2 above*

37. *Koger, Fred Countdown! p. 131*

38. *Bowman & Maslen, see 3 above p. 46*

39. *Ibid. and Bowman, Harold W. & Selwyn V. Maslen 40st B.G. (H) Casualties in W.W.II p. 54-55*

40. *Maslen, see 6 above p. 95*

41. *Closway, Gordon R. 614th Squadron History, Air Operations October, 1944*

42. *Bowman & Maslen, see 3 above p. 48*

43. *See 7 above*

44. *Maslen, see 6 above p. 95 and See 3 above p. 48*

45. *See 7 above*

46. *See 31 above*

47. *See 7 above*

48. *Enclosure to letter, Norman L. Sisson to author February, 1992*

49. *Photocopy of portion of personal log of Jack Healy furnished author as enclosure to letter from Norman L. Sisson February, 1992*

50. *See 48 above*

51. *Freeman, see 20 above p. 111*

52. *See 48 above*

CHAPTER 8 — POLITZ!

Whenever old 8th Air Force bomber crewmen get together they "shoot the bull," recalling combat experiences. During such sessions at their reunions each participant will invariably advance one of his missions that he best remembers above all others. Some recall their most salient mission because it seemed to accomplish so much in the war effort; others recollect missions that were to them most spectacular or in most cases those that were the most terrifying. The early veterans of the 401st from late 1943 speak with awe of Leipzig, Oshersleben and of course, Berlin. Those who came later, during the last nine months of battle, speak as solemnly of targets such as Merseburg and Politz.

So it was that on October 7 the "Maiden" went to Politz with the crew of Lt. W. L. Morton.[1] For some unknown reason that day the Sisson crew flew another B-17, that of my own crew, Fred Babcock's, an aircraft we later named "Miss Gee Eyewanta (Go Home)."[2]

Politz is a northern suburb of the city Stettin, a Polish seaport at the mouth of the Oder River which forms the Bay of Stettin, with access to the Baltic Sea to the north. The target that day was the second largest synthetic oil refinery in German territory which was vital to the Nazi war effort. Other missions that day for the 8th Air Force included additional petroleum targets such as Brux, Ruhland, Lutzkendorf, Merseburg and Magdeburg. With 1,401 heavy bombers in the skies over the Reich, all Groups participated. There were 142 B-17s of the 94th CBW, including those from the 401st, with the "C" wing led by our Lt. Col. W.T. Seawell. It promised to be one of the toughest missions flown by the 401st. It was a ME with the 94th CBW putting up four group boxes, the last of which was a composite group.[3] The 614th Squadron furnished 12 crews in the composite D Group with Lt. Ted Carroll leading the high squadron.[4] En route to the target the composite group overran the 401st and forced the 351st Bomb Group to go wide at the IP. This resulted in the two Groups bombing within 30 seconds of each other[5] while the D Group made a 360 turn at the IP.

That the Germans treasured that target was obvious from the heavy defenses against aerial attack. There were an estimated 270 105mm and 88mm guns protecting the target, and I am sure that did not include all of the weapons defending the greater Stettin area to the immediate south through which our bombers had to fly that day. There was no way to plan a bomb run to avoid heavy flak at such a well defended area. The planners therefore laid out an unusually short eight minute bomb run which, after "bombs away," provided a quick exit north out over the Bay of Stettin and thence to the Baltic Sea, a refuge from those land bound flak guns.[6]

Nathan Picker, Sisson's bombardier, dropped ten 500 pound GPs from 25,000 feet. He recorded the mission in his personal log as "very intense flak...visual... 2 B-17s seen going down...5 lost...all ships damaged... hydraulics shot out...landed at Woodbridge (RAF)."[7] Though the bombing was done visually, a heavy and effective smoke screen had been laid down by the Germans which obscured the target and prevented a bombing assessment.[8]

The flak was ferocious with seventeen of the 142 B-17s either shot out of the sky or unable to make it back to England. Thirty others experienced major damage and another 76 had minor damage. That left only 19 aircraft unscathed. Roger Freeman wrote that it was significant that four of the bombers lost were lead or deputy lead aircraft. He said it was later learned that our own H2X radar emissions from those lead and deputy lead PFF ships had been tracked by the German radar in their range computations, which probably contributed to the accuracy of the flak gunners at Politz.[9] Three of the five 401st aircraft lost that day were from the 614th Squadron.[10] The rest of the 94th CBW losses included seven from the 351st at Polebrook and five from the 457th at Glatton.[11]

The description of the losses of the 401st bombers and their crews provides a graphic picture of the horror of warfare: Pilot J.W. McGoldrick, of the 613th Squadron, reported the loss of the crew of Lt. A.J. Nelson flying "Son of a Blitch". He said: "They received a direct hit in the nose of the aircraft blowing most of the nose off. It went into a vertical dive, hit the ground and blew up." The entire crew was lost.[12]

The 612th Squadron lost the crew of Lt. T.K. Hill who were flying "Boche Buster." Their

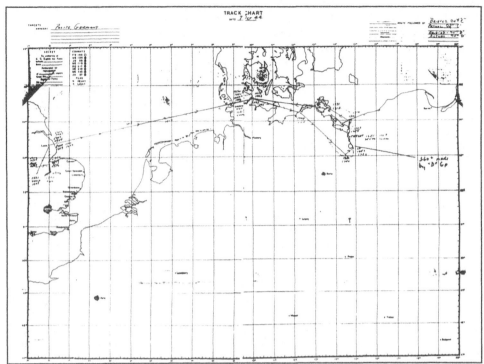

Track Chart for the mission to Politz on October 7, 1944. Note the 360 degree turn executed at the IP by the 94th Combat Bomb Wing Composite Group which was next to suicidal with the intense flak over that target. (Courtesy National Archives)

loss was reported by Lt. L. Lawrence who was himself wounded on January 13, 1945 and died in a French hospital. He said that Lt. Hill's aircraft "was hit by flak over Politz. The #2 engine was hit and feathered at the target. There was a large hole in the forepart of the bomb bay causing the aircraft to lag and lose altitude. It was last seen at 22,000 feet about a mile behind the wing formation." Lt. Hill and his crew made it safely to Sweden where they were interned.[13]

The 614th Squadron crew of Lt. R.W. James flying "Undecided" was also hit by flak over Politz and managed to get to Sweden where they were forced to make a crash landing in a peat bog. Lt. James suffered serious back injuries in the landing and the crew was interned briefly. They made it back to England but were promptly shipped back to the United States in accordance with a treaty between our country and Sweden.[14] The following is a news release made on the return to England of the James crew:

"Seven members of the Flying Fortress 'Undecided' literally had to dig themselves out of the dirt when their aircraft made a 'belly landing' in a soft peat field after two engines had been knocked out over Politz and a third caught fire. The ball turret had been jettisoned along with everything else movable in an effort to lighten the aircraft so it could get to friendly territory, and all of the crew but the pilot and co-pilot crowded into the radio compartment for the landing. When 'Undecided' hit the ground, the soft peat, forced through the opening left by the ball turret, broke down the radio room door and all but buried the crew. No one was injured and all have returned to their organization, the 401st Bomb Group Commanded by Lt. Col. W.T. Seawell, Pine Bluff, Arkansas. "The crew piloted by 1st Lt. R.W. James...was on its tenth mission. Over Politz flak hit No.3 and No.1 engines and the propellers windmilled violently. A few seconds later fire started in No.3 but it was put out with fire extinguishers. The oxygen system was knocked out as were all navigation instruments and big holes were put in the ball turret, the radio room and several gasoline tanks. Another fragment knocked the pencil out of the hand of 2nd Lt. Gerald A. Morris...the navigator. 'We lost 5,000 feet almost immediately' said Lt. James, 'and then came home alone, without escort for an hour and a half. Once two Messerschmidt 109s began to follow us but for some reason they didn't come in to attack. When we landed I think we skidded along the ground for about 150 feet. I saw a big pile of peat in front of me and tipped my right wing into the ground and this swerved us to one side or we would have been buried alive.'"[15] It took them seven weeks to get back to England.[16]

The 614th Squadron crew of Lt. A. Harasyn flying "Betty's Revenge" wasn't as fortunate. They received a direct hit in the nose which killed the bombardier and the navigator. The aircraft went out of control in a vertical dive. Lt. Harasyn reported by radio that his controls had been shot away. Their radio operator left his position and proceeded to the waist area to bailout. Apparently suffering from anoxia, he bailed out without a parachute before his crew mates could stop him. The remainder of the crew got out safely and were POWs.[17]

The fifth crew we lost that day was another 614th crew, that of Lt. H.P. Silverstein who was flying "Cover Girl". Norm Sisson in a 1989 news article related that on the Politz mission his position in the formation was behind and to the left of Lt. Silverstein who was flying deputy lead. He said, "As we were about to drop our bombs on the target a huge burst of flak exploded near the head of our formation. The deputy...lost a wing and exploded in a gigantic fireball... the same burst of flak also shot away the controls of the plane on my right (Harasyn) which went into a vertical dive and crashed..."[18] Lt. R.S. Hubbell, another 614th pilot, said that the Silverstein B-17 received a "direct flak burst in the right wing root adjacent to the bomb bay. The right wing immediately caught fire, the aircraft went down, the right wing came off and the aircraft exploded." Although no parachutes were observed bailing out from the stricken "Cover Girl" it was later learned that the co-pilot, Lt. J.A. Farquhar said, "The plane blew up in midair and I was thrown clear." Also escaping in this miraculous way was the ball turret gunner S/Sgt. D.E. Berhstrom; both parachuted safely to earth and were POWs. The rest of the crew were KIA.[19]

Sisson discussed his problems at Politz in the aforementioned 1989 newspaper interview, "The co-pilot and I were both wounded, and both engines on the right side were knocked out.

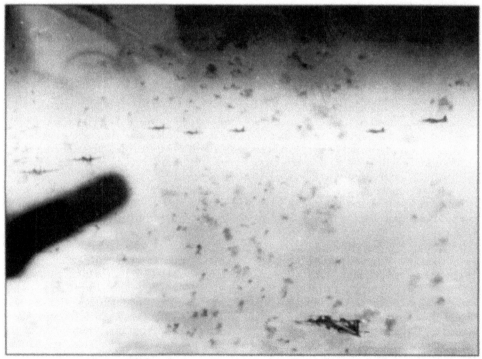

Mission to Politz, Germany. (From 1994 401st Bomb Group Calendar)

The 401st Bomb Group formation over Germany with IW-G "Betty's Revenge" in the left foreground. She was lost with the crew of Lt. A. Harasyn at Politz on October 7, 1944. (Photo from the USAF Collection courtesy of the NASM of the Smithsonian)

Nineteen control cables and two hydraulic lines were severed and I had no elevator control. In order to avoid the debris of the deputy lead plane I had to take violent evasive action, hauling the plane over hard and downward to the left. After a 5,000 foot fall I managed to get the plane flying straight again ... and tried to blend in with the scenery."[20]

Nathan Picker described the Politz mission as the most critical of his tour. He recalled, "... sitting in the nose I was closest to the right wing of Lt. Silverstein's ship and felt the heat from the exploding gas tanks. A few moments later the pilot called out 'we're hit, salvo bombs,' which I did and clipped on my parachute, waiting for the worst." He said the damage to the hydraulic system left them with no brakes so they landed at an emergency RAF base near the coast, Woodbridge, which had extra long runways.[21]

Jack Healy, who flew the previous day with Sisson, was again with them at Politz and his diary provided some interesting comments about that day. "The scuttlebutt about a big one today that I heard yesterday was true. Naturally, no one realized before takeoff how big, or strategically important, this one was. I went again as Lt. Sisson's waist gunner and I never saw so many aircraft or imagined so many could operate and maneuver in an area of air without colliding. We learned later that every plane and crew in England that was flyable – flew." Jack must have been referring to assembly since the rest of the 1st Division and the entire 2nd and 3rd Divisions had other targets. However, Politz was a ME for the 94th CBW. Healy recalled flak over over the Danish Peninsula, and after they crossed the Baltic Sea, over northeastern Germany. He said he had not seen their fighter escort and felt they were lucky not to have needed it. He said, "About ten minutes from the target...from both waist windows I saw the sky ahead ... filling with flak bursts, not only at our altitude, but also for a substantial height above the Group and to a considerable area below it. I thought, if we don't blow up but need to bailout, it will be a long walk to France, dodging 'Jerries' on the ground. I wondered how the guys in the front of the plane and the ball turret gunner were 'enjoying the view' as they had a much better view than I, as the Group approached that black wall of flaming shrapnel. It was accurate, at our exact altitude, full and broad (as) I had seen during my previous 31 missions, although (the) Leipzig/Merseburg area was usually a 'beaut.' The cumbersome chest, stomach and back protective flak suit did not seem too bothersome at the moment." He described the loss of one B-17 which, "received flak in one of the fuel tanks in the right wing which began flaming ... dropping out of formation, the pilot lowered it and began banking to the right ... not low enough to pass under us without colliding. That caused Lt. Sisson to quickly bring our plane higher...The stricken plane passed under us and spiraled down. We noticed five crew members tumble out and the plane exploded...The sight chilled me. After we left the formation the Group went on to the target area without us ... we were stragglers and bait for enemy fighters in the area. I was sure no one on board looked for them as intensely as I. Luckily, no 'bandits' appeared. After some minutes seven of our fighters, P-51 Mustangs, appeared on our right out of the mist...there were exclamations of 'wow,' 'glad to see you, ' 'where have you been?' on the interphone. Stragglers from other Groups joined us and we became the lead plane. We headed for an English base with a longer runway ... because of our useless brakes. Lt. Sisson needed to ease the plane off the runway near the end with manipulation of the right wing engine power and the right rudder allowing the plane to slow and stop in the high grass bordering the runway. The guns and other valuable equipment were removed from the plane; guards were assigned to it until it could be repaired; we were fed at the mess hall and later transported to our base by truck..."[22] Jack Healy recalled the Group had been "well hit" and did not fly the next day.[23] Actually it was a week before the 401st took to the skies again. The weather provided the respite from combat. In addition to the loss of crews and aircraft, those who made it back to Deenethorpe brought seven wounded, three seriously, not to overlook the repairs needed to three B-17s which had major damage and to 40 others which received minor damage.[24]

Jack also provided several clippings from English newspapers after the Politz mission on which he made some personal notations. Above one of these articles captioned "5,000 PLANES HIT GERMANY" Jack printed, "This was a lifetime in eight hrs." According to Sisson's log it was more like ten hours flying time. That same article included the following: "Wing Commander Johnny Baldwin D. S. O., D. F. C., and bar, from Bath, leader of the wing said: 'Bombers were flying through absolutely ten-tenths flak. I saw several hit and go down in flames but I saw no fighters attack them.'" Directing an arrow to this remark Jack wrote: "Flack - Flame & fiery airplanes at 28,500 feet...no foxholes up there."[25]

Copies of Army special orders and general orders are very dull reading even if one could decipher all the military jargon and abbreviations. However, General Orders Number 114 of Headquarters, 1st Air Division, Office of the Commanding General dated February 7, 1945 provides an assessment of one pilot's performance on the Politz mission and two others that have been mentioned heretofore. These orders conferred on Norman L. Sisson the Distinguished Flying Cross and reads in part:

"For extraordinary achievement while serving as Pilot of a B-17 airplane on bombing missions over Germany, 5 September 1944, 19 September 1944 and 7 October 1944. On these operations Lieutenant Sisson demonstrated a high degree of flying skill and exceptional determination."[26]

"Rainbow" wrote me a short note in 1990 which is also appropriate to this chapter. He said; "Forty-six years ago this morning I flew my thirteenth mission to Politz, Germany... they had 355 flak guns around the target and they used all of them. The flak caused the greatest damage tho the German fighters flew through their own flak to get at us. We had 108 holes shot through our plane. One of them thru the left wing just outside the radio room window was large enough to crawl through! The bombardier was hit in the belly with a piece of flak, but it was spent, and while it knocked him away from his bombsight his flak suit saved him from even a scratch...We landed at Deenethorpe, air conditioned with all the holes, flaps shot away from the left side and no radio. We learned that day what war was all about!" He added, "it was so nice, 46 years later to be able to tell about it."[27] "Rainbow" was the co-pilot for Joseph A. Cromer in the 612th Squadron. Joe continued his love of flying after the war and was active in the Confederate Air Force which was devoted to the restoration of World War II military aircraft. He had participated in restoring a U.S. Navy PBY, an amphibian called the Catalina. Sadly, Joe and six others died when that PBY crashed in the waters off south Texas October 13, 1984. "Rainbow" wrote of his respect and fondness for Joe in the "Poop From Group" the 401st newsletter he edits for association members, admitting that he looked upon him as an older brother. "Rainbow" said their B-17 was nicknamed after the Bing Crosby song "I'll Be Seeing You." He said he didn't know who thought up that nickname but, "There was no doubt in my mind that I will meet this man again! So, Joe, I'll Be Seeing You!"[28]

Also at Politz that afternoon was Francis E. Rundell, better known as "Bud." A member of the 614th Squadron he was flying deputy lead in "Hard Seventeen." He said that it was then policy that the squadron formation drop their bombs when they saw the leader drop his. If for some reason the leader had problems and was unable to do so he would signal the deputy leader and all were to drop their bombs when the deputy dropped his. He said that about ten seconds before "bombs away" there was a burst of flak directly in front of his aircraft. A fragment entered the co-pilot's windshield and struck the big red salvo switch located between the pilot and co-pilot. The result was that his bombs were dropped prematurely and half of the squadron dropped theirs when they saw the deputy's bombs fall. He recalls the co-pilot's windshield was completely opaque from the impact of the flak except for a three-to-four inch hole where the fragment entered the aircraft. The cockpit was covered with a white powder, like snow, from the particles which made up the safety glass layers of the windshield. At debriefing back at Deenethorpe Col. Bowman began his remarks with the inquiry, "Rundell, why did you drop your bombs ten seconds early?" Rundell's response was that flak triggered the salvo switch to which the Colonel exclaimed, "I knew those flak gunners were good but I didn't expect them to be so accurate." Later when he saw the bomb-strike photographs, Bud said: "One photograph showed a good cluster of bombs in the target area (dropped on the leader's release); the next photograph showed the bombs dropped on the deputy's release (mine) that landed in the middle of a lake. We had gone all that way to kill a bunch of fish!"[29]

Lt. Morton brought the "Maiden" back from Politz; or I might say she brought them safely back to Deenethorpe. It can be surmised that she like the others were bloodied that day over Germany. Our crew had just arrived at Deenethorpe and the barracks were empty; everybody was at Politz. I had hung up my clothes, made my bunk and was sitting there waiting for my crew to go to the mess hall. The door burst open and a short man walked the length of the barracks to his bunk which was next to mine. He was in the clothes he wore under the heated suit; his face showed more than just fatigue and was grimy with the dried sweat and saliva from the oxygen mask. Although weary he went out of his way to introduce himself to me as Jack Pink, the navigator on the Morton crew. For several minutes he shared with me the moments of terror he had experienced that afternoon almost five miles above the earth. Since I had not yet flown a combat mission I listened with rapt attention to his words delivered under obvious stress and with a tormented look on his face. I later knew Jack to be a rather happy guy but that afternoon he scared me spitless! For all of my 35 missions I remained in constant fear that I would have to go to the Politz area, but I never did. Jack finished his tour in January, 1945 and went home to Rochester, New York.

Major Francis E. Rundell, II. (Photo from the USAF Collection courtesy of the NASM of the Smithsonian)

After the war he returned to Bucknell University in Pennsylvania. After working in private business for a brief period he applied to get into the newly formed U.S. Air Force but was unsuccessful. Instead, in 1948 he went back into the Army as a 1st Lieutenant in the **infantry**! He said he spent 13 months in Korea and came home a Major. He explained he was promoted two grades in a year because he was short! He later saw service in Vietnam as staff secretary for both Generals Westmoreland and Abrams. He retired as a Brigadier General and now divides his time between residences in Florida and the western Pennsylvania mountains. He lived for awhile in Beaufort, South Carolina which is a stronghold of retired Navy and Marine types. He said these guys don't understand why he went into the Army and "I tell them I'm a social climber."[30]

As this chapter came together I recalled the fictional prose of Len Deighton in his novel about the about a P-51 Fighter Group in the air war over Europe titled "**Goodbye, Mickey Mouse**." I have included several paragraphs which describe with greater significance the nature of a heavy bombardment crew during that conflict:

"'B-17s... Fortresses,' said Bohnen as they raised their eyes to a formation of 20 or so planes flying east. He looked at his wristwatch. 'That's a Bomb Group heading for its assembly point. From there they go on to form divisions at an assembly point on the coast, and finally the whole damned task force will be on its way to Germany.'...

"Fairbrother turned his head to see the bombers plodding on toward their target, searching the horizon for the escorting Fighter Groups which hadn't yet arrived. Who could see the bomber crews without admiring the phlegmatic determination which makes other kinds of courage seem no more than temporary lapses of judgement?

"They were the real heroes, the ones who came up here day after day as human targets for every weapon an ingenious, dedicated, and tenacious foe could use against them. So in life the true measure of courage is to fly on despite the tragedies of accident, sickness or failure...

"The lead ship's bomb doors slowly opened. As this plane reached the Initial Point, the sky ahead of it lit up with a box barrage inside which it seemed nothing could survive. Salvo after salvo was fired into the same airspace. All of the planes would have to fly through that great cube of exploding air and flying metal that was now pulsating red and gray like some sort of venomous seabed anemone...

"None faltered. Each plane was no longer under the command of its pilot; the bombardiers had taken control and their eyes were pressed tight to the bombsight trying to recognize the hazy target through the mess of cloud and smoke."...[31]

Combat flyers were an atrociously superstitious lot. The sort of thing that would make one a believer and adopt obsessive habits was often the result of stories about others, such as what happened to Lt. C.L. Barsuk the co-pilot on the crew of Lt. J. H. Singleton in the 614th Squadron. On April 29, 1944 63 bombers out of 618 were shot down over Berlin. Singleton's "Can't Miss" was one of those casualties.[32] They were eventually shot down by fighters and crashed at Leers, near Roubaix, Belgium. In addition to the pilot and the co-pilot the following crew members evaded and returned to allied control: Lt. J. G. Levey, navigator; S/Sgt. W.R. Muse, engineer; and S/Sgt. H.J. Blair, tail gunner. The other crew members perished. The co-pilot, Barsuk, managed to come back to the 614th and was shot down at Politz[33] as co-pilot for Lt. Harasyn. He became a POW. It was my understanding that once an evader got back to England he was not allowed to fly combat in that theater. The theory was that if he should again be shot down, the German interrogators might learn who helped him evade capture before and thus threaten their security and even their lives. Wayne Eveland, writing about his own experience as an evader, said it was for this reason and because he knew too much about the underground that he was unable to resume command of the 614th.[34] We don't know why Barsuk was allowed to rejoin the 401st. Lt. Harasyn's regular co-pilot was Lt. Robert A. Hosley. After being shot down in April Lt. Barsuk next appeared as the listed co-pilot for Lt. Harsyn on September 26, 1944. That same list has Lt. Hosley as co-pilot for Lt. Paul Wittman, apparently a new crew orientation. After

The 401st Bomb Group B-17s above the clouds headed east from England into combat over Europe. Photograph from the USAF Collection courtesy of the NASM of the Smithsonian.

that date until shot down again Barsuk flew with Lt. Harasyn and Lt. Hosley continued to fly as co-pilot with new crews on their first missions and from time to time with Wittman.[35] Another interesting fact was that the Squadron History lists the other evaders, as returning to Deenethorpe in September, 1944 but makes no mention of Lt. Barsuk. The account relates the Singleton crew came down near Brussels, Belgium on April 29 and that those who evaded capture lived with civilians for about three months. They were then passed on to the central underground station in Brussels. Unfortunately, it was a trap. The station had recently been taken over by the German Gestapo and they were running a 1944 version of a sting operation. They told them they were going to be passed on to Paris, but actually they were loaded on a train which was to take them to concentration camps. In the railroad yard Lt. Levey and Sgt. Blair jumped from the train and made their escape. Soon thereafter "patriots" derailed the train and the rest escaped. No other details are available with respect to this interesting episode.[36]

Finally, there was one last poignant comment in the official 614th Squadron History concerning that October 7 mission, "three of our A/C did not return from Politz. That single statement means 27 empty bunks in the Squadron, 27 men whom we ate with, played with and worked with are not here anymore. It is hard to believe that friends are expendable. It is not easy to write off your friends like a broken machine."[37]

Notes to Chapter 8
1. Maslen, Selwyn V. *614th Squadron: Crews - Missions -Aircraft* p. 58
2. Ibid. p. 78
3. Freeman, Roger A., Alan A. Crouchman & Selwyn V. Maslen *The Mighty Eighth War Diary* p. 361-362
4. Maslen, Selwyn V. *614th Bombardment Squadron (H): Squadron History* p. 96
5. Freeman, see 3 above p. 362
6. Ibid.
7. Photocopy of personal log of Nathan Picker furnished author as enclosure toletter from Norman L. Sisson February 13, 1991

8. Maslen, see 4 above p. 96

9. Freeman, see 3 above p. 362

10. Maslen, see 4 above p. 96

11. Freeman, see 3 above p. 361

12. Bowman, Harold W. & Selwyn V. Maslen 401st B.G. (H) Casualties in W.W. II p. 56

13. Ibid. p. 57

14. Ibid. p. 56

15. Microfilm of 401st Bombardment Group (H) records furnished author by the USAF Historical Research Center, Maxwell AFB, AL October 19, 1990 and June 13, 1991

16. Maslen, see 1 above p. 37

17. Bowman & Maslen, see 12 above p. 55

18. Baton Rouge, LA Advocate October 22, 1989

19. Bowman & Maslen, see 12 above p. 57

20. See 18 above

21. Letter, Norman L. Sisson to author March 29, 1991

22. Photocopy of a portion of personal log of Jack Healy with newspaper clippings as enclosure to letter, Norman L. Sisson to author February, 1992

23. Ibid.

24. Bowman, Harold W. & Selwyn V. Maslen Bowman's Bombers p. 47-49

25. See 22 above

26. Copy, General Orders 114, Headquarters, 1st Air Division, Office of the Commanding Officer, 7 February 1945 furnished author as enclosure to letter from Norman L. Sisson February 13, 1991

27. Letter, Ralph W. Trout to author October 7, 1990

28. Poop From Group #46 "Forever Aloft: Joseph L. Cromer August 27, 1919 October 13, 1984"

29. Letter, Col. Francis E. Rundell to author February 9, 1991

30. Letter, Brig. Gen. Jack Pink to author May 31, 1991 and telephone conversation June 3, 1991

31. Deighton, Lee Goodbye, Mickey Mouse p. 118-119, 239, 261

32. Maslen, see 4 above p. 45

33. Maslen, see 4 above p. 93

34. Eveland, I. Wayne Memories and Reflections p. 82

35. Closway, Gordon R. 614th Squadron History loading lists July 18, 1944 -October 7, 1944

36. Ibid. Summary of Events September, 1944

37. Closway, see 35 above Summary of Events October 1944

CHAPTER 9 — TOURING THE REICH

After a much deserved rest following the Politz mission the 401st was back in the skies over Germany on October 14. The Sisson crew and their "Maiden" remained at Deenethorpe that day while the 1st Division put up 326 B-17s. The rest of the Eighth's task force that day included 314 aircraft of the 3rd Division and 248 B-24s of the 2nd Division. The targets included the Gereon and Eifeltor marshalling yards at Cologne with a small force of 90 aircraft going after the marshalling yards at Saarbrucken. The main force of the 1st and 3rd Divisions were targeted at the Gereon yards.[1] Bombing was by PFF with the results unobserved; flak was termed meager and there was no air opposition.[2]

On October 15 the "Maiden" with the Sisson crew on board was ready to go. Their target that day was the Nippes marshalling yards at Cologne. Other 1st Division B-17s went after the Kalk and Gereon yards at Cologne while the main 2nd Division force was assigned to the Eifeltor and Kalk yards.[3] Our Colonel Bowman led the 1st Division with bombing done by PFF. Through a break in the clouds some bombs were observed hitting a built up area of the city, but others reported as strikes on the primary target. As compared to the previous day the Germans were ready and provided intense flak, shooting down four in the 1st Division, doing flak damage to 293 aircraft, with 14 crewmen KIA and ten others wounded in that Division alone.[4]

On that mission the 92nd Bomb Group at Podington, flying with the 40th CBW, was a part of the 1st Division force. Fred Koger, a toggelier in that Group wrote, "Today's strike would be PFF according to the weather officer. We were going to tear up another railway yard, this one at Cologne. The huge Eifeltor Marshalling Yard was a vital transportation link, a main point on the Siegfried Line. Our ground troops had been up against this vaulted defense line for several weeks. The airborne invasion a month earlier was an attempt to make an end run around the north end of the line. That hadn't worked and our guys were going to have to go through it...They shot us up good at Cologne. The flak was heavy and it was accurate. I didn't see any of our planes go down, but they were getting bounced around by close bursts, and so were we. I went through the usual cycle of emotions - anxiety, fear, excitement and finally relief. We came off the target with all four engines running and the Group strung out and scattered. Four P-51s slid back and forth around us like sheepdogs getting the flock back together after the wolves had panicked them."[5]

A newspaper reporting on both the October 14 and 15 missions to Cologne said: "While bad weather curtailed activity by British based heavies yesterday, reconnaissance photographs taken at the weekend attacks on Cologne by the Eighth Air Force Fortresses and Liberators indicated considerable industrial damage and rail lines severed throughout the city. Nearly 5,000 tons of high explosives and incendiaries were dropped on the Ruhr city within 24 hours in the two daylight assaults."[6]

Cologne, German spelling Koln, a large population center, was an important industrial city in the war effort. However, in October 1944 its importance in providing direct support to their ground forces on the western front was critical. Not only was Cologne's railway complex vital to the German industrial might, but it was also a gigantic military supply center with numerous marshalling yards of such proportions that are not easily compared to any city in this country. In 1944 it was the fourth largest city in Germany and the industrial and cultural heart of what was referred to as the Rhineland. So important was this city that it was the target of some 130 bombing attacks during World War II. The bombing missions devastated acres of factories, munitions plants, vital rubber and tool steel works.

The city is bisected by the Rhine River flowing south to north with four bridges to the east bank. Under those bridges passed more than 15,000,000 tons of shipping annually, which made it the greatest inland waterway in Europe. The establishment of a railway center in the city, right on the banks of that important river, was inevitable. Its size and its military significance can be defined by the fact that the rail center was a junction point for the Paris to Berlin rail system, the Rhine Valley system, and railroad lines to Belgium and northern France.

Bomb strikes of the 401st Bomb Group on railyards and rail bridge over the Rhine River October 15, 1944. The 575 foot twin spires of the Cologne Cathedral are visible as pointed black dots just beyond the smoke and the rail complex to the rear of the Cathedral. Courtesy of the National Archives.

A principal landmark and an unmistakable point of reference for the bombardier on a heavy bomber was the famed Cologne Cathedral. It sits majestically, virtually on the west bank of the river, with marshalling yards within feet of its rear walls. Also directly to its rear was one of the railroad bridges crossing the river. The edifice took six centuries to build and was completed in 1880. Considered one of the finest examples of Gothic architecture in Europe, it is easily recognized by its identical twin steeples rising 575 feet above the city. Due to its very vulnerable location during the war it got hit on numerous missions by errant bombs. In the excellent pictorial history of the Eighth titled **One Last Look**, it was reported that William McCarran of the 379th Bomb Group at Kimbolton had been shot down in December, 1943 and became a POW. During his transportation to the Dulag Luft at Frankfort Am Main he saw the great Cathedral at Cologne which he said was undamaged in a city destroyed.[7] Photographs of the Cathedral taken right after the end of the war show it standing alone amid the shells of surrounding buildings, the bridge to its rear down in the river.[8]

When I visited the Cathedral in the mid-1980s it, and its surrounding area, had been completely restored. On the exterior north wall I was able to discern some bomb scarring, but such would not have been readily recognized by the casual visitor. As I looked to the rear of that magnificent place, there was the rail center with no sign of it having been blasted over and over again by allied bombers. Considering its proximity to an important target, it was indeed a marvel that this house of God survived unintentional destruction. The marvel is better appreciated when one understands the math and physics involved in bombing, the technological aspects of PFF bombing through clouds, and most of all the B-17 as a rather unstable bombing platform bobbing around uncontrollably, due to the ever present bursts of flak and prop wash, several miles above its target. These and other elements were inextricably entangled in a typical PFF bomb run. Consider the comments of Lt. W.C. Mannix of the 613th Squadron, furnished Vic Maslen about the bomb run on Cologne on October 15. He was leading the low squadron on that day and said, "Target if visual was a 'hump' type marshalling yard at the bend of the river SE of the city. The PFF target was a rail yard in the center of the built up area on the east side of the river - if it gives good returns; if not, the center of the old city, west of the Rhine..." Describing the bomb run itself he said: "The returns were bright but inconsistent, so that Bill Strong's corrections were rather erratic and we were in a bank to the left at bombs away (my fault actually). Strong got us in there, Rostrom put his pre-set data together with some scanty checking of some ground points through the 9/10ths clouds and hit the toggle at the rule-of-toe rate position and I completed the compensating errors by my left bank which threw the bombs to the right! Results: Excellent results for PFF bombing within 2,000 yards left and 1,000 yards over the actual aiming point." The results were apparently even better because he also wrote that he and his bombing team received a commendation from General Lacey, Commander of the 94th CBW.[9] Good teamwork and a lot of modesty! Bill Strong the "mickey" or PFF operator and C. Richard Rostrom the bombardier were especially commended for their teamwork.

On October 17 the 401st went back to Cologne's rail yards for its third consecutive mission in four days. Although the names of the Sisson crew are on the loading lists for that day, they did not fly that mission. Since Norm has said they never had an abort, one possible explanation was that they were a spare and were not needed.[10] Neither Picker's log [11] or Sisson's [12] lists this as a mission. The 401st was led that day by Capt. Clyde Lewis and bombing was again by PFF due to weather conditions.[13]

After the third trip to Cologne a newspaper reported, "German tank and infantry counter-attacks tapered off yesterday in the Aachen area after a record enemy artillery attack Monday night, while 1,300 British based Forts and Liberators, attempting to ease the ground force problems by shattering the Nazi's chief supply base for their forces near Aachen, struck again yesterday at Cologne 40 miles to the east. For Cologne, focal point of road, rail and river traffic used to defend the Rhineland, it was the third big raid in four days. Yesterday's attack brought to more than 10,000 tons of bombs the total dropped on the city within a week."[14]

After four days off, the Sisson crew took the "Maiden" to Mannheim on October 19. Their target was a factory which manufactured armament and motor vehicles. The lead and low squadrons bombed through partial cloud cover with fair results.[15] The high squadron with Captain D.W. Fesmire as lead bombardier bombed a target of opportunity at Karlsruhr with excellent results. It was his 121st mission![16] That day Picker carried six 500 pound GPs and six 500 pound IBs which they dumped at 26,000 feet. He described the flak as moderate[17] although Sisson rated it with a "star" and added the notation "flak holes".[18] Their assessment of the mission was probably accurate with four of our aircraft suffering major damage, 12 with lesser damage, and two crewmen wounded, one seriously.[19] Officially the flak was regarded as meager and inaccurate which goes to prove it all depends on whose ox is being gored![20]

On October 22 the "Maiden" was aloft again without the Sisson crew. On that day she took the crew of Lt. H.J. Ochsenhirt to Hanover.[21] There were 379 B-17s in the 1st Division force with 171 of that number, including the 401st, targeted on a large plant manufacturing guns and vehicle carriers of all types. The 401st had put up 39 aircraft flying as the 94th CBW "B" group with Maj. D.G. McCree the Air Commander. With poor weather over the continent to the target bombing was done by PFF, results were believed to have been successful. There was very little flak and it was inaccurate with only 15 aircraft in the Division force damaged.[22] This good fortune was not shared by the 306th Bomb Group at Thurleigh which had two of its B-17s collide over the North Sea 25 miles northeast of Great Yarmouth with only one crewman recovered, or by the 305th at Chelveston which had two of its Forts collide, resulting in the loss of all 19 aboard.[23] This mission turned out to be the "Maiden's" last trip in October, but not for the Sisson crew.

On October 25 they flew "Hard Seventeen" to Hamburg. It was a day I remember well; it was my first combat mission. As a part of new crew orientation, Sisson's co-pilot, Hoemann, flew in the right seat beside Fred Babcock, our pilot; our co-pilot, Jack Bousfield, flew as Sisson's co-pilot.[24] The targets were motor transport works and oil industry targets. I remember as we headed south over the North Sea toward Hamburg we passed the island Helgoland. I recalled my last semester in college, just two years before, during a course in

Naval History I learned that Helgoland, only 150 acres in size, was the scene of a great naval victory for the British over the Germans in August, 1914. In minutes I would be in combat with the Germans. The bombing was PFF through 10/10ths clouds; but crews reported heavy clouds of black smoke coming through the cloud layer at about 10,000 feet as they left the target area. Some encountered heavy flak but the 614th Squadron called it meager and inaccurate.[25] Sisson however, gave it his "star"[26] though Picker described it as "heavy flak, inaccurate." He dropped six 500 pound GPs and six 500 pound IBs from 26,000 feet.[27]

On October 26 the Sisson crew was assigned to fly the B-17 with serial number 42-97602 on a mission to Bielefeld with their target an ordnance and supply depot located two miles from the city. It was a PFF mission, as usual.[28] Capt. A.H. Chapman led the 94th CBW "C" Group which experienced no flak or fighter opposition. Later photographs showed that the "Mickey" operators had plastered both MPIs.[29] Picker again carried six 500 pound GPs and six 500 pound IBs which he unloaded at 26,000 feet.[30] Sisson labeled this mission a "milk run",[31] an expression used to describe a mission as an easy one. I have refrained from doing so here except in rare instances. Hypothetically, if only one 88mm shell were fired at an entire group formation, that one exploding shell had the potential for one metal fragment to knock down a bomber and take the lives of its entire crew. That mission might have been labeled a "milk run" for the rest of the group, but it surely wouldn't have been called that by those who were the victims.

A newspaper article summarized the air war activity for the month of October 1944 saying: "Germany got its heaviest blitz last month when 8th Air Force and British heavies unloaded nearly 100,000 tons of high explosives on the Reich, it was disclosed yesterday. Adverse weather limited operations by Fortresses and Liberators to 18 days in October, when the Eighth's losses dropped to a record low - 122 bombers and 69 fighters were dispatched."[32]

Sisson said that when the curtain was pulled in the briefing room on the morning of November 2 revealing the target for the day to be Merseburg there was a "heart rendering groan" from the assembled air crews. He recalled they were told that the target, the I.G. Farben Leuna Plant, was one of the last major synthetic oil producers in Germany.

He also recalled that the briefing officer said that they had increased the flak defenses there by moving guns from other parts of the country, even from as far away as Berlin.[33] The Group that day put up 39 aircraft to form the 94th CBW "A" Group with Capt. A.H. Chapman leading. Sisson's crew had their "Maiden" back. It will be recalled that in the last Chapter Nathan Picker rated the danger of going to Politz with one other target, Merseburg. This would turn out to be his first experience which led to that conclusion.[34]

Merseburg is located in what was then the notorious Leipzig area where numerous other such oil facilities were located. The 8th, which of course included the 401st Bomb Group, was to find it necessary to go to Merseburg again and again! After September 1, 1944 until the end of the war in Europe the 401st bombed other targets in the Leipzig area including Leipzig itself. However, in that period the 8th sent 11 missions to Merseburg. The 401st missed only three of those trips although they flew missions on those days: the first was on September 28 when they were over Magdeburg; the second was on October 7 when they were at Politz; the third one to Bohlen on November 30 was hardly a "milk run." John Hope, Charlie Utter's bombardier, said, "Somebody told me that Merseburg was the graduate school for flak gunners, and I believe it. They fired individually, and you could see one burst a little low and to the left; count to three and you would see another, a little high and to the right. Then count to three and tighten your sphincter because the next one was right under you."[35]

Picker took 18 250 pound GPs which he dropped on a PFF run at 26,000 feet. He noted in his log: "Moderate to intense flak - Tracking - Long run through flak area before and after bombs away - Saw three go down over target in Groups ahead - Lost one - Damage in tail - Fighters."[36] The B-17 "Wolf Pack" flown by Lt. H.L. Oas, Jr. and crew of the 615th Squadron was lost on November 2. S/Sgt. J.J. Geraldi of the 613th Squadron reported, "The aircraft took a direct hit in the #3 engine and pieces were seen to come off. It was last seen just past the target at 26,000 feet. After ten seconds the aircraft went into a vertical dive spiraling down. Three chutes came out of the aircraft in the dive." In an MIA report Lt. Oas said that Lt. W.H. Green, the navigator and Lt. W.M. Mencow, the bombardier, had bailed out ahead of him. He said, "At that altitude they could have suffered anoxia if they did not delay their fall." Lt. Oas was a POW; the rest of his crew were KIA.[37] Another report was made by Lt. John Udy a 615th pilot. He said he was flying on Lt. Oas' wing and reported: "He received a direct hit in the #3 engine causing his aircraft to pitch up into mine. I pulled back on the control column and managed to miss him. This caused a loss in airspeed and I fell behind the formation. I applied full power to get back into formation, and as we watched Lt. Oas' aircraft began to spin down, suddenly, we were hit from behind by three FW-190s. I was doing some evasive action to avoid the flak and I think that prevented us from being shot down. The 20mm shells fired by the 190s went through the right wing and burst in little white puffs approximately 100 yards in front of the aircraft. Our gunners opened up on the 190s and thought they hit them but could not confirm this. We got back into formation and completed the mission."[38] Aside from the heavy and accurate flak on November 2 the mission was memorable also because it was the first time since early September that the Luftwaffe was up in force. They came up to meet the Eighth with about 400 fighters. The Eighth put up 1174 bombers and 968 fighters. Of these there were 460 1st Division and 223 2nd Division aircraft at Merseburg with the 3rd Division hitting a combination of oil and transportation targets in central Germany. Several Bomb Groups in the Triangle 1st were hit hard while unprotected by fighters. The 91st Bomb Group at Bassingbourn lost 13 and our neighbors in the 94th CBW, the 457th at Glatton, lost nine. The 2nd Division lost 26 B-24s and the 3rd Division also lost two aircraft.[39] A newspaper with reference to this mission reported, "On Nov. 2 Eighth bomber - escort fighters scored their greatest single day triumph over the Luftwaffe in the air, shooting down 134 of several hundred German fighters mustered to defend oil targets in the Merseburg area. The bomb crews bagged 53 Nazi aircraft."[40] The official count for that day is impressive: The Eighth's gunners were credited with 36 destroyed, 35 probably destroyed and another 27 damaged. Of these, in the same corresponding categories the 1st Division accounted for 30-33-25. The American fighters claimed a whopping 102-5-25 not to mention our "little friends" got another 25 on the ground.[41] Now, that's more like it! After that scrap the Luftwaffe would pause before attempting to put up another mammoth fighter defense of the Fatherland.

In 1983 during a reunion in England I was reminded of Sisson's description of the apprehension felt at the briefing on November 2 prior to the curtain being pulled disclosing the target for the day. I certainly agree the tension until that moment for every mission was always the same. There we were while others slept, huddled together with our own crew members, each having those private thoughts amid suspense like none other I have since endured. I stood at the rear of that room with Paul Campbell, who had been a pilot and assistant operations officer in the 615th. Even though the building is now a derelict and had been used as some sort of a farm building, we were almost overcome by emotion as we stood there. I then understood why several others did not leave the bus to look at the interior of the place. I was quite surprised at how small it seemed and wondered how all of us could have crowded in there on those mornings so long ago. In a novel written by Robert Denny, who had been a pilot with the 306th Bomb Group at Thurleigh, he described the briefing for Merseburg as follows:

"The air above their heads was thick with cigarette smoke...the men were hunched forward, watching the curtain covering the wall map...the group operations officer...soberly pulled the cord and opened the curtain. The red yarn stretched from England deep into Germany, zig-zagging from leg to leg, leading finally to the initial point of the bomb run...Merseburg. A mass groan pulled from the collective gut, filled the room..."

Denny later described the bomb run itself:

"The bombardier engaged the clutch that coupled the bombsight to the autopilot and began flying the airplane. He made small corrections by turning two knobs on the bombsight. Shutting out the fury that was going on outside, he bent over the bombsight and peered through the telescope. Merseburg lay ahead. A smoke bomb dropped by the wing lead zig-zagged to the ground marking the target. Carefully, Fisk centered

401st Briefing Room 1980s.

the cross hairs of the sight. Now everything was automatic. Computing the instant of release, it would trigger the bomb drop at the right instant...The sky was oily black and seemed to boil around the lead bomber groups ahead. Five hundred flak guns on the ground fired incessantly at the bombers as they moved into range. When their radar screens became jammed by chaff, they switched to preset box pattern of flak coverage. It was like watching an approaching thunderstorm and knowing there was a tornado hiding in it...shrapnel hit the airplane like a giant fistful of stones. The cloud ahead grew larger, blacker more frightening...Explosions burst around the lead squadron. Again the sound of stones being thrown against metal...They were flying through a huge black storm in which the raindrops were flying shards of metal. The B-17 lifted sharply. `bombs away' the bombardier cried."[42]

On November 5 the Sisson crew was aloft with the "Maiden" as the Eighth put up 1,200 bombers against marshalling yards in western Germany. The 1st Division's contribution was 452 B-17s assigned to another of Germany's largest cities, Frankfurt Am Main. Clouds at the IP required a PFF run, but good bomb strikes on the rail yards were observed through a break in the clouds.[43] Flak at Frankfurt was intense and accurate but there was no enemy fighter opposition.[44] Picker recorded that he dropped six 1,000 pound GPs from 26,500 feet.[45] On their return there was a front over Deenethorpe and the 401st had to be diverted to other bases for several hours.[46] I recall weather necessitated my crew being diverted on at least four occasions; and it was never a picnic. Coming home in the late afternoon the crews were tired, dirty and hungry. Returning successfully from a mission it was very discouraging to learn that we couldn't "get in" at Deenethorpe. On November 5 we landed at an RAF base and waited in a large room without adequate chairs for guests who dropped in unexpectedly. I stretched out on the floor, and in my flying togs I was well padded and it didn't seem too bad. At least we were more fortunate than two other crews: one crashed landed at Flambridge and the other had an emergency landing at Great Dunmow.[47] A newspaper account of the mission on November 5 reported, "Not even bad weather now brings any respite for Germany from the crushing bomb loads dropped night and day by the British and American air forces...In 24 hours ending yesterday afternoon 5,000 allied planes struck more heavy blows from the west at Germany's weakening war machine...Important rail junctions at Frankfurt,

Ludwigshaven and Karlsruhr, in the Rhine Valley, through which move military supplies for German defenses in the southern sector of the western front were attacked yesterday by 1,200 U.S. Eighth Air Force heavy bombers, escorted by 650 fighters...30 bombers and 23 fighters have not yet returned but a number of these, including at least six fighters are believed to have landed in friendly territory."[48] Actually, the Eighth lost a total of eight of its bombers on that mission.[49]

After hitting the tactical target at Frankfurt the Sisson crew and their "Maiden" returned to the top priority target, oil. On November 6 they drew as the target a synthetic oil plant at Harburg. The city is located on the southern bank of the Elbe River across from another large and heavily defended city, Hamburg. Capt. A.H. Chapman led the 94th CBW "B" Group on a PFF run with a visual assist; bombing through broken clouds they had excellent results.[50] John Hope, Charlie Utter's bombardier said this "mickey run" was one of the most successful he recalls. He explained that the refinery sat out on a peninsula in the river and for that reason on radar it stood out like a sore thumb.[51]

A newspaper described the mission as follows - "The renewed day-and-night allied onslaught against Germany continued in high gear yesterday when nearly 2,000 heavy bombers plastered oil, rail and other industrial objectives in daylight after two night attacks by RAF Mosquitoes...For the third straight day more than 1,100 Fortresses and Liberators of the Eighth Air Force were dispatched bombing oil plants in the Hamburg-Harburg area, rail yards and other industrial targets in the vicinity of Neumunster and Duisburg, and other objectives in west Germany."[52]

Picker unloaded six 1,000 pound GPs from 25,000 feet. He called the flak light to moderate.[53] It wasn't so light or moderate for the crew of Lt. R.H. Hillestad of the 613th Squadron who was flying "Lady Jane." They had flak damage in the #2 and possibly the #3 engines. They were last reported seen over Cuxhaven (at the mouth of the Elbe River at the North Sea) at 21,000 feet. At 1300 hours the radio operator sent an SOS stating they were preparing to ditch. It was also reported that they made an emergency landing at a Luftwaffe base at Enschede, Holland and became POWs.[54]

There is an important contradiction of the landing at Enschede, located on the eastern border of Holland with Germany. Vic Maslen printed a letter from one Piet Brouwer of Holland which said, "On November 6, 1944 a B-17 of the U.S. 8th Air Force made a wheels-up landing in a large field in the Polder Wieringermeer about 25 miles north of Amsterdam, Holland. The crew of nine were taken prisoners of war. The Germans removed the most valuable parts of the aircraft and then blew it up. An eye-witness remembers the plane had 56 bomb symbols and two victory marks painted on the nose. Towards the end of the war the Germans inundated that part of our country and the aircraft wreck was swallowed by the water. On October 20, 1982, the wreckage was excavated by myself and seven other Dutch aviation enthusiasts."[55] The wreck reported in this letter would have been in northwest Holland, at least 100 miles west of Enschede. Further, Brouwer's report is consistent with the radio report which was heard by another aircraft then over the North Sea as well as the last report from "Lady Jane" over Cuxhaven.[56] That Hillestad and crew landed in the Polder Wieringermeer was confirmed by a recent letter from Fred Campbell, the navigator to "Rainbow." He said that the crew all made it home though the pilot and co-pilot are deceased. In 1988 he visited the crash site and a Dutch family presented him with the gyro-compass from the "Lady Jane" which they have saved for a member of the crew all these years. He said it was an emotional time for him.[57]

On November 8 with Major Leon Stann leading the 94th CBW "A" Group, with Captain Donald Kirkhuff leading the low squadron and Capt. Paul E. Campbell leading the high squadron the 401st went again to Merseburg to bomb the I. G. Farben Leuna refinery. Sisson and crew were aboard the "Maiden" on this mission. Due to a complete cloud cover the PFF bombing results were not observed.[58] Picker dropped ten 500 pound GPs from 24,000 feet. He described the flak as moderate to intense, as might be expected, and further noted: "hit in the nose...613 ship lost."[59] The latter comment was premature. The crew of Lt. R.L. Steele of the 613th Squadron flying "Little Pedro" was hit by flak just before bombs away. Some of his crew were wounded and they endured a fire on the flight deck. Nevertheless, they managed to land safely on an RAF field in Belgium.[60] But "Little Pedro" was finished and had to be left in Europe for salvage.[61]

The degree of protection afforded Merseburg probably had a great deal to do with why the Eighth had to go back time after time. We went there so many times that even today it is hard to find a veteran of the Eighth who didn't share that experience. Fred Koger, the toggelier of the 92nd Bomb Group is very candid in describing his own recollections of the Merseburg experience. He wrote:

"Today, straining through the nose as we turned toward that black hell over Merseburg, I felt I was going to get killed. This wasn't the same fear that I felt on every mission, and it was a profound feeling of helplessness, as if it had just dawned on me how vulnerable we were. And luck, whatever that was, had seemed like a neblulous and flimsy thing to get me through that awesome black gauntlet."

They were leading a later mission to Merseburg when he wrote:

"Today I didn't stare at the black cloud over Merseburg, while dreading the moment we would turn into it. There was no black cloud, just blue sky. We were the first to arrive, and we would test the waters for the six groups that would follow us through. They could watch us and dread the time it would be their turn. The flak didn't start with a few bursts, then build up to a box barrage. Instead it materialized with unbelievable speed, bursting everywhere at once. In a matter of seconds the sky was dirtied with black and I was scrunched up inside my flak suit trying to be as small as possible. I had the same numb feeling that I had before, almost as if I was resigned to the fact that I was going to get killed in a few minutes. And there wasn't a damned thing I could do about it.[62]

On the next day, November 9, the 401st was involved in a purely tactical operation in support of Gen. George Patton's Third Army in the area of Metz, France. It was the only mission of my tour that bombed a target in France. A total of 730 heavies of the 1st and 2nd Divisions had as their targets the reinforced concrete forts on the Moselle River in France. Many of us had fathers, uncles or other kin who served in France during World War I and from them we heard stories of the battle at Verdun. The IP for the bomb run on November 9 was Verdun which left a run of about 50 miles due east to our target. It was a close support mission from a substantial altitude of 25,000 feet. The great concern was for the safety of the ground troops, and a number of steps were taken to protect them from errant bombs falling on those we were there to support.

First, our artillery was to fire "friendly flak." This was to consist of shells with a very distinctive red smoke set to explode at 18,000 feet, every 500 yards along the front line running north to south. Second, 15 silver barrage balloons were spaced 300 yards apart along the line at 2,000 feet. Third, in case of good visibility red and orange cloth markers would be spread on the ground indicating the bomb line. Lastly, radio transmitters were placed on the ground along the line, and when the aircraft passed that point, it would indicate that to the receivers carried by the aircraft. The latter device was the adaptation of an instrument landing system used by American bases.

With smoke and undercast I never saw balloons or the ground markers, and I do not recall the radio technique which Roger Freeman said was the most reliable, but I sure saw that flak. It was indeed red, a shade somewhat like that of a good Bloody Mary. My most conscious recollection was that those things looked a lot higher than 18,000 feet.[63] Bombing was visual with assist of Gee-H, and the results must have been good because we were commended by Gen. Patton and others for superior work which paved the way for the capture of Metz and the eventual breakthrough of our forces on the ground.[64] Picker recorded we dropped eight 1,000 pound SAPs (semi armour piercing bombs). I believe that mission was the only one on which I carried that type bomb load although I do recall carrying 1,000 pound GPs. The SAPs were designed to penetrate the very heavy concrete forts at Metz.[65] The steps taken to protect our ground forces were apparently a success.

Freeman reported that one bomb fell in allied territory without anyone harmed. He said

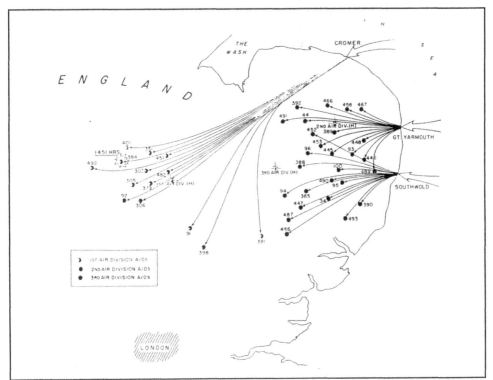

At full strength and particularly during bad weather conditions the number of aircraft returning from combat required a common procedure for their dispersal from the English coast to their respective bases. The chart shows how this procedure was meant to reduce the hazard of midair collisions. From the 8th AF Tactical Development August 1942 - May 1945. Prepared by the 8th AF and the AAF Evaluation Board (ETO).

that it had hung up in an aircraft after bombs away and fell as they were turning back into our territory after bombs away. There were losses that day; eight bombers most of which were lost in takeoffs and landing accidents due to poor weather conditions at our English bases.[66] The horror of those afternoon returns to Deenethorpe still haunt me today. John Hope, Charlie Utter's bombardier, remembers them too. He wrote: "I was scared as often over England on the return as I was over the target; 1,200 planes with tired pilots milling around at 700 feet, trying to make it back to base."[67] There were two Medals of Honor awarded posthumously that day to Lt. Donald Gott, a pilot, and to Lt. William Metzger, his co-pilot of the 452nd Bomb Group, at Deopham Green in the 3rd Division. Flying their B-17, "Lady Janet" they were hit by flak in three of the four engines. Several crew members were seriously wounded and fire trailed from the wing to the tail. Lt. Metzger tended the wounded, and gave his parachute to a gunner whose own had been damaged. Lt. Gott radioed that one of the wounded was not in any shape to bailout so he and Metzger sought to crash land the crippled aircraft in friendly territory. On his final approach at about 100 feet the plane blew up killing the three that were still aboard.[68]

The bad weather contributing, the "Maiden" and the Sisson crew had some time off before their next mission on November 16 to Eschweiler. This was another purely tactical support mission to bomb ahead of the 1st Army then driving toward Cologne.[69] The Eighth was called on to support a planned assault around Aachen, a few miles southwest of Eschweiler. The specific targets were troops and guns only three miles from American lines.[70] The 2nd Division had targets also in the Eschweiler area, and the 3rd Division had similar targets at Duren, a few miles east of Eschweiler. The attacks were designed to be a prelude to the beginning of the allied offensive on the ground.[71] Bombing was done by Gee-H with clouds from 6/10ths to 10/10ths.[72] From all indications the bombs fell within the assigned area.[73] Picker carried 30 250 pound fragmentation bombs dropped from 23,000 feet. He said the flak was light and weather prevented their return to Deenethorpe. He said they landed at a Royal Canadian Air Force (RCAF) base at Ossington where they had to remain for two days before weather permitted them to return home.[74] The 401st suffered no battle damage and there were no casualties - my kind of mission![75]

Notes to Chapter 9

1. Freeman, Roger A., Alan Crouchman & Selwyn V. Maslen The Mighty Eighth War Diary p. 364
2. Closway, Gordon R. 614th Squadron History see Air Operations October, 1944
3. Freeman, see 1 above p. 364
4. Maslen, Selwyn V. 614th Bombardment Squadron (H) Squadron History p. 97
5. Koger, Fred Countdown! p. 138, 140-141
6. Newspaper clippings of unknown publications on unknown dates furnished author as enclosure to letter from Norman L. Sisson February 13, 1991
7. Kaplan, Philip & Rex Alan Smith One Last Look p.1 69
8. Woolnough, John H. The 8th Air Force Album p.197
9. Bowman, Harold W. & Selwyn V. Maslen Bowman's Bombers p.101
10. Maslen, see 4 above p. 97
11. Photocopy of personal log of Nathan Picker furnished author as enclosure to letter from Norman L. Sisson February 13, 1991
12. Photocopies of personal log of Norman L. Sisson and collection of bomb fuse tags furnished author as enclosure to Sisson's letter February 13, 1991
13. Maslen, see 4 above p. 97
14. See 6 above
15. Closway, see 2 above
16. Bowman & Maslen, see 9 above p. 49
17. See 11 above
18. See 12 above
19. Bowman & Maslen, see 9 above p. 49
20. Maslen, see 4 above p.98
21. Maslen, Selwyn V. 614th Squadron: Crews - Missions - Aircraft p. 59
22. Maslen, see 4 above p. 98
23. Freeman, see 1 above p. 369
24. Closway, see 2 above Loading list for October 25, 1944
25. Maslen, see 4 above p. 99
26. See 12 above
27. See 11 above
28. Maslen, see 4 above p. 99
29. Closway, see 2 above Air Operations October, 1944
30. See 11 above
31. Enclosure to letter, Norman L. Sisson to author February, 1992
32. See 6 above
33. See 31 above
34. Letter, Nathan Picker to author March 29, 1991
35. Letter, John Hope to author February 23, 1991
36. See 11 above
37. Bowman, Harold W. & Selwyn V. Maslen 410st B.G. (H) Casualties in W.W. II p.58
38. Bowman & Maslen, see 9 above p. 102
39. Freeman, see 1 above p. 375
40. See 6 above
41. Freeman, see 1 above p. 375
42. Denny, Robert Aces: A Novel of World War II p. 72, 92-94
43. Bowman & Maslen, see 9 above p. 52
44. Maslen, see 4 above p103
45. See 11 above
46. Maslen, see 4 above p. 103
47. Freeman, see 1 above p. 377
48. See 6 above
49. Freeman, see 1 above p. 377
50. Bowman & Maslen, see 9 above p. 52
51. See 35 above
52. See 6 above
53. See 11 above
54. Bowman & Maslen, see 37 above p. 58

55. Bowman & Maslen, see 9 above p. 103
56. Maslen, see 4 above p.104
57. _Poop From Group_ #78, December 1992
58. Bowman & Maslen, see 9 above p. 53
59. See 11 above
60. Maslen, see 4 above p. 104
61. Bowman & Maslen, see 9 above p. 139
62. Koger, see 5 above p. 109, 146
63. Freeman, Roger A. _The Mighty Eighth_ p. 181
64. Bowman & Maslen, see 9 above p. 53
65. See 11 above
66. Freeman, see 63 above p. 181
67. See 35 above
68. Freeman, see 63 above p. 180-181
69. Closway, see 2 above Summary of Events November, 1944
70. Maslen, see 4 above p. 105
71. Freeman, see 1 above p. 382
72. Maslen, see 4 above p. 105
73. Bowman & Maslen, see 9 above p. 53
74. See 11 above
75. Bowman & Maslen, see 9 above p. 53

CHAPTER 10 — A PLACE CALLED MERSEBURG

In the words of Captain Alvah H. Chapman, Jr. "On Tuesday, the 21st of November the 401st Group with the 614th leading, gave the German Air and Ground defenses **all** the odds in their favor and still bored in and put bombs on the target area of one of the most vital targets, the oil refinery at Merseburg."[1]

On that date Captain Chapman led the 94th CBW "B" Group to strike at the Leuna Oil Refinery at Merseburg.[2] Norm Sisson whose crew flew their "Maiden" that day recalled the mission saying, "Here we go again - Merseburg. This was the worst! It was our mission 27 and the Group's 171st."[3] On the souvenir bomb fuse tag from that mission Norm drew two stars indicating the severity of the mission; only one other tag in his collection of 35 shared two stars, the other being Politz.[4] Nathan Picker recorded that they carried ten 500 pound GPs which they were briefed to drop from 26,000 feet.[5] The 614th Squadron put up ten aircraft which included Captain Chapman riding as Air Commander with the crew of Lt. E.W. Mercer. It was the first combat mission for the crews of Lts. Wylie K. White and R.B. Richardson.[6]

Assembly was reported to have been satisfactory and on time but the formation was two minutes late reaching the enemy coast.[7] As they approached the IP a cloud bank caused all Groups to "let down." At the IP they were at 20.000 feet and it was still not possible to remain below the clouds. They flew in and out of clouds and heavy haze on the bomb run at 19,000 feet. The high squadron leader with four other aircraft became separated from the Group formation after the IP, and eventually bombed a target of opportunity at Eisenach, some 100 miles to the southwest of Merseburg.[8] The lead and low squadrons bombed the primary target by PFF and were unable to observe the results.

Flak was accurate and intense. The crew of Lt. Francis E. Rundell, flying as deputy lead, was lost over the target and were MIA. The other members of the crew were: Lt. R.E. Johnson, co-pilot; Lt. R.P. Champagne, navigator; Lt. W.N. Shearer, Jr., bombardier; Lt. Alastair Currie, "mickey" operator; S/Sgt. A.J. Trojanowski, radio operator; T/Sgt. H.B. Mears, engineer; T/

Francis E. Rundell crew.

Sgt. R.E. Ice, tail gunner; and S/Sgt. J.J. Huffman, waist gunner. The last report on their aircraft was that it received a direct hit by flak to the #2 engine over the target. The report said that the prop was feathered with a fire observed on the nacelle. Also it said the aircraft was sideslipped out of formation in an effort to put out the fire, but this was thought to have been ineffectual. Lastly, the report said: "A/C broke up - one or two chutes seen."[9] Also lost was the crew of Lt. R.J. Keck of the 613th Squadron who were flying "Homing Pigeon." Lt. Keck's aircraft had been damaged by flak to the extent that it was forced to straggle, and he was singled out for attack by a German Me-109. That enemy fighter was later shot down by a 401st B-17 resulting in a claim by that B-17.[10] A report by Sgt. L.W. Raymond of the 613th Squadron said: "Keck's aircraft was hit by flak; the #2 engine caught fire and flames were trailing behind the tail. After an attack by a Me-109 the aircraft went down. I last saw it at 10,000 feet and about one mile behind the formation. It exploded at 10,000 feet after rolling over in a steep dive. At least four of the crew bailed out." S/Sgt. R.E. Engler, radio operator, and S/Sgt. E.W. Norr, ball turret, were KIA. The remaining members of the crew including Lt. Keck were POWs. They were: F/O L.A. Istel, co-pilot, Lt. H.W. Freeman Jr., navigator, Lt. S. Shepard, bombardier, S/Sgt. L.V. Stoeger, engineer, S/Sgt. W.T. Metalf, tail gunner, and S/Sgt. E. Fialkowski, waist gunner.[11] The crew of Lt. Paul Sullivan of the 615th had to land in Belgium but later returned to Deenethorpe.[12] The 614th Squadron brought home some wounded on November 21; they were from Lt. Mercer's lead crew, Lt. Leslie E. Gaskins, navigator, and S/Sgt. Edward B. Grasela, waist gunner. On Lt. White's crew Lt. Russell L. Aufrance was wounded on his first mission. Also wounded was S/Sgt. Ernest A. Serafino, engineer.[13]

That day the Eighth had 1149 bombers over Germany. In addition to 421 B-17s at Merseburg and targets of opportunity the other Divisions were also on the line. The 2nd Bomb Division bombed Hamburg. Part of the 3rd Bomb Division bombed a secondary target, the marshalling yards at Osnabruck, while the rest of that force hit miscellaneous last resort targets. The Eighth lost a total of 25 aircraft on November 21, 14 were 1st Bomb Division B-17s. In addition three more crashed in Belgium and one went to Sweden.[14]

An excellent recital of the 401st mission that day is one by a pilot who didn't finish the trip to Merseburg. It is the story of Bud Rundell whose aircraft was lost that day. Bud said he began writing the story of his twelfth, and last mission, while lying on a cot at Camp Lucky Strike, a huge tent city in France for liberated POWs awaiting shipment home, after he was

B-17 the "homing pigeon" lost with the crew of Lt. R.J. Keck at Merseburg November 21, 1944. USAF Photo Collection neg. #C-65643AC courtesy of the NASM, Smithsonian Institution.

Bud Rundell and his parents.

released from Stalag Luft One.[15] He is a good story teller, and I hope he takes the time to write the full story of his Air Force career from which he retired as a Colonel.

"On the night of November 20 I was relaxing around the pot-bellied stove in the 614th Operations hut with Captain Alvah H. Chapman, who was acting C.O., and Captain Donald Kirkhuff, the Squadron Operations Officer. I was the newly appointed Assistant Operations Officer and was learning the business of planning and scheduling aircraft and crews. The business at hand that evening was to learn if I could roast popcorn without scorching it. My crew and I had been flying practice missions over England for two weeks in training for certification as a lead crew and were eager to get on with the actual combat missions. Then the telephone rang. It was Group Operations who wanted a deputy who was certified. I volunteered although I had not commanded a PFF aircraft in combat.

"After the call I walked over to the barracks and told my crew to get some sleep as we were scheduled to fly, and informed our ball turret gunner, Bill Smith, that he would not accompany us since the radar dome replaced the ball turret in the PFF aircraft. I was uneasy but couldn't put my finger on why. I had never thought much about premonition. I had experienced anxiety before missions but this was different, a more intense feeling.

"Breakfast was at 0230...fresh eggs. It seemed we always had fresh eggs instead of the routine powdered variety before a tough mission. We often wondered whether the cook knew the target assignment before the crews learned it later at the preflight briefing. "The briefing at 0330 was uneventful, except for the groan that arose when the target was announced to be Merseburg. Merseburg, Halle and Leipzig were cities sharing important targets; they formed a triangular area where mutually supporting flak batteries were well known for accuracy and intensity. I left my billfold with the operations clerk and caught the truck to the aircraft parking area. After a walk around preflight inspection I was getting in the aircraft when the Crew Chief called to me: 'Don't bother to bring her back here, just park her over on the other side.' He had sweated out 74 missions on his 'baby' and was to receive a bottle of Johnny Walker Scotch whiskey when I brought her back from her 75th mission and he wanted her parked front and center to celebrate the occasion.

"At dawn the takeoff was on time and uneventful. The aircraft, a PFF 'mickey' ship appeared to be in excellent shape. The autopilot worked well and the ship seemed to climb better than most. She was light on the controls and handled nicely. "Then things began to happen. Captain Chapman's lead aircraft had to abort and return to the base. I was left to proceed as leader of the three squadrons through the Group assembly and into the bomber stream. Assembly altitude was changed from 14,000 feet to 17,000 feet. Donning oxygen masks, we led the Group in wide climbing circles around the non-directional radio beacon that marked our assembly point. At the planned wing assembly time we headed toward the area over East Anglia to join the other Groups. I felt mounting concern. Here I was, responsible for not only my crew, my aircraft, and our safety, but also for the performance and safety of 35 aircraft and crews following me. How close should I fly to the Group formation ahead of us if the weather closed in? Should I climb? No; the forecast was for heavy cloud layers at high altitudes. Should I descend? No; Merseburg minimum altitude was 26,000 feet. When should we consider changing to the alternate target? What authority did I have as a leader? "I began to sweat. I had flown as deputy leader five times before, but the leader was always reassuringly there just off my left wing. I breathed a great sigh of relief as I saw Chapman in a replacement aircraft slide into formation just in time to lead us to our correct place in the bomber stream. He would now make the critical decisions that had been worrying me.

"We continued our steady climb on course over the North Sea and past the front lines. When we reached our assigned altitude of 26,000 feet the weather began to look bad. Persistent contrails formed and wisps of cirrus flashed by our wing tips. Over the radio came the clipped message: 'Briefed altitude minus one' so we dropped down a thousand feet. The weather was getting steadily worse and we were flying through thin clouds. Another message and another three thousand foot descent. We broke out of the clouds into the clear but were faced with a solid front of clouds on our level a few miles ahead. 'Briefed altitude minus seven' was the next message. I knew Chapman was reluctant to expose the Group to so low an altitude over so famous a target. But our mission assignment was to bomb an important synthetic oil refinery at Merseburg. Chapman had to make a tough command decision whether to continue to the primary target or divert to an alternate target. `Bandits in the area, bandits in the area' the radio said. No one on my crew saw any enemy fighters, but we all joined all the other planes in tightening up the formation. Each gunner checked his guns to be sure they were in working order. All eyes searched the skies for specks that did not belong to the bomber stream.

"We followed Chapman as he turned on the IP and headed down the bomb run. Pulses quickened. Bomb bay doors opened. This was the part of the mission where seconds seemed like minutes and minutes like hours. The bomb run was usually about five minutes long, that is between the IP and bombs away over the target; but it seemed longer than the four hours it took to go from takeoff to IP. During the bomb run all planes must hold steady in good formation regardless of flak or fighters. Evasive action could not be taken until after the bombs were dropped.

"At the first burst of flak, Lt. Bill Shearer, the bombardier, called for the last oxygen check before bombs away. All crew members checked in positively. The crew acts as a team to get the plane to the target and home safely, but the bombardier is in command during the bomb run. He is responsible for making the trip successful. He manipulates the famous Norden bombsight that is tied into the autopilot which flies the plane while the pilot and co-pilot keep hands off the controls until bombs away. It was found to be more effective in 'pattern bombing' to have the whole formation drop when the lead ship released its bomb load for two reasons: First, the best bombardiers were selected to be members of the lead crews. Second, the effect on the target when all bombs exploded together was greatly enhanced. Since the deputy leader was responsible for dropping his bombs at the exact best time, if the leader had a problem and couldn't release, the responsibility for the deputy lead bombardier was nearly as great as for the lead bombardier. The rest of the squadron would automatically follow his lead on when to drop their bombs. Lt. Rene Champagne, our navigator, reported that we were two degrees left of course and Scottie Currie, the 'mickey' operator, agreed. A train of four bursts of flak appeared too close to ignore. Jim Huffman, the waist gunner, who had the responsibility for manning machine guns on both sides of the fuselage, exclaimed on the interphone: `Wow! If my mother could see me now!' "Red-centered bursts appeared at nine o'clock level. We could tell these German flak batteries were the more effective type with radar-assisted aiming and altitude-sensitive fuses that could be set accurately for the altitude of the target aircraft. Since we were skimming the base of the 19,000 foot overcast, the gunners had excellent reference for setting the fuses. 'Them flak gunners ain't Pfcs, they are Master Sgts!' announced Doc Mears, our flight engineer and top turret gunner. He was interrupted from further observations by Art Trojanowski, our radio operator. 'I have a weather report, shall I read it?' Art was our comedian, a musician and a light-hearted fellow. The joking tone in his voice helped relieve the tension just a bit. Flak was visible on all points of the clock now, and often there were red-centered black puffs between our plane and Chapman's. It was the most intensive anti-aircraft barrage we had encountered in our 12 missions.

"Shortly before bombs away it happened. The ship shuddered once, then again, and on the third jolt, I felt the concussion strike hard on my ear drums. Number two engine had suffered a direct hit. The cowling disappeared, and the mass of metal left was hardly recognizable as an engine. It was on fire with flames streaming past the tail. Number one engine was streaming oil and the oil gauge read zero. I flicked off the fuel shut-off switch and pushed the number two feathering button, brushing Ray Johnson's hand on the feathering button for Number one. I put my finger on the alarm bell switch to give the signal to bail out, but hesitated. The fire wall aft of the engines is supposed to keep an engine fire from spreading to the wing tanks for one minute or more. The fire slowly died out to my great relief.

"At the same time that Ray and I were taking care of emergency procedures, I had started a diving right turn to leave the formation. I had seen a plane explode in tight formation and take two others with it. The angle of bank was getting too steep, and I tried to level off and found that I had no left aileron control. Ray's was still okay so with both of us pushing full left rudder we were able to get back to level flight, drop bombs to lighten the load, start to trim up the plane, and assess the damage. An oxygen check found everyone okay.

"By that time we had caught our breath enough to see what had happened. Number one engine was feathered, number two wouldn't feather and the prop was windmilling slower and slower until it finally stopped; it was frozen in low pitch which caused a lot of drag. Bob Ice, our tail gunner, reported that he had been knocked flat, and when he got up he noticed the whole tail was crooked. Art reported that the bomb bay doors looked like sieves, and his radios wouldn't work. Most of the flight deck instruments didn't work either, but number three and four engines were still running smoothly, although we couldn't get emergency power from them because the superchargers didn't work. From this initial assessment we had complete confidence that the B-17 would take us safely back to France.

"We started to slow down to the recommended B-17 slow cruise speed of 110 mph, but stalled out at 125 mph. We lost about 1,000 feet altitude in recovering and had to continue to fly at 130 mph. I had practiced flying many times with two engines out on the same side, and the good old B-17 always responded well; but with all the damage and added drag encountered, this one couldn't hold altitude at 130 mph. The crew threw out everything possible to lighten the load; the guns, ammunition, extra equipment, anything that wasn't bolted down. The crew formed a line from the radio room to the waist door and passed things out - including Art's parachute, without anyone realizing it; but we continued on a gradual descent on a heading west toward France.

"Ray asked me if I was hurt and pointed toward my left arm. There was a big rip in the sleeve of my jacket and blood stains. I moved my fingers and they didn't seem to be working just right. My flak vest was chewed up on the left edge right over my heart. There was a hole in the side of the plane between the number two engine and me. Wow! Was I lucky! In the heat of the emergency I didn't feel the piece of flak that cut almost to the bone in my forearm and had lodged in the flak vest; but I did feel it as soon as I saw it. It looked deep and Ray told me to go down into the nose and get Bill Shearer to fix it up. I did, and while Bill cut my sleeve off and bandaged the arm, I removed my heated slippers and boots and put on my uniform shoes. Amazingly, I was the only one on the crew to be injured.

"As we continued westward Rene reported we were only making a ground speed of 80 mph due to a very strong headwind. Then an enemy Me-109 was observed flying on our same course about a mile off our right wing. We were lucky again; the big front that was causing the bad weather over Europe was just ahead of us and we plowed into it, grateful for its protection from the fighter. We picked up ice and once the ship shuddered as we approached a stall. We broke out of the overcast at about 5,000 feet; a half hour had elapsed since we had left the formation and were on our own. "I scratched the ice off the inside of the pilot's side window and was surprised to see a hill at about the same altitude as we were. Looking to the right we saw another hill. I had assumed that as we lost altitude and the air became denser we would be able to hold our altitude. I was immediately confronted with a command decision: Do we continue to fly down the valley below us and hope that it had an open end

Retired Col. Francis E. Rundell of the 614th Squadron at Langley AFB during the 401st Bomb Group reunion at Norfolk, Virginia in September 1992.

and the plane would not lose any more altitude, or do we pick out a good place to ditch? I was responsible for our nine lives and we were then too low to bail out. I took the latter choice and gave the signal to prepare for ditching.

"We headed toward a plowed field; I called Art to insure that everyone was in place in the radio room. We made a normal approach with full flaps down; yes, they worked on both sides – lucky again! We touched down with wheels up and slid along smoothly till we lost speed. At about 30 mph the left wing hit a big mound of dirt about 24 feet wide and 20 feet deep. The mound had not been visible from the air and I later learned that it was how the Germans stored potatoes and other vegetables during the winter. As we clipped the top off of the mound the plane slewed around, and as it came to a stop the complete tail assembly fell off. At the abrupt stop I left the seat and bumped my head on the windshield. At any other time I would probably have been knocked out, but I didn't feel any pain and wondered if it was because I was dead. "I unhooked my harness and pulled myself out the side window; I had beaten Ray Johnson out for the first time. We had practiced ditching procedures many times and the training really paid off. I heard a hissing noise that sounded like we were about to explode. Forms were beginning to appear from the radio room hatch and, one-by-one, the men dropped to the ground and stood beside the battered fuselage. Johnson was helping the men out and I was yelling to them to run away from the ship. Johnson threw a thermite bomb into the radio room and we all ran toward the forest which was about 100 yards away. "When we reached the trees, we looked back and found that the thermite bomb had not worked and there were already two Germans on top of the plane. It looked like they were wearing uniforms and were carrying rifles. We couldn't go back and destroy the plane; we were not armed and they were. However, Scotty and Art had destroyed all the secret equipment and materials on the way down. We knew the Germans had B-17s in operating condition and used them in training their fighter pilots on how to attack; but we regretted not being able to keep our plane - however damaged - out of their hands. The Crew Chief wouldn't get his bottle of Johnny Walker for the aircraft completing its 75th mission.

"We stopped in the woods to plan what to do. We took off our outer flying clothes and searched each other for any papers that we thought the Germans could get information from, and buried them. We walked through the woods, crossed a road and railroad track and headed toward the hills that were wooded. A farmer stopped his plowing to watch us pass; nine strangers in various types of clothing plodding along must have been a peculiar sight to him. "After walking a mile or so through the woods we stopped to decide on how to proceed. A group of nine stragglers would be too easy to spot. We decided to split into three groups and go in different directions, hopefully meeting somewhere, some time in allied lands. Johnson, Ice and Huffman, the most athletically inclined who could move faster, were in the first group. Shearer, Currie and Trojanowski were next. Champagne and Mears who already had blisters from their flying boots, joined me to make up the third group. We all shook hands and said good-bye, trying hard not to let anyone notice the tear in our eyes or the tremor in our voices. We took off, not daring to look back.

"We all ended up POWs. The third group was caught at dusk that very day; the second group the following day; the first group hungry and thirsty lasted until the third day when they were fed by a farmer who then turned them in to the local police. All five officers and Trojanowski were sent to Stalag Luft One; the others were not so lucky, ending up in a work camp where they suffered many more deprivations than we did.

"The story of my life in Stalag Luft One is another chapter of my experience in World War II. I'll close the one on Merseburg by saying that I saw all the members of my crew safely returned to allied hands after VE Day. I thank God for looking out for us during all the close calls we had; I also thank all the crew members for their dedication to our country and for making ours the `Best damn crew in the ETO.'"[16]

Bud said that because of the headwind, and the drag, they came down somewhere near Kassel which was where they were taken after their apprehension. From there they were shipped to Oberursel, the Luftwaffe interrogation center near Frankfort, before being shipped to Stalag Luft One.[17] Bud was liberated by the Russians after VE Day and was flown back to France by the Eighth Air Force.[18]

The decision by Captain Chapman to bomb Merseburg from a level recognized as dangerously low may have saved many lives of those flying with the 401st. In the terrible weather conditions that day the 398th Bomb Group at Nuthampstead tried to get over the weather, and at 30,000 feet its 603rd Squadron got separated from the Group. After the 603rd Squadron bombed Merseburg they were at 29,000 feet when 10 FW-190s made a frontal attack shooting down seven of their Fortresses.[19]

When it comes down to the unvarnished truth it is always best to go to the original source of a story, not just to those who were eye witnesses but those who were the major players. In this case I was fortunate in that three of the lead team that day volunteered their recollections of that mission. Alvah Chapman said that the decision he faced that day was "one of the most difficult decisions in my career as an Air Commander." He said that Bud Rundell's observations were right on target and his own which follow are those which are appropriate remarks from the view of the Air Commander: "As Rundell stated, the weather worsened as we crossed into Germany and each 100 miles that we flew closer to the target required us to lower our altitude. Several Groups ahead of us opted not to bomb Merseburg, which was a very heavily defended target, but selected secondary targets. I felt, however, that Merseburg was the primary target and that we should continue even though the prospect of crossing that heavily defended target at 19,000 feet was chilling, to say the least. As most of the Groups ahead of us had diverted to secondary targets, the gunners at Merseburg were ready for us when we started on the bombing run for the oil refineries. The bomb run over Merseburg brought with it the heaviest flak that I have ever experienced in my 37 missions over enemy territory — which included targets such as Berlin, Hamburg, and Frankfurt. "But, to the credit of the 401st Bomb Group, our formation remained tight, and although we took severe losses crossing the target, our bombing accuracy was good as we moved away from the target to start the long flight back to Deenethorpe. What I remember from Merseburg was the support I received from the great pilots of the 401st when I told them that we were going to the primary target even though we were attacking it at 7,000 feet less than the assigned altitude. 19,000 feet over Merseburg in the face of searing flak provided a real test for the 401st. Our pilots and our crews were brave and professional. Many were aware that Groups ahead of us had diverted to the less defended secondary targets. Yet there was only support when I said that we were going in at 19,000 feet! I regret that my good friend, Bud Rundell, was shot down, but I am glad that he returned to write such an interesting story about the mission."[20]

Theodore F. Klefisch was the lead bombardier who said that of his thirty missions the one to Merseburg was special because, first, it was Merseburg, the toughest target in Germany. Second, because we bombed at the lowest altitude of any of his missions; and third, because two of the crew that day were wounded, the only casualties his crew experienced. Ted furnished his thoughts of that day:

"On our way to the target Chapman was informed that clouds over the target were as high as 30,000 feet but there was an opening at 20,000 feet and we might be able to bomb from that altitude. Chapman called me and asked if it was agreeable to me to do that and I said yes. When we went down the bomb run the cloud cover was just as reported, thick clouds above us but scattered clouds below us with some openings to see the ground. "As we approached the target I could see the flak was thicker and more accurate than any I had experienced on any other mission. I was trying to pick out the target and was depending on the radar operator to keep me informed on where the target was. Just before bombs away I heard a load noise and looked behind me.

Gaskins and Smith, the two navigators were lying on the floor. I didn't have time to help them right away because it was too close to bombs away. I then dropped the bombs and tried to see where they landed but could not do so because cloud cover was too thick below us. I then turned and saw that Gaskins and Smith were back on their feet and working at their jobs. "Since I still had control, as the bombardier always did on the bomb run, I told Mercer to start a turn to the right and wanted to give back control to him. Because of the cloud cover and the fact that I had the best seat in the house, Mercer asked me to keep control and help guide us out of there. I looked up and saw a squadron of B-17s on their way to the target about to go over us with their bomb bay doors open and full of bombs. I prayed they would not drop at that point and luckily they did not. Finally, we were in the clear and Mercer took over again. Then I looked back at the target area and saw a huge fireball. Some squadron must have hit the target on the head.

"I called for an oxygen and casualty check. Half our oxygen was shot out; that was the loud noise I heard just before bombs away. Gaskins said he was hit in back of the knee and that was what knocked him down and he took Smith with him. The waist gunner Grasela was hit in the upper leg and I told him that I would come back as soon as possible (bombardiers were the first aid officers on B-17 crews). When I got back there he was lying on the floor and I could see the wound. It was about the size of a silver dollar but not bleeding much. I cut open the pants and put sulpha powder on the wound and a bandage. I asked him if he wanted a morphine shot but he said no. We proceeded to home base but left the formation early because of the oxygen shortage and to get the wounded back as soon as possible. "While we were waiting in the briefing room prior to going to our plane that morning I looked at my first aid kit that was attached to my parachute harness. This was my 23rd mission and I never had to use it up to that time and noted that the cord that secured it was thick and tied very tight. I told someone that if we had to use it it might be difficult to untie it in a hurry. I then cut the cord...that was the only time I had to use it."[21]

Gaskins, now a retired Colonel living in Florida, said that he was the dead reckoning or D.R. navigator. The D.R. navigator used such elements as compass readings, speed and distance from a known point, allowing for drift from the wind, to establish a fixed position. Captain Charles Smith, the Squadron Navigator, was also in the nose as the lead navigator. Gaskins recalled: "We were dropping lower for the bomb run as I had to keep recomputing the wind and altitude data for the bomb run, which was a nuisance. As we dropped lower, I was also aware of the brighter flashes from the flak. They always said that when you could see the red center of the burst they were close! On the bomb run I always stood with my back to the crawl way so as to see the compass better and be able to look over Ted's head to see the target area. The radar operator was feeding a stream of bearings to the target, and for each bearing I would have to give the pilot a new heading to the target. At the same time Smith was working with Ted to confirm the aim-point which was difficult to pick out with the cloud cover.

"Things were going along in a routine way (the usual amount of sheer terror) when I heard a thunderous roar and found myself on my knees with a pain in my right knee. I reached down and felt my leg which was numb from shock and found that it was still there. Man - was I happy! I had a premonition that I was going to be wounded before my missions were over and now I had made it! I had my wound and it didn't seem all that bad...Smith and I got untangled, then heard the damage report about our wounded in the rear of the plane and also were hearing members of the formation calling out `bandits'. As we had two navigators on board, I went back to take over the waist guns for Grasela, the wounded gunner. On the way, I stopped to help dress his wound. As I recall he was a lucky fellow for a piece of flak had gone in low on the outside of his thigh headed for his groin, but was stopped by his parachute buckle. I could see the fighters as specks in the distance, but they never made an attack on our plane. "There was quite a reception party waiting for us on landing as red 'wounded' flares were popping out of the approaching bombers indicating large numbers of casualties. I think that was when I first saw my first General up close. I think it was General Turner standing at the nose of our plane. The medics pulled me out of the waist of the plane and stuck me in an ambulance...I wanted to see what was going on so I popped out the other side and headed back to see a real General...I didn't make it because they caught me again and jammed me back in the ambulance...We took off for the dispensary where they pulled the pieces of cloth out of my knee and applied a bandage before taking off for the main hospital at Molesworth. As soon as we arrived the medics accomplished their triage and that was when I realized the extent of the casualties...I was one of the lesser wounded and was about three quarters of the way down a line of men on stretchers which extended outside the hospital and around the building.

"As my wound was relatively minor, I really didn't appreciate the hospital routine. The first thing I did was limp to the latrine rather than use the blasted bed pan. I no sooner got in than a nurse was pounding on the door telling me I had to come out of there because I couldn't walk. After three or four days of that I went AWOL by grabbing an ambulance returning to Deenethorpe for a little peace and quiet. About a week later we went for our first briefing after Merseburg. I was feeling pretty tough and cocky. I was after all a wounded hero. Imagine how I felt when they pulled up the curtain to reveal the target - the same damned place... the Leuna refineries![22] A week later Colonel Bowman prepared a letter of commendation for the lead crew on the Merseburg mission of November 21 which included the following:

· Captain Alvah H. Chapman, Jr. - Air Commander
· 1st Lt. Elmer W. Mercer - Pilot
· 1st Lt. Leslie E. Gaskins - Navigator
· 1st Lt. Theodore J. Klefisch - Bombardier
· Captain Charles M. Smith - Navigator
· 1st Lt. John T. Dresbach - Mickey Operator
· T/Sgt. Joseph S. Zubrickas - Radio Operator
· T/Sgt. Cecil V. Fowler - Engineer/ Top Turret
· 1st Lt. Leland R. Hayes - Tail Gunner
· S/Sgt. Edward B. Grasela - Waist Gunner

The letter included a verbatim message from the Commanding General of the Eighth sent through the Commanding General of the 1st Bomb Division which read:

"ON 21 NOVEMBER THE 1ST BOMB DIVISION FORMATIONS DISPLAYED OUTSTANDING COURAGE, SKILL AND DETERMINATION IN CONTINUING ON UNDER EXTREMELY ADVERSE WEATHER CONDITIONS TO ATTACK THE VITAL LEUNA - MERSEBURG OIL REFINERY.

"I COMMEND YOU FOR THE DISCIPLINE AND TRAINING WHICH MADE IT POSSIBLE FOR THE 1ST BOMB DIVISION TO SUCCESSFULLY CARRY OUT

THIS   MISSION."...
DOOLITTLE

I consider these words to have been a commendation of all air crews in the 1st Bomb Division who followed Alvah Chapman to Merseburg that day. The message from Doolittle was followed by an addendum from the Commanding General of the 1st Bomb Division:

"WELL DONE...TURNER COMBOMDIV ONE..."

Colonel Bowman's letter to Chapman continued as follows:

"Under the circumstances, your decision to follow the main force into the target regardless of the difficulties, in order to retain the protection offered by the bombers and supporting

The Mercer Lead Crew. Left to right: Lt. Leslie E. Gaskins - navigator, Capt. C.D. Hibbert - copilot, Capt. Elmer W. Mercer - pilot, Lt. Theodore J. Klefisch - bombardier.

fighters was good. Your superior judgment and skill reflect highest credit on your organization and yourself, as well as the members of your crew."[23]

Captain Chapman, in writing, commended the 614th Squadron crews that followed him to Merseburg. During my search for materials for this project many former comrades sent items of memorabilia which were much appreciated. The largest number of one particular item was the poem "Lucky Devils of the 614th" found in Chapter 5. The second item was Chapman's letter written November 23. Included among those commended is the crew of Lt. Babcock, my crew. My copy of that letter, now yellow with age, remains one of my most prized possessions.(Appendix 2)

One of the most unusual stories of the events that day was the fate of a B-17 of the 91st Bomb Group at Bassingbourn. After being damaged by flak over the target the pilot, Lt. Debolt and his crew, bailed out over Belgium leaving their stricken aircraft on autopilot and their wheels down. When they left the B-17 two of its engines were lost and another was on the brink of failure. The valiant bomber continued without crew on a "stable descent and landed itself in a plowed field sustaining only damage to a wing tip and one bent propeller when one main wheel got bogged down and spun the aircraft around. A nearby British Army anti-aircraft crew left their gun to offer assistance and were understandably amazed to find no one aboard!"[24]

The proximate cause of injury and death to airmen and their loss of aircraft due to the enemy was generally two-fold: the relentless attacks of the German Luftwaffe and the concentrated flak from its anti-aircraft batteries. Although the former had shown signs of debilitation, the latter was the unyielding violence of a mortally-wounded nation. The bomber crews when faced with the attack of German fighters, even when they were crippled stragglers, still had the ability to fight back with their many guns. On the other hand, there was something insidiously impersonal and frightening about the explosion of shells fired from miles below with no way for those crews to fight back! Roger Freeman understood the airman's concern about flak when he wrote: "The whole nature of the war fought by the bomber men heightened the individual's concern with flak. Knowledge that the safety and comfort of an English base must be forsaken 30-odd times for the chilling fear of flying into flak was a strain on the most stable character. Those men who became `flak happy' were sent to a `flak home' to rest and recoup before completing their tour..."[25]

Today, almost 50 years since those missions over Germany exposed them to that flak I do not believe there are many still alive who are ashamed to admit the fear they endured.

How they reacted, or more importantly, how they functioned so well in performing their duties under that stress is to their everlasting credit, and without question the product of several factors. To me these factors, not in any order of importance were training, discipline and leadership. Roger Freeman wrote of another contributing aspect to these three factors with the following quotes from men of the Eighth: "The fear of loss of reputation and pride, letting someone down, was much greater than the fear of death. A bomber crew was a team and I think we all worried that we might be the man who let his pals down." Freeman thought these words of John Kirkpatrick would probably be endorsed by the vast majority of men who flew combat with the USAAF. Kirkpatrick said that many airmen found the hours before takeoff to be a difficult time, with apprehension and fear. Freeman also quoted the thoughts of John Greenwood, Group Navigator of the 351st Bomb Group at Polebrook: "For me the worst part of any mission was after being awakened by the CQ, the knock on the door and the light of his flashlight. It immediately hit me with a sinking feeling that stayed with me through breakfast and briefing. This apprehension was engendered by the unknown dangers that lay ahead. Once in the air, that passed, there was work to do and one became resigned to whatever fate had in store that day."[26]

I certainly agree that the pre-mission apprehension and stress had an important impact on most airmen; and I also agree that once airborne there were tasks which occupied the mind of all, some more than others. Although I flew more missions as a bombardier, my last 13 were as a navigator. In the latter position, I felt great pressure with tasks that were so constant from takeoff to landing that the concern for flak was lessened. No only was I busy, I also never had the confidence in my skills as a navigator, and I labored doubly hard as I feared getting my crew lost over Germany. The late Floyd Bilby, our radio operator on Fred Babcock's crew, seemed to manage the concern of flak better than anyone I can recall. He once admitted to me that because he kept so busy at his radio and other duties on our bomb runs, he didn't look out his little window to see the flak. I recall he also said the only time he saw flak was was when we bombed the forts at Metz on November 9, and he looked out to see what the red flak, fired by our troops to mark the bomb line, looked like; after that he never looked again!

I confess I was as frightened as the next guy on all of my missions, but much like Fred Koger I thought that I was going to die on that November 21; and I celebrate that date privately each year. The feeling of helplessness and like Koger, resignation, pervaded my consciousness as we went down that bomb run. The interphone silence after the call "bombs away" was always profound; I likened it to a gigantic gasp of relief by those eight other souls behind me as Fred Babcock wheeled our bird with the formation as we sought to be out of harm's way. I went to Merseburg three times, this one was the worst, not just of those three missions, but of all 35 I flew. After every mission the procedure was always the same and one necessary aspect was the post mission debriefing or interrogation of each crew by Major Wilfred B. "Pop" Fry, the 401st Group Intelligence Officer and his assistants. The pertinent information from these sessions as we downed hot G.I. coffee was incorporated in the written mission reports which still exist in the files of the National Archives. These reports, of course, include the results of the bombing, the enemy opposition, the sighting of German V-2 rocket launchings, information about the loss of aircraft and crews, and so forth. They apparently also wanted to know or accepted information on mission snafus and gripes of various kinds.

In the mission report for the November 21 mission there was a comment by Major Fry which to me was understated, though I am sure it was not intentional. He wrote: "Lt. Babcock who was flying IW-K, 43-38677, reported that the ball turret gunner on the Coleman crew flying IN-H 'Lady Jane II' had handcharged rounds from his guns on the way home without looking behind or below his aircraft. One of the rounds struck Babcock's aircraft." It did a bit more than strike the aircraft; it blew out the Plexiglas nose, penetrating the aircraft tearing a map out of the bombardier's hands as it passed between his knees. The live round was found under the bombardier's seat bent to a 40 degree angle. I know because I was that bombardier! At the moment that projectile came crashing into my space I was still traumatized by the flak at Merseburg. Since we had just passed Ostend, Belgium and were over the North Sea headed home I was beginning to think I had survived Merseburg one more time. The nose of that B-17 was instantly turned into a mess with the unwanted ventilation converting the nose into a wind tunnel with cold rainwater making the compartment uninhabitable.[27] We were all glad that day was over!

Notes to Chapter 10

1. Photocopy of letter captioned "Commendation" dated 23 November 1944 from "Alvah H Chapman, Jr., Captain, Air Corps, Actg. Sq. Commander" to "All Concerned"
2. Maslen, Selwyn V. 614th Bombardment Squadron (H): Squadron History p. 105
3. Letter, Norman L. Sisson to author February, 1992
4. Photocopies of personal log and bomb fuse tag collection of Norman L. Sisson furnished author as enclosure to letter from Sisson February 13, 1991
5. Photocopy of personal log of Nathan Picker furnished author as enclosure to letter from Norman L. Sisson February 13, 1991
6. Maslen, Selwyn V. 614th Squadron: Crews - Missions - Aircraft p. 66,93
7. National Archives, Suitland, Md. Reference Branch, Record Group 18, Mission Reports, 401st Bombardment Group (H)
8. Bowman, Harold W. & Selwyn V. Maslen Bowman's Bombers p. 53
9. Closway, Gordon R. 614th Squadron History Air Operations, November, 1944
10. USAF Historical Research Center, Maxwell AFB, AL, miscellaneous records of 401st Bombardment Group (H) by Squadron on microfilm
11. Bowman, Harold W. & Selwyn V. Maslen 401st B.G.: Casualties in W.W. II p. 59
12. Bowman & Maslen, see 8 above
13. Bowman & Maslen, see 8 above p.54
14. Freeman, Roger A. The Mighty Eighth War Diary p. 384
15. Letter, Col. Francis E. Rundell to author November 4, 1991
16. Enclosure to letter, Col. Francis E. Rundell to author November 12, 1991
17. Telephone conversation Col. Francis E. Rundell and author April 4, 1992
18. See 15 above
19. Bowman, Martin W. Castles in the Air p. 172-173 (Freeman, see 14 above p. 384 reported a loss of five aircraft)
20. Letter, Alvah H. Chapman, Jr. to author June 3, 1992
21. Letter, Theodore J. Klefisch to author May 4, 1992
22. Letter, Col. Leslie E. Gaskins to author May 10, 1992
23. See 7 above
24. Freeman, see 14 above
25. Freeman, Roger A. The Mighty Eighth p. 177
26. Freeman, Roger A. Experiences of War: The American Airman in Europe p. 102
27. See 7 above

CHAPTER 11 — THE WEATHER AND THE ARDENNES

On November 25 another mission was flown to Merseburg by 356 B-17s of the 1st Bomb Division and 388 of the 3rd Division. Meanwhile, the 2nd Bomb Division sent 271 of its B-24s to bomb the marshalling yards at Bingen.[1] Thirty-nine aircraft of the 401st made up the 94th CBW "B" Group with Major D.E. Silver leading. The 614th Squadron flew as the low squadron led by its Operations Officer, Capt. Donald Kirkhuff.[2] The Leuna Plant of I. G. Farben at Merseburg then produced synthetic oil, ammonia and nitrogen, second only in size to the plant at Politz; it was then producing about one-third of the total oil in Germany.[3] The Sisson crew was taking a few days off giving the privilege of flying the "Maiden" to the crew of Captain Arthur R. Seder, Jr.[4] In his own diary Art recorded: "Back to the oil targets after a long layoff - on account of having no navigator. The flak wasn't very bad this time, and we didn't get any battle damage. The P-51s took good care of us, so there was no trouble from enemy fighters although my crew saw a couple of them make a pass at a straggler before they were chased by some of our boys; 10/10 clouds again."[5] His comment about the lack of a navigator was caused by the assignment of his navigator to "mickey" school. On that day his bombardier, Allen H. Crawford, having been certified as a D.R. navigator flew his first mission in that capacity. Because the Seder crew had been designated a lead crew, our rated navigator on the Babcock crew, Lt. Leon F. Stewart, in December joined Art's team. Al continued as the navigator on the Babcock crew.

The mission, the fourth to Merseburg that month, was like others, a PFF bomb drop, but with little opposition from fighters or flak.[6] The 3rd Bomb Division was not as fortunate; they got an intense dose of flak and it was initially thought that they had lost 57 aircraft. They actually had a net loss of eight B-17s with an unheard of number, 30, being forced to land on the continent.[7]

Before he went to Merseburg the first time on November 8, Al Crawford said he was scared and attributed at least some of this to the "war stories" he heard in the barracks and elsewhere. He confessed that on November 25 he was "really scared." He recorded the flak that day as mild, but now almost 50 years later says he can't imagine flak at Merseburg as anything but intense. He noted they dropped five 500 pound GPs and five 500 pound IBs from 26,000 feet that day.[8] As reported, the flak was unusually mild as only four 401st aircraft received minor damage.[9] There was one casualty; sadly, Sgt. J. F. Irvin, the tail gunner on the crew of Lt. F.R. Boddin of the 612th Squadron died of anoxia resulting from an oxygen failure at his position.[10] After all the stress and hard work on that long mission it was particularly frustrating for them to learn that the "bombing was so poor that on November 30 the heavies were once again dispatched to the oil plants." The bombing on November 25 was described as: "one of the poorest displays of 8th Air Force 'precision bombing' resulting in such minor damage that Germany's hottest target – the synthetic oil refinery at Merseburg – was in full production again only 12 hours later."[11] Maybe so but a photograph established they hit something which must have caused a major conflagration from the oily black smoke which billowed through the clouds.

On the next 401st mission on November 30 the Group had a different target but in the very same flak area. The 1st Bomb Division had 301 aircraft, divided between primary oil targets at Bohlen and Zeitz with 116 hitting Merseburg as a secondary target. The 3rd Division had two primaries, the oil targets at Merseburg and Lutzkendorf. Bombing for a welcome change was done visually.[12] Major D.E. Silver led as the 94th CBW "C" Group to Bohlen and reported that although they did bomb visually, a very effective smoke screen obscured the target area. He judged their results as only fair. The lead bombardier said the smoke screen was initiated over Zeitz about ten miles to the south of his target at Bohlen. He was able to use a quarry and a wooded forest north of the target to set up course on the vertical cross hair of his bombsight as well as rate by having those reference points steady on the horizontal crosshair until he found something more definite as he approached the target. He finally saw

Smoke from bomb strikes billow through the clouds on the 401st mission to Merseburg on November 25, 1944. Photograph from the USAF Collection courtesy of the NASM of the Smithsonian.

oil tanks and using them as a reference, he was able to observe the bomb strike on the right edge of the MPI area.[13] The flak was intense and accurate with all but one of the 401st 39 B-17s getting damage from the shrapnel; seven of them major damage. Before getting back to allied lines the Group had 18 stragglers due to flak damage or engine problems. Fortunately, our "little friends" kept the Luftwaffe engaged elsewhere. Five 401st crew members were wounded and one was KIA. The latter was T/Sgt. Dorsey W. Tyree the radio operator on the 614th crew of Lt. Harry W. Thompson; he died from a flak fragment that struck him in the neck.[14] Among those wounded was Lt. Carl L. Hoag, the navigator for Lt. George Cracraft of the 615th Squadron. They were aboard the "Mary Alice" when flak smashed the wooden navigators table sending splinters of wood into Lt. Hoag's face and both eyes. Despite considerable pain and with only one eye usable by propping the lid back with one of his fingers, Lt. Hoag remained at his post. He provided the pilot with the course corrections needed to get them safely back to England. Remarkably, he recovered his sight and continued his combat tour. He was awarded the Distinguished Service Cross (DSC), the second highest decoration for valor given by the United States.[15] It was the highest decoration received by any 401st Bombardment Group crewman.

The Sisson crew was still off that day but the "Maiden" took the crew of Lt. Glenn R. St. Aubyn to Bohlen.[16] A newspaper account described that mission and the days preceding it: "Their blows topped a 36 hour aerial offensive that left the Reich erupting from an average of 10 tons of bombs a minute...The windup blows made November the GREATEST OPERATIONAL WINTER MONTH OF THE WAR...almost 1,300 Fortresses and Liberators of the U.S. 8th Air Force, herded by 1,000 fighters, hurled 4,000 tons of bombs at the oil plants of Bohlen, Zeitz, Merseburg and Lutzkendorf in the Leipzig area 100 miles southwest of Berlin...The targets are in a 40 mile square area defended by a concentration of heavy antiaircraft guns twice the density of that guarding Berlin. It is perhaps the most heavily defended area of its size in the world. In one five mile radius American airmen touched a corner of hell as an estimated 225 ack-ack guns pumped up what veterans described as a solid wall of flak. Weather permitted a good view of the oil plants, and the bombing results were described as very favorable. Crewmen saw large explosions and fire in the refinery areas."[17]

Flying their first mission that day was the crew of Lt. Myron L. King of the 614th Squadron. His toggelier, S/Sgt. R.E. Pyne was among three crewmen reported wounded. The King crew was destined to become more prominent in the story of the "Maiden."[18] King himself recently said: "We never saw anything like what we saw at Bohlen." He said there was no wind that day and you could see the black smoke from flak hanging over Bohlen from 100 miles away. He said that as each Group ahead of them went through that smoke another black line appeared which never fully dissipated, it only turned the skies darker gray.[19]

The events in the life of the "Maiden," and for that matter in the history of the 401st for December 1944, would not be complete without mention of an event described by Capt. Gordon R. Closway, Group Public Relations Officer, "This month brought one of our most severe losses – it does not appear in the Stat records - it was not a casualty - but the loss is keenly felt by the whole Group. We lost Colonel Harold W. Bowman to USSTAF Headquarters. Even a better 'Old Man' could never replace the one we have trained and fought with for more than two years."[20] We were indeed fortunate that Lt. Col. William T. Seawell, one of our own, was chosen to replace him.

Thus, with a new C.O. the 401st was again ready to fly combat on December 4th. By then the Sisson crew was back on board to fly the "Maiden" to Kassel with their target the very important marshalling yards in that city. Capt. Clyde Lewis was the 401st Air Commander leading 39 aircraft to make up the 94th CBW "A" Group; which included ten 614th crews in the low squadron led by Lt. Charles W. Utter.[21] Nathan Picker, Sisson's bombardier recorded that they were listed as a spare that day but filled in for an aircraft that had to abort. He said they carried ten 500 pound GPs and two 500 pound M17 IBs to a bombing altitude of 25,000 feet.[22] The 500 pound M17 IB was described as an "amiable cluster with better ballistics than earlier M11 incendiary cluster bombs. It had a primecord release that could be set to give the desired scatter and became the favored IB during 1944."[23]

On December 4 the 1st Bomb Division dispatched 419 aircraft, with more than 200 going to Kassel and the rest to the marshalling yards at Soest.[24] The usual 10/10ths cloud blotted out the target requiring a PFF bomb run. The flak was described as meager and inaccurate with only seven aircraft in the entire 1st Division force reporting any battle damage. The 401st aircraft suffered no damage.

The next day, December 5, the Sisson crew was again idle but not so their "Maiden." She took the crew of Lt. R.B. Richardson to Berlin. The target was a munitions and tank works of Rhein-Metal Bersig A. C. located at Berlin/Tegal, north-northwest of the center of the city. The 401st put up 39 B-17s as the 94th CBW "B" Group led by Capt. D.A. Currie. The ten aircraft of the 614th Squadron, including the "Maiden" were led by Lt. Charles

Lt. Carl Hoag awarded the Distinguished Service Cross.

W. Utter, as Deputy Air Commander.[25] Takeoff that morning was in darkness as was assembly. The latter was accomplished quickly and despite bad weather the Group departed the Cottesmore Buncher, a radio beacon used for assembly, on time.[26] The 1st Division force of 222 aircraft and the 229 of the 3rd Division had the Berlin target while the 2nd Division sent its B-24s to hit the rail yards at Munster.[27] At Berlin the heavies encountered 9/10s clouds and bombed by PFF. The results were nothing to write home about since later it was determined that the bomb strike was about four and a half miles east of the MPI. With an apparent touch of British humor Vic Maslen wrote "but within the city limits of Berlin."[28] The poor results may have been triggered by malfunctions which left the low squadron lead the only operating "mickey" aircraft; they had to take over as Group lead just before reaching the IP.[29] The 401st did see moderate-to-intense flak, but it was apparently not too accurate since no damage was reported and thankfully there were no casualties.[30] Although the 401st was unscathed the 1st Division lost three and the 3rd lost nine B-17s. It sure wasn't a "milk run".[31]

For the third consecutive day the 401st was briefed for a major target. On December 6 the 1st and 3rd Divisions again teamed up for another assault on the Leuna oil refinery of I.B. Farbenindustrie at Merseburg.[32] The 401st, as the 94th CBW "A" Group, was leading the 1st Division force with Lt. Col. Burton K. Vorhees as the Air Commander with Lt. Charles W. Utter as his deputy. For the second time in its combat history the 401st was able to put up 51 aircraft. The feat was without question a magnificent accomplishment by our ground crews. All of the many facets of preparing each B-17 for a mission have to be considered in light of the fact that they had put up 39 aircraft on each of the two previous days. The 614th had 12

Left — Lt. Col. William T. Seawell, right — Col. Harold W. Bowman. USAF Photo Collection neg. #65599AC courtesy of NASM, Smithsonian Institution.

aircraft flying as a screening force which included the "Maiden" with the Sisson crew on board. The purpose of the screening force was to fly ahead of the main Group formation and drop "chaff" which consisted of packets of fine strips of metallic foil that were dropped in the target area to disrupt radar used in computations by enemy flak gunners. The screening force flew to the windward side of the target area and dropped its chaff which may have had some impact on the accuracy of the flak guns. However, eighty-one aircraft in the 1st Division were damaged by flak[33] and though none were lost, the 3rd Division lost four of its aircraft.[34] Nathan Picker, on the "Maiden," called the flak meager to intense over the target at 27,000 feet.[35] Sisson gave the mission his one star for the intensity of the opposition.[36]

Although neither the Sisson crew or their "Maiden" were on the mission to Merseburg on December 12, it was an historic one and worthy of mention in this story. The plant was the largest hydrogenation plant remaining in Germany producing synthetic fuels, lubricants, fixed nitrogen products and various organic

Collage demonstrating the work of highest quality, performed under the most adverse conditions, by 401st ground personnel who kept the B-17s ready for combat. Photograph from the USAF Collection courtesy of the NASM of the Smithsonian.

chemicals. The mission on December 12 was the eighteenth to Merseburg in 1944, and the last by the Eighth, although other such refineries in the immediate area such as Zeitz and Lutzkendorf were bombed in 1945. All of the previous attacks had delayed and reduced its capacity to produce, but the eighteenth mission left it with only ten percent of it normal production.[37]

The RAF conducted "crippling" night attacks on the facility in December, January and April, 1945. But on February 14 Lt. Robert Dixon of the Eighth's 25th Bombardment Group (R) flew a photo reconnaissance mission to Merseburg in an RAF Spitfire with an interesting report. Making his fourth run over the Merseburg plant at 12,000 feet he was hit by flak. Preparing to bailout he told the three P-51s flying as his escort: "Listen to this carefully. There are ten chimneys down there. Only one is smoking. This plant is inoperative..." Those words, even today, warm the heart of this old bombardier. The campaign to cripple the German oil industry was almost over.[38] It has been said that the oil campaign was one of the Eighth's greatest accomplishments; one which was waged concurrently with many other strategic and tactical operations. The effort by the Eighth

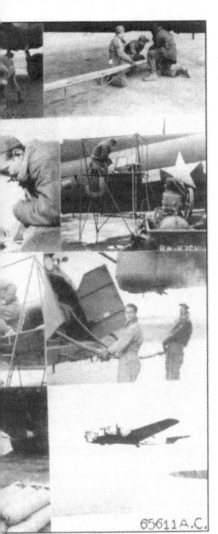

65611 A.C.

forced the Germans to use every possible means to try to halt it.[39]

The "Maiden's" next mission was to Kassel on December 15 with the crew of Lt. Paul F. Wittman. For three days the Eighth had been shut down because of bad weather; and this was only the beginning! It was still bad when the 401st took off for Kassel.[40] The 401st was part of a force of 318 aircraft with their targets being rail facilities and an armored vehicle factory.[41] The Group was the 94th CBW "C" Group led by Maj. D.G. McCree as Air Commander and Lt. Charles W. Utter, as deputy leading the high squadron. They had been given a rail target as their assignment. Only 11 aircraft of the entire 1st Division claimed flak damage.[42] The 3rd Division lost one B-17 on its mission. Several other Eighth aircraft were forced to land in Europe and one had to ditch in the North Sea. In poor visibility returning to England three more aircraft and their crews were lost.[43] In fact the weather was so bad that the 401st could not get into Deenethorpe and was diverted east to land at Old Buckenham, home of the B-24 453rd Bombardment Group, near Norwich.[44]

December had brought the worst winter to England in 50 years, snow and ice along with frigid temperatures as low as five degrees Fahrenheit, not to mention fog. It was the latter above all the rest that concerned the Eighth.

By December the Germans had their collective backs up against two walls. From the fall of Stalingrad the Russian offensive had moved relentlessly westward, and the Normandy invasion in June by the allies had created a second front. The Nazi war machine could not contain the renewed Soviet vigor enhanced by American lend-lease equipment and supplies. From October 1944 the Axis satellites: Romania, Bulgaria, Finland and Hungary had capitulated and Germany itself was in peril on that front. The invasion of France, followed by the breakout of allied troops, found those powerful forces well-entrenched; and invasion of the Fatherland threatened from the western front too. Before the allies could cross the Rhine River they were destined to fight one last major battle, a last stand German offensive. It has been said the objectives were to cut the allied front in two and move west to the North Sea blitzkrieg style, to capture badly needed fuel reserves of the allies. In retrospect, this battle orchestrated by Adolf Hitler himself was an act of futile desperation. Even if the Germans won the battle, they could not have turned final defeat into victory; and sadly, it inevitably cost so many lives on both sides.

On December 16 Field Marshal Karl von Rundstedt's Panzer Divisions attacked, breaking through the allied front in the Ardennes forests of Belgium creating a "bulge" in the lines from which the fight became known as the "Battle of the Bulge."[45] The horrendously bad weather on the continent was shared in England and air operations slowed, then stopped, then were limited, then stopped again for that week when the bombers of the Eighth were so badly needed. Von Rundstedt's ground commander, Field Marshal Walter Model, capitalized on the heavy fog and his blitz drove the allies back, almost to the Meuse River. In the process they cut off the Belgian town of Bastogne and encircled the U.S. 101st Airborne Division. In time General Patton's 3rd Army fought its way through and relieved the

The damage to the I.G. Farben Leuna refinery at Merseburg by Eighth Air Force mission during 1944 and 1945 is surveyed by American military in May 1945. Photograph from the USAF Collection courtesy of the NASM of the Smithsonian.

Americans who were under siege. For some days there were grave concerns; the weather was on the side of the Germans.

On December 16 only the 3rd Bomb Division could get airborne. They were able to put only 115 aircraft over Europe to bomb the railroad yard at Stuttgart and a target of opportunity at Beitingheim. The weather and related mishaps, with the loss of aircraft and lives characterized the mission.[46] The next day was worse. The only aircraft of the Eighth in the air that day were from the very specialized 25th Bombardment Group (R). It dispatched four Mosquitos over the continent and four of their B-17s to the Atlantic and the Azores on weather reconnaissance missions. The Eighth was determined to find suitable weather which would permit the heavies to pound the German communications and supply network to the front.[47] The hope was that their presence overhead would encourage those allies on the ground, in the snow, to resist until help arrived. The 2nd and 3rd Bomb Divisions were located east of the bases of the 1st in the Midlands. The weather in East Anglia was generally an improvement over that "enjoyed" by the Triangle First. Even so on December 18 the bombers of the 2nd Division had to be recalled because of extensive clouds, presumably over the continent. The same was true for some units of the other two Divisions. Somehow the 1st Division got a respectable 385 aircraft up to bomb the Kalk marshalling yard at Cologne and secondary communications as well as other tactical targets at Coblenz, Kaiserslautern, and Bonn. The 3rd Division had 220 aircraft up to bomb the marshalling yards at Mainz. The 94th CBW, including the 401st, and two Groups of the 40th CBW were all grounded.[48]

On December 19 the weather remained bad. Nevertheless, the Eighth managed to make a fair showing in view of the crisis. The 1st Bomb Division sent a small force of 144 B-17s to bomb six different tactical targets; in addition 24 other aircraft bombed the marshalling yards at Coblenz. The 2nd Bomb Division had a more credible showing sending 312 B-24s to bomb two tactical targets and the marshalling yards at Ehrang. Gee-H was the bombing method

Maintenance work by ground crews continued at Deenethorpe day and night during December 1944 with snow and ice along with extreme cold which was described as the most bitter winter in England in 50 years. The aircraft shown with the IY call letters are 615th Squadron aircraft. Photograph from the USAF Collection courtesy of the NASM of the Smithsonian.

used at the tactical targets and H2X elsewhere.[49] The 401st made up the 94th CBW "A" Group led by Lt. Col. Edwin W. Brown with forty aircraft. The Sisson crew and the "Maiden" remained at Deenethorpe. The weather was so bad that the three squadrons became separated and bombed independently.[50] The lead squadron bombed the target at Coblenz, the high squadron a target at Schleiden and the low squadron a target of opportunity at Stadtkyll. The latter two targets were west of Coblenz near the Belgian border of Germany.[51] The only losses that day were B-24s of the 2nd Bomb Division; one crashed during assembly and another was abandoned near Brussels.[52]

Allen Crawford remembers that mission well. It was the first he flew as the navigator with my crew. I continued to share the nose of our B-17 with him until after February 3, 1945 when I was drafted to fly as a navigator on another crew for the rest of my tour. On that day we flew in the high squadron which bombed Schleiden in support of our ground forces.[53] Another reason our crew remembers that mission was because it culminated in the "mother of all diversions." The Group was diverted that afternoon to several bases. Twelve of ours put in at an RAF base at Tangmere, near London. Another 20, including our bird, landed at Predannack, an RAF Coastal Command base on Lizard Point, in Cornwall. To give a better understanding as to how desperate we were for a place to land, it was as far west and south as one can go and still be in England. I remember it as being as close as I could get to the good old U.S.A., not far from Lands End.[54]

The base was right on the ocean. I was very impressed with the rugged beauty of the sheer cliffs and the surf crashing on the rocks below. It is wild country with quaint villages. The area is noted for the green serpentine like marble, much like the material used to make the soda fountain counter tops of my youth. I always wanted to revisit the area on my peacetime trips but other commitments and the remoteness of the area prohibited doing so. The visit was not an educational tour however. This diversion was not like others, not for just a few hours or even an overnight stay. We were stuck there for four days until the afternoon of December 23. The 25th Bombardment Group (R) continued to fly its weather reconnaissance missions over the North Sea, out into the Atlantic and to the Azores from December 20 through December 22. At Predannack accommodations were less than spartan and the food far below G.I. standards, although it was the best our hosts could offer 180 uninvited guests. We arrived there on the afternoon of December 19; we were tired and dirty. We had no toilet articles and no change of clothing, and the clothes we arrived in were soiled to say the least. On the last day, Leon F. Stewart, our former navigator, who was then flying with Art Seder, made me an offer I couldn't refuse. He had with him some British pounds and had rented a fantastic bedroom at a lovely inn in the village close by the base and offered to share it with me. When we arrived I thought I had never seen a more beautiful bed in my life. We were deciding who was going to use the bath across the hall when we were alerted to return to the base immediately. Alas! we never even got on that bed and had to forfeit our investment. We learned that Deenethorpe was again open to traffic so all aircraft independently raced north across England toward home. It was late afternoon and I should add that our B-17, "Miss Gee Eye Wanta, (Go Home)" had lost all of its exterior lights and those in the interior of the nose compartment to flak damage on December 19.

Just before we arrived in the area of Deenethorpe, Flying Control advised that the base was again closed to traffic and diverted us toward East Anglia. By this time it was getting dark. We had been given the name of a base, possibly Ordeneck, and a temporary compass heading east. Al loves to tell the rest of the story of that three hour flight. He gave me the map and asked me to locate the coordinates of the base to which we were diverted; we were both working with flashlights by this time. According to Al I incorrectly gave him coordinates east of the Greenwich line instead of to its west. When he finally got a navigational fix using the Gee box he found we were over the Wash, a large body of water off the North Sea. He gave Fred a 180 degree compass heading south to bring us back over land and East Anglia. By this time we were a hazard flying around in the dark without exterior lights. Through a hole in the clouds Fred spotted the unique funnel shaped lights typical of British built air bases. These systems provided two lanes of lights on the ground which curved and converged leading to the end of the runway, providing a final approach for the aircraft.[55] We landed, learning we were at Great Massingham, an RAF Mosquito base, located a few miles east of Kings Lynn. I was always fascinated by the Mosquito. It was a sleek and very versatile aircraft with a very unconventional plywood fuselage. It was effectively used as a night fighter and as a reconnaissance aircraft.

Al recalls many of the pilots there were trained to fly in the United States and couldn't have been more hospitable to nine dirty and hungry Yanks. They saw to it that we were able to get a shower even though we had to don our dirty clothing. Still without shaves we were treated to drinks at their Officer's Club and dinner followed. Our enlisted men were also given the royal treatment at the Non Commissioned Officer's (NCO) Club. Al recalls that they were guests at a party there given by the WAAFs, the British female auxiliary to the RAF. We really had a fine evening and I think it was all due to my bonehead blunder that got us there. On our way to the billet provided for the night we stopped off at the NCO Club to be sure that our guys were taken care of. The base was stood down for Christmas and the party there was in high gear; I am sure we were the last persons our Sergeants wanted to see. As we were leaving I heard a commotion accompanied by cheers and a fanfare by the dance band. Out on the dance floor came a tall flying Sergeant of the RAF; he was there to dance and was encouraged by cheers from the crowd. His partner for the dance was the biggest defeathered goose I had ever seen, quite dead of course, which he swung around by its very long neck. I have often wondered if that poor fowl made it to the table for Christmas dinner.

We retired for the night confident that we would never have to fly the next day. Wrong! They found us; I believe the call came from Capt. Don Kirkhuff, the Operations Officer of the 614th Squadron. It was to be a maximum effort because the weather was finally going to clear for us to hit the Jerry where it hurt. We were given the altitude, the exit point on the English coast and the time we had to be there to rendezvous with the 401st Bomb Group as it headed out over the North Sea toward Germany. The mission that day has been described as follows: "On Christmas Eve 1944 the Field Order at all bases called for a maximum effort, to meet which most groups put up all available aircraft, including war wearies and even assembly ships. Doolittle wanted to throw as much weight as he could against the German airfields to prevent any missions being flown by the Luftwaffe in support of the German land forces in the Ardennes. However, controllers had to work overtime at some 3rd Bomb Division bases that were still congested with 1st Division Fortresses. Many had landed there after the mission on December 23 when their own bases were 'socked in.' Visibility was still poor and it led to many accidents on takeoff ... despite these setbacks, the 8th was able to mount its largest single attack in history with 2,034 heavies participating...Crews were told that their route was planned on purpose to go over the ground troops positions for morale purposes."[56] Our crew was uniquely different; we were not on an Eighth Air Force base. We had no gas and found that the equipment for servicing the Mosquito would not be able to fuel our B-17. We also didn't have bombs; I couldn't see making that trip to Germany unless I was going to drop explosives on the enemy. Al said we were a sorry sight that morning in the RAF briefing room. I am sure we were and speaking for myself, I didn't feel very well after partying late. We looked at the map and found that there was a B-24 base less than ten miles south of us. It turned out to be Wendling, home of the 392nd Bomb Group. We popped in unannounced as they were preparing to takeoff; I believe they had already started their engines. We parked our bird, and as Al and I dropped to the ground from the nose hatch, a jeep pulled up and a very irate and red-faced Major demanded: "What the hell do you think you are doing?" He was naturally very upset that we had landed at that most unfortunate time.[57] By that time our engineer, T/Sgt. Carroll "Bud" Caldwell, had joined us and suddenly he and the Major grabbed each other like long lost brothers. It turned out that they had been Noncoms together in the prewar Air Corps. The Major was the Group Engineering Officer at Wendling and when he heard our story he couldn't do enough for us. While they serviced our aircraft he transported us to the Mess Hall where we consumed one of the best breakfasts I can ever recall woofing down; fresh eggs and all the trimmings, even the G.I. coffee tasted delicious. As Al and I both recall they provided each one of us with a pack of Lucky Strike cigarettes. After a week of our existing on the very stale British Players, that Major had made nine friends for life. By then it was time to leave our new-found friends. We were gassed up; the best they could do with the hoist for B-24s was to load eight 500 pound GPs in my bomb bay. I felt it was better than going to combat empty, which were our instructions![58] Finally, the Eighth was able to play a significant tactical role in the Battle of the Bulge.

The force was led that day by the 3rd Bomb Division followed by the Triangle 1st with their targets eleven airfields east of the Rhine River. The 2nd Bomb Division followed to bomb 14 communications centers west of the Rhine.[59] Fred Babcock got us to altitude and to the position at the English coast about ten minutes before our rendezvous time, and we circled and watched the bomber stream for the 401st Triangle S to no avail. We finally opted to join the 379th Bomb Group from Kimbolton flying with them as "tail end Charlie" in "Purple Heart Corner" to bomb Friedberg.[60] This town should not be confused with Freiburg, a larger city in southern Germany. Friedberg is located about 50 miles east of Coblenz. The mission was uneventful, but after we bombed and turned back to the west, I was in awe of the number of bomb strikes identified by their smoke markers. In whatever direction I looked, there were bomb strikes everywhere from that vast armada of four engine bombers. The Christmas Eve mission was the only one for which I had no briefing. It was only some days later that I learned the 401st effort was divided between two different targets, both rail objectives with main force going to Coblenz and another squadron going to Darmstadt. The Coblenz portion included those like ourselves who were scattered around England, that bombed visually with bomb strikes observed in the MPI area. The other squadron, led by Capt. D.A. Currie went to Darmstadt. They also bombed visually but their results were mostly unobserved.[61] The Coblenz leader had to abort and the deputy, leading the high squadron, took over for the bomb run. They ran into meager but accurate flak for a 27 minute period before reaching the IP and found it continuing on the bomb run and thereafter. The experience left them with 24 damaged aircraft and two wounded crewmen. The "Maiden" which had been idle since December 15 was a part of the mission to Coblenz with the crew of Lt. J.E. Fondren on board. The really sad note that day, which spread quickly throughout the bases of the Eighth Air Force, was the death of Brigadier General Fred Castle, C.O. of the 3rd Bomb Division's 4th CBW. Gen. Castle was flying that day with the 487th Bomb Group at Lavenham when the aircraft he was flying was fatally hit by flak. He took over the controls from the pilot to give the uninjured members of the crew the chance to bailout. Most of the crew escaped before a wing tank exploded putting him in a spin, the B-17 crashing near Hods, Belgium.[62] Gen. Castle was the highest ranking officer in the Eighth to be awarded the Medal of Honor.[63] Roger Freeman said of Gen. Castle: "As a man to whom duty was paramount he would have wanted nothing better than to be remembered as the only General in his country's history to die in a direct act to try and save the lives of his subordinates."[64]

We had flown our mission with the host Group, and before we even saw the coast of

England Fred peeled off and we barreled across England like the proverbial horse headed for the barn. The weather was still foul and Al remembers our approach to Deenethorpe with considerable detail. He said we were over very heavy clouds, and with the help of the Gee box he got a good fix for a heading to the base. Fred called Flying Control which authorized one landing attempt down through the soup.[65] He brought her down with Al's assistance while I kept staring down from the nose straining to see some sign of mother earth. I know we were less than 50 feet off the ground when swirling fog separated and the first thing I saw was a neighbor's cow looking up at me. I stared back, then looked up and saw the end of the runway; Fred had only to make a fraction of a correction to line her up. We were on the runway with one of the smoothest landings ever. We had no more than left the runway when the tower advised the whole Group that the base was closed again and diverted them to some other base. We were the only crew that got into Deenethorpe that Christmas Eve. I do not believe we were debriefed, at least I do not recall anything except arriving back at my barracks. I remember Jack Bousfield, our co-pilot, and myself entering our cold and empty barracks. My bunk was covered with mail and Christmas packages. It was heartwarming to see what had accumulated during that absence of a week, but I left it all there. I got out of the clothes I had worn for six days, bathed, shaved and donned my best uniform. I quickly packed some necessaries in a musette bag and rushed to the 614th Orderly Room. I got a pass, and without dinner left on the bus to Kettering. There I caught the next train to London. London was my haven; I knew that I had to get away for a day or so. I spent a very pleasant Christmas Day, but that week before December 25, 1944 was the most unusual of my life. The mission folder for December 25 contains an unusual sheet on which there were handwritten notations that bore no signature. The notations brought to mind the atrocities committed on allied troops in the Ardennes which were published in the newspapers at the time; they were obviously words of caution given the 401st crews that were briefed at Deenethorpe before that mission. They said: "P.W. keep in the woods, travel by **night** toward allied lines. If near front lines beware of Germans in American uniforms and equipment. Stay away from children, approach older people and foreign workers."[66] Major Alvah Chapman, Jr. as Acting Squadron Commander of the 614th Squadron directed a letter which commended those on the crews of that Squadron for their particiaption in operations between December 19-26, 1944 (Appendix 3).

Even more unusual is the account of the bombing of Coblenz in December, including Christmas, from the German point of view. Charles W. Utter had correspondence with a Dr. Helmut Schnatz of Coblenz about these attacks and visited Dr. Schnatz in 1983. Thereafter Dr. Schnatz wrote a book on the bombings of Coblenz which occurred in 1944 and 1945. A translation of pertinent pages from the book provide an insight only to some of the problems which resulted from the bombings. After describing some of the damage done to the rail facilities by raids on September 19, 21 and 25 Dr. Schnatz summarizes, "It can be assumed that the entire railroad transit traffic in the region of Koblenz was heavily disturbed in the week following 19 of September, if not at times completely stopped. For instance the line on the left side of the river Rhine south of Koblenz was newly repaired on the eve of September 22 but on September 25 it was again disrupted. The undertaking, which due to the large number of airplanes in action had a depressing effect on the population, achieved its purpose..." The text of an allied warning to the German population attributed to the "Superior Allied Command" (probably a leaflet from the Supreme Allied Command) warned them to stay away from street crossings, rail sidings, railroad switchyards, power stations, manufacturing plants and military installations. Such leaflets from Eisenhower's Headquarters were dropped with regularity in Germany during late 1944 by B-17s and B-24s of the Night Leaflet Squadron (406th Bomb Squadron) of the Eighth Air Force. Dr. Schnatz said these warnings were "to create a panic" and that "these intentions were not without success." My response to this is not intended to be a disclaimer since our top leadership may have had some secondary psychological warfare purpose in mind when they ordered these raids, particularly the one on Christmas Eve. However, I doubt this was ever the actual motive. The primary objective in late 1944, and paramount after the German counter-offensive of December 16, was to bomb transportation facilities such as the railroads that were used to move men and supplies to the front just west of Coblenz. Actually, these targets had been high priority before the Battle of the Bulge began and were of greater importance to the allies in the last two weeks of the year. Dr. Schnatz fails to appreciate that his city was in the immediate path of a shooting war. Dr. Schnatz wrote of a flight of six B-17s coming from the west to Coblenz on December 24th. He said: "The six B-17s belonged to the 614 Squadron under their Squadron Leader Charles Utter, nowdays newspaper publisher in Westerly, in the State of Rhode Island in the U.S.A.. The Squadron dropped their bombs on the railroad Station Koblenz-Lutzel...For Koblenz the terror had not yet come to an end because 20 minutes after Utter's attack the 390th BG and the two other Squadrons of the 401st Group came from the west and again hit the switchyard station, using it as a casual target..." He later said "...there, most assuredly, was no Christmas spirit felt outside the battered traffic installations. Damage to the tracks caused on December 22 by the English attack had just been eliminated. Now, again, the lines were blocked. At the switchyard station Koblenz-Lutzel, traffic had been halted by 35 direct hits, presumably, for 48 hours. The Main Railroad Station had received two direct hits, at the Mosel Railroad Station a transport train had been hit, the line to Trier had been blocked. On the right side of the Rhine, in Pfaffendorf, a switch tower had been destroyed." Our bombs had been seen to strike the target area. It appears that the raid created the kind of havoc that was intended.[67]

The Eighth didn't let up for Christmas; the 3rd Bomb Division sent 248 aircraft to bomb eleven communication centers west of the Rhine River. The 2nd Division sent 174 of its birds aloft to bomb railway facilities, rail bridges and communication centers in the same area. They bombed visually with Gee-H assists, losing four aircraft in this continuing support of the ground forces in the Ardennes. On December 26 the efforts of the Eighth were again restricted by the weather. The 2nd and 3rd Bomb Divisions were able to get only 151 aircraft off to hit rail targets in the area of the Battle of the Bulge.[68]

On December 27 bases of the Eighth were hampered by freezing rain and fog, but all three Bomb Divisions were able to put 575 aircraft over western Germany to bomb marshalling yards, rail bridges and rail junctions in support of the allied battlefront.[69] The 401st was able to provide 36 B-17s, getting back in the action as the 94th CBW "C" Group. Major Alvah Chapman flew as Air Commander with the Mercer crew.[70] It was so cold that morning that a number of aircraft engines refused to start and some aircraft had to be scrubbed. At briefing it was said that the purpose of the mission was to disrupt enemy lines of communications and the flow of supplies to the battle area.[71] The specific target for the Group was the marshalling yards at Gerolstein, about forty miles south of Bonn and less than 30 miles inside the German border with Belgium. The rail lines from Gerolstein were carrying heavy traffic into Belgium to support the German counteroffensive. Weather from the coast on in was clear permitting a good visual bomb run. The target was easy to spot because of a wooded area that stood out against the snow. Bombing results were excellent; 50 percent of the bombs were within 1,000 feet of the MPI and one-hundred percent were within 2,000 feet.[72] Returning home to Deenethorpe that afternoon was again hazardous. Ground fog and haze made the runways difficult to find. Colonel Seawell took over the trailer at the end of the runway to help Major Charles Baldwin in the tower get our birds down safely. It took two and a half hours to land all our B-17s but it was done without an accident – real teamwork![73] Earlier in this chapter I mentioned that the November 30 mission to Bohlen was the first for the crew of Lt. Myron L. King and that they would become more prominent in the life of the "Maiden". Destined to come to know each other much better in the weeks to come the King crew took the "Maiden" to Gerolstein on December 27 for what was their seventh mission. Although the flak was called meager, 83 of the 232 1st Bomb Division aircraft were flak-damaged. Enemy fighters were not seen although our "little friends" claimed 29 victories in the air.[74]

The next day the 401st had a mission to bomb the marshalling yards at Rheinbach. They had 39 aircraft to make up the 94th CBW "A" Group with Capt. Clyde Lewis as the Air Commander. Deputy was Lt. Charles W. Utter leading the 614th Squadron's twelve B-17s in the low squadron. They bombed by Gee-H over 10/10ths clouds with unobserved results. Of the 379 aircraft in the 1st Bomb Division only two reported any flak damage.[75] The Sisson crew was back that day flying the "Maiden".[76] Picker carried eighteen 250 pound GPs and two 500 pound IBs which he dropped from 22,000 feet.[77]

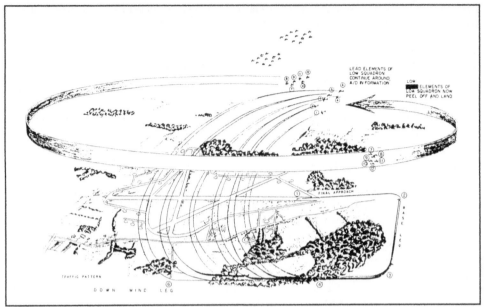

On many afternoons in England in 1944 and 1945 weather conditions were consistently poor, fuel was getting low and frequently there were wounded aboard. With so many aircraft in the skies all trying to get home a standard landing procedure was necessary. Bear in mind there were 38 B-17 Bomb Groups and 21 B-24 Groups as well as 15 Fighter Groups in the Eighth many of which were aloft at the same time. The Chart for landing procedure depicts the low squadron in the landing pattern with the lead and high squadron of a Bomb Group circling to follow in turn. 8th AF Tactical Development August 1942 - May 1945. Prepared by 8th AF and AAF Evaluation Board (ETO).

On December 29 the Eighth sent 784 heavy bombers to west Germany to again bomb communications and railroad facilities. The 1st Bomb Division had a total force of 304 B-17s of which 144 including the 401st had as their target the marshalling yards at Bingen on the Rhine River.[78] Lt. J.J. Brown led the high squadron with ten aircraft of the 614th which included the Sisson crew on the "Maiden".[79] Picker's bomb load again included 18 250 pound GPs and two 500 pound M17 IBs which were dropped from 22,000 feet. He also noted: "flak to and from target. Visual. Good results temp 22,000 -30".[80] The high squadron put 98 percent of their bombs within 1,000 feet of the MPI. The lead squadron missed by 2,000 feet and the low squadron by 4,000 feet.[81] The success and the failures may be in some way related to the following recollections of the high squadron lead bombardier. The bomb run was all visual and Lt. William F. Schiefer said, We had 10/10ths clouds until we got to about 40 or 50 miles from the target." He said the clouds may have had something to do with the lead and low squadrons changing their heading coming in from the north instead of from the west northwest. He continued: "Because my pilot did not follow them, I had to sweat out whether my bombs would miss them." He said he felt it would be safe to drop as they passed under him, but watched as the bombs fell, relieved when his bombs passed the other squadrons. He said he was so relieved that he didn't continue to watch for the bomb strike, but belatedly had the impression that he had a good hit on the target.[82] The mission report for the day said, "the target was clearly visible and the bombing results were excellent."[83] Sisson rated the mission flak with his single star which placed it the category of being "downright hazardous".[84] The 1st Bomb Division lost two of its B-17s with 134 of the 304 aircraft damaged; 27 of the 401st 36 were damaged by flak. Somehow the flak was officially described as moderate.[85]

On December 30 the Eighth showed its strength and endurance by putting up 1,257 bombers for attacks on more rail and communications centers.[86] Among the 1st Division targets were the marshalling yards and a rail bridge at Kaiserslautern. The 401st formed the 94th CBW "A" Group led by Capt. D.A. Currie. The "Maiden" that day carried the crew of

Lt. Wylie White. "Whitey" was a barracks mate of mine and a great guy. The members of his crew and mine have remained friends down through the years. They had 10/10ths clouds at the target and bombed by Gee-H; the results could not be observed. The flak was reported to have been light with only six aircraft in the entire force lost; two of those through a midair collision in the target area.[87]

A newspaper article at the time reported the following concerning this mission:
"For the eighth day running Rundstedt's supply railways in western Germany were hammered yesterday. More than 1,300 U.S. Flying Fortresses and Liberators covered by large forces of fighters, attacked the yards at Kaiserslautern, Mannheim and Kassel as well as at other points. Eight American bombers are missing."[88]

On New Year's Eve the Eighth again made a show of force with 1,259 bombers over Europe. The 3rd Division departed from the tactical targets for some strategic targets such as oil and other industrial objectives at such places as Hamburg and Misburg. It would appear from this that the tide was beginning to turn in the Battle of the Bulge. The 1st and 2nd Bomb Divisions remained committed to the tactical ground support effort. The Triangle 1st was dedicated to rail and communication targets along the German supply routes such as Krefeld, Neuss and Monchen-Gladbach, all further north from those previous targets which had been directly east of the struggle in the Ardennes.[89] The 401st was targeted on the marshalling yards at Krefeld. They formed the 94th CBW "B" Group under the command of Major Alvah Chapman. The target was partially visible but Gee-H was used for bombing. It was reported that the target was missed with the bomb strike being to the right of the MPI.[90] A newspaper article published at the time said:

"In their final blow of 1944 – the ninth in as many days the Eighth Air Force yesterday dispatched more than 1,300 heavy bombers, escorted by upward of 700 fighters, to smash a variety of strategic and tactical targets in Germany including six rail bridges over the Rhine and Moselle in the Coblenz area... Other targets were oil refineries, airfields and communications, as well as U boat pens.
"Yesterday was the second straight day in which the Eighth sent out more than 1,300 Fortresses and Liberators. Saturday's large scale operation saw the heavies, covered by 650 Mustangs and Thunderbolts, strike at German communications lines behind the battlefront for the eighth consecutive day...
"In the first enemy fighter opposition encountered by 8th fighter pilots the bomber-gunners claimed shooting down an additional 26 enemy fighters..."[91]

Although the 1st Division made out quite well with no losses from flak and only 29 of its aircraft damaged, the 3rd Division wasn't as lucky. A Luftwaffe fighter attack shot down 27 B-17s; out of its 526 aircraft 288 had battle damage.[92] The "Maiden" stayed in the nest that day. The 401st closed out the year with its 188th combat mission; the last three weeks were climactic. During that time the medium and heavy bombers blasted the German salient in Belgium with more than 100,000 tons of bombs. The Germans began their withdrawal December 27 and the "bulge" was eliminated in January.
With the advent of 1945 "Germany was no longer an industrial nation. Its transportation facilities were at near collapse. Its airfields were packed with aircraft which had no fuel. The entire Third Reich was crumbling from within and without..." Rundstedt later said:

"Three factors defeated us in the west where I was in Command. First, the unheard-of-superiority of your air force, which made all movement in the day-time impossible. Second, the lack of motor fuel - oil and gas - so that the Panzers and even the remaining Luftwaffe were unable to move. Third, the systematic destruction of railway communications so that it was impossible to bring one single railroad train across the Rhine. This made impossible the reshuffling of troops and robbed us of mobility."[93]

The "Maiden" and the rest of the flock, and their crews had good reason to look with satisfaction to the New Year. On January 1, 1945 the three Bomb Divisions of the Eighth Air Force became known as Air Divisions. This would mark the last structural change in the World War II development of the "Mighty Eighth."[94]

Notes to Chapter 11
1. Freeman, Roger A. *The Mighty Eighth War Diary* p. 386
2. Maslen, Selwyn V. *614th Bombardment Squadron (H): Squadron History* p. 106
3. National Archives, Suitland Reference Branch, Record Group 18, Mission Reports, 401st Bombardment Group (H)
4. Maslen, Selwyn V. *614th Squadron: Crews - Missions - Aircraft* p. 73
5. Letter Arthur R. Seder, Jr. to author January 27, 1991
6. Maslen, see 2 above p. 106
7. Freeman, see 1 above
8. Letter, Allen H. Crawford to author March 30, 1992
9. Bowman, Harold W., Selwyn V. Maslen *Bowman's Bombers* p. 54
10. Bowman, Harold W., Selwyn V. Maslen *401st B.G. (H): Casualties in W.W. II* p. 60
11. Bowman, Martin W. *Castles in the Air* p. 173
12. Freeman, see 1 above p. 388
13. See 3 above
14. Bowman & Maslen, see 9 above
15. Freeman, Roger A. *B-17 Fortress at War* p. 102
16. Maslen, see 4 above p. 3
17. Newspaper clippings from unknown publications on dates unkown from personal scrapbook of Allen H. Crawford loaned the author during 1992
18. Closway, Gordon R. *614th Squadron History*, Air Operations November, 1944.
19. Interview of Myron L. King by author, Nashville, TN June 9, 1992.
20. Maslen, see 2 above p. 109
21. Maslen, see 2 above p.109-110
22. Photocopy of personal log of Nathan Picker furnished the author as enclosure to letter from Norman L. Sisson February 13, 1991.
23. Freeman, Roger A. *The Mighty Eighth War Manual* p. 225
24. Freeman, see 1 above p. 390
25. Maslen, see 2 above p. 110
26. See 3 above
27. Freeman, see 1 above p. 391
28. Maslen, see 2 above p. 110
29. See 3 above
30. Bowman & Maslen, see 9 above p. 57
31. Freeman, see 1 above p. 391
32. Freeman, see 1 above p. 392
33. Maslen, see 2 above p. 110-111
34. Freeman, see 1 above p. 392
35. See 22 above
36. Photocopy of personal log of Norman L. Sisson and collection of bomb fuse tags furnished author as enclosure to letter February 13, 1991.
37. Rust, Kenn C. *Eighth Air Force Story* p. 43
38. Freeman, Roger A. *The Mighty Eighth* p.200
39 See 37 above p. 44
40. Maslen, see 2 above p. 112
41. Freeman, see 1 above p. 395
42. Maslen, see 2 above p. 112
43. Freeman, see 1 above p. 395
44. Maslen, see 2 above p. 112
45. Bowman, Martin W., see 11 above p. 176
46. Freeman. see 1 above p. 396
47. Ibid.
48. Freeman, see 1 above p. 397
49. Ibid.
50. Maslen, see 2 above p. 113
51. Bowman & Maslen, see 9 above p. 58
52. Freeman, see 1 above p.397
53. Photocopy of official 614th Squadron Mission Record Card of Captain Frederick H. Babcock furnished

author as enclosure to letter November 26, 1990

54. *Bowman & Maslen, see 9 above p. 56*
55. *See 8 above*
56. *Bowman, Martin W. see 11 above p. 177*
57. *See 8 above*
58. *Ibid.*
59. *Freeman, see 38 above p. 201*
60. *See 3 above*
61. *Bowman & Maslen, see 9 above p. 58*
62. *Maslen, see 2 above p. 113*
63. *Freeman, see 38 above p. 201*
64. *Freeman, see 1 above p. 404*
65. *See 8 above*
66. *See 3 above*
67. *Schnatz, Helmut <u>Aerial Warfare in the Region of Koblenz 1944/45: A Description of its Course, its Effects and its Background</u>; translated pgs.1-9 furnished author as enclosure to letter from Charles W. Utter February 19, 1992*
68. *Freeman, see 1 above p. 405*
69. *Freeman, see 1 above p. 406*
70. *Maslen, see 2 above p. 114*
71. *See 3 above*
72. *Ibid.*
73. *Bowman & Maslen, see 9 above p. 56*
74. *Maslen, see 2 above p. 114*
75. *Ibid.*
76. *Ibid.*
77. *See 22 above*
78. *Freeman, see 1 above p. 408*
79. *Maslen, see 2 above p. 115*
80. *See 22 above*
81. *Bowman & Maslen, see 9 above p. 58*
82. *Letter William F. Schiefer to author June 19, 1991*
83. *See 3 above*
84. *See 36 above*
85. *Maslen, see 2 above p. 115*
86. *Freeman, see 1 above p. 406*
87. *Maslen, see 2 above p. 115*
88. *See 17 above*
89. *Freeman, see 1 above p. 410-411*
90. *Maslen, see 2 above p.116*
91. *See 17 above*
92. *Maslen, see 2 above p.116*
93. *Sunderman, James F. <u>World War II in the Air: Europe</u> p. 251, 257*
94. *Bowman, Martin W., see 11 above p. 180*

CHAPTER 12 — THE STAUFFER CREW - MORE LUCKY DEVILS

The December 6 mission to Merseburg was the last that Lt. Eugene E. Hoemann flew as co-pilot for Norm Sisson. On December 27 he was assigned as the first pilot on the recently arrived crew of Lt. David H. Stauffer. It was the policy to provide a new crew with a combat veteran co-pilot on their first mission . The reason for this was to provide a new crew with combat expertise from takeoff to landing and the new co-pilot would gain experience by flying with a veteran crew. The Stauffer crew provided an interesting difference since they were trained for combat on the B-24. Stauffer flew as copilot with the more experienced Sisson crew for six missions beginning with the December 28th mission to Rheinbach. Of those six missions three were on the "Maiden." After Hoemann finished his tour January 10th Stauffer returned to his crew as its first pilot for another 19 missions together.[1]

The following is part of the story of the Stauffer crew which includes two incidents I feel appropriately demonstrate the teamwork of aircrews but also illustrate how those young men in battle, far above the earth, could rise above stress and pain to perform their duties and care for each other. I believe these young men of the Stauffer crew were typical of all those "Heaven Hellions" of the 614th Squadron.

Dave, who came from Highland Park, New Jersey now resides at Bethesda, Maryland. Between 1990 and 1992 we corresponded and most of the material contained in this chapter came from his letters and enclosures.[2]

In mid-August 1944 Dave Stauffer was at Westover Field, Massachusetts where he obtained the services of three members of his crew: William P. Eidemiller, known to Dave as "Buzz" and also known as "Buss," who would later be the toggelier or the bomb dropper and nose turret gunner (they never had a rated bombardier); Arthur L. Wright, an armorer-gunner and their ball turret gunner; and Lt. Edward C. Haake, copilot.

On August 19 they arrived at Chatham Field, Savannah, Georgia where they met more of their crew: Howard J. Smith, engineer-top turret gunner; Howard Tuchin, radio operator; Libero L. Laura, waist gunner and William J. Dobson, known as "Dobby," tail gunner.

At Chatham Field they began their combat training as a B-24 crew. I found this highly unusual and do not recall another such crew without B-17 training ending up assigned to a Fortress group in combat. In September the crew was rounded out with the addition of their navigator, Lt. Thomas E. Burns.[3] In August Dave had written home indicating his crew had adjusted into a team when he said the following about the enlisted personnel, "the whole bunch – the six of them – are living together in beds side by side ... and they go everywhere together. Its a great sight seeing them come up the road together smiling and eager to get started."[4] During their training in the skies over Georgia Dave was obviously proud of his crew as he complimented them in another letter home, "You should see our men shoot. They put a couple rounds in the water, wait a second, then aim and put a couple more splashes right smack among the first burst. My engineer really knows his airplane and makes a fine dependable crew-chief, a hundred percent better than most I've seen here. The instructor-engineer who first checked him out in the air here on a B-24 said he was tops. Howard Tuchin is very eager... and is always cheerful. The tail gunner, "Dobby," ... is turning out to be most stable and dependable – a crack shot, cool as a cucumber, a good man...without the need of others around to check on him... Ed Haake, copilot, is a fine flyer, he does very well at formation flying... which is exhaustive work." In another letter he wrote, "Tom Burns, our navigator, is a wonderful fellow – a really conscientious worker who knows his stuff and wants to do his job as well as possible..."[5] By November the "phases" of their combat training complete, the Stauffer crew left the country on board the Queen Elizabeth, arriving in the United Kingdom late that same month destined to join Bowman's Bombers at Deenethorpe. Dave wrote home in a positive vein of their conversion to the Flying Fortress as follows, "It will be as much a surprise to you as it was to me when I found myself in a bomber unit flying the other heavy bomber. It will be a little difficult at first...and I'll probably fly the first few missions as a copilot, but all in all its not a bad deal. There are several good reasons for being quite pleased about the change. Just now – and for another eight days or so including Sundays – we attend ground school on an all-day schedule..."[6] That letter was written on December 5 and in less than two weeks they were flying combat over Europe.

Of his missions with Sisson Dave said: "I remember Sisson well – a happy and competent person. He had some rough missions before that last one on January 7..."[7]

Their first mission together as a crew was an historic mission to Berlin on February 3, 1945 which is the subject of Chapter 14.[8] It was on their tenth mission together that the Stauffer crew experienced the first of two of the most unforgettable incidents of their lives. On February 24 they were on board IW-K bombing an oil refinery at Harburg. The 401st put up 36 aircraft to form the 94th CBW "A" Group. The Air Commander was Lt. Col. Seawell riding with the lead crew of Captain J.J. Brown of the 614th Squadron. Due to complete cloud cover at the target the Group did a PFF run, by squadrons, and all "Mickey" operators reported their equipment worked perfectly for a good run at the target. Moderate flak was accurate as the 401st made its run, and out of the 26 aircraft of the 1st Air Division that were damaged 13 were 401st aircraft.[9] An indication that the bombing was successful were reports from crews who saw black smoke coming through the clouds at 12,000 feet as they were departing the target area.[10] On board IW-K, the navigator, Tom Burns of Tarentum, Pennsylvania had just recorded the word flak in his log at bombs away. An instant later a piece of shrapnel from one of those German shells ripped upward into the aircraft and through his desk, leaving a gash on his knee and cutting off the tip of his little finger.[11]

In 1990 Dave wrote that after bombs away they were pulling away from the target trying to clear "a blanket of bursting shells. One puff of black after another appeared around the planes. Then came the first dull thud." He recalled, "The elevator trim tabs became inoperative, and the rudder almost so, as cables were cut. We used added force on the controls to hold the plane in formation. Another thud followed the first and then another and another. The oxygen system was threatened, and intercom communication established that Bill Dobson, the tail gunner, had passed out. Arthur Wright came out of his ball turret to revive him with emergency flow from a waist tank. Either flak in the engines or the extra power forced upon them to hold position at high altitude resulted in all four superchargers shutting down at about the same time. The resulting loss of power made continued flying at high altitude impossible. Other problems also made an immediate descent to lower altitude necessary. These included the lack of oxygen in the tail and the malfunction of the prop governor on the number four engine. With no oil under pressure to hold the propeller at a constant pitch and rpm we faced the prospect of the propeller 'winding up,' spinning at such speed that it shakes the plane and threatens to fly off, possibly cutting through the plane. More than once the propeller was brought back to normal rpm by pushing and releasing the feathering switch, but when this failed to return the governor to normal function, we feathered completely and continued on three engines. Meanwhile, our copilot, Ed Haake, had called the lead plane of our squadron and very briefly given the reasons for our leaving formation."[12]

Dave neglected to say that as he left the formation he, himself, began to lose consciousness from a lack of oxygen. The engineer, Howard J. Smith, from Monroe, Louisiana managed to revive him and got portable "walk around" bottles of oxygen to those crew members who were in danger of being killed by anoxia. From the same barrage of flak that wounded Lt. Burns, the waist gunner Libero L. Laura, of Winthrop, Massachusetts suffered a leg wound from flak fragments. Apparently, the same shell caused about 100 rounds of their own .50 caliber ammunition to explode directly behind the tail gunner's position.[13] Burns had passed out from lack of oxygen and Haake left the flight deck, crawled down into the nose compartment to revive him and to provide first aid for his wounds.[14] Brute strength was needed to keep their crippled B-17 on the straight and level. In addition to the feathered number four engine and the loss of superchargers the number two engine had been hit but was still providing some power. To add to their woes the number one fuel tank had been hit, with the loss of fuel badly needed to get them to England. Burns refused further first aid, remained in the nose and undertook to navigate them back home. Aside from his wounds he endured cold and wind through 25 holes in the nose. To make matters worse, all of his navigational instruments had been knocked out and his charts were covered with his own blood. "Buzz" Eidemiller helped Burns, who was unable to write, by making log entries. Burns relying somewhat on D.R. navigation and somewhat on his memory, directed them through partial overcast, around known flak areas and eventually out of enemy territory.[15]

Dave said that he did not know whether they had been protected by fighters early on, they had been much too busy to notice, but when they reached the North Sea two Navy planes were flying on their wings. The loss of fuel was beginning to become a problem. He said: "Our engineer, Howard Smith, was watching the fuel gauges and from his recent measurements, announced what we had already feared – that the gas supply would probably not last to the English coast. Alternating at the controls, Ed and I coaxed the plane along, sacrificing altitude for speed and fuel preservation. We pointed toward the nearest tip of the English coast with hard pressure of both feet on the left rudder. Beneath us in the channel, we were told later, were three air-sea rescue boats ready to pick us up if we were forced to ditch."[16] Dave continued, "Tom... picked our way across England in such a way that we could land into the wind on our Deenethorpe base without need of a turn. From a distance of about 15 miles, Ed or I called ahead to the tower, described the plane's condition and fuel situation, informed it that we had wounded men aboard, and requested clearance for straight in landing. When the wheels were lowered, we found that one of the tires appeared to have been hit by flak. This would require that the plane's 38,000 pounds or so of weight would have to be held over the good wheel with throttle and brake as long as possible to avoid a ground loop and a blocking of the main runway. An ambulance was waiting as our plane dragged to a stop. It carried off our navigator and gunner while a tow car removed our plane from the narrow landing strip so that our arriving formation, circling above, could come in and make their landings."[17]

On later examination it was determined that there were over 100 holes from flak in their aircraft. Their radio operator, Howard Tuchin, had narrowly avoided being a casualty, if not a fatality. It was learned that as he stood and bent over his radio receiving set a chunk of flak from below entered the aircraft, sliced through his metal seat, the seat cushion and his parachute. It continued on its path cutting control cables and severing a steel girder before exiting through the top of the fuselage. After the mission they picked out more than 50 .50 caliber machine gun slugs that had lodged in "Dobby" Dobson's flak suit from the exploded ammunition.[18] In addition to the Purple Hearts earned by the wounded, the navigator, Tom Burns, was awarded the Silver Star for gallantry in action and Dave Stauffer was awarded the Distinguished Flying Cross.[19] At the time Dave Stauffer said, "Never has a Fortress crew done a more beautiful job than my crew did at such a critical time...mere words of praise fall short of telling the story."[20] The B-17, IW-K, was patched up to take the Stauffer crew to Chemnitz on March 3rd and other missions; she flew combat with other crews up to and including the 401st's last mission on April 20 before flying home on "Operation Home Run."[21]

Concerning their experience on February 24 Dave wrote home four days later saying: "A couple days ago I mentioned in a V-mail that I was very proud of each man on the crew - not mentioning that there was a special reason for it. However, since then I've learned that Hospital Service called the folks of the two crew members who received injuries as a result of flak, so I'll let you know the details to reassure both you and any of the parents that start worrying. Shorty (Libero Laura) got hit in his left foot which broke no bones. He's jumping about on crutches now – a couple days after it happened...Tom Burns was a little less fortunate and was hit in the little finger of his right hand. The end of the finger will be lost but he is quite resigned to it and jokingly says he never did put that finger to much use anyway. He also got a nick in the other hand and a cut on one knee. We see them every day or so and they are in fine spirits...They're at a big hospital about ten miles from here."[22] During Tom Burns recuperation I was privileged to fly with them as their navigator to Schwabmunchen on March 4. On March 11 Dave wrote home as follows, "Tom, Ed and I are getting a little vacation in a rest house located somewhere in southern England. The rest of the crew is also getting a week's stay at a similar place probably not far from here. These houses are beautiful estates being run by the Red Cross temporarily. Four or five Red Cross girls are live wires around

here. About 25 fellows are in various stages of the seven day period. Most crews get this before they finish up. We're a little bit past the half-way mark."[23] We called these places flak houses and it is a good bet that our bosses thought the Stauffer crew deserved that week after the Harburg mission. They may have stayed at Standbridge Earls where my crew spent a week in February over my 21st birthday; it was delightful! Within a month of the February 24 incident the Stauffer crew had another hair-raising experience. This one involved another aircraft of the 614th Squadron; one with an illustrious history. She was IW-F, 42-97395, well known by her nickname "Chute the Works." My own memories of that lady warrior are very good since I was on board for four of my missions. On November 5, 1944 with the Babcock crew I flew "Chute the Works" to Frankfurt Am Main for our fifth mission, and we flew her again on that historic mission to Berlin on February 3, 1945. The real reason I recall that B-17 was I was on her when we went to Essen March 8. It was my third mission as a navigator and I was flying with the crew of Robert M. Stehman.[24] I had been drafted, against my will and my better judgement, to fly as a navigator. I had this awful premonition that I would get lost over Germany, and all alone, would not be able to find my way back to Deenethorpe. The mission itself I do not recall; it was either uneventful or I blocked it out of my mind, still unconvinced that I had any skill as a navigator. On our return we were surprised to see a small gathering when we parked "Chute the Works" on her hardstand. When we emerged from the aircraft we were made to line up with the ground crew for a photograph under her nose to commemorate her 100th combat mission which she had just successfully completed. My last mission on IW-F was with the crew of Lt. H.W. James on March 22, a milk run to Barmingholten where we bombed military barracks near the Rhine River. It was a visual bombing with good results and very little flak which damaged only one 401st aircraft.[25] One other note concerning my lack of prowess as a navigator; the training provided at Deenethorpe was more complete than I had received as an Aviation Cadet and much more practical - my diploma, the "Eighth Air Force D.R. Navigation Certificate" was dated six days before I finished my combat tour, and after I had already flown ten missions as a navigator. I guess they were waiting to see if I could find my way back home before they issued the Certificate. (Appendix 4)

On March 25 the Stauffer crew was briefed for a mission on "Chute the Works," her 111th mission. I recall the weather was gross from the ground up that morning. As we climbed through that terrible weather in the darkness, our assembly altitude was changed repeatedly as we were unable to get over the freezing rain, snow and heavy clouds. I recall another aircraft flashing by the nose of our ship so close I don't know how we didn't collide. I gasped with shock as it was gone as fast as it came out of the darkness. I later recall some of the crew saw a flash of light which we assumed was a mid-air collision. Shortly after 7:00 A.M. the mission was scrubbed because of the weather and we were recalled. Somehow all of our aircraft but one, "Chute the Works", got back down safely; she never got that 111th mission.[26]

That morning Stauffer had a substitute navigator, copilot and waist gunner. Lt. William M. Bruce, was their navigator in place of the recuperating Tom Burns; Bruce had been Lt. R.B. Thompson's bombardier and was a certified "Lucky Devil" in that crash landing of "Hard Seventeen" in Belgium January 10 described in Chapter 5. Bryan Cosden was Dave's copilot that day with Ed Haake out with a sinus infection. Edward Grasela, wounded at Merseburg on November 21, was the waist gunner in place of the recuperating Libero Laura who was also wounded February 24.[27]

Dave recalled that the entire 1st and 3rd Air Divisions, 737 aircraft, were airborne for the mission on March 25 and all but his aircraft got down safely after recall. From another 401st B-17 IN-J, "Homesick Angel," most of the crew bailed out after the pilot accidentally hit the bailout alarm bell.[28] Dave's description in his own words best relates the horrifying details of the flight that morning: "Following our usual practice, our crew ...assembled for breakfast at 2:00 A.M. and briefing at 3:00 A.M....We took off in forbidding weather a little after 5:00 A.M. before dawn, and climbed through heavy clouds towards our assembly point. We saw no other planes after we left the runway. As we climbed and circled, the air grew increasingly bumpy. The plane's position instruments that depend on air pressure began to act suspiciously as freezing blocked the Pitot tube. One or two of the gyros began to spin uncontrolled, as I am sure they did in many of the planes about us. When we started to dive

"Chute the Works" — 100th mission to Essen March 8, 1945. Back row left to right: M/Sgt. William E. Royal - ball, Sgt. George E. Bacon - radio, Lt. George H. Menzel - navigator, Lt. Frank R. Bush - copilot, Lt. Robert M. Stehman - pilot, Sgt. Albert F. Petrowsky - tail, Sgt. Harold R. Crowe - engineer. Front row left to right: Sgt. Maurice E. Batemen - waist, Sgt. Sherman Oatman - Ass't. Crew Chief, M/Sgt. Charles Barker - Crew Chief, Sgt. Herman Pennala - Ass't Crew Chief, Sgt. Loren P. Shaw - tail.

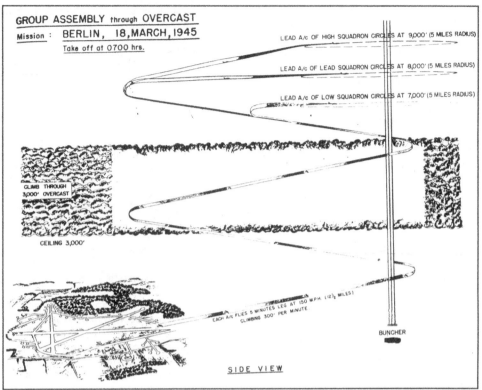

GROUP ASSEMBLY through OVERCAST

Mission : BERLIN, 18, MARCH, 1945

Take off at 0700 hrs.

LEAD A/c OF HIGH SQUADRON CIRCLES AT 9,000' (5 MILES RADIUS)

LEAD A/c OF LEAD SQUADRON CIRCLES AT 8,000' (5 MILES RADIUS)

LEAD A/c OF LOW SQUADRON CIRCLES AT 7,000' (5 MILES RADIUS)

CLIMB THROUGH 3,000' OVERCAST

CEILING 3,000'

EACH A/c FLIES 5 MINUTES LEG AT 150 MPH (12½ MILES)
CLIMBING 300' PER MINUTE

BUNCHER

SIDE VIEW

Early morning takeoffs were frequently done with bad weather complicated often by darkness. This required a standard procedure for Bomb Groups to use to avoid midair collisions and to facilitate assembly of each squadron above the bad weather. The buncher was a radio transmitter. 8th AF Tactical Development August 1942 — May 1945. Prepared by the 8th AF and AAF Evaluation Board (ETO).

and turn and climb again in worsening weather, we began to realize that the one instrument still available to us for blind flying, the gravity-controlled artificial horizon, was giving us false readings...Still attempting to climb above the weather, we gradually lost all ability to fly straight and level. Our altimeter reading moved through thousands of feet, up and down, with alarming speed. We could no longer determine whether the plane was level, climbing, or diving during the tight turns we were feeling. Cosden had a brief turn at the controls as the plane became increasingly unmanageable. With the plane in tight turns while rising and plunging in heavy turbulence, and no way to determine our attitude in the sky, I gave the order to bailout. "There was no effort that I can recall to break the strictly enforced radio silence. Some of the crew were able to 'abandon ship' in short order. When I started down from my seat, the plane entered a sharp turn and I was stuck between the pilot and copilot seats. Afterwards I learned that when I reached back to straighten the plane's flight, it allowed Tuchin, the radio operator pinned to his chair, and tail gunner Dobson pinned in the tail of the plane, to move towards the escape hatches. As the plane straightened out and began another turn, I was propelled down through the cockpit toward the left side escape hatch, the forward entrance door. As I fell through the opening, I thought I saw one of the crew just inside the hatch. Later, when our nose gunner, Eidemiller, failed to appear, I was afraid that it might have been he and that he had failed to jump. Actually, he followed me out, I believe, and broke an ankle landing in a tree over a roadway. He was located and returned to a hospital separately.

"On our way down, the plane was radioed several times by the flight tower of a nearby airfield which was evidently being buzzed by our unmanned plane. As we descended through snow, the plane made several passes below us and then crashed in a plowed field almost under us. The explosion of its heavy bomb load blew us back upwards in our downward glide. According to Air Force records, the crash occurred at 5:45 A.M. one-and-a-half miles north of Saltby...

"Once on the ground, several of us assembled at the sight of the crash. It was light by then and many spectators from what I seem to remember as a farming landscape joined us in curiosity. I recall walking through the debris, anxious over the possibility of detecting the odor of burnt flesh. About the largest piece of airplane in sight was a tire. Very soon a British crash crew of some sort arrived and urgently ordered us out of the crash site. Some of us owe our lives to them. We had no sooner withdrawn to a distance than a remaining bomb or two, probably deeply buried, blew up. Fortunately, no one to my knowledge was injured by the blast.

"Eidemiller, I think, was the only crew member seriously hurt in the jump. The so-called wound recorded on my army record was simply a cracked sternum caused by the yank of the opening parachute as it jammed a colt revolver into my chest..."[29]

One other story about that incident was furnished by Robert M. Stehman. Bob said that Bill Bruce had a bunk next to him and told him that after he bailed out he landed on the back of a sheep. He said the sheep took off with him on its back and ran into a haystack knocking Bill off. He said that he was so scared he sat there and defecated for 30 minutes.[30] In retrospect I have come to believe that the aircraft that narrowly missed ours that morning was "Chute the Works" and it was she who buzzed the tower of a nearby airfield. After such an illustrious combat record the bomber was like a mortally wounded and crazed animal, just trying to stay alive. "Chute the Works" had flown 82 missions without an abort, beginning on April 24, 1944. On the next mission she returned with an engine failure, and from that time on through her 110th mission did not have another abort.[31]

"Chute the Works" like the "Maiden" has been kept alive through a painting. She is depicted as the secondary subject in a painting titled "Purple Heart Corner" by aviation artist A. Ric Druet. She wears her 401st plumage well and her 614th lettering, IW-F, proudly as seen inside the front cover.

After the war Dave Stauffer returned to college at Amherst and later studied Chinese at Yale before going to China as a base manager and sometime pilot for Civil Air Transport. He returned to the States in 1948 earning a PhD. in Latin-American studies. After a short teaching experience including a stint at Union College he had a career with the State Department. He and his wife also spent some years on a an education project of the Peace Corps in the British Honduras now known as Belize.[32] As for his war experiences it is fair to say that Dave Stauffer and his crew are certified "Lucky Devils." Dave himself, having flown on three of her missions, is one of the "Maiden's" heroes.

Notes to Chapter 12

1. Maslen, Selwyn V. _614th Squadron: Crews - Missions -Aircraft_ p. 31, 78, 82
2. Press release of _Stars and Stripes_ sub-captioned 401st Bomb Group dated February 24, 1945 furnished author as enclosure to letter dated February 5, 1991 by David H. Stauffer
3. Notes by David H. Stauffer during September, 1990 for a crew reunion which contain abstracted material from letters between crew members and their families in 1944 - 1945; furnished author as enclosure to letter from Stauffer June 22, 1992
4. Ibid.
5. Ibid.
6. Ibid.
7. Letter, David H. Stauffer to author April 2, 1991
8. Maslen, see 1 above p. 82
9. Maslen, Selwyn V. _614th Bombardment Squadron (H): Squadron History_ p. 134
10. Bowman, Harold W. & Selwyn V. Maslen _Bowman's Bombers_ p. 66
11. See 2 above
12. Copy of article captioned "The Raid of February 24, 1945" prepared by David H. Stauffer September 16, 1990 furnished author as an enclosure to letter from Stauffer February 5, 1991
13. See 2 above
14. Ibid.
15. Ibid.
16. See 12 above

17. Ibid.
18. See 2 above
19. See 3 above
20. See 2 above
21. Maslen, see 9 above
22. see 3 above
23. Ibid.
24. Closway, Gordon R. <u>614th Squadron History</u>, loading list March 8, 1945
25. Maslen, see 9 above p.147
26. Maslen, see 9 above p.149
27. Copy of article captioned "'Chute the Works' Bailout March 25, 1945" prepared by David H. Stauffer September 21, 1990 furnished author as enclosure to letter from Stauffer February 5, 1991
28. Maslen, see 9 above p. 149
29. See 27 above
30. Letter, Robert M. Stehman to author June 27, 1992
31. Closway, see 24 above, Summary of Events, March, 1945
32. Telephone conversation, David H. Stauffer and author July 14, 1992

CHAPTER 13 — A NEW YEAR
A NEW CREW FOR THE "MAIDEN"

Captain Gordon R. Closway, Public Relations Officer of the 401st and an original member of the 614th Squadron, chronicled its wartime history. He was prophetic when he wrote about the combat operations of the Group for the first month of 1945, "January weather permitted 13 missions, most of them PFF and G-H, most of them of tactical value to the ground forces. Just as before D-Day, we are striking rail junctions and bridges behind the German Army, and the months operations indicate another big push coming."[1]

I do not recall celebrating the advent of the New Year, probably because I was in bed long before midnight since we were scheduled to fly the following morning. On New Year's Eve I had seventeen missions under my belt which was a long way from finishing a combat tour. Also, looking at the map of Europe, particularly in light of the "Battle of the Bulge, I did not anticipate an early capitulation of the German Government. Author Martin W. Bowman later commented on the New Year with the optimism of one looking back over history, without the threat of being second guessed. He said, "January, 1945 marked the 8th's third year of operations and it seemed as if the end of the war was in sight. The Ardennes breakthrough was on the verge of failure and Germany had no reserves left. In the east, the Red Army prepared for the great winter offensive which would see the capture of Warsaw and Cracow and take the Soviets across the German border..."[2] There was still a lot of geography between the Rhine and the Oder.

On New Year's Day the primary target for the 401st was Derben, Germany, an oil storage dump. The 94th CBW "C" Group was made up from the 401st with Major R.J. White as Air Commander.[3] The 1st Air Division that day was pointed at oil facilities, rail bridges and junctions in western Germany. Out of 451 committed aircraft 292 bombed the Henschel marshalling yards at Kassel while the others due to heavy clouds chose various targets of opportunity at Coblenz, towns north of that city and several in the immediate area of Kassel.[4] The primary and secondary targets were obscured by clouds so the 401st went on to a last resort target. The lead squadron used PFF with a visual assist to bomb the marshalling yards at Elz, north of Kassel while the high and low squadrons bombed the Hadamar Railroad yards at Kassel. One factor of importance was the recorded ground speed over Germany at 328 mph[5] due to high wind velocity. Considerable flak was encountered that day with 22 of the 401st bombers damaged. One of those sustained such serious damage that it had to land and be abandoned on the continent.[6] Our Fortresses were ignored by the Luftwaffe which had plenty of other fish to fry. A screening force of 12 aircraft of the 92nd and 305th Bomb Groups for the 40th CBW were late in their rendezvous with their escorts and were jumped by FW-190s and lost five B-17s. The Luftwaffe strafed an allied airfield at Brussels where many Eighth fighters and bombers had just put in with damage and other difficulties. A dozen were set on fire and others were left badly damaged by the German attack.[7] This strafing attack, called "Operation Bodenplatte," was of great cost to the Luftwaffe which lost many of its veteran pilots, "Experten" formation leaders.[8] A small force of 11 B-17s of the 1st Air Division hit an oil refinery at Magdeburg and were in turn hit by the German Luftwaffe which shot down two of the bombers.[9] The "Maiden" that day carried the crew of Wylie White. As mentioned in Chapter 9 "Whitey" was one of my barracks mates. He was a very big, muscular and ruggedly handsome guy whose physical presence commanded respect. It wasn't uncommon to see "Whitey" spend his evening sitting on his bed absorbed in embroidery. Not one person ever had the courage to poke fun at him for his needle and thread pastime.

That mission to the Kassel area was a close shave for the "Maiden" and for the members of "Whitey's" crew. The featured actor of that story is Edwin R. Cranz, the waist gunner on the White crew. Eddie and Allen Crawford on our crew had a special relationship. They had both been in infantry training at Camp Wheeler in Georgia and later in the Air Force at Keesler Field in Mississippi. They really became friends on the military train from Keesler to the

College Training Detachment at Marshall College in West Virginia where they were roommates. They were separated at the Classification Center when Eddie was "washed out" because he was a quarter of an inch too short. Eddie went on to gunnery school while Al became a bombardier. They literally ran into each other in front of the 614th Squadron Orderly Room when Eddie, having that moment arrived at Deenethorpe with the White crew, jumped off the truck and into Al almost knocking him to the ground. They have remained good friends to this day.[10] Many of us have told Eddie's story many times and Al got to the point that he was convinced that he was White's navigator that day. Although he did fly two missions with White he was with me on Babcock's aircraft. Strangely, Babcock was flying White's B-17 "Gambler's Choice" that day. Eddie said they had been in heavy flak that day, and at one point he bent over for some reason and was aware of a noise of sorts which caused him to straighten up and look to his rear. He said on the floor he saw a rip in a parachute bag belonging to Art Viescas, the ball turret gunner, and assumed that a piece of flak had caused it. The air above and in the vicinity of the parachute bag was a billowing cloud of white powder. He suddenly realized the cloud was nothing but pulverized sugar from a large cache of hard candy which Art had saved from the bags of goodies we were provided with on each mission. I recall each bag contained two large very good oatmeal cookies, the hard candy, and a Hershey chocolate bar among other things. With breakfast at 2:00 A.M. it was a long day until the evening meal and those goodies surely were enjoyed on the way home from Germany. Eddie knew that Art was saving the candy to make "points" with English lassies, and he suddenly thought the destruction of the cache was funny. He was laughing hysterically when he received an intercom call from their engineer/top turret gunner, Paul Whitney. Paul's voice was concerned and asked Eddie if he was alright; Eddie assured him that he was fine. At that point Paul told him to look over his head. Eddie confessed that he was shocked and amazed to see a hole in the roof of the fuselage just over his head that was two feet square.

Paul with his turret facing the tail had seen the hole and was concerned that Eddie had been hit. They determined that an 88 mm shell had entered the "Maiden" from below, tore through the parachute bag, missing Eddie as he was bent over, exiting over his head, exploding harmlessly above them. Fortunately, it did not do irreparable damage to the

"Maiden U.S.A." flying on the wing of IW-B with wheels down for a landing at Deenethorpe. Courtesy of Ralph W. Trout.

aircraft controls.[11] It will be recalled that White's bombardier, Lt. Russell L. Aufrance, was wounded on his first mission, that unforgettable one to Merseburg November 21. "Skip," as he is called, said that the flak they encountered on New Year's Day was light but accurate as they crossed the front lines. He said there were several shells that exploded just beneath the "Maiden" and bounced her around before the one that almost got Eddie. He said the shell in exiting the aircraft creased a hydraulic line, but did not sever it; it did sever some of the control cables to the tail.[12]

The rations provided each aircrew member, which I described as goodies, reminds me of another story. There is a notation in the Mission Reports for the November 6 mission to Harburg by Major Wilfred B. "Pop" Fry, the Group Intelligence Officer, of a complaint by Lt. George S. Schaunaman. During the post mission debriefing Lt. Schaunaman said there was a shortage of rations that morning and his crew received "no cookies or candy." The remark might seem humorous today but believe me, it was deadly serious to those combat crews in 1944. In the same report "Pop" recorded another complaint by Lt. B. Weinstein, a navigator, who reported there had been no fire built in the navigator's briefing room that A.M.[13]

The damage sustained by the "Maiden" on New Year's Day was the most serious she suffered during her lifetime. She was grounded for several days to the care of a more than reliable ground crew who would make her fit again.

The Eighth sent over 1,000 aircraft to bomb rail and communications targets in west Germany on January 3. The 1st Air Division's 421 B-17s hit rail junctions, marshalling yards, and communications centers at various locations.[14] The 401st was briefed to hit a marshalling yard at Hermulheim. Actually, there were two targets there, yards designated Hermulheim East and Hermulheim West.[15] Sisson's crew, in the absence of their wounded "Maiden," was on IW-O that day. Nat Picker said he dropped 12 500 pound GPs from 25,000 feet.[16] Solid undercast over the target prevented any observation of bombing results; they had no enemy opposition, no battle damage or casualties.[17]

The Sisson crew went out again on January 5 on "Shark Tooth" as a part of a screening force to drop chaff for the protection of the bombing force that followed. The 1st Air Division's 379 Fortresses hit six primary targets including airfields, communications centers and rail facilities. The 401st was part of a force of 96 aircraft which bombed their secondary target, the marshalling yards at Coblenz.[18] Picker said that he dropped his chaff from 25,000 feet and called the raid a "milk run" even though two Me-110s made a pass at the formation.[19]

On the following day the Eighth made Gee-H and H2X attacks by 778 bombers on western German communications and rail facilities. The 1st Air Division's 422 aircraft were divided between three primary and two secondary targets.[20] The 401st put up 36 aircraft to form the 94th CBW "B" Group with Lt. Col. D.E. Silver as the Air Commander.[21] They were a part of a 72 B-17 force to bomb a communications center at Kempernich.[22] Sisson that day, still without the "Maiden," flew a 615th aircraft, IY-C.[23] The entire Eighth only lost one aircraft to the enemy that day although they had two crash on takeoff, one went down with mechanical difficulties and another made a forced landing in Europe.[24]

The Sisson crew will always remember January 7, 1945. It was the day that they flew their 35th mission and finished their combat tour. It meant they were going home! It was only fitting that the "Maiden" was again in shape to share that final mission with them. That day the Eighth continued its tactical support of the western front by bombing communication centers, rail targets and an oil storage depot. The 1st Air Division put up 351 B-17s which bombed five different targets.[25] The 401st was a part of a force of 110 bombers which bombed a communications center at Bitburg. Major Clyde Lewis was the Air Commander of the 94th CBW "C" Group and the PFF plotting showed the 401st scored a "shack," bombardier parlance for a "bulls-eye." There was little flak and of the total 985 aircraft of the Eighth that day only 28 received any battle damage.[26] Picker celebrated the last mission by dropping twelve 500 pound GPs; he noted it was his fourth "milk run" in a row.[27]

Norm Sisson had a lot to say about that last mission. "The mission was estimated to be 8 hours flying time... weather for takeoff was clear and cold. Visibility was excellent, a daylight takeoff. The 614th Squadron aircraft were lined up on the taxi strip, one behind the other, all props turning. The line of aircraft moved at a steady pace up to the point of takeoff on the runway. When it came our turn for the takeoff roll I remarked to the crew on interphone – 'last takeoff in this war.' This did not turn out to be true. On the takeoff roll I noticed a vibration in engine #2. After we were airborne, about 200 feet, a section of cowling flew off engine #2. Our altitude for bombing that day was to be 27,000 feet. The air at that altitude was extremely cold in the month of January. I knew that one could not control the cylinder head temperature without the movable cowl flaps. We did not want to abort. We were very proud of the fact that we had completed 34 missions without a single abort.

"Immediately, I called the Tower and told them of our problem. I explained that we wanted to go on this mission and could do so with a repair in a short length of time. I requested the Tower to notify our crew chief of our problem and have them standby for our return with a new section of cowling. I requested permission to land as soon as possible.

The Tower worked our landing around the remaining aircraft taking off for the mission. After a high speed landing with full fuel tanks and bomb load, we made a full speed taxi to our hard stand. The crew chief was standing by with the replacement cowling. As soon as the aircraft stopped...the crew chief moved the engine stand into place. All the crew stayed in their positions except Peter Carter, the engineer. Peter assisted in the installation of the new cowling. Engines were all shut down to top the tanks with gas. As soon as the cowling was replaced we were cleared for takeoff. "By this time the Group had formed up and were over the North Sea. After takeoff, the engines were reduced from full power to high power to catch up with our Group. Laverne Crossen, our navigator, gave me a heading...Using high power, our Fortress, "Maiden U.S.A.," performed superbly and began passing the bomber stream. Escort aircraft would fly down and look us over. We caught up with our Group as they were crossing the coast...we slid into our element lead position and the squadron adjusted their positions." Norm said that the rest of the mission was uneventful, and opined that because the "Maiden" was so airworthy and because of the conscientious crew chief they were able to finish their tour of 35 missions without an abort.[28]

Lt. Eugene Hoemann, Sisson's copilot, finished his missions three days later making it possible for Dave Stauffer to regain his position as first pilot of his own crew, which was explained in Chapter 12. On January 7 a photograph was taken of the Sisson crew on the wing of their "Maiden" to commemorate their last mission.

Sisson was promoted to Captain during that month and the crew was sent home and went their separate ways. Norm himself, after a long leave, returned to duty teaching emergency procedures to new B-17 pilots at Hobbs Air Force Base in New Mexico. He said he soon found this to be more dangerous than combat and he volunteered for another combat tour. He had completed B-29 transition with a new crew at Shreveport, Louisiana to go to the Pacific when the war ended. He was separated from the military and was able to earn a degree in engineering and one in law before being recalled to active duty for the Korean War. He spent five more years on active duty, the last assignment flying B-47s in the Strategic Air Command (SAC),[29] before returning to civilian life. He remained in the Reserves and was later retired as a Colonel. Today he resides at Baton Rouge where he recently retired as General Counsel for the Louisiana Department of Transportation and Development.[30]

After the end of World War II Norm Sisson lost track of his combat crew. Concerted efforts to find them only reinforced the knowledge that we have become a very mobile society. He was able in recent years to locate Nathan Picker and they have remained in touch with each other.

Nathan Picker's personal log provided some detail to the Sisson missions for which I am appreciative. Norm said that Nat was very artistic and often sketched unusual ground installations during missions which were well received by our intelligence personnel. After the war Nat became a sign painter and had his own business in New York. He is retired, residing in Ocala, Florida. According to Sisson, he and Nat went on leave together looking for girls, and recalls Nat "always got the good looking ones."[31]

Sisson described Eugene Hoemann as being fearless and an excellent pilot. Like many bomber pilots he had wanted to fly fighters but was too tall. Norm said that Hoemann handled stress very well and recalled one incident where his excellent reaction to crisis may have saved their lives. He said, "A B-17 was hit and slid into our formation. The damaged

```
                    LOW SQUADRON 94TH C GROUP


                    LT. BROWN              7 JAN 45
                    CAPT. SEDER
                    LT. TURK



                    614 SQDN          612 SC JABWOCK
                                      613 IN MACRO
                                      614 IW GOLFCLUB
                    BROWN             615 IY BUZZARD
                    IW G  8259

            KING                  SEDER
            IW O  7602            SC P  1891


        614 SQDN                      612 SQDN

        SISSON                          COX
        IW A  6508                    SC B  1662

    RICHARDSON        MORTON        CAMPBELL          MARTIN
    IW T  8646        IW B  7151    SC D  6992      SC N  6506

            ST AUBYN
            IW F  7395

        COLE          HOEMANN
    IW K  8677        IW N  8738


            SPARES
            FONDREN
            IW X  8565
                            Spare PFF IW C 8033 Disp 3
                                VIS IW R 7780 Disp 4
                            Grnd Spares IY P 8758 Disp 30
                                    IN F 6313 Disp 39
                                    SC C 9993 Disp 13
```

The 401st low squadron making up the 94th Combat Bomb Wing "C" Group for the mission to Bitburg on January 7, 1945. This was the 35th mission for the Sisson crew completing their combat tour.

Fortress was low on the right side and I couldn't see the danger. Hoemann immediately grabbed the controls with such force that it stung my hands and maneuvered the aircraft out of danger."[32] Sisson said that during the period he was flying with SAC his wife sent him a newspaper clipping which reported that Hoemann had been killed in a B-47 crash that had taken place during a refueling operation.[33]

Sisson's engineer, Peter J. Carter, became an M.D. after the war and practiced medicine for some years at Fort Worth, Texas. He attended several 401st reunions including the one at Savannah in 1986. Since then, he temporarily dropped out of sight and efforts by Sisson to contact him had been unsuccessful.[34] He did show up at the 1992 reunion in Norfolk. During

Sisson's crew on the wing of their "Maiden" on January 7, 1945 after the completion of their final combat mission to Bitburg. Standing left to right: Nathan Picker - bombardier, Lavern Crossen - navigator, Dave Stauffer - copilot, Norman Sisson - pilot. Seated left to right: Jose Torres - waist, Calvin J. Stevens - ball, Andrew Haluck - radio, Peter J. Carter - engineer, Francis T. Ritchie - tail. Courtesy of Norman L. Sisson.

conversation at the reunion Dr. Carter recalled that the crew chief for the "Maiden" was Edward Nepyjwoda. It was determined that Mr. Nepyjwoda resided in England for many years but efforts to contact him were unsuccessful.

Sisson's tail gunner was Francis T. Ritchie who had been a coal miner in Pennsylvania before the war. He wanted to become a radio announcer. Sisson said he was a good student of the English language and had excellent diction so he may have achieved that goal. Sisson said Calvin J. Stevens, the ball turret gunner, was a Mormon from Salt Lake City, Utah. Norm described him as having been a very religious person. Jose M. Torres, the waist gunner, was from Houston, Texas. Norm considered Jose to be a good soldier and an excellent gunner. When the post-mission whiskey before debriefing was passed out, Jose would drink those portions that some of the crew did not consume and generally ended up at his barracks half-drunk. He said it was also rumored that Jose would shoot one hole in the roof of his barracks after each mission.[35] The Department of Veteran Affairs informed Sisson he was deceased.

During his search to locate other crew members the Department of Veterans Affairs also forwarded a letter from Sisson to the last known addresses of Laverne Crossen, Andrew S. Haluck, and to Calvin J. Stevens and Francis T. Ritchie. Norm received no reply from them.[36]

The departure from Deenethorpe by the Sisson crew left the "Maiden" without a crew she could call her own. That situation was quickly corrected. By then the Myron L. King crew had 14 missions and they were pleased as punch to have their own B-17; they were already acquainted with the "Maiden" since the lovely lady had taken them to Gerolstein on December 27.

Like the Sisson crew, and most others, the King crew was a cross section of America. There were two from California, one from Texas, Pennsylvania, New Mexico, Ohio, Indiana, New Jersey and one who called both New York and Tennessee home. After numerous telephone conversations with Myron King for more than two years I went to Nashville, Tennessee and on June 9, 1992 spent seven hours with him as we taped an interview for this story. The following background material about Myron and his crew came from that interview, unless otherwise documented.[37]

Myron Lyzon King is best described as a soft spoken southern gentleman, but one who can be quite passionate in his expression of love for his country, American art and his hatred of Soviet Communism. In getting to know him it would be easy to conclude initially that he is a pure product of the American south, born and bred. That is only half-true. He was born in 1921 at Hampton Bays, Long Island, New York, in the heart of the fashionable "Hamptons" out on Long Island. His father, Walter King, was internationally known as a designer and milliner of ladies hats. His shop, "Lyzon" was patronized by the well-to-do ladies of the social register. The southern half of his heritage and upbringing came from his mother who was from Chattanooga, Tennessee. For his entire youth Myron lived on Long Island during the spring and summer and then for the rest of the year they were residents of Chattanooga. Myron said he became very experienced at school transfers, having moved back and forth between New York and Tennessee schools each year. After high school he attended David Lipscomb College at Nashville for two years until he enlisted in the Army Air Force Enlisted Reserve Program in the spring of 1942. At the end of that school year he returned home to Chattanooga, and while waiting for the call to active duty in early 1943 he attended the University of Chattanooga for one semester.

Myron followed the usual pattern for that period of time: he had basic training at Miami Beach, College Training Detachment experience at Western Kentucky State Teachers College at Bowling Green and then went to the Cadet Classification Center at Nashville where he was selected for pilot training. He then became a member of Class 44-D with preflight at Maxwell Field, Montgomery Alabama. His flight training followed with Primary at Union City, Tennessee, Basic at Searcy, Arkansas and Advanced at Blytheville, Arkansas. He won his wings and his commission as a Second Lieutenant on April 15, 1944.

Myron learned how to be a B-17 driver at Columbus, Ohio and then went on to Plant Park in Tampa, Florida where the crew was assembled for combat training at Avon Park, Florida.

Myron said on several occasions that he had an excellent crew and as he spoke of them individually he described each with high praise.

His copilot, William J. Sweeney III was from the Philadelphia, Pennsylvania area and before entering the service had completed the pre-medical program at Marysville College, Tennessee. Bill entered the military through a program that earned him a commission. He was in Myron's class at Maxwell as a Student Officer as opposed to being a Cadet.

Myron recalled that Sweeney was the top of their class in preflight, and was so talented all the way through pilot training that he should have been made a first pilot with his own crew. It was Myron's understanding that after Bill won his wings he was held back for two classes until a spot in fighters could be found for him, which he had earned with his excellent record. Unfortunately, an Inspector ordered that he be given an immediate assignment; as a result he ended up a copilot on the King crew. Myron commented that while this was a personal wrong to Sweeney it was a definite plus for him and the rest of the crew. Because of his ability Bill took a lot of the weight off Myron from time to time, in addition to his being a good pilot in his own right. After the end of the war Sweeney attended medical school and for many years has practiced medicine as a well known gynecologist and obstetrician in New York City. One of the crew members said that he has a textbook written by Sweeney and though he does not understand it, obviously is proud to own it. Myron said that Sweeney has frequently appeared on television news as an authority in his field of specialization.

Richard I. Lowe, their navigator, was reared at Roswell, New Mexico. He was described by Myron as an exceptional navigator who would have been an asset to any lead crew and to have him on his crew was a real bonus. Myron said Richard was a big, tall, handsome young man, normally a quiet person with an agreeable personality. Locating Richard took more than a year. (I must give credit for ultimately finding Richard to Philip A. Reinoehl, the ball turret gunner, who gave me the first clue as to his whereabouts.) Richard said that after being separated from the service at Santa Ana, California in November, 1945 he returned home to New Mexico and married, Jeanette. He worked as an assistant manager in a grocery store in Roswell for several months until Jeanette twisted his arm sufficiently to convince him to return to school. He earned an electrical engineering degree at New Mexico A&M and worked for nine months for the El Paso Electric Company at less than he had earned in the grocery store. He then went to Pearl Harbor as a civilian electrical engineer in the Navy's public works department for three years. He then spent seven years in the hydro-electric department of a mining company in Peru. Returning to the United States Richard earned an MBA degree at Harvard University. For the next 17 years he was associated with the Doble Engineering Company near Boston. He was thereafter employed by the Hartford Steam Boiler Inspection and Insurance Company in Connecticut. Now retired in Bloomfield, Connecticut he continues to work as a consultant for the latter concern which activity took him on an extensive trip in southeast Asia in 1991 and in 1992 on several trips to Mexico.[38]

The King crew originally had a rated bombardier whose name was Richard Smith. Before leaving Avon Park he was reassigned and replaced by a gunner who would drop the bombs; the position came to be called the toggelier. This was not uncommon at the time since the Eighth had squadron formations releasing their bombs, not by bombsight, but on the bomb release of the squadron leader. The crew replacement in that position was a combat veteran, S/Sgt. Robert E. Pyne, who came from Oakland, California. Pyne had served a combat tour in the Mediterranean Theater and had flown 80 missions as a gunner. He had been returned to the States and had an assignment as a gunnery instructor. He told the King crew that this bored him and he volunteered for another combat tour. One member of the King crew said Pyne never expressed or in anyway indicated fear in combat. On the contrary, Pyne would never don his flak suit and would wait until he saw flak before he would even put on his flak helmet. The records reflect that Pyne received a wound on his first mission with the King crew but there is no corresponding record that he received a Purple Heart.[39] Myron recalled that he was wounded and is sure that Pyne never received the Purple Heart. He said, "We were so busy flying missions the matter was probably forgotten and knowing Pyne, he probably could have cared less." The crew lost track of Pyne after the war and recent efforts to locate him ended with information from the Department of Veterans Affairs that he died May 19, 1979.[40]

Ernest S. Pavlas was the King crew engineer and top turret gunner. Myron recalled Ernest was a most proficient engineer on whom they relied to keep them in the air. He said that when he was off duty Ernest palled around with Pyne. Pavlas was from Caldwell, Texas and after the war was in the insurance business in Houston. He later purchased an insurance company and in 1955 moved to Austin. He and his wife had three daughters and he is now retired, still living in Austin. On several occasions the author spoke to Ernest but he refused to discuss his military service. His daughter and son-in-law, Mr. and Mrs. Harold Perry of Richardson, Texas have been helpful but were unable to get Ernest to talk of his experiences with the King crew.

King's radio operator was Patsy DeVito of Long Branch, New Jersey. Like Pyne, he too is deceased, having succumbed to emphysema in February, 1990.[41] Myron recalled that Patsy said that his mother had made him speak Italian as a youth.

He said Patsy had a good sense of humor. Once while airborne and speaking on the interphone he said: "I wonder why they have those big fans on those four motors...you'd think rushing through cold air would keep the motors cool without them." After the war he worked on Government radar at Fort Monmouth, New Jersey and for several years at Rome, New York. His widow, Rosemary, still resides at Long Branch.

Philip A. Reinoehl, the ball turret gunner, came from Brazil, Indiana where he still makes his home. After he returned home from the war Philip was employed as an automobile mechanic but later became involved in the repair of farm equipment. He and his wife reared six children and identical twin foster daughters. He is now retired and resides on his own farm. He once visited Patsy in New Jersey, has stopped by to see Myron on his way to or from Florida and for awhile kept in touch with Richard Lowe and his wife.[42]

The waist gunner on King's crew was K. Hampton Speelman. He prefers to be called and addressed simply as "K." He was born in Michigan but lived most of his youth in Toledo, Ohio until his family moved to Fostoria, Ohio in 1940. "K" said that during his senior year in high school the Army Air Force offered a program for enlisting while still in school in the Enlisted Reserve Program. He passed the aviation cadet written examination, but failed the physical examination due to a perforated ear drum suffered in a wrestling match at school two weeks prior to the examination. He said he was later drafted when another physical examination determined that his ear had healed itself. He went to Keesler Field for basic training and still trying to make the Aviation Cadet program, he finally made it to the College Training Detachment at Wittenburg College in Ohio. While there the Cadet program was being cut back and he requested aerial gunnery school in preference to wherever else he might end up in the Army. "K" got his gunnery wings at Kingman, Arizona in the same class as Phil Reinoehl, and they were both sent to Florida where they ended up on Myron King's crew. After the war "K" studied engineering at the University of Toledo until he had to withdraw and go to work due to his wife's pregnancy. They went back home and he was employed in the ceramic laboratory of the Autolite Spark Plug manufacturing facility. He continued to be employed there for more than 35 years until his retirement in 1982 as an Engineering Supervisor. Since then he and his wife have traveled extensively and remain very busy. "K" does volunteer work for the American Association of Retired People (AARP), for a TAX-AID program assisting elderly and low income taxpayers, serves as President of a nursing home auxiliary, works as an instructor in an adult literacy program, tutors elementary school students and much more. He and his wife Rita have four children. Their service in their community is a fine record of good citizenship.[43]

George E. Atkinson, King's tail gunner, was probably the youngest member of the crew. He was born September 15, 1925 which made him just 19 by a few months when he flew combat. His home before the war was South Pasedena, California. After the war he got into construction work and eventually had his own construction business in Alaska. He still makes his home in Anchorage but winters at San Carlos, Mexico on the west coast of the Baja Peninsula. George does not like to write letters and prefers to use the telephone, which he does frequently. He has been enthusiastic in his assistance to the author and a good friend. His own personal experiences could not have been told in Chapter 19 without his recollections and the documents he made available.

After the King crew successfully finished their training at Avon Park they traveled to Hunter Army Air Field at Savannah, Georgia. There they were assigned to a new B-17 which they would ferry across the Atlantic Ocean to England. During their short stay in Savannah they were hauled from their beds one night because of a hurricane which was threatening the coast. The object was to evacuate those priceless aircraft to Shreveport, Louisiana where they would be out of harm's way. After the storm passed they flew back; Myron confessed that en route they buzzed his future wife's home in Nashville and his parent's home in Chattanooga. He admits that on the latter ferry job he almost went in Lookout Mountain. They ventured a little out of the way to Savannah but I am sure it had a positive morale impact on the folks in Tennessee. They say that confession is good for the soul; Myron also admitted that while in Basic in Arkansas he buzzed the Chapel at the college his future wife, Eleanor, attended. He said the noise of that Vultee Vibrator caught the attention of those attending the Chapel service.

They departed Savannah in a new B-17 headed for Maine on their way overseas and to combat. On the way up the east coast they had another opportunity to buzz ... this time it was Bill Sweeney's home in Pennsylvania. The first leg of their journey, after leaving Maine, was to Greenland. The late Fall weather almost snowed them in for the winter. They were told that they had only an eight percent chance of getting cleared out of there; they were grounded for ten days with very bad weather. Each day they watched an older pilot go out on a weather reconnaissance mission in a Mosquito bomber. Myron recalled that one day the pilot

Myron L. King and crew at Hunter AAF, Savannah, Georgia 1944. Standing left to right: Patsy DeVito - radio, R.E. Pyne - togglier, Ernest Pavlas - engineer, K. Speelman - waist, George E. Atkinson - tail, P.A. Reinoehl - ball. Kneeling left to right: W.J. Sweeney III - copilot, Myron L. King - pilot, Richard I. Lowe - navigator. Courtesy of George E. Atkinson.

returned from his mission and said, "There are old pilots, and there are bold pilots, but there are no old bold pilots."

After that lengthy delay they were cleared for the next leg of the trip to Meeks Field, Iceland. After King was told by Richard Lowe that they had passed the point of no return, they ran into a tremendous front with clouds towering thousands of feet above them with no way around or over them. He said when they hit that front the aircraft was flipped up virtually 90 degrees spilling all of the gyros on board, leaving him with a ball and bank indicator and a magnetic compass that was off about 35 degrees. The snow was so thick that the wing tips were obscured from his vision. Myron said they called Iceland for guidance and were told to go down to 300 feet and fly under the weather. From then on about every five minutes a disembodied voice from Iceland would give them a new heading. Myron said that years later when he was visiting Sweeney in New York they reminisced about that day over the North Atlantic. Using his acting skills entertaining Myron's children, Sweeney mimicked first himself and then the Iceland tower. Pretending to have a microphone he shouted "Iceland! Iceland! Tell us what to do!" then very calmly he assumed the role of the Tower, "B-17 – go down a little lower." With great passion Sweeney radioed back, "Iceland! What do you think this is, a sub? We're already in the water!" They did make it to Iceland safely that day, and Myron said all nine of them were kissing the ground before the propellers stopped turning. He claimed that ordeal was worse than any combat mission they flew in the months ahead.

I was far more fortunate when the Babcock crew crossed the Atlantic on the same route a month and a half earlier. There was already an accumulation of snow at Goose Bay, Labrador on October 1, our first stop. I will never forget my impression of Iceland. The temperature was cold, the weather cloudy, foggy and damp. Its terrain was dominated by gray and black boulders, a very depressing impression. As we flew east into the sun over the clouds the following morning I told the crew on the interphone: "I hope I never see that place again, unless I'm going the other way."

401st Bomb Group low squadron bomb strikes on a synthetic oil refinery at Sterkrade January 22, 1945. Note the snow and the black smoke in the MPI area to the lower left and late release bomb strikes to the right of the MPI and beyond. Courtesy of the National Archives.

The King crew delivered the B-17 to a depot in Wales and after several days at a replacement depot in that area they arrived at Deenethorpe in early November, 1944 and were assigned to the 614th Squadron.

On January 10 the King crew boarded the "Maiden" to bomb a fighter base at Euskirchen, west of Bonn, then on the western front.[44] The entire Eighth concentrated on rail facilities, bridges and airfields. That morning snow and high winds over Europe created havoc. The 401st bombed by Gee-H, but a break in the clouds permitted observation of our bomb strikes at the edge of the airfield and on an adjacent railroad and autobahn.[45] A bright note was the fact that only two of our aircraft had battle damage from German flak.[46] I previously commented that one man's "milk run" was or could have been another's catastrophe. One of those two damaged aircraft was "Hard Seventeen" with the crew of Lt. R.B. Thompson. Their crash landing in Belgium that day was one of the "Lucky Devil" yarns in Chapter 5. We must have been very fortunate that day since the overall losses were ten B-17s, evenly divided between the 1st and 3rd Air Divisions. That figure was further punctuated by more disaster with crash landings, bailouts and accidents.[47]

The "Maiden" took her new boys out again on January 13 to bomb a rail bridge at Maximiliansau. The 401st furnished the 94th CBW "B" Group led by Major Jere Maupin. The Triangle First provided 315 B-17s and 159 of those bombers dropped 477 tons of bombs on that Maximiliansau bridge.[48] The weather was unusually clear with visibility unlimited (CAVU), permitting visual bombing. Although the lead squadron's bombs landed beyond the target, both the high and low squadrons hit the MPI scoring a "shack."[49] The results were surprisingly good considering the fact that the 94th CBW lead was forced to swing wide at the IP to avoid turbulent prop wash from an interfering Bomb Group. This left the lead bombardier 94 seconds for his bomb run and probably had an adverse effect on those behind him.[50] A near miss was experienced by the crew of Robert B. Campbell on IN-J "Homesick Angel." They said a single B-17 from another Group had dropped its bombs over their formation, some of which fell through within feet of their aircraft.[51] I can really appreciate their fright; it also made me very uncomfortable when I had another bomber pass directly overhead with its bomb bay doors open and its "eggs" hanging there waiting to be dropped.

After flying five missions in eight days the King crew got some time off. While they were gone the "Maiden" went out on January 17 with the crew of Lt. Ken J. Hartsock. Frank Mendez, ball turret gunner for Ken, passed along the sad news of Ken's untimely death. In January, 1982 Ken was the manager of a Tuscon, Arizona bank when he was murdered during an attempted bank robbery. The perpetrators, two brothers, both had atrocious criminal records. A news account reported that Ken was stabbed to death after coming to the aid of a female teller who had been stabbed ten or more times. They described Ken, then 63 years of age, as a "good man" and "like a father" to those who knew him well.[52] The mission on January 17 with the Hartsock crew was to Paderborn. Some of the Eighth's effort that day was back to strategic targets with the 3rd Air Division hitting oil refineries at Hamburg and Harburg. The 1st Air Division remained committed to tactical work. A force of 397 Fortresses, including those from the 401st, hit the marshalling yards at Paderborn; another Group bombed a rail viaduct at Bielefeld/Schildesche.[53] The Paderborn target was actually a secondary target with the primary at Altenberken passed up because of solid undercast. Bombing was done by PFF and the results were not observed. Crews that day said the mission was a "milk run." [54]

By January 21 the King crew was ready to go back to work again and the "Maiden" was ready to provide the transportation. The 401st was assigned a tank park as its target at Aschaffenburg southeast of Frankfurt am Main. Before the bomb run the "mickey" and Gee equipment on the lead and deputy lead aircraft were found to be inoperative, which required J.J. Brown, the high squadron leader, to take over the bomb run at the last minute.[55] A complete cloud cover obscured the target and the Group did a PFF run on the town's marshalling yards. Major D.G. McCree led the 94th CBW "C" Group with 36 aircraft. No flak or enemy opposition was experienced.[56] The 1st Air Division force totaled 379 aircraft with 257 of that number pounding Aschaffenburg with 756 tons of explosives. Only one 1st Air Division aircraft was lost that day though the 3rd Air Division lost six at Mannheim.[57]

They were up again the following day; this time to bomb the synthetic oil refinery and chemical works of the Ruhr-Chemie A.G. at Sterkrade. The 401st put up the lead and low squadrons for the 94th CBW "A" Group with Major Eric de Jonkheere as Air Commander. The lead squadron bombed visually while the low used Gee-H with a visual assist.[58] Actually, the Gee-H operation turned visual with only three minutes before bombs away. The lead bombardier saw the southernmost corner of two buildings in the target area and synchronized on them. All ships salvoed hitting the MPI very well.[59] Bombing results were excellent.[60] There was heavy flak at Sterkrade with 20 B-17s of those two squadrons damaged.[61] Five of the 167 aircraft of the 1st Air Division were lost at Sterkrade.[62] The flak there was classed as moderate at bomb release continuing for five minutes with accurate clusters.[63]

It was the last mission for the King crew with the "Maiden" for the month of January. The King crew was with the Group on January 28 to Cologne's marshalling yards flying "Shark Tooth." It was the 200th mission for the Group!. In February we celebrated the achievement with a huge party. The leading VIP guest was none other than Lt. Gen. James H. Doolittle, the 8th Air Force Commander. There were speeches followed by music and entertainment in Hanger #1 along with refreshments: 1,000 gallons of beer and 5,000 American hot dogs![64] The King crew finished up the month flying that grand old girl "Chute the Works" to Bad Kreuznach on January 29.

Notes for Chapter 13
1. Closway, Gordon R. 614th Squadron History, Summary of Events, January, 1945
2. Bowman, Martin W. Castles in the Air p. 180
3. Maslen, Selwyn V. 614th Bombardment Squadron (H): Squadron History p. 119
4. Freeman, Roger A. The Mighty Eighth War Diary p.412-413
5. National Archives, Suitland Md. Reference Branch, Record Group 18, Mission Reports, 401st Bombardment Group (H)
6. Bowman, Harold W. & Selwyn V. Maslen, Bowman's Bombers p. 60

7. Freeman, see 4 above p. 413
8. Maslen, see 3 above
9. Freeman, see 4 above p. 412
10. Enclosure to letter, Allen H. Crawford to author March 30, 1992
11. Letter, Edwin R. Cranz to author April 15, 1991
12. Enclosure to letter, Russell L. Aufrance to author February 27, 1991
13. See 5 above
14. Freeman, see 4 above p.415
15. Ibid.
16. Photocopy of personal log of Nathan Picker furnished as enclosure to letter, Norman L. Sisson to author February 13, 1991
17. Bowman & Maslen, see 6 above p. 60
18. Freeman, see 4 above p. 416
19. Maslen, see 3 above p. 120
20. Freeman, see 4 above p.417
21. Maslen, see 3 above p.120
22. Freeman, see 4 above p.417
23. Maslen, Selwyn V. 614th Squadron: Crews - Missions - Aircraft p. 78
24. Freeman, see 4 above p. 417
25. Freeman, see 4 above p. 418
26. Maslen, see 3 above p. 121
27. See 16 above
28. Enclosure to letter, Norman L. Sisson to author February 12, 1992
29. Ibid.
30. Baton Rouge, Louisiana Advocate October 22, 1989
31. Letter, Norman L. Sisson to author February 12, 1992
32. Ibid.
33. Letter, Norman L. Sisson to Ralph W. Trout August 5, 1987
34. See 31 above
35. Ibid.
36. Ibid.
37. Interview of Myron L. King by author at Nashville, Tennessee June 9, 1992
38. Letter, Richard I. Lowe to author September 16, 1991
39. Closway, see 1 above, Air Operations November, 1944
40. Telephone call by author to Regional Office, Department of Veteran Affairs, Atlanta, GA, September 4, 1991
41. Telephone conversation, Mrs. Rosemary DeVito and author October 2, 1990
42. Telephone conversation, Philip A. Reinoehl and author October 4, 1990
43. Telephone conversation, K. Hampton Speelman and author August 26, 1990 and an undated letter, Fall 1990, Speelman to author.
44. Maslen, see 3 above p. 121
45. Ibid.
46. Bowman & Maslen, see 6 above p. 60
47. Freeman, see 4 above p. 421
48. Freeman, see 4 above p. 423
49. Maslen, see 3 above p. 122
50. See 5 above
51. Ibid.
52. Tuscon, Arizona Daily Star January 9, 1982
53. Freeman, see 4 above p. 425
54. Maslen, see 3 above p. 123
55. See 5 above
56. Maslen, see 3 above p. 123
57. Freeman, see 4 above p. 427
58. Maslen, see 3 above p. 123
59. See 5 above
60. Maslen, see 4 above p. 123
61. Bowman & Maslen, see 6 above p. 61
62. See 5 above
63. Freeman, see 4 above p. 428
64. Bowman & Maslen, see 6 above p. 62

CHAPTER 14 —
A BIG DAY AT "BIG B"

From their entry into World War II Americans were single-minded in their determination to bring her enemies down to defeat. For many a symbol of their victory was to be the devastation of the enemy capital cities – Tokyo and Berlin. It became important for those of us in the Eighth who had chosen to be bombardiers to be able to say "I bombed Berlin." Other targets might have been tougher but "Big B" was the ultimate. I went there twice; the first time, February 3, 1945 was the special one for me. It turned out to be my last mission as a bombardier and it my last mission on the crew of Fred Babcock, who has remained my life-long friend. I remember that mission vividly, not just for these reasons, but also because it was such an awesome display of military air power. That day the sky over Berlin was as clear as a bell and I had the opportunity to see it all and still do my job – drop bombs on such a top-priority target. Many of us considered the bombing of Berlin that day to have been a historic mission.

Roger A. Freeman provides a background to the operation on February 3, 1945. "To assist the Russian offensive, attacks were planned on Berlin, Leipzig, Dresden and other places in the east where disruption to communication centres might hamper retreat and reinforcement. With dismal weather prevailing it was not until February 3rd that an opportunity arose to implement such a mission. Berlin, which had not had a visit in strength from the Eighth Air Force for two months, was selected, the large Tempelhof marshalling yards being the primary objective for the 1,003 B-17s of the 1st and 3rd Divisions..."[1]

The targets had a very important strategic purpose as pointed out by Freeman, but Martin W. Bowman wrote of another agenda to this strategy. "...Marshal Zhukov's Red Army was within 35 miles of Berlin and the capital was jammed with refugees fleeing from the advancing Russians. The raid was designed to cause the authorities as much havoc as possible..."[2]

That day the 1st Air Division task force was led by Col. Lewis E. Lyle, the C.O. of the 379th Bomb Group at Kimbolton. The 401st put up 36 Fortresses to make up the 94th CBW "B" Group with Capt. J.R. Locher as the Air Commander flying with Captain Bill Riegler in the left seat.

The 614th Squadron put up the high element in each box.[3] My crew, Lt. Fred H. Babcock's, led the high element in the lead squadron with Lt. R.B. Richardson on our left and Lt. R.E. Moran on our right. The low squadron high element was led by Lt. G.H. St Aubyn with Lt. Wylie White on his left and Lt. Dave Stauffer on his right. In the high squadron the high element was led by Lt. R.B. Thompson with Lt. Ken J. Hartsock on the right wing and Lt. Myron King in the "Maiden" on the left wing.[4] (Appendix 6)

The Babcock crew that day was flying that grand old lady warrior "Chute the Works" that went down on the morning of March 25 in the Stauffer story chronicled in Chapter 12.[5]

Takeoff at 6:55 A.M. that morning in the darkness was normal under excellent weather conditions. Squadron and Group assemblies over the Cottesmore Buncher were done in fairly good time. There was some delay, possibly due to the fact that it was the first assembly in darkness in some time and with some newer less-experienced crews. The Group departed the Buncher on time, flying the briefed course over England. We made control point #1 on time but were about five miles south, caused by Groups jammed up on the Division assembly line as the Division left England at Folkstowe. Our correct position, number eight, in the column, was obtained a few miles out over the Channel. The 1st followed by the 3rd Air Division was on course but six and seven minutes late at control points #2 and #3 respectively. As the bombers made landfall with the European Continent they encountered meager flak and began to have between four and six-tenths cloud coverage which increased as they moved across Germany. Just before they reached the IP, Buckeye Blue, weather reconnaissance aircraft reported bombing could be done visually. Our bombing altitude was to be 26,600 feet. The temperature there was a minus 43 degrees with a 75 mph wind from the west.[6]

The mission was a public relations officer's dream! There were more than 1,000 Fortresses creating a bomber stream that stretched continuously from the Dutch coast all the way to the target, Berlin, the capital of Hitler's Third Reich. There were over 500 fighters in the air to escort the heavies with their bomb load totaling 2,266 tons, constituting the largest single raid by the Eighth on a single target![7]

I remember the trip to the IP as routinely uneventful but was very conscious of the ten-tenths cloud cover as we headed into eastern Germany. The meteorologists had a banner day! They said there would be clouds all the way but that there would be clear skies for the bomb run. Sure enough, as we turned north to the IP and onto the bomb run from the south there was the most unusual break in the clouds. There was a clear swath along the briefed bomb run, wider than the city of Berlin, all the way north of the city. It was not just cloudless, there was no undercast or haze; it was as clear as it could ever be, just plain old CAVU. Our navigator, Allen H. Crawford said, "It was like a giant hand reached down and took a handful of clouds away right over Berlin so we could see to bomb..."[8]

As we flew northeast on the 42 mile bomb run the sky became increasingly black with exploding shells. Al stood just behind me and watched the unfolding panorama before us during those crucial minutes. He wrote, "As the bomber stream turned north on the bomb run I recall the flak was very intense. Our Group leader was very 'battle wise' and pulled our Group up close to the Group ahead of us. They took most of the track flak barrage as we passed over the drop point at 11:13 A.M."[9] Officially the flak was reported as follows: "moderate to intense, accurate for altitude and deflection, appearing to consist of barrage, which became continuously pointed type fire two minutes before bombs away and tracked formation for approximately six minutes."[10] On that bomb run we saw B-17s drop beneath us, some mortally wounded like one I saw on its back falling like a stone, and others struggling for control and survival as they had left their formation. There was also the sobering sight of parachutes drifting beneath us toward the German capital city below. There was so much going on, and Al was constantly banging on my shoulder to point out one horrifying sight after another. I finally dropped our bombs, and our B-17 lifted perceptively with the lightened load and Fred got us the hell out of there. From the IP to the target it was an uncharacteristic bomb run with the visibility described. The bombardier picked up the Tempelhof Airdrome to the right of course, then located the marshalling yards in front of the target, and finally, the target itself. The assigned MPI was covered by smoke from the previous bombing and was not seen. Using the RAF grid the bombardier was able to synchronize on a point short of the target, and then roll the indices (on the bombsight) back to point it at the assigned MPI. He then double checked the rate (the horizontal crosshair of the bombsight) by using the target photograph and locating points on a line with the MPI and outside the smoke area. The AFCE (Automatic Flight Control Equipment) worked OK, and bombs were salvoed by the lead B-17 of the lead squadron with the lead squadron dropping with a 150 foot intervolemeter setting. The high and low squadrons met with the same conditions and bombed in like manner also using the RAF grid to bomb through smoke. Although the high squadron strikes were unobserved, the lead squadron observed strikes in the smoke which covered the target, and the low squadron bombs were seen to fall right into the smoke over the MPI.[11]

Al wrote of one event that I had almost forgotten as he described that bomb run. "I remember seeing a couple of Forts going down...I can still feel the sigh of relief as we left Berlin and headed for England. We had been on the return leg about one and a half hours and we could still see the bombers on their way to Berlin. About this time a P-51 flew in close to our left wing, gave us a 'thumbs up' sign and, while sitting there, looking at us in our bomber, he disappeared in a mighty explosion, leaving only debris falling from the sky..."[12] He was there one moment and then a second later he was gone. That night I wrote a V-Mail letter home to my family. I was still mind boggled by what I had been through that day. I am afraid my words were a violation of censorship rules, but it was as though I had to tell them something of what I felt. I said, "We worked today. Someday I hope to tell you of the events.

It was the most thrilling thing I have ever participated in. Tomorrow it will be in your papers. It was more than likely on the radio tonight. It was a super colossal show."[13] (Appendix 5) Newspapers at the time furnished a spectacular account of the remarkable events of the day:

"Berlin, black heart of Nazi Germany was still in flames last night from the 2,500 tons of high explosives and incendiaries which upward of 1,000 Flying Fortresses of the U.S. Air Force cascaded at midday on military, governmental and communication targets in the center of the capital.

"In Berlin at the time were 3,000,000 starving shivering refugees, who fled before the advancing Red Army from reconquered Poland, from Silesia and Brandenburg. Swedish correspondents declared in midnight messages that thousands of these wretched people, unable to find shelter from the bombs, were killed where they stood...The devastating attack on Berlin was over in three quarters of an hour.

"It was an awesome climax to a procession of bombers and fighters, which set out in mid-morning, eventually miles over sea and continent."

Another story on the same page as the above reported that Colonel Lewis E. Lyle of the 379th Bombardment Group (H) at Kimbolton had led the entire task force to Berlin on February 3. The article contained some remarks by Colonel Lyle:

"Over Berlin there was no cloud at all when we arrived and it was a real treat to see the German city so clearly..." His bombardier, Major Edwin H. Millson said, "We approached the capital through thick cloud and ran into a sea of clear weather." Col. Lyle remarked that as he turned from the far side of Berlin he could see the rest of the Groups dropping their bombs, 'and it looked like as if someone with a giant rake was tearing the heart out of the city'...He was a quarter of the way back to England before he passed the tail end of the great procession of outward-bound bombers.'"[14]

Vincent Browne, the engineer on the crew of the late Ken Hartsock, is also deceased. His wife, Carolyn, wrote to say how much Vincent loved the Air Force and the B-17. On another note she furnished the following story of that day which I know many of my old comrades will relate to. She said, "One of the crew urinated in the bomb bay and the doors became frozen open. He went out and manually closed it, then took his gun and was ready to kill 'the son of a bitch who pissed in the bomb bay.' Over the years no one identified the culprit but I never tired of hearing that story..." As all B-17 crew members know it was mighty cold in that open bomb bay five miles over Berlin and to close those doors manually was not as easy as it might sound.[15]

The 401st did not come out of that sky unscathed with four of its bombers receiving major damage and 17 others minor damage from flak. The Mission Summary Report also has the following brief statement: "A/C 44-6508 failed to return having notified leader over target he was heading for Russia." The "Maiden" and the King crew were in trouble and before the day was over they were listed as MIA.[16] From "Missing Crew Reports" there were some additional details, "First Pilot Myron L. King in A/C 44-6508 was last seen over Berlin headed east as the formation turned north...moderate to intense flak burst caused failure of two engines although no fire started...Two engines out, according to the pilot, who called the Group Deputy Leader on VSF, stating he was going to Russia...Aircraft under control...Last sighted last contacted by radio Capt. Robert L. Stelzer O-461320."[17] Captain Stelzer was the 401st Deputy Group Leader that day but does not recall the above. By way of explanation he wrote, "I always felt that when you went over Berlin it was a special kind of mission. This was were all the trouble originated, and at the same time scared the hell out of you. I honestly cannot recall much of anything about the mission of February 3, 1945. I do remember on one of the Berlin missions we were briefed that the flak would barely reach 25,000 feet and we were about 26,000 to 27,000 feet and it was bursting a couple of thousand feet above us. When you are getting shot at like we were when you flew over Berlin – I am not sure your brain thought much more than how the hell can I get thru this one; and as soon as you landed at Deenethorpe you tried to forget all the unpleasant part of the mission."[18]

The loss of the "Maiden" and her crew also meant a shattered record for the 614th

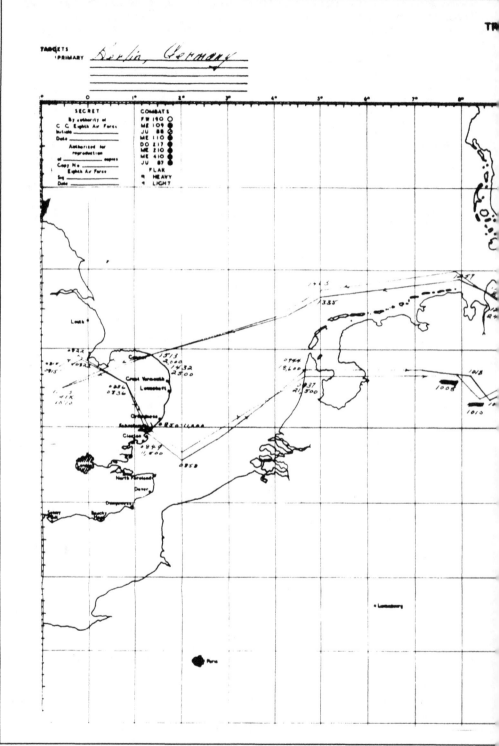

Track Chart for the mission to Berlin February 3, 1945. Note the preparer incorrectly listed the date as January

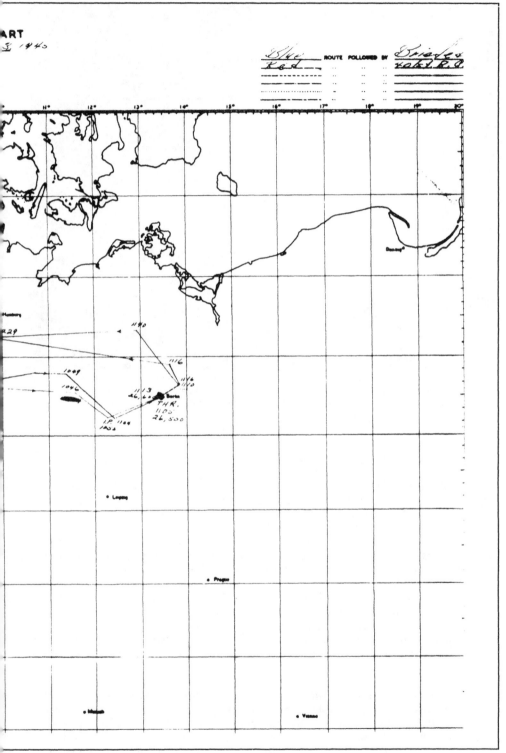

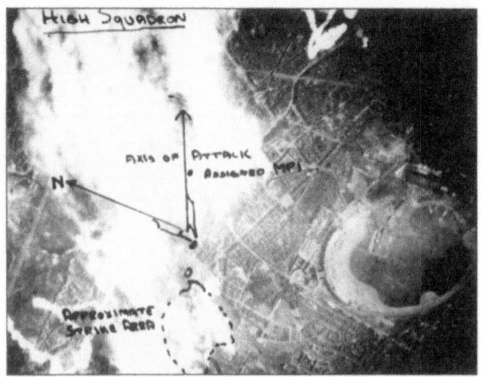

Two photographs of the 401st on Berlin February 3, 1945. The targets were the Tempelhof Marshalling Yards and German Government buildings in central Berlin. Left photo of the high squadron bomb strikes shows a large circular area to the right which is the Tempelhof Airdrome much as it appears on maps today. Right photo shows the bomb strikes of the lead and the low squadron. Bombing into the smoke from the strikes of the lead and the low squadron. Bombing into the smoke from the strikes of many bomb groups ahead of the 401st hampered accuracy. Courtesy of the National Archives.

Squadron which had had a remarkable record of 31 consecutive missions without a loss.[19]

Don Anderson, tail gunner on Hartsock's crew, provided his recollection of Berlin that day, "While we were on the bomb run, an anti-aircraft battery was tracking our formation. The burst of flak that most concerned me were very close to ...the tail section where I was the gunner. At first, I turned my head to protect my eyes but then realized that if it hit, the flak would go right through my head, so I decided I might as well watch. It dawned on me that as soon as the bombs were released the formation was to turn...and we would fly directly into the flak. Death seemed inevitable, but my feeling was not fear so much as resignation. Would the next burst of flak bring us down, or would it be the one after that? Several B-17s were hit, and many were going down. We hoped to see parachutes, but realized that anyone bailing out was supposed to free fall as far as possible to help avoid being shot by German fighters. Suddenly, it was bombs away, and at that instant the flak bursts stopped. We banked away and returned home safely, but what a trip it was. I was 19 years old."[20] Don Anderson furnished a newspaper article which included other details of that devastating raid. It said in part:

"...reports streamed in yesterday of a city left burning and staggering while the sound of Red Army gunfire rolled across the level eastern approaches to the German capital...Photo interpretations of the raid by the 8th, however, revealed smashing blows dealt military and government offices, railroad yards, and industrial objectives in the heart of the city. Pictures showed fire and smoke in almost unbroken mass over an area two miles long and one mile wide...The Air Ministry received eight direct hits

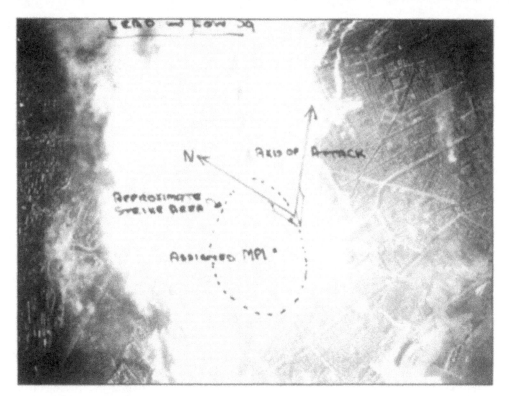

and other buildings surrounding the Ministry, including the Reich Chancellery, Ministry of Propaganda and Gestapo Headquarters were smothered under 18 concentrations of high explosives. Five railroad stations were hit and the Tempelhof marshalling yards and nearby Tempelhof Airdrome suffered some damage. The Deutsche Gas Works got a terrific blow...T/Sgt. Clifford Whipple, radio operator from Syracuse New York, reported this item about Saturday's deluge of TNT: 'before we left Germany I tuned in to a propaganda broadcast from Berlin. The announcer said that every man, woman, and child is out fighting the flames, with the Russians only 70 kilometers away...'"[21]

"Skip" Aufrance, Lt. Wylie White's bombardier, said that on the way home from Berlin they noticed a B-17 flying low over the North Sea. Concerning that incident he wrote as follows: "The unidentified B-17 was seen to ditch and sank in a few minutes still in eyesight of the European coast. We dropped out of formation and, after searching for several minutes, we spotted a life raft with about five men in it who were frantically waving as we flew over them. We radioed the British air-sea rescue unit and while waiting for it to come we watched out for possible German units to come out; none came. After a few minutes two rescue units came and dropped smoke flares to determine wind direction and speed. One plane was carrying a boat underneath. It dropped down close to the water going toward the raft and dropped the boat. The boat stopped a few feet from the raft. After the flyers got into the boat and got it started, the two rescue planes flew low over the boat to show the boat the direction to travel...We flew in a northwest direction as indicated by the planes and, after a few minutes, we spotted a larger boat heading toward the flyers...When returning to the States after completing my missions I was on a ship, primarily with flyers. While telling each other our war stories, one man in one of the groups heard me tell of this incident and said he was one of the flyers on the raft. He, of course, was most profuse in his thanks."[22] "Skip" also provided a postscript to the story of the February 3 Berlin raid; this story from an eyewitness on the ground that day in Berlin. He said that after the war while he was a student at Bowling Green

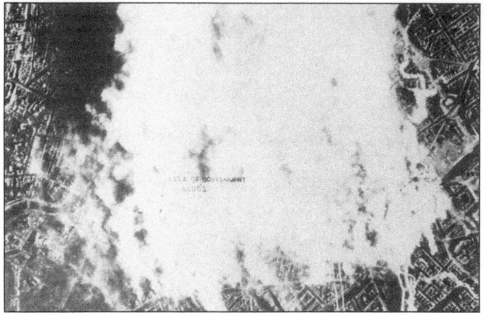

Berlin February 3, 1945. Note the targeted area of the German Government buildings.

State University in Ohio, he met the wife of a fellow student. He said she was in the first group of German war brides to arrive in the U.S. after the war. "She had been the secretary for one of the Mayors of Berlin. After she eventually heard that I had been a flyer in the 8th Air Force, we discussed the war. She said the February 3 bombing of Berlin was very vivid in her memory and the worst she experienced during the war."[23]

What happened to the "Maiden" and her crew? This is a saga which now can be told in its entirety principally by Myron, his crew and others. The following, however, is mostly from an interview with Myron at Nashville in 1992 which has been confirmed by others on his crew with the help of Government records.

Myron recalled: "After bombs away over Berlin the "Maiden's" number two engine was running away and I kept trying to feather it without success. Philip Reinoehl, in the ball turret, reported something strange coming off the wing behind the ailing engine. It looked to me like a black rubber mattress was wrapped around the wing and appeared to be six to eight inches thick. I realized it was oil from that engine, which in the sub zero temperature exposed to the 150 mph wind had frozen; what Reinoehl reported were frozen chunks which had broken off. I had about given up on getting the prop feathered when it began to slow and I was able to feather it before it wrenched itself off. Then the number four engine began running away but I was able to feather it without any problem. I was sure we could not make it back to England due to the strong wind and did not want to go to Sweden for fear we might not be able to make it across the Baltic Sea. Further, I knew we were within 40 miles of the Russian front and thought heading east was the best option and the most logical choice to get us back to England faster than going through the process of being interned in neutral Sweden. From our bombing altitude with a particularly strong tail wind I radioed our intention to go east and began to let down, picking up speed to 250 M.P.H. indicated, and we were past the front lines in ten minutes and over Russian occupied Poland. "Several American fighters checked out our condition and waved goodbye as they turned back toward Berlin. We had coordinates for an emergency field that had been given to us at briefing, but when we reached that location we found nothing but a plowed field. We continued on east with the belief that we would there find an adequate landing field which would accommodate a heavy bomber. We flew around the city of Warsaw and were horrified at what we saw below. Virtually every building in the city seemed destroyed with only some walls and chimneys still standing. The runway of the airport was completely bombed out, and we could observe civilians filling in bomb craters in the grass parallel to the runways for future use as a runway; it was not anywhere near ready for us to land there. As we continued to search for a place to land we observed the roads into the city from the east were jammed with refugees, mostly on foot but some with carts, all trying to get back into that devastated city." (Future chapters will provide a link between the crushing of Warsaw and the fate of Myron King) Myron said that as they looked down on that beleaguered city "we little realized we were flying right into a political hornet's nest."

As they circled the city the "Maiden" suddenly found herself in the gun sights of a Soviet fighter. Myron said, "The Russian made three passes, and I later learned from him personally how close we were to having been shot out of the sky. The pilot told me that on each pass he had taken up the slack on the triggers to his 20 millimeter cannon and questioned himself: 'Nazi?' and then again to himself: 'No, American.' On his third pass I fired a flare and lowered my wheels; this convinced the pilot that we were Americans.

"He escorted us to his base, a very small fighter field which was nothing more than a plowed field, very short, with ditches about every ten feet or so across the landing area covered with ice. "I knew we had to get down and I threw caution to the wind. I ordered the crew to assume their positions in the radio room in accordance with practiced ditching or crash landing procedures; there they sat on the floor crammed body to body from the bomb bay bulkhead facing rear. Since the landing area was very short I was determined to use every bit of it and set the aircraft down just inside the fence at the edge of the field. After we hit the ground and began to roll across the field there were these very loud explosion-like noises. It turned out to be broken ice from the ditches we crossed which flew up hitting the underside of the "Maiden." I was very concerned at the time that the force of the ice might damage the flaps. Actually, I think the force of the ice may have helped slow us down sufficiently to bring us to a stop before the end of the field."[24] They had landed! The "Maiden" with the stamina of the will to survive, on only two of her engines, had carried them across Poland to a base southeast of Warsaw called Kuflevo, near Minsk Mazowiecki. They were about 600 miles from Berlin. They had crossed a battle-torn land recently reoccupied by our ally, the Union of Soviet Socialist Republics.

In the work on this book I have read stories of other bomber crews cast into similar situations as the King crew, and even seen pictures depicting the hand of friendship of members of the Red Army. I have also come across other stories of their deep suspicion of the presence of downed American airmen and even brutal treatment without any basis for such actions. The King story isn't so much about brutality by the Russians, but their treatment of the crew falls into that category. I am sorry to say that our own military and our own country ignored the way they were treated by the Russians. Our military toadied to their officials who used their perverted sense of statecraft to disguise their real intentions; their actions in complete disregard for legal and human rights of the individual.

Notes to Chapter 14

1. Freeman, Roger A. _The Mighty Eighth_ p. 208
2. Bowman, Martin _Castles in the Air_ p. 183
3. Maslen, Selwyn V. _614th Bombardment Squadron (H) Squadron History_ p. 127
4. National Archives, Suitland Reference Branch Record Group 18, Mission Reports 410st Bombardment Group (H)
5. Maslen, Selwyn V. _614th Squadron: Crews - Missions – Aircraft_ p.4
6. See 4 above
7. Maslen, see 3 above
8. Enclosure to letter Allen H. Crawford to author March 30, 1992
9. Ibid.
10. See 4 above
11. Ibid.
12. See 8 above
13. V-Mail letter, author to Mrs. H.G. Menzel February 3, 1945
14. Newspaper clippings from unknown publications on dates unknown from personal scrapbook of Allen H. Crawford loaned the author during 1992
15. Letter, Carolyn C. Browne to author January 27, 1991

16. *See 4 above*

17. *National Archives, Suitland Reference Branch, Microfilm #4474 Record Group 92, MPCR #12213*

18. *Letter, Robert L. Stelzer to author January 19, 1992*

19. *Bowman, Harold W. & Selwyn V. Maslen* Bowman's Bombers *p.63*

20. *Letter, Donald S. Anderson to author August 14, 1991*

21. *Newspaper clipping from Stars and Stripes published in England on a date unknown furnished author as enclosure to letter from Donald S. Anderson August 14, 1991*

22. *Enclosure to letter, Russell L. Aufrance to author February 27, 1991*

23. *Ibid.*

24. *Interview of Myron L. King by author at Nashville, Tennessee June 9, 1992*

CHAPTER 15 — HOSPITALITY FROM OUR ALLY?

The "Maiden" and her crew were safe, on the ground, in Poland. As it turned out for all of them, the war was over. They still had much to do and a long way to go. They found themselves on a dirt field in the middle of nowhere, a land fought over several times and just recently a battleground taken from the German Army by the Russians.

Richard Lowe said they got out of the aircraft and were soon surrounded by many people, military and civilian, none of whom spoke a word of English. Through gestures they managed to convey the message that they were all very thirsty for a drink of water. Richard said they were each quickly provided with a tumbler full...of vodka! Thinking it to be water he took a big swallow of what was his first taste of vodka. "What a shock to take a large swallow only to discover the truth."[1]

The rest of this chapter was furnished during an interview with Myron L. King June 9, 1992 unless otherwise documented. He said that the crew was taken to an underground headquarters for the air base, an earthen room supported by timbers which reminded him of motion pictures which depicted an underground command post in World War I trench warfare. The Russians sent for a high-school girl who could speak a little English to act as an interpreter for them. Myron explained, through this girl, who they were and how they happened to be there. The Russians then became very cooperative, particularly after they were told that they had just bombed Berlin. There was a radio communications system in this underground room which was in constant use. It was his understanding that they were trying over and over to get clearance from their superiors to allow King to fly to Lublin, Poland where the Russians said they could get one hundred percent octane fuel for their aircraft. During the conversation the Russians said something to the young girl and then began to giggle among themselves while the girl blushed and was obviously embarrassed. They then learned that the Russians had asked her to find out if Americans had "front-line wives" and, if so, they would provide them with female companionship for the night. Myron said that he politely refused the offer, for the entire crew, much to the disappointment of Sgt. Pyne.

He said they were billeted separately in small homes with Polish families. These were square structures with thatched roofs and thatched walls which were covered with boards. Each had four rooms heated by a central fireplace which was open to all four rooms. Myron said the pilot who intercepted them, apparently the commander of the base, was billeted with him and he obtained a photograph of this officer who wrote his name, Jaskulsky Vikenty Ivanov, on the back of the photograph with his address in Kiev.[2]

"K" Speelman recalled the night of February 3 as follows, "We were taken to a nearby town, fed well, and treated to a dance. The band consisted of a banjo and an accordion and, although they were not good, they were eager to play for us. After the dance...Patsy DeVito and I were escorted to a Polish home, where members of the household were told that they should provide a place for us to sleep. Patsy and I spent a long time that night talking to those people through a neighbor who could speak English."[3]

Myron said that the next day Pavlas supervised some Russians who assisted him in making some repairs to the "Maiden," and he spent the time trying to get the Russians to obtain clearance for them to fly to Lublin. They never received a clearance and were never told why. He said that on their arrival the previous day he had given the names of each of the crew members to the Russians to notify the American Embassy that they were safe. No notification was ever given and their families were only advised by the U. S. Army that they were MIA.

By the afternoon of February 5 Pavlas had the "Maiden" airworthy and, with the entire crew on board, King began to pre-flight the engines. During the pre-flight a Russian C-47 buzzed the field and then landed, parking right next to the "Maiden." Sweeney left the aircraft while Myron finished shutting down the engines. As Myron left the "Maiden" and walked over to the Russian aircraft, Sweeney was already trying to converse with a Russian General. Standing between Sweeney and the General was a young man, about 19, who none of them had seen before, who was acting as an interpreter. Myron said that he and the rest of his crew believed the interpreter was with the Russian General. Through this interpreter they explained who they were and their desire to get back to England. They told the General that had been informed that Lublin would have a runway which could handle a B-17, and that they could get fuel there to continue their journey. The General said they would not be able to get a clearance for Lublin without giving any explanation; they later learned of a political development which had made Lublin a closed city.

Myron and his crew did not know that on July 22, 1944 radio Moscow announced from liberated Polish territory the formation of the communist directed Polish Committee for National Liberation. A few days later that committee moved from the town of Chelm near the Russian border to Lublin, about 40 miles west, where it became known as the Lublin Committee.[4] On December 31 the Lublin Committee announced that it was the Provisional Government of Poland, and on January 5 the Soviets recognized the new regime they had orchestrated.[5] This action by the Soviets triggered an international controversy with the other allies at the highest levels which might well be called the beginning of the "cold war." Myron was later made to understand that the reason they were not permitted to go to Lublin because it had been made a closed city for the protection of the new communist government from the Polish underground, loyal to the Polish Government in London and favored by the U. S. and the British. He said the Russians wanted them out of the area because the Lublin Government was then being moved along the road to Warsaw, only several miles from them at Kuflevo. Myron was accurate in this since it was at the Yalta Conference during the same week in February that Stalin referred to the puppet government of Poland as the Warsaw Government.[6] The appearance of the Russian General at Kuflevo was probably no accident; he probably was told to get them out of that area for security reasons.

The General said that he would escort them to Lida, in the Soviet Union, where they could get fuel and proceed to the American base at Poltava in the Ukraine. Myron recognized that a takeoff from the field at Kuflevo was a risk because it was a plowed field and very short for a B-17; he said it would be necessary to lighten the aircraft by removing heavy equipment and flying with only a skeleton crew to include the pilot, copilot, engineer and navigator. The General agreed to take the equipment and the rest of King's crew on his C-47. It was then late afternoon and the General said he would not fly at night. Myron said everyone around there helped, and there was much confusion as Americans and Russians raced back and forth between the two planes. Anything that could be moved – machine guns, flak suits, ammunition, were all put on the Russian plane along with the rest of Myron's crew. As Myron ran up his engines, a piece of cowling flew off one of the engines. He sent Pavlas back to the rear of the aircraft to be sure that if it had struck the tail it didn't do any damage. When he returned to the flight deck to report no damage he told Myron that the interpreter was on board. Myron said that at that moment Richard Lowe was coming to the flight deck from the nose to assume a crash position in the radio room for the takeoff. He told Richard to tell the interpreter to get off the B-17 and get on board the General's aircraft. But it was too late; the General had already taxied out ahead of them and there was no way to stop him. Myron said that he then made the decision to take the interpreter with them so that he could rejoin the General when they arrived at their destination.

The field they were using for a runway was about 2,000 feet long. By comparison, the main runway at Deenethorpe was 6,000 feet and the other two were 4,200 feet. Not only was Kuflevo field just dirt, it was also in the most impossible condition, with those irrigation ditches about every ten feet which were covered with ice. Myron said that the runway was a slight inclined plane, and he chose to takeoff downhill with a slight tail wind. He said, "I locked the brakes, broke the seal...had it in war-emergency before letting the brakes go, and she was shaking like a vibrating machine." At the end of the field they were not airborne and they hit the edge of a road which was raised. It acted like a ski jump, bouncing them into the air about 100 feet. Myron said that when they bounced off that road Sweeney instantly had the wheels up and the flaps down. He said they began to mush in, and their props actually hit the ground covered by about one foot of snow. They remained barely aloft as they crossed the neighboring field, and Myron had to turn her about 15 degrees to go between two groves of trees. He said, "Then with all that power she went up like a rocket...when she went up had to be for me the most thrilling point without duplicating another war...I was so thrilled to be flying."

As he pulled back on the throttles his elbow hit the interpreter who had apparently come forward during the takeoff. He told Myron that he wanted to go to London; that he had an uncle who lived there. Myron said that at that moment he knew they were in trouble. It had become clear that this person was not in the General's party. He said that his first thought was to put a parachute on him and throw him out of their B-17. During the flight the interpreter stayed to the rear of the bomb bay, in the radio room by himself. The crew kept an emergency bag in the radio room which included items of clothing. Apparently, due to the cold, the interpreter found clothing in that bag which he put on over his own clothing for warmth. This was a two-piece set of flying clothes consisting of a heavy A-10 alpaca and wool jacket and trousers.[7] These bore no rank or insignia of any kind and could not be considered to be a military uniform. Probably due to approaching darkness the General did not go on to Lida but landed at an air base at Szczuczyn, Poland. Szczuczyn is located about 105 air miles north northeast of Kuflevo. Myron recalled it was almost dark when they arrived there and the base trained lights on them to assist their landing. He said as he made his final approach, the very tall fir trees beside the base covered with snow were silhouetted against the darkening blue sky, creating a beautiful sight. He said he was reminded of that sight many years later by some of the scenes in the motion picture, Dr. Zhivago. He said this was a fighter-bomber base and some of the Russian-made aircraft looked as if they were built in someone's backyard. The runway was a lend-lease steel mat which was a definite advantage over Kuflevo. After they had come to a stop, a Russian in a small vehicle came to the aircraft and through gestures and some Russian words indicated all but the aircraft commander were to leave the aircraft. Through other gestures Myron was told where to park the "Maiden," and the vehicle departed with Sweeney, Lowe and Pavlas. After parking the aircraft he went through the aircraft and discovered the Russian interpreter seated at the radio operator's desk. Myron confessed that he didn't then know what to do about this person who called himself Jack Smith.

He had hoped that when Jack discovered they were not in England he would have just disappeared. Myron said Jack did not want to leave the aircraft but when he insisted, the young man accompanied him to the operations building where he found his entire crew waiting. The General and his party had disappeared and were not seen again that night. He described the building as a very large mansion with columns very similar in appearance to the White House in Washington, D. C. No one present could speak English and no one questioned who the interpreter was, apparently assuming that he was a member of the crew. Soon after their arrival ten places were set for them and they were fed and given vodka to drink. After the meal they were taken to a room where there were ten beds prepared for them to spend the night. Although the interpreter called himself Jack Smith, "K" Speelman, the waist gunner, recalled that some of the crew also referred to him as "Jocko."[8]

Myron said that he understood that as the aircraft commander he had the responsibility to decide what to do with this stowaway. Exercising this responsibility he made the decision to take Smith to Poltava where he would be dealt with by American authorities. He pointed out that after getting fuel on the following morning, they expected to fly directly to Poltava which was in Russia, not in the direction of England. Richard said that after they landed at Szczuczyn he confirmed that Jack Smith was not in the General's party, and that "was when the trouble began." He also said he did not know how that person came by the name Jack Smith, nor did anyone on the crew suggest that they take him with them.[9] In a statement signed by Richard Lowe in 1945 he said Jack Smith at Szczuczyn purposely attached himself to their crew. He thought Jack Smith was obviously trying to give the Russians the impression that he was a member of the crew but said, "As far as I know none of the crew gave him any active cooperation in this matter."[10] Myron said that during the evening of their arrival at Szczuczyn, February 5, while in their room Smith again expressed the desire to go to England to see his uncle. On the following morning the crew returned to their aircraft for the purpose of transferring their equipment and other belongings from the Russian C-47. They were then advised that the weather was not good enough for them to be given a clearance that day. It was the first of many days that they were told they could not depart because of weather conditions. It was obvious to the King crew that this failure to clear them for flying then and later was a ruse to detain them. That day Myron and Richard walked to a nearby village to look around. The rest of the crew remained behind and spent some time with some of the Russian pilots assigned to the base. Jack Smith had gone to a barbershop on another floor. While he was there the Russian General who escorted them from Kuflevo came in and saw him in the barbershop. After the General left, armed Russian soldiers entered the building and took Jack Smith away. Myron and Richard, unaware of this, returned to find the building guarded by soldiers with machine guns. The crew had been told they could not leave the building, and when Myron entered he was taken to another room by a Russian who wanted to know who was on their aircraft. Myron wrote down the name of each crew member and beside each name the position that person held on the "Maiden;" he included the name of Jack Smith as a second waist gunner. A Russian mechanic who spoke some English was brought into the room to act as an interpreter. He pointed to each name on the list and asked, "Amerikanski?" and to each Myron replied "Da" until he reached the name Jack Smith and then Myron said: "nyet." Still pointing to the name Jack Smith the interpreter inquired: "Polish?" and Myron indicated he did not know. The room had a large map on the wall and Myron was asked to point out where Jack Smith had boarded their aircraft. Myron explained that his nine-member crew on February 3 left England and after bombing Berlin lost two engines and flew to Kuflevo. On February 5 they left Kuflevo escorted by the Russian General and discovered Jack Smith, the General's interpreter, on board. Myron said after he realized that Jack Smith was not in the General's party, he decided to take him with them to the nearest American authorities for violation of regulations that prohibited unauthorized persons from riding in American military aircraft. Myron said Jack Smith was then brought into the room, and he had the impression that Jack Smith was "wise" to what was going on. As they removed Jack from the room he said to Myron, "Pray for me." Myron said he did not know the purpose of confronting him with Jack. That was the last time he or any of the crew ever saw of Jack Smith.

The following day Myron was returned to the same room and was asked to prepare a written account of the details furnished the day before, incorporating everything he knew about Jack Smith. Myron said at the end of the statement he wrote in big letters the word "FRIENDS." The Russian General arrived with another Russian who didn't speak English too well but carried an English-Russian dictionary with him. This interpreter then translated Myron's statement aloud as the General, who appeared grim at first, began to nod his head with approval after each sentence. After the complete statement was read, the General expressed his satisfaction with Myron's explanation and indicated that this was purely a local incident which he would handle at this base, and Myron should forget about it. During this interchange Myron said he and the General were having trouble communicating with each other. At one point the General, saying something in Russian, became very excited, drew his pistol and came around pointing it in Myron's back. Later they found another interpreter who explained that the General was only trying to say that Jack Smith would have shot Myron in the back.

Myron said that after Jack Smith was taken into custody on February 6, he and the crew were kept under armed guard in their room and their movements were very restricted for several days. They were later allowed some freedom of movement, but it was made clear that they were not going to be allowed to leave Szczuczyn. During the period of time they were confined to their room the entire crew on one occasion was told to strip for a shower. Those that did not want to take a shower were made to strip anyway. He recalled that Sweeney was quite concerned because he had several passports in his jacket pocket which Jack Smith had given him. King said he had been unaware of this. He said he does not recall whether these were passports or identity papers. He did not know what name or names appeared on these documents, does not recall seeing them and doesn't know what happened to them. He said it was obvious that the Russians arranged the shower as a ruse to search their clothing.[11]

"K" Speelman said, "A guard was placed near the door of our one room and our travel was restricted...I can honestly say that after a few weeks of this confinement I sure would have liked getting out of there." He recalled that some of the Russians shared their candy bars, cigarettes and tobacco.

He remembered one Russian navigator who later served as their interpreter who took them to a house which served as a theater where they saw a movie, "Jungle Book" in English with Russian subtitles.[12]

George Atkinson, the tail gunner, recalls the treatment and conditions in Poland to be more severe. He said, "Our quarters were a dirt hut with straw beds and the most filthy of conditions. I remember going to the outhouse and between holes there were feces that were there for days. I was scared but too young to panic. The armed security and internment lasted six weeks...I never thought I would see my family again, and after a month they were sure they would never see me again. I remember under armed guard helping Polish loggers pick up the limbs of trees and load them on wagons. The food was terrible, in my estimation, and I lost 30 pounds in six weeks. When we finally arrived at Poltava I remember Americans brought us roast beef, cheese, butter and bread and other foods of which I could eat about two bites and became sick."[13]

After several days at Szczuczyn the King crew was permitted to go out to the "Maiden" each day to run her engines. The Russians, to deter their takeoff, without a clearance, parked huge earth rollers in front of the aircraft. The rollers were used to compact the snow. Myron said that on the eastern front the Red Air Force was successful because they used these rollers on the runways rather than try to keep the runways clear by removing the snow with plows. Richard Lowe said that at one point they decided to leave without a clearance since they found they were able to roll the rollers away. They planned to leave the next morning but the base was fogged in. When they got to the "Maiden" later that day the rollers were returned along with a snow plow parked blocking their path. Richard said they found this amusing and kidded the Russians that their aircraft was so advanced that it could go backward. They must have believed them because the following day the Russians dug a big ditch behind the "Maiden," completely blocking her in.

He also recalled that when they regularly requested clearance to leave, they were always told "the weather is too bad." After some good weather arrived Richard said he remembers they would all look up at the sky and give their own weather report. He said George Atkinson would say, "Ten/tenths clear... LETS GO!"[14] Myron has a published photograph of the Russian rollers which were half again as tall as a man standing beside one of them. He said the Russians were so concerned that they would try to roll them away from the aircraft again that they stood them on end so they could not be moved without the use of heavy equipment.[14]

Myron said that after several weeks of this the Russians said they had received a telegram from Moscow which said they could leave whenever the weather permitted. When the weather became clear they then told Myron that the runway at Poltava was unserviceable.

During this time they were able on several occasions to visit a nearby town. During such visits Poles who could speak English questioned them about the welfare of one of their crew that had been wounded. Myron said that they would respond that they were all alright and none of them had been wounded. The Poles would then say that they had heard one of them had been shot. On another occasion the navigator on the General's C-47 came to their room in an advanced case of inebriation and pointed to the spot where Jack Smith's bed had been; he then pointed his forefinger and thumb as though it were a pistol, conveying to the crew that Jack had been shot. Myron said that they never had any information about the fate of Jack Smith. He opined that if he were executed by the Russians, they did not have to plant the story with Polish citizens unless they wanted the story spread around for some nefarious purpose. Myron said considering the facts in 1945 and the history of the Soviets since that time, he has some doubts that Jack Smith was executed.

With the advances of the Red Army it soon became apparent that the base at Szczuczyn would have to be moved further west. Much of the equipment, supplies and ground personnel had been moved by ground transportation. Conditions there became progressively worse during the moving period.

At Szczuczyn food was running out it got so bad that the crew broke out one of the

*"Maiden U.S.A. at Poltava, U.S.S.R. March 1945. This photograph was selected by Roger A. Freeman to represent the 401st Bomb Group in the plates depicting all Eighth Air Force Bomber and Fighter units in his book **The Mighty Eighth**. The artist, R.G. Smith, copied the paint work from that plate. USAF Photo Collection, Courtesy of NASM, Smithsonian Institution.*

"Maiden's" inflatable rafts and removed the K-rations for sustenance. The Russians had informed King that when their aircraft moved to the new base they would escort them, flying their own aircraft. They had told Myron there would be no runway at the new base and the mud was nine inches thick. Myron said there was no way he would land the B-17 wheels down on that kind of a field and if he were forced to accompany them, he would have to go in wheels up. The plans were then changed. The Russians were to fly to Lida and they went along. Myron said the weather was poor but they arrived at Lida without incident.

Lida is about 150 miles further east in the Soviet Union, almost due south of Vilnius, Lithuania. The King crew found things a lot different at Lida. They were provided an entire apartment for quarters with three Russians to wait on them. Undoubtedly those three were there to spy on the crew for the Narodnyi Kommissariat Vnutrennyhl Del (NKVD), the Soviet seurity police, later known as the Komitet Gosudarstvennoy Bezopasnosti (KGB). The King crew ate, not at the regular officer's mess, but with the Colonels and Generals. Further, every meal was a banquet and Myron said they were all treated like kings, no pun intended I'm sure. They were given a tour of the base at Lida and were permitted to examine the Russian aircraft; they in turn permitted the Russians to inspect the "Maiden." While at Lida she was closely guarded by Russian soldiers, and their quarters were provided with a guard armed with a machine gun. I am sure these sentries were not used to protect the "Maiden" or the crew but to insure they did not escape from Soviet custody. Nevertheless, Myron felt the treatment was "on the up and up" and that the Jack Smith incident had been forgotten. Finally, after five days at Lida they were cleared to fly to Kiev 300 miles to the southeast. Myron said that when they encountered no bad weather en route he opted to fly on to Poltava another 150 miles further southeast of Kiev.

They made the flight without incident and on March 18, 1945 were back on an American base after 43 days of being MIA and held against their will by the Russians. In fact, Federal regulations were amended to classify those held in captivity by an allied power as POWs.[15] Myron said that when they arrived at Poltava the Americans had no idea who they were. On that day Poltava cabled the Spaatz and Doolittle Headquarters, the United States Military Mission to Moscow (USMM) and the 401st Bomb Group of the arrival of the King crew, listing each member by name, rank and serial number. After furnishing the route they had flown and their stops en route the cable stated: "Aircraft needs minor repairs and will be flown to home station by crew within four days, weather permitting. No information on this aircraft or crew had been received from the Russians at this base although crew was advised by the Russians that Poltava had been notified promptly that they were safe."[16] It would appear that the ordeal of the King crew was over, but it wasn't; not by a long shot!

Notes to Chapter 15

1. Letter, Richard I. Lowe to author September 16, 1992
2. Interview, Myron L. King by author at Nashville, Tennessee June 9, 1992
3. Enclosure to undated letter, K. Speelman to author Fall, 1990
4. Harriman, W. Averell & Elie Abel *Special Envoy to Churchill and Stalin 1941-1946* p. 333
5. Ibid. p.323
6. Toland, John *The Last 100 Days* p. 14
7. Freeman, Roger A. *The Mighty Eighth War Manual* p. 245-246
8. See 3 above
9. See 1 above
10. National Archives, Washington, D.C., Record Group 334, Records of Interservice Agencies; Military Mission To Moscow 1943-1945, Cables in the Case of King, Myron L. Item #11 page two of statement, first page missing, signed Richard I. Lowe
11. See 2 above
12. See 3 above
13. Veterans Administration form 21-4138 Statement in Support of Claim signed George E. Atkinson dated 9/27/90 furnished author by George E. Atkinson.
14. See 1 above
15. Letter, D'Wayne Gray, Chief Benefits Director, Department of Veterans Affairs, to U.S. Senator Ted Stevens August 14, 1990 furnished author by George E. Atkinson
16. Cable Poltava to Spaatz, Doolittle, info Hill and 401 Bomb Group March 18, 1945 T-3114

CHAPTER 16 — POLTAVA, U.S.S.R. ... AND FRANTIC

During World War II the United States briefly used three air bases in the Soviet Union which were established as the Eastern Command under General Spaatz's USSTAF. The headquarters for the Eastern Command was located at Poltava, the largest of these three bases in the Ukraine. The purpose of the bases was to serve aircraft of the 8th Air Force in England and the 15th Air force in Italy when they flew missions deep into Germany and German-occupied territory in eastern Europe. The concept was designed to provide a place for bombers and fighters to land, refuel and rearm their aircraft, so they could fly another mission on their way back to their home bases; thus they became known as shuttle missions.

Shuttle missions were flown between June and September, 1944. The 401st Bombardment Group (H) never was called on to participate in them but I do recall hearing about a base at Poltava some time in early 1945. When we were briefed for missions to eastern Germany we were each given an American flag about five-by-seven inches, laminated in plastic to which a ribbon was attached to wear around the neck so that the flag hung on one's chest. On the reverse side of the flag was a message in Russian which identified the wearer as an American and an ally. The idea was to provide some measure of security for air crews who went down in Soviet-controlled territory. Rumors had persisted that some of our airmen had been killed or wounded and mistreated by Russian troops. About the same time I recall that we were told that if we ended up in Russian-occupied territory we should try to get to the American base at Poltava and they would arrange for transportation out through the Middle East. I had some idea that Poltava was in Iran and it wasn't until after the war that I learned that it is about 150 miles east of Kiev in the Soviet Ukraine.

The negotiations to obtain the three bases tells a story of American effort to initiate close collaboration with the Soviet Union, our ally in the fight against the original Axis Powers, Germany and Italy. That story provides a picture of deviousness and obstructionism by the Russian leadership in their dealings with outsiders, even wartime allies. It is the story of years on end of frustrations, where "yes" meant "maybe" and "maybe" should be understood to mean "nyet," Russian for "no." It is also a tale of inumerable incidents, many manufactured by the Soviets, and others based on partial truths or outright disinformation by the Russians to create an anti-American climate and discourage American presence inside Russian borders. The sad experience is important to this story because of the involvement of Poltava in what happened to Myron King and his crew while in Poland and Russia.

Efforts of the United States to assist the Soviet struggle against the forces of Adolf Hitler began with President Roosevelt before we became entangled in the war ourselves. In the summer of 1941 Roosevelt said it was of "paramount importance to the safety and security of America" that we provide all manner of munitions to Russia.[1] In the Spring of that year lend-lease legislation had been passed by the Congress,[2] in August the President ordered shipments of both fighter and bomber aircraft to the Soviet Union[3] and in November the Russians were declared eligible for lend-lease.[4] Such were the first steps toward what the President envisioned as Soviet-American collaboration.

In 1941 the War Department planning, even before our entry into the conflict, looked toward the uses of bases in the Soviet Far East to provide the United States with bases from which aerial bombing attacks could be made on an otherwise invulnerable Japan in an anticipated war with that country. General Henry H. Arnold, wartime commander of the AAF, in a letter to the White House said that should the "undesirable" war with Japan come, a promising way to victory would be through the "exercise of air power over the Japanese industrial system and the inflammable cities of Japan." It was pointed out that bases in the Vladisvostok, U.S.S.R. area put almost all of Japan within reach of American bombers.[5] Initial consideration of such a plan had to be masked out of respect for the Russian-Japanese Neutrality Treaty of 1941. The opening gambit we used was an effort to obtain information under the guise of surveying air and cargo delivery routes of war materials from Alaska across the Soviet Union to their fighting front against Germany.[6]

It was General Arnold himself who first proposed the idea of shuttle bombing. He suggested that President Roosevelt appeal to Marshal Stalin for terminal bases in Siberia, from which in a war with Japan we could bomb Japan from the Philippines and fly on to Siberia for a turn around mission. The U.S. General Staff opposed this approach to Stalin because they feared the plan would leak out and upset the ongoing U. S. peace negotiations with the Japanese.[7]

After Pearl Harbor and the entry of the U.S. into the war against both Japan and Germany, the Russians were still not willing to involve themselves in a war against Japan by providing us bases in their country from which we could bomb Japan.[8] They even saw through the facade of our seeking information on cargo and ferry routes across Siberia, rightly believing that our persistence was "for other than aircraft delivery purposes."[9] America was not deterred and our interest in bases near Vladisvostok remained constant, becoming more determined after our defeats in the Pacific placed the Japanese mainland far out of reach of our air power. However, in October, 1942 the Soviets approved an Alaskan-Siberia ferry route for aircraft but remained openly resistant to further collaboration, particularly in the Far East, which could have involved them in a war with Japan.[10]

After the German surprise attack on Russia in June, 1941 Stalin wasted no time begging for help from the United States. In July of that year he told Harry Hopkins, a close confidant of the President, that he would welcome American troops "on any part of the Russian front under complete control of the American Army." During the same month he also made a similar desperation overture to British Prime Minister Winston Churchill in seeking a British military force for the Russian Caucasus, north of the Caspian Sea.[11] In August, 1942 Churchill proposed an Anglo-American air force for the Caucasus. General George C. Marshall, Chief of Staff, recommended against American participation in such a project.

The idea, code named VELVET, continued to be discussed until December of that year when Stalin ended it by saying that the emergency for which it had been needed had since passed.[12] It is interesting that the members of the British and American staffs which made up the mission to Russia on VELVET suspected the Soviets had no intention of permitting a foreign military presence on their soil. They did not want foreign troops fraternizing with theirs and were suspicious of any power being in close proximity to their oil resources.[13] A very interesting comment was made by General Elmer Adler, Commander of the 9th Air Force Service Command, who was a member of that VELVET mission. He suggested that bases in European Russia might offer substantial advantages for heavy bombardment against targets in central Europe.[14]

In 1941 the British had provided RAF air cover for lend-lease convoys on the Murmansk run and in 1943 offered to do so again. After the offer was accepted by the Russians, supplies and personnel were sent to Murmansk. At that point Russia objected to the revision of British personnel needed to operate the project, from 500 to 750. After recriminations the Russians would not permit the project to be established so the British forces returned to the UK.[15] That experience is typical of the "made difficulties" which were common in every effort to collaborate with the Soviets except one – their acceptance of lend-lease.

In December, 1942 General Arnold proposed to General Marshall the use of western Russia for bombing eastern Germany and its satellites, and, the ultimate use of Siberia as a base of operations against Japan.[16] General Albert C. Wedemeyer, head of the Operations Division of the War Department, did not agree with Arnold's position. He believed that collaboration initiatives were not the responsibility of the U.S. and that collaboration with the Soviet Union "has been and will continue to be determined by the Russians..." Speaking of Russia he said, "She does not trust us and, realistically viewed, she certainly understands our sudden friendly interest is a selfish one." He added that if we negotiated with them it should be with our full understanding of these facts, and we should remain "ever alert to counter oriental cunning."[17] These were very prophetic words.

The unfavorable impact of the English weather on operations of the Eighth in the winter of 1942-1943 led General Marshall to express to General Arnold interest in shuttle bombing and temporary operations from dispersal airfields. In his concern over the bombing offensive not being interrupted by adverse weather he suggested "possibly Sicily or other areas."[18] His concern related to the Casablanca Directive which came out of the Casablanca Conference of allied leaders in January, 1943. That decision ordered a bombing offensive from England to destroy German military, industrial and economic systems and to undermine German morale.[19] The Directive was given the code name POINTBLANK and was most frequently referred to as the Combined Bomber Offensive (CBO).[20] The CBO established target priorities, and heading the list were the Luftwaffe and the German aircraft industry.[21] These and the other targets and the respective level of importance given them by the CBO were quite similar to the targets and their rankings in the AWPD-42 described in Chapter 4.

In April, 1943 General Carl A. Spaatz, then commanding the AAF in North Africa, referring to the CBO, said: "The most critical targets in Germany lie within range of the UK and not within the range of other bases. Thus, this throws the weight of the attack in the near future to that which can be supported from UK bases." Both Spaatz and Arnold believed bases in Italy could be used for bombing Germany, and this potential advantage was the major reason in July, 1943 to invade Italy.[22]

On August 17, 1943 the 8th Air Force conducted the first shuttle mission. The target was a Messerschmidt factory at Regensburg. The force suffered horrendous attacks by fighters from Holland to the target, not to mention flak. After bombs away they crossed the Alps into Italy letting down over the Mediterranean Sea toward bases in north Africa. Their major problem after bombing their target was to make their fuel last to destination. Once in Africa their problems were profound. They lacked aircraft repair parts and mechanics; fuel had to be pumped by hand from drums. The weather service was poor and crew accommodations were inadequate. Delays in getting the force back to the UK resulted in illnesses such as dysentery and malaria among air crews. General Curtis Lemay, the commander of the force, was critical of the operation in his official report and concluded, "Some other theater isn't much interested in your war, so you can't depend on another command furnishing you with adequate service."[23]

During a visit to England in September, 1943 General Arnold discussed the idea of shuttle missions with General Ira Eaker, then heading the VIII Bomber Command. Eaker was generally opposed to the concept of shuttle missions to Russia but conceded that intelligence reports indicated the Germans were moving aircraft manufacturing plants east, out of the range of his bombers in the UK.[24]

Lt. Gen Barney M. Giles, Chief of the Air Staff, in September, 1943 envisioned a three-way shuttle between Italy, England, and Russia which he believed would enable the Eighth to bomb Germany when the UK suffered bad weather, to rearm and refuel, bombing targets on the way back to either England or Italy. He opined that the Russians might be more favorably disposed to such a plan which did not contemplate establishing an American base in Russia. He also said such a project would create closer ties between American and Soviet forces, "as well as helping the political situation."[25] While still in England General Arnold had ordered General Giles to do a study on the Russian shuttle idea for him to consider when he returned to Washington. That study concluded that the idea was "tactically desirable" but anticipated difficulties in its implementation. The study was aware that Russia did not want a contingent of British or American troops to enter Russia and believed there was no change in this policy.[26] On his return, Arnold told General Lawrence Kuter, his Assistant Chief of Staff, that he did not want anything to do with the shuttle project and to file the study done by Giles. Apparently, his rejection of the idea at the time was then based on a planned allocation of American-made bombers to Russia, which he was opposed to as he considered that to be a "diversion of force" from the CBO established by the Casablanca Directive.[27]

Other developments may have affected Arnold's decision at the time. There were personal disagreements in the American Embassy at Moscow, which involved Brig. Gen Philip R. Faymonville, the American lend-lease representative, Brig. Gen. Joseph Michela, the Military Attache, and Admiral William H. Stanley, the Ambassador. It was believed that these internal problems had created an unfavorable view of this country among the leaders of the Soviet Union, which may have impacted the idea of collaboration adversely.[28]

Ambassador Stanley resigned in May, 1943 and W. Averell Harriman was selected by the President to be the new Ambassador. He already had experience in dealing with the Russians on lend-lease and military procurement matters.[29] Before going to Moscow Harriman moved to correct the internal problems. He combined Faymonville and Michela's existing offices into the Unites States Military Mission (USMM), that organization to be headed by a General Officer of the Army who would work "in close cooperation with, and under the Ambassador."[30]

Many will recall Roosevelt's famous and frequently used wartime objective, "unconditional surrender." Our military leaders on a policy-making level had no problem with prosecuting that kind of war. General Officers at the time found stepping over the line into the political and diplomatic aspects of waging a war to be distasteful and a distraction from their full attention to the military objectives. General Adler, mentioned earlier as a member of the VELVET mission, expressing the apolitical view of the professional military leader wrote to his wife from Moscow:

"This political game is not to my liking. The way of the soldier is so much more direct."[31]
The creation of the USMM placed those assigned thereto and those for whom they labored in Washington into that political arena and its diplomatic circus whether they liked it or not.

Harriman, the President and his confidant Harry Hopkins believed the USMM could provide a new approach to U.S. relations with the U.S.S.R.. But more to the point, Harriman and General Marshall believed the objective of the USMM would be to gain the confidence of the Soviet military "in order to gain the fullest cooperation from the Soviet Government in our military and political objectives."[32] That belief took on greater significance as time passed.

The selection of Brigadier General John R. Deane was important to the above objective of the USMM. He had been Secretary to the Joint Chiefs of Staff and was knowledgeable as to Anglo-American planning.[33] More significant than his professional credentials was the fact that he and Harriman viewed ultimate American-Soviet collaboration against Japan as their "major objective." Such a position left the conflict with Germany, and the CBO, to be of secondary importance to our Ambassador and the military head of the USMM. Deane said he viewed air bases in western Russia, for shuttle missions, to be a "proving ground" for the air operations which would later take place from Siberia.[34] Deane was later described by George F. Kennan, Charg' d'Affaires under Harriman, as, "...a senior military aide of the highest quality: modest, unassuming, scrupulously honest, fair-minded and clearsighted."[35]

By late September 1943 General Kuter's staff had prepared a document for Deane and Harriman to take to Moscow for negotiating the shuttle project which suggested shuttle missions between London, Rome and Smolensk. The proposal no longer included the offer of allocating American-made bombers to the Soviet Union, which may have had something to do with General Arnold favoring the project.[36] Probably more important in Arnold's approval, and an important factor to the political and diplomatic leadership of the United States, was an observation by Harriman; the Ambassador fascinated General Arnold with the view that shuttle bases in European Russia would be useful as a "condition precedent" to securing bases in the Russian Far East from which Germany could be bombed.[37]

General Deane arrived in Moscow on October 18, 1943, the day before conferences began with V.M. Molotov, the Soviet Minister, and others.[38] During discussions on October 20 Deane stressed the objectives of the CBO as they were related to the cross-channel invasion of Europe and their importance to the Soviets. He then apparently took the Russians by surprise by advancing the shuttle proposal, which requested the use of Soviet air bases from which our aircraft could operate.[39] It had to come as something of a surprise when Deane received an approval "in principle" from Molotov two days later.[40] Approval of the necessary details, including the bases to be used, and final approval of the entire project would not be as easy.

Deane's proposal was designed to be exploratory. Caught off guard by Molotov's approval, he had to get instructions expedited. They arrived October 26th [41] and included the following main points:

1. Shuttle missions would be flown when "special weather and operating conditions" existed.
2. Requirements included five bases in the north and five in the south, situated for coverage of targets from England and Italy; those bases to be revised capitalizing on advances (moving bases west with Red Army advances).
3. Bases to accommodate up to three wings of aircraft on one mission.
4. Total ground personnel, both Russian and American, to be slightly less than 1,000.
5. Russia to provide fuel, oil, bombs, ammunition and housing.[42]

On November 15 Deane met with General A.I. Antonov, then Deputy Chief of the Red Army General Staff, for the first time. Deane described his reception as very cold when he asked about the shuttle proposal. Antonov said he had received no instructions from Molotov on the subject.[43] On the following day Harriman approached Molotov and asked that he get a staff officer to discuss details of the airfields that were available for the shuttle project. His efforts then and later were unsuccessful up to the Teheran Conference of allied leaders in late November. Harriman followed up Deane's efforts with a letter to Molotov on November 18 which expressed his disappointment that no progress had been made on this issue.[44] Without the benefit of Soviet input General Arnold ordered Kuter to prepare shuttle plans using only the guidelines in the briefing paper which had been prepared for Deane and Harriman before they had left for Russia in September.[45]

The Teheran Conference began on November 27. During that high level meeting Roosevelt mentioned the shuttle proposal to Stalin and gave him a short memorandum on the subject, asking for his support. The same day Arnold met with Stalin and in their discussion, surprisingly, he offered him 300-400 B-24 bombers on a quid pro quo basis for air bases in western Russia for the shuttle bombing of Germany and German occupied territory. Stalin's reaction to this was not clear except that Arnold expressed surprise that Stalin did not follow up on the offer of aircraft.[46]

Deane returned to Moscow from Teheran optimistic, but there was little progress on the shuttle project for two months.[47] Finally, on December 26 Molotov gave Harriman a written reply for the President to his memorandum presented to Stalin at Teheran. Basically, it was another agreement "in principle" which said that before final approval of the shuttle project could be given, the bases to be used would have to be agreed to and the plans for their use would have to be coordinated with the Soviet Air Force Command.[48]

After several days transpired, Harriman told the President that we were getting a "complete runaround" from the Soviets on military proposals. Harriman then wrote a letter to Molotov on December 31 complaining, listing 15 proposals advanced by the U.S. designed to hasten the end of the war; at the top of that list was the shuttle proposal. After setting forth the history of these proposals he asked for prompt action on them by the Soviet Government. Privately, he told the President that he believed the Soviet inaction was not ill will but "bottlenecking" inside the Kremlin.

Molotov replied to Harriman that their military had been instructed to deal with the American proposals. Deane was then contacted by the Soviet General Staff; he said it was the first time they contacted him on their own initiative.

They met January 10, 1944. During that meeting General N.V. Slavin, Deane's liaison with the General Staff, asked for "an accurate statement" of what was involved in the shuttle proposal. Deane then gave him a restatement of the instructions on the proposal he had received from Washington on the previous October 26. Added as a carrot on a stick, Deane said that shuttle bombing would facilitate advances by the Red Army by hitting German supply centers on their front and offered valuable, up to date, photographic reconnaissance of the front.[49]

On February 2, 1944 Harriman met with Stalin and during their meeting they discussed the military proposals made by Roosevelt at Teheran, particularly the shuttle bombing proposal. Stalin's main concern was the role of the Soviet Union in this project. They had a detailed discussion as to supplies, who would be responsible and how supplies would be provided, the ground staff that would be needed to support the bombers, and the type of airfields needed. With respect to the personnel needs, which later became a point of contention, Harriman said that some American specialists would be needed but this would depend on the wishes and the convenience of the Red Air Force. Stalin agreed to the plan to handle 150-200 bombers initially, which could be increased later. Harriman responded, "This is perfect." Official Washington was not only pleased with this breakthrough but believed that it also meant that after the Soviets declared war on Japan we would get the Siberian bases that we wanted there.[50]

The shuttle project had been given the code name BASEBALL but that was soon changed to FRANTIC.[51] James Parton's biography of General Eaker, **Air Force Spoken Here**, describes the new code name as a "wry acknowledgment of the breakneck pace" needed to organize the project in a four-month period after the approval by Stalin.[52] General Deane described the code name as "a masterpiece of understatement."[53] Three days after the approval by the Soviet leader, Harriman and Deane met with Marshal A.A. Novikov, head of the Red Air Force, and members of his Staff. Their discussions included very general concerns about the type, location and number of airfields that would be needed for FRANTIC. During these discussions Novikov made it clear that the defense of such bases would be the responsibility of, and would be provided by the Soviet Government.[54]

General Spaatz, by then Commander of USSTAF, sent a mission to Moscow to assist in the selection of airfields for the FRANTIC project.[55] The three chosen for this effort were the following:

✈ Colonel John S. Griffith, Mission Commander - Former Director of Maintenance, Air Service Command.[56]

✈ Colonel Alfred A. Kessler - Former C.O. 95th Bombardment Group (H) and C.O. 13th CBW, 8th Air Force.[57]

✈ Colonel Paul T. Cullen - Former C.O. 7th Photographic Group, 8th Air Force.[58]

Spaatz charged them with the responsibility to locate bases for shuttle bombing missions and for photographic reconnaissance with an overall mission to "sell the ability and power of the American air (forces) to the Russians." He and his staff met with these three officers on February 8 when he made clear his intention to keep control of USSTAF operations in the Soviet Union. He told Griffith, as mission commander, that he was his personal representative to the Soviet Union to be "working with but not under Deane;" he pointed out that Griffith would be responsible for military decisions whereas Deane was a representative "for diplomatic purposes." Griffith's party was then ready for departure for Moscow, but typical Soviet delay in the issuance of visas prevented them from leaving until February 17th.[59] It will be recalled that the Casablanca Directive laid out POINTBLANK for the CBO, with top priority targets for heavy bombardment being the Luftwaffe and the German aircraft industry. It will also be recalled that ARGUMENT followed with its all out campaign in February, 1944 to gain the air superiority necessary for OVERLORD, the European invasion on June 6, 1944. The missions of "Big Week" were described in Chapter 4 when 3,300 sorties of the Eighth were flown, dropping 6,000 tons of bombs on German aircraft industrial facilities.[60] Not only did they gain the air superiority they sought, they also made the prospect of shuttle missions more attractive.[61]

When the Griffith party arrived in Moscow they obtained a different perspective for their mission from their briefings by Harriman and Deane as well as from later conversations. Contrary to what they had been told by Spaatz, they were informed that the primary objective of FRANTIC was to set a "precedent" by establishing operations against Europe on Soviet soil for later gaining bases in Siberia for operations against Japan. The Ambassador and Deane let it be known that, from their point of view, that they considered the strategic and tactical advantages of FRANTIC to be last in importance.

To Harriman and Deane, even of greater importance, was the desire through FRANTIC collaboration to improve relations and morale among the fighting men of both the U.S. and the U.S.S.R..[62] The difference of opinion led to a rivalry over control between those who would handle the air operations of FRANTIC and those who would make the political arrangements with the Russians. The AAF personnel "wanted to get on with the flying and ignore the delicate negotiations and appeasement tactics Deane knew were necessary." General Marshall was drawn into the differences and overruled Spaatz, placing "Griffith under Deane while he was in the Soviet Union."[63] Thus, complete control of the Eastern Command was to be shared by USSTAF with the USMM, headed by an Amry General lacking expertise in military aviation strategy.

The mission headed by Griffith met with Colonel General A.V. Nikitin, representing the Red Air Force and Colonel General A.K. Repin, Red Air Force Chief of Aviation Engineering. The Americans wanted bases closer to the front than Poltava and Kharkov which were at the range limits for the B-17. They were told this would not be possible because airfields and facilities for personnel close to the Kiev salient had been destroyed by the Germans during their retreat. Griffith suggested that 2,000 persons would be needed as a ground staff, one third of that number would be American personnel.[64] Kessler and Cullen had inspected the airfields at Poltava and Kharkov and reported they were unsuitable.[65]

Meanwhile, Griffith's staff of specialists for the mission in support areas of ordnance, supply, transportation and medicine were being assembled and were ready to leave for the Soviet Union February 27. Again, no visas were forthcoming from the Soviets; this was frustrating for the Americans whose only objective was to fight and win the war.[66] On March 16 Nikitin reported that all airfields west of Kiev were filled with Russian aircraft. In addition to the airfield at Poltava the Russians offered two other locations, Mirgorod and Piryatin; these were fifty and one hundred miles respectively west of Poltava on the railroad between Poltava and Kiev.[67] In view of the American previous rejection of Poltava it would appear that acceptance of these bases were the best they could get from the Russians. Those three became the Eastern Command with headquarters at Poltava.

On March 17 the members of the American mission discussed intelligence and personnel matters with the Russians. On the latter issue the Russians said that 700 Americans on the ground staff at FRANTIC bases would be sufficient. Forced to negotiate from that figure the Americans revised their figure from 2,150 Americans to 1,250, agreeing that the difference would be made up by Russians substituting for some of the needed American specialists.[68]

The conference on March 17 was the last one until late that month. During that period an agreement was finally entered into on the subject of visas, although the problem with the Russians continued to be a source of friction for the duration of FRANTIC. The Soviets agreed to issue group as opposed to individual visas for incoming American personnel, yet there continued to be excessive delays in the issuance of the group visas and delays in permitting entry for persons for whom visas had already been issued. Also granted was authority for American aircraft to airlift supplies from Teheran to Poltava, although this was limited to thirty such trips for that purpose. It was obvious that the Soviets would not approve every request made by the Americans, but their refusals seemed to be based on making a point rather than whether the requests were completely valid. For example, they refused a request for a weekly round-trip flight from Poltava to Teheran for needed supplies; later they agreed to provide the service themselves.[69]

It isn't surprising that the initial differences between Griffith and Deane, that is the military view as opposed to the political/diplomatic view described earlier, became greater points of contention. Their disagreements led to Deane's request that Griffith be relieved. Such requests, and there were others, were normally honored without discussion.

Deane said that Griffith lacked the temperament and personality to work with the Russians. Glenn Infield, author of **The Poltava Affair**, probably provided a much more honest appraisal of the differences when he wrote: "Not everyone assigned to the project had the patience, tact, and diplomacy to work with the Russians. It was much too one-sided, with the United States `backing down' at every meeting in an effort to keep the project alive."[70] Deane's sense of Griffith may have been accurate but the problem was apparently a much deeper one. Griffith had continued to represent Spaatz on the FRANTIC project with his preoccupation on the European war and the aims and deadline of the CBO which was so vital to OVERLORD. Deane, on the other hand, was first and foremost dedicated to the concept that FRANTIC was the "precedent" to securing those bases in Siberia for the war with Japan.

Colonel Griffith, to Deane and Harriman, was not a team player, at least he wasn't a player on **their team**. For example, Griffith made it clear in his dealings with the Russians that the operation of the three bases of the Eastern Command would be vested in an American commander. As it turned out there would be two commanders one American and one Russian although it was difficult at times to tell whether the base was an American operation at all. Griffith reportedly communicated such problems to Spaatz and the result was an inevitable conflict with Deane. It appears the conflict culminated in the inspection report which Griffith prepared on the status of the three bases. He said that all were devoid of any facilities including water, sewage, and power systems. The only building left standing by the retreating Germans was a partially-destroyed barracks then in use by the Russians. He said the Russians' lower standards required the Americans to provide their own sanitary, medical, housing and messing facilities. Although he did not say the report was inaccurate Deane thought the report presented "too gloomy a picture" and asked that Colonel Griffith be recalled. Spaatz approved the request and Deane's recommendation that Colonel Kessler be named as Griffith's replacement. Kessler must have been the kind of team player that Deane wanted because he became the deputy commander of the Eastern Command and was promoted to Brigadier General. Colonel Cullen became deputy commander for operations.[71]

During April and May problems, both major and petty ones continued to bedevil the Americans but operational planning somehow continued. Even getting the Soviets to advance their own preference for bombing targets of value to their Army brought one delay after another. They were, however, quick to reject American suggestions as to targets which were of interest to the CBO. Nevertheless, by mid-May, 1944 the three bases were sixty-five percent ready, with remaining work not vital to further delay FRANTIC operations.[72] Arriving in time for the first FRANTIC mission was the commander of the Eastern Command, Major General Robert L. Walsh. Walsh was also named to head the Air Division of the USMM under Deane; this put him on Deane's team and necessitated his being in Moscow much of the time.

In late May a final conference was held in England at which it was decided to fly the first FRANTIC mission prior to the OVERLORD invasion of Europe. It was hoped that this would cause the transfer of Luftwaffe units from the west to the east and by so doing help the cross-channel invasion. There was also a decision to give priority to targets to be bombed from FRANTIC bases chosen by the Russians. For the first mission the Americans chose German Heinkel aircraft plants located at Riga, Latvia and Mielec, Poland. The Russians disapproved with the inexplicable reason that those targets were "within the Russian sphere of influence." Instead, they suggested targets in the area of Bucharest and Debrecin, Hungary. They were insistent on these targets even though Deane pointed out to Lieutenant General N.V. Slavin, that those places could be bombed from Italy without having to resort to bases in Russia. Slavin refused to compromise and Deane recommended that we back down again, with the ever present optimism that once operations began they would be allowed more freedom of action in target selection as well as on all other questions.[73]

The first operational mission, known as FRANTIC JOE, was flown on June 2, 1944 by 130 B-17s escorted by 64 P-51s of the 15th Air Force[74] With Genral Eaker, then commanding the Mediterranean Allied Air Forces (MAAF), leading the force.[75] The conflict with the Russians over the target for the day resulted in FRANTIC JOE being characterized as "a mission going somewhere and a target being found en route."[76] The specific targets were marshalling yards and locomotive works at Debrecin, Hungary. Though legitimate targets, they were certainly of no value to the CBO.

There was considerable hoopla attached to the arrival of the force when it landed at Poltava, American and Russian journalists were on hand and wrote featured stories on the event. Among the dignitaries were Harriman, his daughter Kathleen, Generals Deane, Walsh, and Kessler on the American side. Russians present included General Slavin, Lt. Gen. Dimitri D. Grendal, Chief of Intelligence and Reconnaissance for the Red Air Force and Gen. A.R. Perminov, then commanding the Russians at Poltava. During the arrival festivities General Eaker presented Perminov with the Legion of Merit.[77]

Bad weather kept Eaker from an early return to Caserta, his headquarters in Italy. During that time his force flew a mission from Poltava to bomb an airfield at Galatz, Rumania returning to Poltava.[78] Eaker was becoming anxious to leave Poltava in light of Russian reports that there had been an increase in German photographic reconnaissance of the area. He felt his aircraft were vulnerable and the antiaircraft defenses of the three bases inadequate.[79] On June 11 he led his force out of Russia bombing an airfield at Foscani, Rumania near Bucharest on their return to Italy.[80]

Following FRANTIC JOE, which was perceived as a success, and the news of D-Day on June 6, many believed that further collaboration would follow including securing those bases in Siberia.[81] Apparently, General Arnold thought the time was ripe for some straight talk with the Russians when he wrote to Deane on June 4. He said it was time for strong presentations to the Soviets that "combat conditions under which our aircraft and personnel will be operating necessitates immediately dispensing with red tape and technicalities which have hampered FRANTIC operations to date." He listed such difficulties as haggling over visas, a ceiling placed on the number of personnel admitted to the Soviet Union for FRANTIC, delays in clearing flights into Poltava, and delays in clearing photographic aircraft from and to the UK.[82]

Hoping to capitalize on the high level of American-Soviet amity following FRANTIC JOE and the invasion of Europe, Harriman met with Stalin on June 10. Knowing the Russians still wanted to obtain American-made heavy bombers it was decided to treat this on a quid pro quo basis. In return for the bombers Harriman wanted a commitment on the bases in Siberia. Stalin was surprisingly agreeable even discussing the types of bases required, and advised Harriman that there were six or seven airfields in the Vladisvostok and Sovietskaya Gavan which were suitable for use by AAF bombers. He even went further to discuss the need to begin prompt stockpiling of fuel and other supplies. He said subsequent discussions would start promptly but would not set a date for such discussions.[83] When nothing happened for six weeks General Deane spoke to General Antonov, who received the information on Harriman's conversation with Stalin coldly. Several months would pass before the Russians would begin planning with the Americans.[84]

Operational work for further FRANTIC missions continued during the above protracted negotiations with the same Russian problems, as well as some new ones. For example, they would not agree to establish permanent air corridors over their occupied territory for the protection of our photographic reconnaissance aircraft. They were concerned that the Germans would use these for the Luftwaffe to make attacks. They offered to provide corridors for each mission with a mandatory ten-hour notice, this resulted in attacks on our aircraft by Russian fighters and by ground-fire. Other problems included a breakdown in the exchange of weather data, as previously agreed to, and in the transportation of large amounts of supplies in contemplation of the expected expansion of FRANTIC and various base needs such as winter housing for personnel.[85]

On June 15 Spaatz wrote Deane requesting the Russians provide one new airfield further west, down from four airfields previously requested and told him to keep the pressure on for locations closer to the front. At the same time he asked that the Soviets approve additional American manpower commensurate with the expansion of FRANTIC. These requests were passed on to General Nikitin who responded favorably. Nitikin suggested that Deane press the Red Army General Staff on these requests, but that they not approach the Soviet Foreign Office except as a last resort.[86]

On June 21 the Eighth participated in FRANTIC II; their target was the Ruhland Oil Refinery south of Berlin. It was a force of 137 B-17s and 63 P-51s that landed at the Eastern Command bases late that day. Again, their arrival was well covered by the allied press and similar warm greetings were exchanged between the American and the Russians present.[87]

What followed was a disaster! Late that evening the German Luftwaffe bombed the base at Poltava; two Americans were killed and 12 were wounded.[88] In its last major victory the German Air Force destroyed or damaged beyond repair 47 B-17s and three other aircraft. Of the remaining 30 Fortresses at Poltava, only six were ready for a mission on June 25. In addition there was a corresponding huge loss of bombs, many different types of ground vehicles, ammunition, and 200,000 gallons of aviation fuel. The aircraft at Mirgorod and

Piryatin were not attacked; those at Mirgorod were dispersed to other fields before the Germans returned the next night to bomb that location effectively destroying large numbers of bombs, aviation and other fuel reserves.[89]

All reports agree that the Russian antiaircraft fire was absolutely ineffective. It was said that their guns were obsolete, of deficient caliber and lacking radar. Although they fired thousands of rounds they hit nothing; the Luftwaffe apparently unconcerned took no evasive action. It was reported that Russian night fighters took off but there was no indication that they engaged the enemy. During the prolonged attack the Russians would not permit American fighter aircraft, most of which were at Piryatin, to takeoff and go after the Germans.[90] It was later established that the Germans had shadowed the incoming American force and photographed the bases at Poltava and Mirgorod. From German Air Force archives it would appear the Germans had high level intelligence concerning FRANTIC II independent of the reconnaissance conducted on June 21. One report states General Rudolf Meister, Commanding Officer of the IV Fliegerkorps, gave the order to attack Poltava on June 21 before the Americans had landed at Poltava.[91]

The attack was described as a "triumph for the Germans and the worst defeat of its kind since the Japanese had caught MacArthur's B-17s on the ground at Clark Field in the Philippines December 8, 1941."[92] Without question it was the greatest loss of aircraft on the ground suffered by the Eighth. General Eaker was right when he was concerned about the security at Poltava.

Although there were no official accusations by either nation, there were unofficial comments which ran very deep in criticism of the Soviet Union. Many Americans were suspicious of Soviet action, or the lack of action, during the raid. The Luftwaffe aircraft were described as roaming the skies dropping bombs and butterfly mines at will. One American officer quoted General Kessler as saying, "in two hours Stalin could have ordered Yak fighters from a dozen airfields in the area - if he wanted to."[93] One account said that by the next morning the question uppermost in the minds of Americans at Poltava was, "Had Stalin double-crossed the United States, as many had predicted he would?"[94]

The defeat was more than the immense loss of aircraft, supplies and equipment; having suffered the attack on the ground with no way to fight back was a bitter pill for the Americans. American leadership, particularly in Washington, apparently did not share the suspicions of those who believed the Soviets permitted, or even invited, the attack on the Eastern Command. Their fixation to secure bases in Siberia may have been the reason no one demanded an explanation from the Soviets for the lack of adequate defense which they themselves insisted they would provide.[95]

On June 26 the remnants of FRANTIC II left Russia. The force reduced to seventy-two B-17s bombed the oil refinery at Drohobycz, Poland en route to Foggia, Italy on their way home to England.[96] The disaster at Poltava forced the Americans to reevaluate the entire FRANTIC project. This was the purpose of a conference held at the MAAF Headquarters, Caserta, Italy in early July, 1944. Present at that conference were Generals Deane, Walsh, Eaker and Colonel F.J. Sutterlin, the project officer for FRANTIC. Still hoping to expand FRANTIC they planned for personnel requirements at the three existing airfields and optimistically another base in the Kiev–Vinnitsa area, further west from the Eastern Command facilities. They decided that for obviously practical reasons, until lost fuel, bombs and other lost supplies could be replaced, they would continue FRANTIC missions of solely fighter and fighter-bomber aircraft.[97]

It would not appear that the conference, in its reevaluation of the project ever considered ending it then, cutting our losses and getting out of Russia as soon as possible. Although the results of FRANTIC JOE and FRANTIC II were not great, and the losses on June 21 only capped the trials and tribulations endured in trying to work with the Soviet hierarchy, it must be recalled that those present at Caserta knew both Arnold and Roosevelt were sold on FRANTIC as the "precedent" to securing bases in Siberia.

Aside from the determination of those in Washington and the tunnel vision of those in the American Embassy in Moscow and the USMM, there had to be misgivings of those at the Eastern Command and at USSTAF from a purely military point of view. After the attack

Colonel Sutterlin, the project officer, in a radio message to USSTAF said, "Conditions regards planning abruptly altered by enemy last night. (We) are now faced with the problem of whether political advantage worth the price of maintenance..."[98]

In a report, Major Reynolds Benson, A-2 Officer of the Eighth's 45th CBW, following the FRANTIC II mission pointed out that there was a sparsity of targets for the bombers when they were in Russia, and the majority of other targets en route to Russia were closer to England than to Eastern Command bases. He also pointed out that all north Germany, Prussia and Posen could be bombed from England easier than from the Soviet Union. He said Vienna, Austria, Budapest, Hungary, the Ploesti – Galati – Bucharest triangle in Rumania, Sofia, and Constanta, Bulgaria were within reach of the 15th Air Force in Italy. He noted this left a small area in Poland and the Baltic States which could not be bombed from either England or Italy, and the Russian offensive made those areas of little concern as bombing targets. Major Benson's report established beyond any question that the FRANTIC project was too costly for the results achieved. The report was known to Spaatz and Arnold but the decision to go forward with FRANTIC was made in spite of sound evidence and common sense that it was not worth it. Washington was not ready to give up on the collaboration effort even though all evidence at that point persisted that they were pursing a hopeless goal.[99]

Pursuant to the Caserta conference FRANTIC III became operational with a bombing mission on July 22, 1944 with 72 P-38s and 41 P-51s from Italy attacking airfields in the Buzau-Zilistea area near Ploesti, Rumania.

On July 25 they flew another mission from the Eastern Command bases attacking an airdrome at Mielec, Poland, returning to the bases in the Russian Ukraine. On the following day a greater portion of that force returned to Italy including a mission to Bucharest, Rumania on the way. The rest of that force, fourteen aircraft, returned to Italy after an attack on Kecskmet, Hungary on July 29. The statistics for FRANTIC III could be considered good with 64 German aircraft destroyed in the air, 56 on the ground, not counting probable aircraft destroyed, rail equipment, trucks and other vehicles claimed by the fighters.[100]

FRANTIC IV was another fighter, fighter-bomber operation on July 31 involving 77 aircraft from the 15th Air Force. The weather was so bad that neither targets or statistics were recorded. Poor weather also affected the missions from the Eastern Command although they were able to attack an airfield at Foscani, Rumania on August 4. The force on its return flight to Italy on August 6 attacked targets in the area of Zilistea, Rumania.

With the lack of fuel, ordnance and other supplies for bomber operations after the German attacks on the Eastern Command in June, there appeared to be a valid reason for the deployment of fighter, fighter-bomber missions of FRANTIC III and FRANTIC IV. It was hoped that these missions would also salvage some form of future collaboration with the Soviets and belay German efforts to use the disaster of FRANTIC II to divide the U.S. and the U.S.S.R..[101] However, at this point a decision was made to discontinue any further fighter, fighter-bomber shuttle missions because of American losses (12 lost and eight down over Soviet occupied territory), plus the fact that appropriate targets were not available nor had FRANTIC III or IV contributed to the basic purposes of the project.[102]

Spaatz felt the Caserta conference established the USSTAF primary interest and responsibility for Eastern Command operations for the first time[103] as opposed to the USMM political/diplomatic control of the command after the Deane - Griffith confrontation. General Deane remained the optimist, he felt the disaster of FRANTIC II could rebound to our advantage, cementing a U.S. - U.S.S.R. relationship with the Soviets more acquiescent to American requests.[104] At that point we had requested Soviet approval for an American night-fighter squadron with support personnel and three battalions of radar-controlled antiaircraft batteries for security of the Eastern Command bases, even though that responsibility had belonged to the Soviets.[105] Base security remained a real concern since intelligence reports claimed the Germans had moved 300 additional aircraft to the Russian front after the advent of FRANTIC.[106]

Bomber operations were resumed with FRANTIC V on August 6 with an 8th Air Force mission to bomb a Focke-Wulf aircraft factory at Rahmel, Poland, north of Gdynia. The 78 B-17s were escorted by 64 P-51s on what was termed a routine mission with no enemy fighter opposition and excellent bombing. On August 7th they flew a mission bombing an oil refinery at Trzebinia, Poland, again with excellent bombing. On the following day they were up again bombing airfields at Buzau-Zilistea on their way to Italy before returning home to England.[107]

Deane's proposal for the expansion of FRANTIC had been made in July, 1944 and Nikitin promised to support it. At that time he suggested that Deane also present the entire program to the Soviet Foreign Office. It will be recalled that this was contrary to the advice he had given Deane in June when he said that Deane should only approach the Foreign Office as a last resort.[108] Harriman did present the whole plan to Molotov the same day who said he would take it up with Soviet military authorities. The same evening Deane discussed the plan with General Slavin who was alarmed at the increase in American military personnel contemplated by the expanded FRANTIC plan. He requested a reduction, which request was forwarded to USSTAF; Spaatz refused to reduce the number since the increase involved the large defensive contingents needed for base protection.[109]

On August 9 Harriman sent a cable to General Marshall for General Deane, then in the United States, in which he said that he thought relations with the Soviets continued to be more frank and cordial, although there were annoying delays and suspicions on the part of the Soviet Foreign Office and other areas of Government. He said he remained optimistic about the fulfillment of their long-range agreement.[110]

Yet by this time there had been ample evidence that the Soviet Union was about to, or already had, ended any policy of collaboration with the United States. A good clue for any observer were incidents which had begun to take place months before. Prior to the FRANTIC II disaster there had been many stories of the unusually good relations between the Americans and the Russians at the Eastern Command bases. Both military and civilian Russian and the American ground and flying personnel had gotten along fairly well. Then a documented story of anti-American Russian abuse of Americans and some of their own people was furnished by Lt. Hanlon E. Davies.

Davies had been reassigned from the Eastern Command to England in July, 1944 at the request of the Russians who did not want him there anymore. It was believed that the initial basis for their objection to this officer was the fact that Davies had been employed before the war as an investigator for the Dies Committee, better known as the House Un-American Activities Committee of the U.S. House of Representatives chaired at one time by Congressman Martin Dies. Lt. Davies report documented that between July 3 and July 18 there had been thirty-five incidents of verbal and physical attacks on Russian women seen in the company of off-duty American military personnel, most of these incidents having occurred in the city of Poltava, many at a city park close to the Poltava base. It was determined that the incidents usually involved the same man and woman as leaders of a group of attackers.

One such incident involving this man and woman is interesting. The couple, leading a group of Russian civilians, were attacking an American and his Russian female companion. An American Army sergeant nearby who spoke Russian asked two Soviet Army officers to intervene; they did so, but quickly withdrew when the leaders spoke to them and displayed a leather-encased identification card. Other sources writing of this same incident furnished other details. One source said the male leader said to the American's female companion: "Yes, I see you are with an American, our friend today, but probably our enemy tommorow."[111] Another source said the couple had identified themselves as NKVD agents and said they were acting on orders of the Kremlin.[112] When General Spaatz read the Davies report he was disturbed and said this was the first indication that USSTAF had of any problems of this type at the Eastern Command bases. It was an obvious change from the open friendliness which had existed between persons of both nations during June, less than one month before.[113]

It was said that the files of the Eastern Command contained numerous investigative reports which reveal too striking a similarity in the pattern of the vast number of these incidents to have been accidental.[114] Interestingly, during the research on this story the files reviewed did not disclose such reports. The fact that Spaatz was disturbed and surprised by the Davies report raises a question why such a pattern of Russian conduct was not being furnished to USSTAF? It also raises another question - was that pattern of conduct furnished to the USMM? If so, was this anti-American activity covered up for political/diplomatic considerations? Whatever, these incidents provided the first evidence of a new party-line out of Moscow.

The American staff at Poltava were said to have taken a wait-and-see position on this apparent change in the policy of collaboration. However, Col. Paul Cullen, acting in General Walsh's name, restricted all American personnel to living and working areas on the bases during hours of darkness, and recommended that if they went to any of the nearby towns during the day, they only do so in pairs. Cullen issued this order after an American G.I. was physically attacked by Russians when he intervened in the defense of an assaulted Soviet female who was in his company. [115]

The scenario being played out included another clue, this involving international politics, on the highest level, which made Soviet intentions on the future of collaboration quite clear. It also was followed by the most serious breach between the western allies and the Soviet Union.

The Soviets were determined to exercise complete control over eastern Europe and insure that post-war governments of those states were favorable to the Soviet Union, which is to say that those countries would have communist governments. During the period of the German-Soviet Union Nonaggression Pact of 1939 Germany and Russia had divided up Poland. During their occupation of that part of Poland the Russians executed thousands of Poles and deported to the Soviet Union an estimated one million they suspected were anticommunist.

After Hitler attacked the Soviet Union in June 1941 the Russians agreed to recognize the Polish Government in exile also known as the Polish Emigre Government headquarted in London. This action was a ploy to get military and other help from the west. As the Red Army eventually pushed the Germans out of their own country and then Poland itself Stalin began to think in terms of a new government for Poland. In 1944 he created a communist-dominated faction in "liberated" Poland called the Committee of National Liberation which became located at Lublin, Poland. Stalin then broke with the London Poles and endorsed the puppet group which became the post-war communist government of Poland.[116]

In July, 1944 the residents of Warsaw could hear the Red Army artillery and they could see the Red Air Force overhead each day. They began to believe that they were about to be liberated from Nazi occupation. Inside Warsaw was General Tadeusz Bor-Komorowski who headed the Armja Krajova (A.K.), which was the Polish Secret Army or Home Army. It was an underground army of 40,000 partisans loyal to the Polish Government in Exile.[117] General Bor became convinced that the time was ripe for the Home Army to rise up and retake the city from the Germans. He then relied on several broadcasts on Soviet radio, the first on July 29 which encouraged the Poles saying: "Poles, the time for liberation is at hand! Poles to arms! Make every home a stronghold in the fight against the invader! There is not a moment to lose!" A similar message was monitored the following day urging the people of Warsaw to assist the Red Army in crossing the Vistula River which divides the city east and west. They were that close to entering the city, and with the Red Air Force controlling the skies, General Bor on August 1 ordered his Home Army to attack the Germans. In 48 hours they won back two-thirds of their city. Feeling liberation within their grasp the populace celebrated.[118] But, they had been tricked by the Russians! The Red Army guns were suddenly quiet and the Red Air Force was no longer seen in the skies over Warsaw. The Soviet radio was also quiet. General Bor felt they could hold out for seven days without supplies or a renewed offensive by the Red Army. But military help from the Russians was not forthcoming; Warsaw was trapped and was being purposely abandoned to the German Army by the Soviet Union.[119] The Germans incessantly bombed the city with artillery day and night, Stuka dive bombers attacked the city relentlessly and the German tanks pushed the fiercely resisting Home Army back. Until the middle of August, British and Free Polish RAF flights dropped supplies to the beleaguered city, but the losses to the Luftwaffe and German flak guns ended that effort. General Spaatz proposed a shuttle mission to drop supplies to the Polish city but this was rejected by Stalin. Meeting with Harriman and Deane on August 15 Stalin refused to permit American or British aircraft to land in Russia after dropping supplies over Warsaw. Stalin's convoluted thinking blamed the Warsaw crisis on the Polish Government in Exile. Molotov echoed Stalin's position, and despite the Soviet radio broadcasts to the Polish people, Molotov said his government did not want to associate itself, directly or indirectly, with the Warsaw "adventure."[120]

Once Stalin was confident that help for the inhabitants of Warsaw was too late to save them from the vengeance of the Germans, he agreed to permit a shuttle mission to make a supply drop on the city. Problems delayed the effort until September 18 when 93 B-17s escorted by 73 P-51s of the Eighth made up FRANTIC VII to fly supplies to the citizens of Warsaw. It was estimated that only 50 percent of the supplies fell within the city; the operation was already too little and too late thanks to Stalin.

General Bor's Home Army surrendered to the Germans on October 5, 1944.[121] Glenn Infield devoted an entire chapter in his book **The Poltava Affair** to the treachery of Stalin as related to the battle for Warsaw. He titled that chapter "The Tragedy of Warsaw". In that chapter he said that General Bor could not conceive that Stalin was so cold-blooded that he would plan a trap for the Polish people that would cost the lives of 250,000 men, women and children.[122] Not only had he planned it, he insured it by ordering his military not to take Warsaw which was opened to them by the courageous Home Army. Infield described that tragedy as the first clear indication of Stalin's ruthlessness and said, "Until the Warsaw affair Stalin's true attitude toward the United States was clouded and confused. During the Warsaw affair the answer became crystal clear." It appears that Stalin felt little or no guilt for the massacre at Warsaw, but as time passed it seems he was furious at having been caught bringing about such a diabolical incident. This perhaps explains Stalin's anti– American attitude toward our presence in Russia which had surfaced in July of that year.[123]

The total FRANTIC history provides fact upon fact, incident upon incident, that Stalin did not want us there to begin with, obstructed every effort at collaboration, and instigated dirty tricks to make our presence less than desirable. He wanted us to leave! To the Western mind the direct course would have been for the Russians to say that our presence was no longer desired in their country. Instead they used indirect and often dirty tricks to make a statement and convey a message. Molotov gave Harriman a lesson in Soviet deviousness when they met on September 17 on the matter of a supply mission to Warsaw. Harriman said that as he was about to leave, an irritated Molotov, passed the most incredulous comment, saying that the Soviet Air Force was proposing to revise the agreement on the FRANTIC bases. He then had the temerity to add that the bases had been granted the Americans for the summer (1944) only, and Russia had an acute need for them and wanted them back.[124] Harriman reported to Secretary of State Cordell Hull that Molotov and Vishinsky were men "bloated with power" who felt they could force all countries, including the United States, to accept their decisions without question.[125]

General Spaatz did not have to be in Moscow to tell which way the wind was blowing. In early August he became angry and sent an ultimatum to the Soviets on the expansion plans for FRANTIC. After he heard of Molotov's comment to Harriman, Spaatz said that FRANTIC was a "thorn in the side of Stalin" that the Russian leader wanted removed.[126] Or as Infield said, he no longer needed foreign troops on his soil and he wanted the Americans out.

Strangely, Harriman still believed it to be important to find a way to work with the leaders of the Soviet Union.[127] After a conference at Capri, he persuaded Spaatz that the Eastern Command should be reduced in size rather than disbanded. Spaatz and others expressed doubt as to the validity of Harriman and Deane's assumption of the value of FRANTIC at that time. Spaatz's approval to continue the project in such a reduced state may have been based on his reluctance to be the one who ended FRANTIC, considering Arnold's and Roosevelt's interest in American-Soviet collaboration in the war with Japan.[128]

Arnold on August 30 agreed to reducing personnel at Poltava to 200 men and giving up the bases at Mirgorod and Piryatin. The latter bases were to be closed on September 30; the excess American personnel were to leave Russia by November 1.

FRANTIC VI was flown on September 11 with 75 B-17s and 64 P-51s making up the 8th Air Force task force. Their bombing target was the Wandererwerke small arms plant at Chemnitz which they damaged heavily by excellent bombing. On September 13 they bombed the Royal Iron and Steel Works and the Mavag Armament Works at Diosgyor, Hungary on their way to England via a stop-over in Italy.[129]

The supply drop to the Poles in Warsaw on September 18 by FRANTIC VII was followed by that force bombing the locomotive repair sheds and transshipment center at Szolnok, Hungary the next day on its way to Italy and then home to England. It was the last FRANTIC mission.[130]

Although no further FRANTIC missions were contemplated, the base at Poltava remained important to the AAF. Missions to eastern Germany, with fighter escort all the way, were now all in a day's work for the bomber crews of the 8th and 15th Air Forces. Those bomber crews and their "little friends" in fighters looked at Russian-occupied territory and the base at Poltava as sanctuary when battle damage made their return to England and Italy impossible. Poltava was important in the rescue of our flyers downed in a strange land and in processing them out through the Middle East to their home bases.

General Spaatz became further irritated with the Russians. After the "Tragedy of Warsaw" Soviet displeasure was reflected swiftly and regularly through restrictions placed on all Americans in Russia. Some examples: American flights would be grounded without a reason given, American rescue teams were not permitted to service American aircraft known to have made forced landings in Poland, American practice of removing sick and wounded air crew members from Poltava to Teheran for better care was halted by the Russians.[131]

Worse than that, it wasn't uncommon for the Red Air Force to shoot down American aircraft. One incident is typical of such occurrences. Lt. James D. Ayers of the 15th Air Force bombed the Oswiecim Oil Refinery in Poland on September 13. Hit by flak over the target they lost the left inboard engine, their aileron controls were shot out and their fuel line was severed. Ayers lost 8,000 feet before he was able to regain control of the aircraft. He knew full well that he could not get back to Italy and headed for an emergency field at Rzesvow, Poland. En route their fuel supply was almost gone when Ayers spotted an airfield at Dembetzen, Poland and decided to land. He descended slowly from 15,000 feet to 3,500 feet when they were shot out of the sky by Russian Yak fighters. As they drifted down in their parachutes, Russian ground troops fired on them but did not hit anyone. Russian soldiers rounded them up and treated them as German prisoners. It took considerable time to convince the Russians that they were Americans, and more time before they were transported to Poltava. General Walsh protested the treatment but Soviet officers ignored his complaints completely. They intimated that any Americans on Soviet soil or territory controlled by the Soviet Union could expect such treatment.[132]

Finally, on December 16 General Antonov told General Deane that Soviet forces would need all of their air bases in Siberia and an American force would not be able to operate from there. Deane, said Antonov had "let loose a bombshell" and objected; on December 19 he was advised that Antonov's decision was final. Harriman and Deane must have, at long last, realized that their aims in the Far East and further collaboration with the Soviet Union were dead.[133]

Operation FRANTIC may have ended, but the rescue of downed airmen in Soviet-controlled territory and the withdrawal from Poltava remained a delicate task. Infield said in his book that this period was even more frustrating and discouraging than approval of the project and the establishment of the three bases. Every move by the Eastern Command was questioned or halted by the Russians. "Ugly incidents became a daily occurrence, some so serious that it took considerable tact and discipline" for General Walsh to control the angry Americans under his command.[134]

Harriman and Deane, from the very beginning to the very end, were considerably more optimistic in their estimates of Soviet intentions on collaboration than was warranted in light of Soviet action, or the lack thereof. Their reports on collaboration helped reinforce an unfortunate tendency for those in Washington to believe what they wanted to believe.[135] A great portion of this chapter relied on the doctoral dissertation of Dr. Thomas A. Julian. James Parton, who authored the biography of General Eaker said that Julian's work was "by far the most detailed on the subject of collaboration with Russia and said it is a "must" for any student of U.S. – U.S.S.R. relations since World War II. Julian wrote the following terse comment in his conclusion on the collaboration effort at Poltava: "The Soviet cooperation in FRANTIC in retrospect must be considered as a tactic rather than as a change in policy."[136] He explained that the Soviets from the beginning delayed approval of FRANTIC, clearly intended to discourage the U.S. The persistence of Harriman and Deane, and Roosevelt's expressed interest in the project to Stalin at Teheran caused Stalin to give in. Once, however, the European conflict was no longer in doubt, and his control over eastern Europe was virtually secured, Stalin wanted us out of the Soviet Union.

In September, 1944 Harriman expressed his thoughts on collaboration to Secretary of State Hull. He said in part that once victory in Europe was in sight, the Soviets reverted to less accommodating policies they intended to follow. He said that these included the nature of their participation in world affairs and the isolation of Soviet people from outsiders. With respect to the latter he said the NKVD and the "party" never liked the idea of our troops coming onto Russian bases. He suggested that these influences were brought to bear to close the bases as soon as possible.[137] However, it was Joseph Stalin who set policy in such matters and the NKVD and the communist party merely carried it out.

Deane believed the end of FRANTIC operations in September signaled a decline in relations with the Soviet Union as related to Poltava. He said this was aggravated considerably by the deterioration of relations on a political level because of the dispute over the Warsaw situation which manifested itself in restrictions on American personnel on the bases in the Ukraine.[138]

Deane provided his own explanation as to the reason for a breakdown in their cooperative efforts at Poltava. He said Stalin did not want us in the Soviet Union to begin with and made it next to impossible to work with them. He said one of the reasons they wished to remain aloof from the outside world was the fear that the people would be contaminated by the representatives of capitalism. Deane used Poltava as an example of what happened. "When the Americans came they brought with them refinements of maintenance equipment about which the Red Air Force had not even dreamed. They paraded their shiny monstrous refueling trucks, their snow plows, their fire-fighting apparatus, and their wreckage-disposal trucks. In the infirmary were surgical instruments, sterilizing machines, dental chairs and other equipment on a scale hitherto unknown in Russia. Then there was the American soldier with his chocolate bars, cigarettes and other attractions for the Russian girls which lured them away from their own men. This experience made it seem certain that contacts with foreigners could only sow the seeds of discontent, which would weaken the cohesiveness of the Soviet nation during the war and in the future."[139]

The foregoing is undoubtedly true, but we were fools in the eyes of those in the Kremlin. Infield wrote, "Under orders from President Roosevelt, Deane, Walsh, Kessler, Spaatz, Harriman and other military and diplomatic personnel were constantly compromising and backing down in the face of strict regulations, flat refusals, harassing tactics, and rude treatment by the Soviet officers with whom they had to negotiate or the Kremlin party leaders who often made the final decisions."[140] This unfortunate treatment of our representatives was not confined to the major military and diplomatic personnel, but included the combat personnel who by misfortune ended up east of Germany and the G.I.'s who were assigned to the Eastern Command.

The story of Poltava, and in particular, the change in Soviet policy after FRANTIC II had a direct relationship to the accusations made against the crew of Myron L. King. It is important to bear in mind that our own military and diplomatic persons in the Soviet Union remained conciliatory with the Soviets even though they had all the substantive evidence of Soviet acts of ill will, small and great, for over seven months prior to the "Maiden's" landing in Poland on February 3, 1945.

Notes to Chapter 16

1. Julian, Thomas Anthony, *Operation Frantic and the Search for American – Soviet Military Collaboration, 1941-1944* p. 13
2. Julian, see 1 above p. 39
3. Julian, see 1 above
4. Deane, John R. *The Strange Alliance* p. 88
5. Julian, see 1 above p. 20

6. Ibid.
7. Julian, see 1 above p. 21-22
8. Julian, see 1 above p. 23
9. Ibid.
10. Julian, see 1 above p. 31-32
11. Julian, see 1 above p. 38-39
12. Julian, see 1 above p. 55
13. Julian, see 1 above p. 52, 56
14. Julian, see 1 above p. 58
15. Julian, see 1 above p. 60-61
16. Julian, see 1 above p. 67
17. Julian, see 1 above p. 67-68
18. Julian, see 1 above p. 88-89
19. Julian, see 1 above p. 83
20. Parton, James *Air Force Spoken Here* p. 263
21. Julian, see 1 above p. 86
22. Julian, see 1 above p. 90
23. Julian, see 1 above p. 95
24. Julian, see 1 above p. 96
25. Julian, see 1 above p. 97
26. Julian, see 1 above p. 99
27. Julian, see 1 above p.101-102
28. Julian, see 1 above p. 107
29. Julian, see 1 above p. 107-108
30. Julian, see 1 above p. 108
31. Julian, see 1 above p. 57
32. Julian, see 1 above p. 109
33. Julian, see 1 above p. 110
34. Deane, see 4 above p. 107
35. Kennan, George F. *Memoirs 1925-1950* p. 231
36. Julian, see 1 above p. 102-103
37. Julian, see 1 above p. 110
38. Julian, see 1 above p. 112
39. Julian, see 1 above p. 113
40. Julian, see 1 above 114
41. Ibid.
42. Ibid.
43. Julian, see 1 above p. 116
44. Julian, see 1 above p. 116-117
45. Julian, see 1 above p. 118
46. Julian, see 1 above p. 123-124
47. Julian, see 1 above p. 127
48. Julian, see 1 above p. 128
49. Julian, see 1 above p. 129-130
50. Julian, see 1 above p. 133-135
51. Julian, see 1 above p. 135
52. Parton, see 20 above p. 392
53. Deane, see 4 above p. 107
54. Julian, see 1 above p. 137
55. Julian, see 1 above p. 145-146
56. Strong, Russell A. *Biographical Directory of the Eighth Air Force 1942-1945* p. 104
57. Ibid. p. 120
58. Ibid. p. 85
59. Julian, see 1 above p. 146,149, 152
60. Bowman, Martin W. *Castles in the Air* p. 119
61. Julian, see 1 above p. 147
62. Julian, see 1 above p. 155-156
63. Infield, Glenn B. *The Poltava Affair* p. 24
64. Julian, see 1 above p. 156-157
65. Julian, see 1 above p. 164
66. Julian, see 1 above p. 159
67. Julian, see 1 above p. 167
68. Julian, see 1 above p.1 68-169
69. Julian, see 1 above p. 170
70. Infield, see 63 above p. 36
71. Julian, see 1 above p. 171-174
72. Infield, see 63 above p. 49
73. Infield, see 63 above p. 53, 56-57

74. *Infield, see 63 above appendix Summary of Bomber Operations and Summary of Fighter Operations June 2, 1944*
75. *Infield, see 63 above p. 57*
76. *Julian, see 1 above p. 205*
77. *Infield, see 63 above p. 73-78*
78. *Infield, see 63 above p. 100*
79. *Julian, see 1 above p. 208*
80. *Infield, see 63 above p. 108*
81. *Julian, see 1 above p. 209-210*
82. *Julian, see 1 above p. 211*
83. *Julian, see 1 above p. 218-219*
84. *Julian, see 1 above p. 220*
85. *Julian, see 1 above p. 221-223*
86. *Julian, see 1 above p. 224-225*
87. *Julian, see 1 above p. 226-227*
88. *Julian, see 1 above p. 228*
89 *Infield, see 63 above p. 156, 163*
90. *Infield, see 63 above p. 162*
91. *Infield, see 63 above p. 139, 230*
92. *Parton, see 20 above p. 405*
93. *Infield, see 63 above p. 160*
94. *Infield, see 63 above p.154*
95. *Infield, see 63 above p. 234*
96. *Infield, see 63 above appendix Summary of Bomber Operations June 26, 1944*
97. *Parton, see 20 above p. 408-409*
98. *Parton, see 20 above p. 407*
99. *Infield, see 63 above p. 168-169*
100. *Infield, see 63 above appendix Summary of Fighter Operations July 22, 25, 26, 1944*
101. *Julian, see 1 above p. 230*
102. *Infield, see 63 above p. 178-179*
103. *Julian, see 1 above p. 243*
104. *Julian, see 1 above p. 231*
105. *Julian, see 1 above p. 232*
106. *Infield, see 63 above p. 173*
107. *Infield, see 63 above p. 181-182*
108. *Julian, see 1 above p. 244*
109. *Julian, see 1 above p. 245*
110. *Julian, see 1 above p. 268*
111. *Julian, see 1 above p. 268-269*
112. *Infield, see 63 above p. 207*
113. *Julian, see 1 above p. 269*
114. *Ibid.*
115. *Julian, see 1 above p. 271*
116. *Infield, see 63 above p. 190-192*
117. *Infield, see 63 above p. 192*
118. *Infield, see 63 above p. 193-194*
119. *Infield, see 63 above p. 195*
120. *Infield, see 63 above p. 196-199*
121. *Infield, see 63 above p. 205*
122. *Infield, see 63 above p. 193-194*
123. *Infield, see 63 above p. 190*
124. *Julian, see 1 above p. 283*
125. *Julian, see 1 above p. 288*
126. *Infield, see 63 above p. 208*
127. *Julian, see 1 above p. 288*
128. *Julian, see 1 above p. 290*
129. *Infield, see 63 above p. 200*
130. *Infield, see 63 above p. 200-203*
131. *Infield, see 63 above p. 206*
132. *Infield, see 63 above p. 211-212*
133. *Julian, see 1 above p. 339*
134. *Infield, see 63 above p. 211*
135. *Julian, see 1 above p. 347*
136. *Julian, see 1 above p. 348*
137. *Julian, see 1 above p. 308*
138. *Deane, see 4 above p. 123*
139. *Deane, see 4 above p. 296*
140. *Infield, see 63 above p. 229*

CHAPTER 17 — AN ACCUSATION LACKING CREDIBLE EVIDENCE

Myron's memory during my interview with him was remarkably consistent, not only with the recollection of his crew members but also with the records of the USAAF and the USMM. This is true of the events that occurred during the weeks of their interment by the Soviets which he related in Chapter 15, but also of the events after their arrival at Poltava in 1945.

After the USMM was notified by cable on March 18 that the King crew had arrived at Poltava, a subsequent cable was sent to Moscow advising that the King crew was cleared to fly the "Maiden" back to England via Bari, Italy on March 23.[1]

On March 19 Myron was interrogated by Captain William Fitchen, AC, an intelligence officer. The report relates to their bombing of Berlin, details of the damage to their aircraft, their efforts to find a place to land in Poland, their stay at Kuflevo, the trip to Szczuczyn and Lida and the flight to Poltava. No mention of the Jack Smith is made in the report.[2]

Apparently in response to the cable from Poltava which reported the arrival of the King crew, but before receiving the Fitchen report, the USMM requested the crew be questioned as to the long delay between their landing in Poland and their arrival at Poltava, the reason for flying to several locations as well as any information as to their activities during that period.[3]

The response to the USMM the same day provided the details requested with still no reference to the incident involving Jack Smith.[4] On March 25 the King crew was given a flight plan to leave Poltava for the return flight to England on the following day or the next flyable day thereafter.[5] The following day the flight was postponed for one day with no reason stated for the delay.[6] On March 26 the Eastern Command at Poltava cabled Major General Edmund W. Hill, by then head of the Air Division of the USMM and Commander of the Eastern Command, stating General Kovalev, the Soviet Commander at Poltava, said the King crew was delayed by Soviets at Moscow, and the "reason for the delay should be known to us."[7] General Hill responded the next day saying, "It is apparent Soviets feel they have justified complaint against crew of B-17 number 446508." The message noted that the information furnished by Poltava which explained the detention of the King crew in Poland "indicated that complaint is all on American side." He requested a formal investigation be conducted to determine if Soviets had any complaint against the King crew. He also suggested that it would appear logical to form a new crew from personnel not involved in this incident and send the B-17 back to England.[8] It would seem that General Hill at this point was trying to protect the rights of the King crew. But why did he request a formal investigation without first having had, or requested, a formal complaint from the Russians? Unless General Hill and/ or others at the USMM had knowledge of a Soviet complaint before it had been received, it would seem that this was a premature request. After all, at this point the investigators had no specific allegations to prove or disapprove.

On the same day, March 27, Major General John R. Deane, head of the USMM, cabled Colonel Thomas K. Hampton at Poltava. The message was classified TOP SECRET and directed Hampton to prefer charges against 1st Lt. Myron L. King. It appointed Lt. Col. James D. Wilmeth investigating officer to investigate charges when directed by Deane in a subsequent communication.[9] Why did this suddenly become a "big deal" and why was it suddenly upgraded to a TOP SECRET classification? At this point there were no allegations against King. Why Wilmeth? Since he became a major figure in this story it is most appropriate that he be described at this point. Lt. Col. James D. Wilmeth GSC, 019519, a 1934 graduate of West Point, served in the infantry until 1937 after which he became a tank officer. A Battalion Commander when he was sent to Moscow in 1944, he was probably selected due to a reputedly good knowledge of the Russian language. While assigned at the USMM he made statistical studies of the Far East situation, was a U.S. POW contact officer and compiled an historical record of the USMM. In February 1945 he headed a POW contact team which was sent to Lublin, Poland to give aid to a number of our liberated military personnel who had been freed from German POW camps but were unable to return to military control; many were in need of medical care. The team also included Lt. Col. Curtis B. Kingsbury, MC, a physician, and Corporal Paul Kisil, an interpreter.[10]

The Wilmeth team had gone to Poltava on February 14 so as to be ready to proceed by aircraft to Poland when cleared by the Russians. It took until February 28 before they were cleared and were able to fly to Lublin. On their arrival they were specifically told they could remain in Lublin for ten days and were confined to the city itself. After the ten days expired they remained, with the knowledge of Gen. Deane, although six different times they were told by the Russians to leave.[11] They were finally forced by the Russians to leave Lublin and on March 28 arrived at Poltava. That day Wilmeth advised Deane by cable: "Wilmeth arrived; brought Kingsbury because without complete change in Soviet attitude his presence in Poland would be ineffective. Will come to Moscow first plane. Any work I can do here?"[12] Subsequent communications indicate that General Deane picked Wilmeth to investigate charges against King probably because of Wilmeth's gratuitous offer to be of service at Poltava. Subsequent facts indicate Deane should have countermanded his own order.

The investigation of the Jack Smith incident is set forth in a three-page report signed by Major Donald S. Nicholson, AC, dated March 28. It basically is the same as the recollections of King and others, with the following exceptions taken by King. Nicholson reported that on the evening of February 5 the interpreter again made known his desire to accompany the crew back to England; so far this is accurate. He then said the following which King and Lowe say is incorrect; that the crew decided that if this could be done without becoming known to the Soviets, they would comply with the interpreter's desires. Nicholson continued, saying that since the interpreter's name was unpronounceable to the American crew and, since he had gained their sympathy and confidence, they allowed him to keep the flying clothing he had acquired and gave him the alias Jack Smith. According to Nicholson, the crew also agreed they would treat the interpreter as a member of their crew and try to maintain the impression among the Russians that he was an American.[13]

Myron said that to his knowledge no such decision was made by the crew, either individually or collectively, and Nicholson was not furnished such information. He said that five of the crew members had practically no contact with Jack Smith except when they ate together and slept in the same room on February 5. He pointed out that no conversations had taken place with Jack Smith other than the few comments with Pavlos during the flight from Kuflevo, and his own with Smith after the plane had landed at Szczuczyn when he ordered him to leave the aircraft. He further said that he does not recall Jack Smith giving them his real name, does not believe they gave him the alias, and assumes that name was his own invention.[14] Nicholson's report also said that King said Jack Smith wore a British uniform under the flying clothes he found on the B-17. Myron said he did not know what Smith had on under those flying clothes. In subsequent testimony co-pilot Bill Sweeney said that Jack Smith wore a jacket under the flying clothes he got from their emergency kit. He called it a British uniform garment because Jack Smith had come over to him that evening at Szczuczyn and made him look at the buttons.[15]

The last paragraph of the Nicholson report digresses from being investigatory, arriving at conclusions which are inconsistent. He said: "King and his crew could not be held responsible for transporting Smith to Szczuczyn, the incident having arisen from a very reasonable misunderstanding. By failing to notify the Soviet authorities at Szczuczyn of Smith's presence, by allowing him to keep American flying clothing, and by listing him with Soviet authorities as a member of their crew, King and his crew have created reasonable grounds for suspicion on the part of the Soviets."[16] On the basis of the facts thus far known one could ask, "Where's the beef?" Certainly such a suspicion, as Nicholson called it, does not constitute the evidentiary basis for a General Court Martial. From the following actions it appears that the Eastern Command at Poltava and the USMM in Moscow didn't have their act together. Although the USMM had ordered charges be brought against King by its cable on March 27, the Eastern Command issued Special Orders on March 29 for the King crew to proceed to London (appendix 7). This seems to be a case of the right hand not letting the left know what was going on, surprising since there were only 200 permanent-party personnel plus those transient folks left at Poltava. Those orders for the King crew departure were canceled; had they left Poltava, a decision by a Court Martial in England or anywhere else other than the Soviet Union would have ended differently.[17]

On March 30 Poltava suggested to the USMM that King be charged with a violation of the 96th Article of War. The specification, which was subsequently the subject of changes through cables back and forth between Poltava and Moscow, related to the transportation of Jack Smith on the "Maiden" and his failure to surrender that person to the Soviets at Szczuczyn, which conduct was to the "detriment and prejudice of the military service of the United States."[18] At this point what appeared to be still lacking was just how those actions were to the detriment and prejudice of our military. Some of the cable traffic back and forth provides a picture of indecision by our military authorities in Moscow. On March 30 the USMM amended the specification of "willful neglect" by King in not surrendering Smith to say that he did "willfully conceal from Soviet authorities that he had transported as stowaway Polish subject from Warsaw to Szczuczyn, Poland and did thereby bring discredit on the Military Service of the United States."[19]

On March 31 Wilmeth cabled the USMM saying that because King was the only American present at having given false testimony (to the Russians) a charge of "willful concealment" would be difficult to substantiate and would probably result in acquittal. This message suggested a modification to read "failure to disclose" which could be proved, and added "I will bring you details or send by Kingsbury if I am ordered to remain here."[20]

Without any notification, or ever stating a reason, the Soviets on March 30 grounded all American aircraft in the Soviet Union.[21] On April Fools Day the plot grew thicker with a cable from Wilmeth to General Deane. He said, "Soviets still holding all flights" and to avoid delay he would follow with a more detailed report of the King investigation. (No trace could be found in Archival records of such a detailed report of an investigation) He then cautioned that the interrogation of King and the report of Major Nicholson were done before King was warned of his rights. Those documents show actual offense of "willful concealment" but case not "court proof" because the accused cannot convict himself on his false statement to Russians, and there are no other witnesses. He added that, "No crew member will testify as to complicity in plot to permit concealment because such testimony would incriminate himself." It is interesting that Myron and George Atkinson cannot recall any crew members on the "Maiden" ever being interrogated except for the four who were on the B-17 to Szczuczyn. Wilmeth raises the specter that the Soviets needed to be appeased saying, "If the trial needed for political reasons only, then try as charge stands. If King must be punished, then charges must be able to stand without necessity of Soviet testimony, which, I presume is neither desirable nor forthcoming." He added that the phrase in the specification "stowaway a Polish subject" cannot be substantiated and should read "alien" and the place "Warsaw" to be changed to read "vicinity of Warsaw."[22] Interestingly, they also eliminated the word stowaway.

The next day a scorching cable came back from the USMM which denied King was to be tried for political reasons. In an apparent effort to keep the record clean, the USMM, which ordered King charged, then turned around and put the responsibility on those at Poltava. The cable said, "If he is to be tried at all, he should be tried for an offense which brought discredit on the military service of the United States, and has hampered our operations, for which he would deserve punishment."[23] It is quite clear that the USMM, and General Deane in particular, by those words had decided that King was guilty, was singularly responsible for the Soviet grounding of U.S. aircraft, and was to be punished. If he had a reason for such strong feelings he certainly was not passing it along to his investigator. That is clear from the response sent by Wilmeth on April 3 to Major General Edmund W. Hill, who had replaced General Walsh, to be passed on to General Deane that he was not being told the whole story of Soviet displeasure. Wilmeth said, "Not knowing the extent of result of King's act I am not in a position to judge its seriousness and to evaluate need for punishment, but looking at this matter from a purely practical viewpoint, trial would consume time of many officers and men whose services are more urgently needed in other occupations. To use this time in forcing a pilot's own crew to convict him of a deed in which all were involved, and the consequences of which could not be foreseen at the time of commission, does not serve the interests of the Government as well as to get the unified crew back to service at the earliest opportunity. My recommendation is to withdraw the charges. If you do not concur then see my number 65 for rewording, according to the degree of seriousness. If charges 'to the prejudice of order and discipline' recommend Special Court. If 'discredit of service' then General Court."[24]

The following day the USMM disapproved Wilmeth's recommendation and advised that King would be tried by General Court Martial and requested that Colonel Hampton recommend composition of the Court.[25] On April 5 the USMM advised that a General Court Martial would meet in Moscow, about 500 miles from Poltava. This change of venue would indicate the King Court Martial was going to be a showcase trial for the benefit of the Soviets well beyond the purpose of determining the truth and dispensing justice. The cable to Poltava on that day said the Court was to include officers from the Mission and two or three air officers from the list to be recommended by Hampton and that Wilmeth would be the Trial Judge Advocate or prosecutor. The message ended with an unusual comment, "If King is tried before this Court, he may of course select his own defense counsel, although one will be appointed, probably from Poltava, as permanent Defense Counsel, in the Court."[26]

Between April 4 and April 11 there were at least ten cables between the USMM and Poltava dealing with the composition of the Court, with many persons suggested and apparently rejected, until they selected those who were to try King. Some of the officers were downed fliers at Poltava, waiting to get out of Russia. Others were permanent party, staff officers, at either the USMM or at Poltava. It is interesting to note that each name submitted included that officer's military arm. While it would appear at first glance that they may have been trying to reach some kind of a balance for fairness, when looked at closely it was more like a stacked deck against Myron L. King.[27] Finally, the selection process seemed to have satisfied the USMM and their batting order was awesome. A short resume of those involved is as follows:

The President of the Court was Colonel Moses W. Pettigrew, GSC, 06976. He was in charge of the Japanese Order of Battle Section of the Military Intelligence Section of the General Staff. General Deane called him our outstanding expert on that subject. Arriving in Russia in April, 1944 he developed a continuing relationship with the Russians which lasted until the war ended. Deane said that Pettigrew saw to it that every bit of Japanese intelligence was promptly turned over to the Red Army; in return Americans received information on troop movements in Manchuria.[28] Considering the lack of cooperation from the Soviets on almost everything except their acceptance of lend-lease and their anxiety over their neutrality as related to the Japanese, it is rather obvious who got the better of that relationship.

As already stated Lt. Col. James D. Wilmeth had been personally chosen by Gen. Deane to be the trial judge advocate. Assisting Wilmeth in the prosecution of the case was Lt. Serge J. Dankevich O-1944653, AGD as his assistant. From prior cable traffic from Wilmeth at Poltava it appears Dankevich was assigned to the USMM.[29] Two officers were recommended to be Myron King's defense counsel but were rejected by the USMM. Captain Roger M. Trimble who was soon to be promoted and replace Col. Thomas K. Hampton as the American C.O. at Poltava and Lt. Col. M.L. Alexander, who with Hampton, was relieved of his duties and left Russia April 12.[30] Finally chosen by the USMM was Lt. Col. Curtis B. Kingsbury, MC, O-480818, the medical doctor who was a member of Wilmeth's team at Lublin, Poland.[31] (One might consider their relationship to constitute a conflict of interest in this case). Chosen as assistant defense counsel was 2nd Lt. Leon Dolin, AC, O-2069206, a navigator with the 487th Bombardment Group (H) of the 8th Air Force.[32] He had been shot down on March 18 on a mission to Oranienburg and was the only graduate lawyer and member of the bar present at King's trial.[33]

The other members of the Court were: Lt. Col. H.W. Robb, AC, of the 463rd Bombardment Group in the 15th Air Force,[34] a combat transient at Poltava who Myron recalled, was upset that he had been chosen for this assignment, probably because it delayed his departure and return to Italy. Later he was upset when he had to leave Moscow after the trial ended before the Soviet May Day parade, as he had an invitation to sit in the main grandstand to observe the festivitives.[35]

Lt. Col. F.W. Crandall, CE, O-903156 was either a staff officer at Poltava or at the USMM. Since he was first suggested in a USMM cable to Poltava he was probably assigned at Moscow.[36]

Major Kern C. Hayes, Inf. O-281779, was the law member of the Court whose duty was to rule on questions of law during the trial including motions by counsel.[37] A cable from Poltava to the USMM said: "Trust you appreciate Hayes, the law member, is not a lawyer, but simply an officer with more General Court experience than anyone from here."[38] It will be recalled that he had one year of law school when he quit to enter the Army; he was assigned to the USMM and was a member of a POW contact team. At the start of the trial Hayes was challenged by a defense motion since he was not a lawyer; the motion was denied.[39] Major John C. Light, Ord., O-281779, was assigned to the USMM and was listed in a communication on May 20 as having been appointed along with Col. Pettigrew as the Foreign Claims Commission under the supervision of Gen. Deane.[40] Major R.E. Conner, AC, O-428003 of the 78th Fighter Group of the 8th Air Force was also apparently a combat transient.[41]

On April 10 General Deane was advised by cable that King had been served with the charges against him[42] which read as follows:

"**CHARGE**: Violation of the 96th Article of War. SPECIFICATION: In that 1st Lt. Myron L. King, 401st Bomb Group, 614th Bomb Squadron, did, in Poland, on or about 5 February 1945, while, as a Senior Pilot, operating an American aircraft under the auspices of the Soviet Army, transport, without proper authority, an alien from near Warsaw to Szczuczyn, and did, thereafter until such alien was removed by Soviet authorities on or about 6 February 1945, permit this alien to wear U.S. Army flying clothes, and to associate himself with the American aircraft's crew under the name 'Jack Smith' known to be an alias, thereby bringing discredit on the military service of the United States."[43]

It was previously mentioned that all American aircraft in the Soviet Union were grounded on March 30 without explanation. They were still grounded on April 11 when a cable was sent to the USMM which said: "Wilmeth wishing you were here with us for Eastern Command's first anniversary celebration. We remain in confinement - signed Wilmeth and Kingsbury."[44] The use of the cable facility for such a message was a frivolous abuse by Wilmeth which would have brought a reprimand for someone of lesser rank and privilege. Another example of this was a cable Wilmeth sent to General Deane which requested, "You notify Lt. Dankevich I will persecute the case; he will be responsible for the court administration and preparation of court records. He should rehearse the requirements with the court steno and court orderly until they are both experts."[45] The use of the words "persecute" and "rehearse" seem to be facetious and improper when considering the fact that he is discussing the military future of a fellow officer. It would probably be claimed that the use of these words were typographical errors in sending the message but I find that difficult to accept after reviewing hundreds of messages sent between Poltava and the USMM.

On April 15 a cable from Poltava advised General Spaatz that all American aircraft remained grounded by the Soviets for the sixteenth consecutive day, except one ATC transport for Teheran that day. It is quite possible that the excepted aircraft may have been carrying Ambassador Harriman who left Moscow four days after the death of President Roosevelt, April 12, 1945. The Ambassador was en route to attend the United Nations Conference at San Francisco, California which was held April 25-26, 1945.[46]

On April 14 Wilmeth advised the USMM that the Court would need King, Sweeney, Lowe and Pavlas for the trial. It is noted that these were the only crew members on the "Maiden" when she flew from Kuflevo to Szczuczyn with Jack Smith as a stowaway. Wilmeth, the appointed investigator of the Jack Smith incident, and the other so-called investigators completely ignored the rest of King's crew who spent as much time with Jack Smith at Szczuczyn as those Wilmeth specified he wanted for the trial. It is an indication of a slipshod investigation that none of the five others were even interviewed at any time! Wilmeth's message also suggested that a clearance be obtained for the other five crew members so they could proceed back to England.[47] It was not granted. It is difficult to understand Wilmeth's suggestion; it would appear that he wanted the rest of the crew out of Russia before King was tried.

The grounding of American aircraft by the Soviets also complicated the question of getting those at Poltava who were needed for the trial to Moscow. A clearance was received for their travel on April 18 [48] to Moscow. Myron recalls the trip was on a Soviet aircraft due to the grounding of the American aircraft. He said that after their arrival he did not recall spending any time in the preparation of his defense and specifically recalled no conferences with Lt. Col. Kingsbury, his counsel, even though they were there a week before the trial commenced. Myron explained that there wasn't much to prepare for. He had been made to understand that the Soviets were upset because of the Jack Smith incident, and that this was the basis for his facing a Court Martial; he was not afforded details. Before the trial began he had come to believe that the best thing for him and his crew would be to do whatever would please the Russians. He said he told those involved in the Court Martial that whatever it took to clear up this problem suited him...even a dishonorable discharge. He reasoned this would satisfy the Russians who considered that to be a very severe penalty. Myron believed that if he was given a dishonorable discharge it would be reviewed immediately back in the United States and the verdict would be overturned. When asked if he thought before the trial that he was being set up, he said that he did. He had been told that Ambassador Harriman, prior to his departure for the United States, had assisted in the preparation of the written reprimand which he received after the trial. He discussed the makeup of the Court. The entire Court of ten members included only three who were of the AAF; one of those was the assistant defense counsel. Of the six voting members, only two were of the AAF. Of the same ten persons seven were assigned at the USMM or the Eastern Command at Poltava. Myron said he thought these odds were against him, and he also thought inter-service prejudice against the AAF entered into the matter. He added that since there appeared to be no urgency or concern in formulating any trial strategy with his Counsel he spent the weekend sightseeing in Moscow.

Richard Lowe recalled the following, "While, in retrospect, the Jack Smith affair may have had something to do with the decision to subject Myron to a Court Martial, I think the main reason for that decision was to arise from the next series of events." He enumerated several things that he believed were "the kinds of events which had a bearing on the Russians forcing the Americans to Court Martial Myron." First – King being allowed to fly from Lida to Poltava. Lowe was convinced, as was Myron, that the Soviets planned to keep them with them when they moved to their new base closer to the front. Second – Poltava's main mission after the end of FRANTIC was to pick up downed American air crews. The Russians failed to report the King crew down and safe even though they had repeatedly requested that this be done. This was not just a slip of the mind or a Russian SNAFU (situation normal, all fouled up); it was a purposeful action over a seven week period. Third - There had been trouble between the Americans and the Russian "in charge" at Poltava which grew out of an incident where an American officer returning to Poltava from Teheran landed without a Russian clearance after being denied such clearance several times. (This incident happened about the time of the Yalta Conference of the Allied Powers and will be further explored during an examination of Myron's trial).

Richard said that he no longer recalls details of the trial itself but said: "...it is my firm belief that the Americans were determined to find Myron guilty to appease the Russians."[49]

During their stay in Moscow the King crew was billeted in different locations and Myron recalled that quarters were very hard to come by. He said that he had "makeshift quarters" at the Red Cross. When they were at the Embassy Building they took their meals there, which was a decided improvement over what they had to eat while they were in Poland. The Embassy Building was on Mokhavaya Street, next door to the National Hotel; it overlooked a Square covering what would be three or four city blocks in the United States.

Directly across this Square was the west wall of the Kremlin.[50] The Ambassador's residence, Spaso House, is located a mile from the Kremlin. It was built by a wealthy merchant before the Russian Revolution and had been taken over as the Ambassador's residence in 1933. General Deane wrote that Ambassador Harriman had made Spaso House the American Center; its 13 bedrooms were usually bulging with VIP American guests.[51] Since the King Court Martial was moved many hundred miles to Moscow for no other reason than to make it a showcase trial for the Soviets, for additional drama it was only fitting that with the Ambassador gone that the trial be held at Spaso House. Myron described in great detail the splendor of that residence which was featured in the January, 1988 edition of Architecture Digest.

After their arrival at Poltava the King crew must have felt their ordeal was over; they were again among their own countrymen, their own Army. Then they were betrayed by those they felt would be their defenders, their pilot charged with a most despicable offense, of bringing discredit on the uniform that he wore. Leon Dolin, Myron's assistant defense counsel, agrees with Richard Lowe and remains convinced today that the Americans were determined to find Myron King guilty to appease the Russians. After the kind of hospitality the King crew received from our so-called ally and a not-so-great welcome from their fellow Americans in that foreign land, could Myron King expect a fair trial and simple justice?

Notes to Chapter 17

1. Cable Poltava to Hill at USMM March 18, 1945 T-3113
2. Interrogation form and attached report of William Fitchen, Captain, AC March 19, 1945
3. Cable USMM to Poltava March 21, 1945 M-23331
4. Cable Poltava to USMM March 21, 1945 T-3174
5. Cable Poltava to Spaatz, Eaker, Twining, Doolittle, info Hill March 25, 1945 T-3243
6. Cable Poltava to Spaatz, Eaker, Twining, Doolittle, info 401 Bomb Group, MILMIS Bucharest, Hill March 26, 1945 T-3268
7. Cable Poltava to Hill March 26, 1945 T-3274
8. Cable USMM to Poltava March 27, 1945 M-23463
9. Cable USMM to Poltava (Wilmeth's eyes only) March 27, 1945
10. National Archives, Washington, D.C. Record Group 334 Records of Interservice Agencies; Military Mission to Moscow Box 18 Personnel and Deane, John R. The Strange Alliance p. 195
11. Deane, see 10 above p.195-196
12. Cable Poltava to USMM (Deane for Crockett) March 28, 1945
13. Report of Donald S. Nicholson, Major, AC, Investigation of Incident Involving First Lt. King and Crew March 28, 1945
14. Intereview, Myron L. King by author at Nashville, Tennessee June 9, 1992
15. Record of Trial of Myron L. King by General Court Martial April 25-26, 1945, United States Military Mission, U.S. Embassy, Moscow, U.S.S.R., Spaso House p. 16
16. See 13 above
17. Special Orders No.46, Headquarters, Eastern Command dated March 29, 1945
18. Cable Poltava to Hill March 30, 1945 T-3356
19. Cable USMM to Poltava March 30, 1945 M-23549
20. Cable Poltava to USMM March 31, 1945 T-3388
21. Cable Poltava to Spaatz for info Deane April 15,1945
22. Cable Poltava to USMM (message 65 from Wilmeth) April 3, 1945 T-3405
23. Cable USMM to Poltava April 2, 1945 M-23599
24. Cable Poltava to Hill (message 69 from Wilmeth) April 3, 1945 T-3439
25. Cable USMM to Poltava April 4, 1945 M-23641
26. Cable USMM to Poltava April 6, 1945 M-23713
27. National Archives, Washington, D.C., Record Group 334, Records of Interservice Agencies; Military Mission to Moscow 1943-1945 Cables in the Case of King, Myron L. (Items numbered 20-23, 26-27, 29, 30-32)
28. Deane, see 10 above p. 238-239
29. Cable Poltava (Kowal for Wilmeth) to USMM (for Deane) April 12, 1945
30. Cables Poltava to USMM April 4, 1945 T-3457 & USMM to Poltava April 9, 1945 M-23756
31. Cable Poltava to USMM (for Deane) April 10, 1945 T-3533
32. Ibid.
33. Enclosure to letter, Leon Dolin to author July 21, 1945
34. Cable Poltava to USMM (for Deane) April 10, 1945 T-3534
35. See 14 above

36. *Cable USMM to Poltava April 9, 1945 M-23756*
37. *Ibid.*
38. *Cable Poltava to USMM (Olsen for Roberts) April 13, 1945 T-3588*
39. *See 33 above*
40. *Cable AGWAR Washington, D.C. to Moscow (Foreign Claims Commission) May 20, 1945*
41. *See 34 above*
42. *See 31 above*
43. *See 15 above p. 4*
44. *Cable Poltava to USMM (to Olsen for Spaulding, Roberts and Crockett) April 11, 1945*
45. *Cable Poltava to USMM (From Kowal for Wilmeth to Deane) April 12, 1945*
46. *Cable Poltava to Spaatz (From Trimble for info Deane) April 15, 1945*
47. *Cable Poltava to USMM April 14, 1945 T-3598*
48. *Cable Poltava to USMM April 18, 1945 T-3651*
49. *Letter, Richard I. Lowe to author September 16, 1992*
50. *Deane, see 10 above p. 6*
51. *Ibid. p. 8-9*

CHAPTER 18 — A MOSCOW TRIAL ... A KANGAROO COURT

Many of those persons who were intimately involved in the King Court Martial trial in Moscow are deceased. Myron L. King, himself, has gratuitously told his side of the story, and others on his crew have furnished their recollections; all of these agreed as to what happened during their days and weeks in Russian-occupied Poland.

It was of particular satisfaction to me that Leon Dolin, who was King's assistant defense counsel in Moscow, came forward and volunteered to provide an account of what happened to King in April, 1945. His version is quite important because on many important issues his memory of the trial is in more detail than that of King. Further, his involvement lifts the curtain to provide, for the first time, good reason to believe that Myron King was found guilty before he was even tried, based on an unsubstantiated complaint of the Soviet Government. His recollections also serve to confirm the author's opinion that King was offered as a sacrifice to appease anti-American officials high in the Soviet bureaucracy and to appease the ire of Marshal Stalin himself who probably intentionally misrepresented the facts of the King incident to Ambassador W. Averell Harriman.

Leon Dolin is a native of Brooklyn, New York and a first generation American of Polish parents. He is an attorney and Certified Public Accountant who resides at Lawrence, New York not far from his native Brooklyn. Before he entered the military service in World War II he had completed his legal education at New York University and was admitted to the practice of law in New York State during a "delay in route" before going overseas. Leon was commissioned and won his wings as a navigator and, as was set forth in Chapter 17, his crew was a part of the 487th Bombardment Group (H) at Lavenham, England, in the Mighty Eighth.

I had enjoyed a lengthy telephone conversation with Leon in July, 1992[1] after which he wrote a short letter [2] and a statement which provides his story of the King trial.[3] In his letter he said, "You have my full permission to blast the bums and at least get an apology from the Army" for their prosecution of Myron King.[4] Leon recalled the February 3, 1945 mission to Berlin when King was forced by battle damage to fly the "Maiden" east into Russian-occupied Poland. He recalled correctly that all of the B-17s of the Eighth that day went to Berlin and the B-24s went to Magdeburg. He said that his Group that day was briefed on how to say "I am your friend" in Russian in case they too had to fly east from their target and were given coordinates for an emergency landing airfield at Lodz, Poland.

Leon said that on March 18, 1945 his B-17 was badly hit over their target at Oranienburg, northwest of Berlin, and they, like the King crew had done in February, headed east. They were pursued by a Luftwaffe fighter which added some more damage to their aircraft before turning back west. They had been told that the Red Army was at the Oder River, and once they were east of it the order to bailout was given. Two Russian fighters made passes at them in their parachutes. Two of his crew were killed and the Russians gave his pilot their "dog tags" and some personal stuff but would not let him see the bodies. Once on the ground Leon was picked up by a Red Army Mongolian infantry outfit which spoke no Russian, much less any English. He said the "I am you friend" spoken in Russian meant nothing as they proceeded to "beat the crap out of me and prepared to shoot me." Fortunately, a Soviet officer in a tank arrived and interceded, taking him to their headquarters. There the political commissar understood Leon's German; all then became friendly. He was reunited with the rest of his crew and two days later the Russians flew them to Lublin, Poland. At Lublin they joined up with Lt. Col. James D. Wilmeth, Lt. Col. Curtis Kingsbury and their interpreter. They were the trial judge advocate and defense counsel respectively at the King trial.[5] Leon described both of the these officers as "spooks", the vernacular for spies, meaning they were in Lublin on an intelligence mission.[6] He said he personally saw reports on their desks which concerned location and movement of Red Army units, their armament, their morale and other matters. He said he knew they were there ostensibly to assist liberated American POWs, but all he ever saw them do was give the former POWs shots. He believed their principal mission in Poland was to gather intelligence.[7]

About a week after their arrival at Lublin they left for Poltava with the Wilmeth team, arriving at Poltava March 28.[8] Leon recalls that about April 10 or 11 he was ordered to report to a room at Poltava where he found Wilmeth and Kingsbury alone. They asked if he was a lawyer, which he acknowledged but when asked if had any trial experience, he said no. Determining that he did not know Lt. Myron King, they asked if he had any objection to serving as assistant defense counsel to Kingsbury at a Court Martial trial in Moscow. He said he had no objection and was told that because he was the only American lawyer in Russia his services were needed. Leon said they then emphasized that it was nothing important; they just wanted to have at least one lawyer there.[9] During that discussion Leon learned King was the "accused" and some of his crew were to be used as witnesses against him. He said he raised questions then about the legal propriety of such a plan because of the absence of other corroborating evidence and was told not to concern himself that "it was all taken care of."[10]

A cable was sent to Gen. Deane in Moscow on April 10 which advised that "accused wants Kingsbury and 2nd Lt. Dolin, O 2069206, AC, 487 Bomb Group, 837 Bomb Squadron, a combat man with legal experience, as defense counsels."[11] Leon said that days later he was off to Moscow where he met King, Sweeney, and two others of King's crew, the navigator and the engineer. He was given a set of orders which listed all the officers to serve on the Court Martial, a copy of the charge and the specification, and a copy of the Army Articles of War.

At the Embassy building he was permitted to review the file on the King case which was classified SECRET. He was not allowed to have any copies of the contents of the file which was not permitted to be before the Court during the trial. In that file he recalled seeing a statement made by Admiral Clarence Olsen of the USMM that the charge against King "was another Slavinism." Lt. Gen. N.K. Slavin was the Assistant to the Chief of Staff, Red Army General Staff. He was Gen. Deane's liaison contact with the Red Army General Staff.[12] That relationship with the USMM apparently did not prevent Slavin from being disagreeable to Americans; he was also described as a very class and rank conscious officer in the Russian classless society.[13] Leon said the file also contained correspondence between Roosevelt, Harriman, Eisenhower, Eaker and others on how to brief crews so as to avoid trouble.[14] He said that Lt. Col. Kingsbury made no attempt to review the file even after he told him about the material he had seen. Further, Leon reviewed Lt. King's story with him before the trial but Kingsbury, the lead defense counsel, did not even discuss the case with King; this is consistent with King's story.[15]

The trial began on April 25, 1945 at Spaso House, the residence of the American Ambassador in Moscow. All members of the Court Martial detail were present.[16] The first five pages of the trial transcript set forth miscellaneous administrative information. This includes an affidavit signed by Captain George Fischer, AC. The document includes a statement of Fischer, under oath, that he personally signed the charges and specifications against King and, "he has personal knowledge of the matters set forth in the specifications and investigated the matters set forth in the specifications of the charge and that the same were true in fact, to the best of his knowledge and belief." Fischer was assigned as Adjutant at Eastern Command Headquarters at Poltava.[17] Of all the materials reviewed in the research done on this story there was no information which disclosed any investigation conducted by Captain Fischer in the King case. The affidavit also contradicts information previously reported that Gen. Deane by cable March 27 appointed Wilmeth to be the investigator in that case; this was reiterated in another cable March 29.[18] The only instance in this case when Captain Fischer's name can be recalled was his certification of "true copies" of cables in a cable file compiled for the King trial. The effort to have Fischer listed in the record may have been because it might seem awkward in the record for Wilmeth to have been both the investigator and prosecutor of King; it was also a question of ethics. Besides, it was best to downplay Wilmeth as much as possible since the facts will show that his refusal to leave Lublin when the Russians demanded could have resulted in a charge against him under the same Article of War. The affidavit, if improper, is another factor which raises the question whether the trial of King was corrupted before it even began. In addition to the aforementioned five pages of miscellaneous material, the trial transcript consists of ninety-three pages of testimony and six more setting forth trial exhibits and other administrative information.

The trial was held in a paneled room with a ceiling about two stories high. It was on the first floor adjacent to a large ballroom.[19] Leon Dolin said that at the outset he asked for a change of venue which he based on "obvious outside pressure"; the request was denied. It is also interesting to note that there is no mention of this request in the transcript, or of many other objections Dolin said he made during the trial. A cable from the USMM to Poltava on April 6 said the Court Martial was "being appointed to meet in Moscow." There must have been some concern about the propriety of moving the trial to Moscow since a cable dated April 16 from the Adjutant General in Washington to Moscow said: "Please use your own discretion as to change of venue for King's trial."[20] It is interesting to note that neither this cable, or the message from Moscow to Washington, D.C. requesting advice on the venue question were included in the cable file for the trial. Did those in the Moscow Embassy and the USMM fear that moving the trial more than 500 miles from the Eastern Command base at Poltava to the Soviet capital would be construed as a showcase trial for the Russians and a denial of justice? In one of his volumes on the 401st Bombardment Group our historian Vic Maslen said the Russians "demanded that Lt. King be Court Martialed in Moscow; and, to the disgrace of the representatives of the USAAF in Moscow, they agreed ..."[21] However, the decision to do so was not the responsibility of officers of the USAAF in Moscow, but rather of Maj. Gen. John R. Deane, not of the USAAF but the U. S. Army Commanding General of the USMM.

Also before the trial got underway, Dolin objected to the Court as it was constituted. He said it was improper to name as the law member, Major Kern Hayes, who was not a lawyer. This objection was also denied. Dolin said that Kingsbury, a medical doctor and the lead defense counsel, told him to shut up, cause no trouble and everything would be OK.[22] Again, no mention is recorded in the transcript that an objection was made to Maj. Hayes serving as the law member, and it will be evident that the part he played in the trial favored the prosecution through consistent decisions not based on the law or fairness. Leon said that when he objected to various matters during the trial he was repeatedly told by Kingsbury to sit down and shut up. Very few of Dolin's objections and none of such admonitions Kingsbury recorded in the transcript.[23]

The first witness to be called was Lt. William J. Sweeney, King's copilot. In all material statements Sweeney's testimony was consistent with the story as told by Myron King in Chapter 15. Some of that testimony is summarized and quoted here because it provides an appreciation of the weakness of the case brought by the military of the United States against King.

With respect to the events at Kuflevo on February 5, Sweeney testified that after the Russian General landed and parked his C-47 right next to the "Maiden," he was the first to exit their aircraft via the nose hatch. He said as he approached the General, the interpreter that they came to know as Jack Smith was standing with the General and proceeded to act as the interpreter for the Russian. He said that he had never seen Jack Smith in the three days they had been at Kuflevo, and from the circumstances of his appearance with the General he concluded Jack Smith was in the General's party. How he got there remains a mystery to this day. If he had not landed with the General there is a question left unanswered: where did he come from and how did he show up at that particular time?

Sweeney said the General would escort them out of Kuflevo but was in a hurry to depart because he said he would not fly at night. This led to a lot of confusion because they had to strip as much weight from the B-17 as possible if they were going to be able to make it on takeoff from such a short dirt field. He said, "everybody was trying to help us transfer our flak suits, ammunition etc. to the other plane. There were Russians and Americans in and out of both aircraft and running back and forth between them." He said the confusion was such that Jack Smith could have hidden on the aircraft. Here Sweeney and later witnesses could have been more convincing; All Jack Smith had to do was to be the last person on board when the transfer of equipment and crew to the C-47 was completed. All of the crew aft of the bomb bay were to fly with the Russian C-47. Since all crew members assigned forward of the bomb bay, which included all on the skeleton crew that day, normally entered the aircraft by way of the nose hatch they would not have seen anyone from the radio room to the tail. There were doors at either end of the bomb bay, that is between the flight deck and the radio room. There would have been no need to hide; once the waist hatch was closed Jack Smith had the rest of the aircraft to himself. The only reason he was discovered before they took off was because Lt. King sent Sgt. Pavlas to the rear to insure that no damage was done by a piece of engine cowling which flew off when they were running up the engines prior to takeoff. Only two members of the Court, Lt. Col. Robb and Lt. Dolin would have been familiar with B-17 crew positions and how they normally entered the aircraft.

Without any variation, both Lts. King and Lowe agreed with Sweeney's testimony that once Jack Smith was discovered on board their aircraft, it was too late to get him off and on the Russian C-47 which was preparing to takeoff.

Sweeney said it was the General's decision that they land at Szczuczyn rather than continuing on to Lida as planned. He said it was en route that they first realized that Jack Smith was not a member of the General's party when he commented to Sgt. Pavlas that he had an uncle in England and wished to go there.

Sweeney testified that Jack Smith was the only name he knew this person by, and, although he never said what his nationality was, he did not think he was an American.[24] It was obvious that Wilmeth was trying to get Sweeney and the other witnesses to say that they knew Jack Smith was an alias and that he was Polish. He was unable to do so.

In Sweeney's testimony the only discrepancies with other sources were as follows: Lt. Leon Dolin said that on one occasion he recalled Sweeney telling him that Jack Smith confessed to him that he was an agent of the Polish Emigre Government in London.[25] Over the passage of years such a statement could have been made in a different context; Sweeney may have meant that he suspected Jack Smith was an agent based on Soviet accusations that he was. There was one other unexplained piece of information about Sweeney's contact with Jack Smith. Richard Lowe recalled that they were once forced to disrobe at Szczuczyn for showers, even if they didn't wish to bathe. He said they assumed this was to permit the Russians the opportunity to search their clothing. Myron King recalled this same incident in Chapter 15 saying that Sweeney had several passports or other identity papers Jack Smith had given him which were in his jacket when they disrobed for the showers.

Sweeney's testimony and that of his crew members who also testified provides not one iota of evidence, direct or circumstantial, that Jack Smith was intentionally smuggled on board their aircraft; nor was there any evidence from any other witness during the trial to this effect. On the contrary, all testimony is clear that he was a stowaway. Sweeney said that during the flight to Szczuczyn King resolved they would take Jack Smith with them to Poltava and turn him over to American authorities. He said all they needed at Szczuczyn was fuel, and that they expected to reach Poltava that night or the next day.[26]

An interesting exchange concluded the questioning of Sweeney. Wilmeth wished to introduce as an exhibit a document signed by Sweeney.[27] (Appendix 8) The statement accurately follows Sweeney's testimony of what happened on the flight to Szczuczyn on February 5 and the arrest of Jack Smith on February 6. Leon Dolin objected to the admission of the exhibit claiming that such a document is not admissable on direct examiniation by the prosecution when the witness who made the statement is in court and able to testify. He continued that Wilmeth was using the statement to impeach his own witness, attacking his credibility. He said that for Wilmeth to do so would require a showing that Sweeney was a hostile witness which could not be adduced from his testimony. Wilmeth argued that he was not trying to impeach the witness but was trying to "conciliate his statements with the statement in the charge sheet to the effect 'Jack Smith,' a name not known to be his own." The objection of the Defense was again not sustained by the law member and the document was admitted as Exhibit #1; Dolin objected to the ruling.[28] Wilmeth claimed Sweeney's testimony followed the statement he signed with the exception of a slight misunderstanding over the last ten words which in the above quote. He then asked Sweeney to testify as to the circumstances under which he signed that statement. Sweeney responded Jack Smith was the only name that he knew the interpreter by and no one ever said what his nationality was. He said they did not believe when they signed the statement that it would assume the magnitude that it had. He added, "although we knew no other name than Jack Smith, we just thought it was probably wasn't his real name." Sweeney completed his testimony by pointing out that the statement he signed was dictated by Wilmeth and presented to him to sign without giving him an opportunity to make a statement of his own.[29]

After Sweeney was excused Wilmeth asked the Court to take judicial notice of the Army regulation which pertains to the subject of the illegal wearing of the uniform. He read a portion of that regulation AR600-40 par. 26 into the record which said that it would be unlawful for a person, not an officer or enlisted man, to wear the "duly prescribed uniform" of a branch of the military or "any distinctive part of such uniform."[30] To call or to infer that the flight clothes, without any form of rank, without any unit designation or insignia, to be a duly prescribed uniform or a distinctive part thereof is fallacious!

Lt. Richard I. Lowe, the navigator, was the next witness called by Wilmeth. His testimony in every way was in agreement with King's story and the testimony of Sweeney. As in Sweeney's case Wilmeth made an effort to get Lowe to testify that the crew knew Jack Smith to be an alien and that they knew his name was not Jack Smith. Lowe said he could not swear Jack Smith was an alien and said: "So far as I know, his name was Jack Smith."[31]

Lowe was followed as a witness by S/Sgt. Ernest S. Pavlas, the engineer, and the only enlisted man on the skeleton crew that flew the "Maiden" to Szczuczyn on February 5. On direct examination he said that he learned from other crew members that the interpreter was called Jack Smith and he began to use that name also. Since he was called as a witness by Wilmeth it was strange that Wilmeth asked Pavlas very few questions, particularly since it was Pavlas who discovered Jack Smith on board their aircraft and reported it to Lt. King. The defense asked Pavlas if, to his knowledge, there has been a conspiracy to transport on their aircraft a member of the Polish underground who was wanted by the Russian authorities; he responded: "No sir." Apparently realizing Wilmeth had forgot, Col. Pettigrew as President of the Court, had Pavlas testify as to finding Jack Smith on board before takeoff which coincided with the testimony of the other members of the crew. Pavlas then advised the Court that after they were airborne he went to the rear of the aircraft to check the tail, wing etc. and found Jack Smith in the radio room. He said it was then that Jack Smith told him he had an uncle in London and wanted to go see that relative. He said he then reported this information to Lt. King. [32]

The next witness was Major Howard W. Taylor, AUS, the aide-de-camp to Gen. Deane and Deputy Chief of Staff for the USMM. He was called to identify a letter, in the Russian language, from Gen. Antonov to Gen. Deane which was dated March 30, 1945. Wilmeth then called as a witness Capt. Henry Ware, AUS, the official interpreter for Gen. Deane, to provide the Court with a translation of that letter. [33] Capt. Ware also identified the writer as General A.E. Antonov, Chief of the Red Army General Staff. Basically, the letter charged that American personnel in Russian occupied territory had rudely violated the order established there by the Red Army and did not live up to the elementary rules of a relationship between friendly nations. The letter cited three examples of such conduct: the incident involving Lt. King, and the case of 1st Lt. Donald R. Bridge of the 15th Air Force in Italy and that of Lt. Col. James D. Wilmeth in Lublin. (Appendix 9)

Bridge, a B-24 pilot in the 459th Bombardment Group (H) of the 15th Air Force on March 22, 1945 bombed Prague and thereafter, running low on fuel, returned to a designated emergency airfield at Mielec, Poland. The crew was detained there until March 24 when they took off, despite the lack of clearance, and returned to their base in Italy. Bridge, on the basis of the Soviet complaint in the Antonov letter, was tried by General Court Martial at 15th Air Force Headquarters on April 19, 1945. He was found guilty of one specification under the 96th Article of War. That specification included the wording that Bridge disregarded the signal to prohibit takeoff, and wrongfully and in direct contravention of recognized flight discipline and control did take off from Mielec. It continued to say that his conduct might prejudice the relationship between the United States and its ally, the U.S.S.R. He was sentenced to be reprimanded and to forfeit $100 of his pay per month for six months. As the aircraft commander who was responsible for that aircraft and for his crew, Bridge found himself in a war torn-land, interrogated at length at Mielec and detained by Russians, circumstances which have made anyone suspicious of the intent of those who professed to be his ally. His actions therefore were understandable, and he did what he believed was in the best interests of his crew. Later in 1945 an effort was made by a member of the U.S. Congress to reopen the Bridge case; it was rejected by the U.S. Army. His conviction should today be overturned and the $600 plus interest from 1945 should be paid to him by a grateful United States.[34]

The third incident in the Antonov letter involved none other than Lt. Col. James D. Wilmeth, whose choice as the trial judge advocate against Lt. King represents a conflict of interest and an apparent effort to cover up his own possible culpability. He was accused of refusing to comply with the Russian request that he leave Lublin, Poland on March 11, 1945. Gen. Antonov's letter, after summarizing the three incidents described all three incidents as facts which he considered to be a rude violation of the elementary rights of our friendly mutual relationship. Gen. Deane later wrote that Wilmeth was "invited" by the Soviets to leave Lublin not once but on six different occasions.[35]

The defense objected to the admission of the Antonov letter as an exhibit for the record because to do so would injuriously affect the rights of the accused. The defense also questioned the translation as a more severe form inadvertently used, referring to language differences best described by Gen. Deane who wrote, "Some of our differences with the Russians spring from the language difficulty. Russian is a more precise language than English. In Russian there is more apt to be a word to express each different shade of meaning. In English the same word not only has different meanings, but inflections on words and their relations to other words in the context connote different thoughts. Thus a Russian translation into English often appears blunt and unnecessarily offensive, while an English translation into Russian is likely to result in an interpretation not intended."[36]

Another objection to the admission of the Antonov letter was that author of the letter was not present to testify and be subjected to cross-examination. The defense said that the locale of the Court had been moved over 500 miles for the convenience of the Russians to appear. The defense further said, "They have been requested to be here by the Commanding General of this Mission to give, as properly should be given, their own testimony. If they wish to absent themselves, then this type of testimony should properly be excluded." Before the objection could be ruled on Wilmeth said that prosecution was not trying to prove the statements in the letter but was trying to show that it became necessary for an official of the Red Army to write a letter in derogatory terms about the act the accused committed. Lt. Dolin responded, "We have had no notice of what the letter contains; no means of knowing whether this letter is derogatory. The Court cannot take judicial notice of the letter since it has not been introduced as evidence." Major Hayes, the law member, overruled the defense and admitted the letter as Exhibit #2.

According to the transcript Wilmeth began to read portions of the letter but did not indicate what portions were read and which were not. The defense again objected saying that the fact that displeasure was shown in the letter by Gen. Antonov was based on a number of instances, not just the one involving Lt. King and said, "The rights of the accused are affected injuriously by the reading of these extracts." Wilmeth responded, "The other cases mentioned in the letter do not form a part of this trial." His strategy saved him the humiliation of reading into the record Soviet criticism of his own conduct, which also would have been shared by Lt. Col. Kingsbury, the defense counsel, who was on Wilmeth's team in Lublin. Strangely, the transcript reported no ruling on the defense motion, which may have been sustained since the extracted portions read do not appear on the record.[37]

The choice of Wilmeth to prosecute the King case in light of his being listed in the Antonov letter on the same level of conduct as Lt. King and Lt. Bridge is incredulous to say the least. The history of the Wilmeth incident in Lublin, after his return to Poltava needs to be further explored. In a cable from the USMM to Poltava on March 29 General Deane advised that he desired charges be brought against King and appointed Wilmeth to be the investigator of the King incident. He also said, "Desire that he (Wilmeth) be held at Poltava until his departure from there has been authorized by me."[38] It was subsequently revealed that the Antonov letter dated March 30 was not received by General Deane until April 1.[39] How the

General anticipated the Soviet complaint is not known from the trial transcript, the cable traffic or other materials. From this particular message it appears that he was trying to keep Wilmeth out of Moscow, which also would indicate he may have known Wilmeth was to be included in the Soviet complaint before he received the letter from Antonov. Two days later Deane cabled Wilmeth that if the investigations were complete he could return to Moscow. However, by then all American flights had been grounded and Wilmeth was stuck at Poltava.[40]

On the change of venue two communications reveal contradictory information being given to Gen. Slavin, Assistant to the Red Army Chief of Staff. On April 11 Deane sent a letter to Slavin advising him of the plans to try Lt. Donald Bridge and Lt. King. He said that King would be tried in Moscow and added, "I am not having the case tried in Poltava because I feel that officers of the U.S. Military Mission who do not have knowledge of the facts and who are not acquainted with the individuals involved can judge the case without prejudice."[41] Deane was saying that the Eastern Command officers and the combat transients at Poltava, who were in the main Army Air Force personnel, would not render a just verdict. Making such a statement to a high ranking official of another government, even an ally, I think was reprehensible. Gen. Deane virtually admits he set Lt. King up to be convicted. He left Moscow during the second week in April for a trip to Washington, D.C. from which he did not return until May 6. How he got out of Russia when all American aircraft were grounded is not documented but it can be presumed he traveled with the Ambassador who left about four days after the death of Roosevelt on April 12.

His explanation for having the trial in Moscow must have intrigued Slavin when Slavin met with Brig. Gen. Frank N. Roberts of the USMM on April 17. Slavin requested clarification as to whether they wanted to have the King trial in Moscow or in the United States. Gen. Roberts said they intended to hold it in Moscow and that Gen. Deane decided to do so because there were not enough officers at Poltava to carry out the trial; it was with the idea of expediting matters that Moscow was decided on. Slavin thanked Roberts for his clarification and said, "the matter is clear now." He said he would respond that day if the Soviet Union objected to a Moscow trial, perhaps by telephone, by just saying "no objections."[42]

There were at least twelve other officers recommended by Poltava to serve on the Board which was to try King, and I would wager at least another twelve could have been found among the combat transients at Poltava who would not have known Myron King and would have given him a fair trial.

The certified copy of the April 6 cable prepared for use during King's trial omitted the following: "request you inform Wilmeth that I (Deane) saw Gen. Golubev this evening and he promised to do what he could toward obtaining authority for Wilmeth to return to Moscow. He should return as soon as such authority is received."[43] Lieutenant General K.D. Golubev headed the Repatriation Commission, and since Wilmeth was a POW contact officer he may have known Golubev. Regardless, it would appear that Deane may have been involved in some damage control efforts on the complaint made against Wilmeth in the Antonov letter. What other reason would there have been to delete that portion of the cable from a certified "true copy"?

On April 9 Wilmeth sent a cable to Deane in which he suggested, "It might help if I saw Kovalev (Soviet Commander at Poltava) and explained without argument, debate or bitterness" the reason that he failed to leave Lublin when ordered to do so six times. Wilmeth said he believed his problem originated with Kovalev. Wilmeth concluded by asking, "Can Kingsbury and Kisil, who are guiltless, be separated from my sin?"[44] On the same day Wilmeth in another cable to Deane expressed deep appreciation for Deane's strong support and said, "I know you realize there are two sides to every story and you are getting only one."[45] In response, Deane cabled Wilmeth on April 10, and said that with respect to the Soviet complaint on Wilmeth, "I feel they are seizing on this incident and exaggerating the importance they attach to it because of the overall situation, both political and military."[46] Deane was thus able to condone the conduct of an immediate subordinate but would not extend the same rationale to King and Lt. Donald Bridge who were veteran combat pilots.

Wilmeth, continuing to keep the cable traffic busy replied the same day to Deane, "I suspect now the issue was trumped up … I regret that I allowed an issue to develop. I wanted to stop short of creating an incident, but overshot. However, I feel as you do, the charge presented is not the crime committed."[47] This was the last communication which relates to the complaint against Wilmeth, although the subject was raised briefly during the King trial over the objection of Wilmeth.

Wilmeth was very concerned that the Russians would learn of his association with the King case. In a cable to General Roberts on April 17 (because Deane was absent in the U.S.) Wilmeth said, "Unless you have already done so, I suggest that you do not connect Kingsbury and myself with the King case when asking for transportation for us. I think the Soviets would suspect you of chicanery in trying to use the Court as a vehicle for their (re)lease of my party as an admission by you that my party is guilty of some offense. Request you keep me informed of action taken."[48]

The Antonov letter having been admitted as an exhibit, Capt. Ware was questioned further. He said that in his capacity as Deane's interpreter he attended a meeting between Deane and Slavin about mid-April 1945 (note Deane left for the U.S. about mid-April). He said that during that meeting Slavin expressed a reaction to the alleged act of Lt. King. There was an objection to this testimony by the defense because of the failure of the witness to document the date of the meeting, which they noted was at least some 69 days after the alleged incident. No ruling was found in the transcript on this objection and as Capt. Ware continued, the defense again objected on the grounds that the testimony was hearsay. Wilmeth again responded that he was not trying to "prove what he said was correct, but only that it was said." Again the law member overruled the defense. Ware then said that Slavin considered King's alleged acts to be "an infringement or violation of an allied relationship, or a relationship between allies. And, furthermore, it consisted of a violation of the order established at airdromes and areas occupied by Soviet forces."

Wilmeth then asked Capt. Ware if Slavin expressed himself as to what would be the outcome of such acts? The defense again objected to this question as hearsay saying, "We are in a locale where this testimony can be properly given. We are 200 yards from the Kremlin." The law member interceded to ask Wilmeth what it was he was trying to bring out by the course of this questioning. Wilmeth responded, "I am trying to bring out that the act Lt. King committed was of such a character that Soviet officials at official meetings and in official correspondence took note of it and reported on it as being a violation of the order of the Soviet Union and the order they had prescribed for Soviet-occupied territories and hence a reflection on good relations between the United States and the Soviet Government." (Wilmeth was attempting to establish that King's alleged act, as charged, brought discredit upon the military services of the United States) The law member then said, "The Court will take judicial notice of the impracticability of summoning the witnesses and therefore accepts the testimony into evidence. The objection is not sustained."

Capt. Ware then continued that Slavin said, "As a result of recently-occurred incidents it was necessary for the Soviet General Staff to take action to protect themselves against the recurrence of such alleged acts." Ware said the alleged act of Lt. King was mentioned specifically in that regard. On cross-examination Ware said the Soviet reactions were not due to one incident, that is the alleged act of Lt. King. He denied ever having heard of the expression "Slavinism," apparently with respect to anti-American and/or obstructionist utterances of Gen. Slavin, but did agree from his years in the Soviet Union that the Russians have different standards and different social values than Americans. Although denied by Capt. Ware and later by Admiral Olsen, then acting head of the USMM in Deane's absence, Leon Dolin said he saw the reference to "Slavinism" in the King file he reviewed at the Embassy before the trial. He recalled the appellation was attributed to Olsen but probably was commonly used within the USMM by those who had contact with Gen. Slavin.[49]

On further examination by members of the Court Capt. Ware said he could name four incidents which caused Slavin's reaction, but said Slavin implied there were many others which were not furnished to American authorities. He was asked if Slavin provided any scale as to the degree of the various offenses, and he said that the King incident was given "particular stress because of the alleged implications with our supposed attitude toward a government which is friendly to the Soviet Union in an area which the Red Army forces are occupying." (This is an oblique reference to the Lublin communist government of Poland established by the Soviet Union mentioned in Chapter 16)[50] In his testimony Ware confused the facts in the Lt. Donald Bridge incident, previously discussed, with the case of Russian Captain Morris I. Shenderoff.

Shenderoff was drafted into the Red Army in 1941 and served in an engineer battalion in the retreat to Moscow and the defense of that city. He claimed to have been wounded and then injured when he was run over by a tank. He then eventually transferred to the Red Air Force. He said he had served at Poltava when the Eastern Command of the USSTAF was established there. In December 1944 his unit was transferred to Kecskemet, Hungary where he said he headed a department which recorded repair work done on Soviet aircraft. He said that several American B-24s made emergency landings at Kecskemet including one of the 454th Squadron (15th Air Force) which required repairs. He said the pilot was a Lt. Raleigh and the copilot a Lt. Wilkins. He said that he was encouraged by Lt. Raleigh to stowaway on his B-24 which he did when the aircraft departed on March 22, 1945. He was turned over to American authorities on arrival at Bari, Italy the same date. He was detained at a Segregation Compound and was interrogated by American authorities. The 15 page interrogation report of Shenderoff's background shows that he claimed to have been born at Cleveland, Ohio June 8, 1912, and claimed U.S. citizenship through his father's naturalization in 1921. If born in Cleveland he would have been a citizen regardless of his father's naturalization. He listed eleven relatives by the names Krasnick and Zimmerman, who he said were last known by him to be residents of Chicago. He said his father was a successful building contractor in Cleveland and had a lawyer by the name of Moldavar. He named associates of his father in the building business by the names of Sturman, Wilensky and Levinson. Shenderoff said his father, who had been a political revolutionary opposed to the Czar, returned to Russia ostensibly for a visit in 1926, then prevailed on the family, his mother, sister and himself, to visit him in Russia in 1927. He said his father was executed by the Soviets in 1936 as an "English spy"; that his sister died in 1929 and his mother in 1944. Shenderoff furnished many details of his unsuccessful efforts through 1938 to return to America. The interrogation report is replete with facts which render the Shenderoff story verifiable if true.[51]

Nevertheless, within three weeks of his arrival in Italy, a cable to Moscow from Washington, D.C., signed "Marshall" advised that Shenderoff was not a U.S. citizen. Deane then wrote to Slavin advising that Shenderoff was being held in Italy, and said they were awaiting Soviet desires as to where they wished him to be delivered in the Soviet Union.[52] On demand of the Soviets, Shenderoff was transported on an American aircraft, in custody, to Moscow arriving there April 12, 1945. On that day in the presence of Major General Edmund W. Hill, the Chief of the Air Division of the USMM, Shenderoff was turned over to Soviet officials and driven away.[53] The National Archives files contain a copy of a "receipt" dated April 12, 1945 in which it was stated that on that day custody of Captain M.I. Shenderoff of the Red Army was turned over by Lt. Col. David V. Anderson, representing the USMM, to an officer representing the Red Army. It was signed "Major Storbanov."[54]

Myron King said that while he was in Moscow he heard that Shenderoff was shot the day that he arrived there. King also heard that the U.S. "traded" Shenderoff for a clearance for Ambassador Harriman's aircraft to leave Russia about April 17 to attend the United Nations Conference at San Francisco later that month.[55] All American aircraft were still grounded. The decision to return Shenderoff to Russia was to send him to certain death. It also raises the question as to how much checking was done in such a short period of less than three weeks to determine if Shenderoff was or was not a citizen.

The next witness at the King trial was Edward Page, Jr., Second Secretary, American Embassy, Moscow and a resident at Spaso House. Page testified that he served as interpreter for the Ambassador and at times did "general political work." He said he attended a meeting April 15, 1945 between Ambassador Harriman and Marshal Stalin which was also attended by various interpreters. The Defense objected to this testimony as being totally hearsay, also pointing out that the meeting occurred 69 days after the alleged incident and that other incidents could have caused or affected the reaction of the Soviets. The defense further said:

"the rights of the accused are injurously affected by such testimony. The locale of the Court is convenient for Russian witnesses to appear." Wilmeth responded as before saying, "The purpose of the witness is to show that at official meetings Soviet reaction of a certain character was expressed … this is a first-hand witness to such a reaction." The objection was again overruled by the law member.

Mr. Page then testified, dropping the other shoe as it were, that he recalled Stalin saying, "It appeared that American aircraft were coming into Soviet-controlled territory for ulterior purposes." Page said Stalin then more of less defined such "purposes" saying they were "dropping supplies, wireless sets and getting in touch with the Polish underground." Harriman asked for the facts of such a charge and was told by Stalin that they would be forthcoming. Stalin continued by saying that General Deane had undoubtedly informed the Ambassador of the case of an airplane coming down "on the pretext of engine trouble, had received help and hospitality of the Russians and had immediately flown off with a Pole on board."

Dolin, for the defense, pointed out that the real thrust of Stalin's comments did not apply to the King incident in that there was no proof of dropping supplies and wireless sets, nor was there proof of King being in touch with the Polish underground. He then asked Page if it weren't true that after that statement by Stalin, Gen. Antonov said he did not know what was going on in the King case or whether Rear Admiral Clarence E. Olsen, Chief of the Navy Division of the USMM, was present and referred to the allegation by Stalin as a "Slavinism"? Page denied that either Antonov or Olsen were present at that meeting. Dolin then indicated that there had been another meeting when the expression "Slavinism" was used by Admiral Olsen.[56] In 1992 Dolin recalled having seen a document in his pretrial review of the file at the Embassy which recorded such a comment attributed to Admiral Olsen.[57]

During Page's testimony he was questioned by the Court and it was brought out that Stalin did not identify Lt. King as the pilot in his allegation, and as Major Light of the Court said in an inquiry, "That is rather an assumption that he was referring to the King case." No recorded response was made to this comment by Light.

Also, in responding to a question by Major Conner of the Court, "Isn't it possible he had reference to another incident?" Page replied: "I could not say definitely; he just gave it as an incident." Further, in response to a question by the Court President, Col. Pettigrew, whether the dropping of supplies to the Poles was the concern of Stalin at the time, Page said, "No, I would say it was the general subject of assistance to the underground, the bringing in and out of agents." Again, as Dolin previously pointed out, the King crew had nothing to do with such activity nor was there any evidence of such presented in the trial. Dolin was told by Page that he did not know how many American aircraft had come down in Poland during the months prior to this trial.[58] Later, Dolin tried unsuccessfully to get an admission from Wilmeth confirming what he heard at Lublin and at Poltava that some fifty American planes went down behind Soviet lines in that period of time and any of those crews would have caused the Soviet displeasure. Wilmeth said, "I can't deny the possibility. On the other hand, I can't testify to anything definitely that would indicate the possibility."[59]

Col. Pettigrew further questioned Page who said he did not know how many incidents formed the basis for Stalin's comments. Pettigrew pointed out that the allegations of dropping supplies and wireless sets to the Polish underground was more or less a general statement. He then asked Page: "He did not offer any proof?" Page replied: "No, not to the Ambassador." Lt. Col. Crandall of the Court asked if the Ambassador had given Stalin a detailed explanation of the matter and the response was: "No, I think the Ambassador wanted the proof first."[60]

Page's recollection of who was present at that meeting was somewhat faulty. Patrick J. Hurley, Ambassador to China, had stopped over in Moscow on his way to Chungking and accompanied Harriman to his meeting with Stalin on April 15. In a book by Harriman and Elie Abel the facts of that Harriman-Stalin meeting were garbled. The King incident was described as follows, "At the height of the Polish crisis, an American air crew on a rescue mission from the Poltava base had made matters worse by smuggling out a young Pole disguised in a GI uniform. The immediate Soviet response was to order the grounding of few planes that remained at Poltava and 163 airmen who had landed there in planes crippled by German gunners or had been evacuated to safety after crashing in Poland. Stalin made a great deal of alleged smuggling escapade when Harriman went to see him on April 15 ... Hurley was aghast when Stalin accused the American Air Forces of having conspired with the anti-communist Polish underground against the Red Army, and Harriman thundered back, 'You're impugning the loyalty of the American high command and I won't allow it. You're actually impugning the loyalty of General Marshall.' For all his toughness, Hurley was shocked by Harriman's blunt words, but Stalin replied in a mollifying tone. 'I would trust General Marshall with my life,' he said. 'This wasn't he but a junior officer.' ... On the way back to Spaso House, Hurley exclaimed that he had been afraid Harriman would come to blows with Stalin during their contretemps over the grounding of the Poltava airmen."[61]

Of course King was hardly on a rescue mission from Poltava on February 3 while dropping twelve 500 pound bombs on Berlin; he did not smuggle a Pole on board his aircraft and that person was not wearing a GI uniform. The entire trial transcript is loaded with efforts to prove that the grounding of American aircraft was based on Soviet displeasure over the King incident; it was never established that that incident or any other one specifically triggered the Soviet action. Further, the Soviet reaction was not "immediate" following the King incident, but 55 days after King was forced to land in Poland on February 3.

The next witness at the King trial was Admiral Olsen, who in addition to his position as Chief of the USMM Navy Division, was acting head of the USMM while Deane was in the United States. When asked if he were acquainted with Lt. King, Olsen said: "I have never seen the accused." He said he first learned of the incident about April 1 when Gen. Deane received the letter from Gen. Antonov. He claimed to have a superficial knowledge of the case until Deane left Moscow for the United States. On April 16 the Ambassador informed him of the allegations made by Stalin on the evening before and directed him to arrange a meeting with the Red Army Chief of Staff (Antonov) as soon as possible. He said the purpose of that meeting was, "to demand evidence to support the allegations made against the U.S. Army Air Forces by Marshal Stalin the night before."[62] He said that he was able to arrange such a meeting later the same day. Harriman left for the U.S. about April 17.

Olsen's testimony parallels a typed recording of the meeting which was held at Red Army General Staff Headquarters at 9:00 p.m. April 16 but provides other pertinent details not included in his testimony. Present with Olsen from the USMM were Brigadier Generals Frank N. Roberts and William L. Ritchie and Capt. Henry Ware. With Antonov were Gen. Slavin and Major Yevsikov. Olsen told the Russians that the comments made by Stalin to Harriman "constituted a most serious charge, and that we want to have all the information pertaining to it."

Olsen sidetracked his own request for proof at that point by asking Generals Roberts and Ritchie to speak to these allegations as representatives of Generals Marshall and Arnold respectively. Roberts said that Marshall would be distressed by the "accusation and would want to take drastic measures." Ritchie said Arnold would be shocked by such an accusation and said the Air Force system would not permit "political activity or ulterior motives that would embarrass our ally." Both statements seem to presume the accusations by Stalin against King were true, or at least King was guilty of something. Such presumption of guilt was expressed by Ritchie who said there had been a few isolated cases of our crews doing "foolish and stupid things on the spur of the moment. These individuals are being dealt with by Court Martial." Ritchie did however emphasize the need for "concrete proof of deliberate acts by American Air Force personnel so that it may be properly evaluated by both sides..."

Antonov responded that he was pleased with their assurances that ulterior motives were not involved, and if incidents had occurred, these were exceptions by "undisciplined crews" and he would convey such comments to Marshal Stalin. He then said he had already reported a number of incidents to Gen. Deane, with an apparent reference to his March 30 letter. He said that "perhaps there was further information of a nature about these incidents that he himself did not yet know about" and added that he would try to explore all the details of any other possible incidents and inform the heads of the Mission.

Olsen's subsequent comments were in error, not based on facts he should have known.

In addressing the "accusation of collaboration with the Polish underground" he brought up the King incident identifying it as, "the incident where Captain King took a Polish subject on his plane for the purpose of taking him away from Poland."

First, King was not a Captain; second, neither King nor anyone else had any proof as to Jack Smith's nationality, for which reason the charge had to be amended to describe him merely as an "alien." Lastly, and most importantly, King did not "take" Jack Smith on his plane for the purpose of flying him out of Poland. All evidence agrees that Jack Smith was a stowaway and to imply that they planned to help him get to England is ridiculous. The fact was that after Szczuczyn they were going the other way, east into Russia. With such superficial knowledge of the facts Olsen should have confined himself to his instructions to demand proof. Instead he said that it was his personal conviction that King's acts were "without political motives" and that King had no reason to suspect "sinister connections this person may have had as an agent of the London Polish Government." Olsen made matters worse when he told Antonov, "what help had been given this Pole had been for purely personal reasons to help out a man who had made friends with certain members of the crew." This comment was not based on fact.

It was late afternoon on February 5 when Jack Smith acted as interpreter for the Russian General, providing no service to the King crew. During the flight to Szczuczyn he had a few words with S/Sgt. Pavlas and after they landed a few words with Lt. King when he was ordered off the aircraft. That evening he ate with the King crew and was billeted with them that night. The next day the Soviets arrested him, less than 24 hours after he met the King crew, hardly time to form any fast friendships with a stranger who spoke little English. Such inaccurate and unsubstantiated comments by Olsen were prejudicial to King. Antonov then said that after the incidents he furnished Deane in his letter, "especially the case with King," the Soviets decided to take action to prevent such incidents in the future. Antonov responded to a comment by Olsen that the grounding of American planes was preventing those aircraft from getting back into combat by saying he did not believe that the action "had materially affected the United States combat air force action, since only a few planes were involved." He went on to say that in the King case it was "self-evident" that Jack Smith was a Pole and he had passed himself off as a member of the King crew. He continued that Jack Smith "admitted he was a Pole and that he had ulterior motives. Finally, this Pole had tried to run away to avoid being detained." Here was another point to request again proof of Antonov's statements but it was not done.

Antonov then began to rehash the other incidents he had included in his letter to Deane. He called the second case that of Lt. Donald Bridge and curiously skipping the Wilmeth case, called the third incident that of Capt. Shenderoff. Deane's damage control apparently removed Wilmeth from a controversy that could have impacted his own command. Olsen then pointed out that none of the cases involved assistance by Americans in furnishing supplies to the Polish underground, and he requested definite information as to the exact place, time and date where such occurred so that they could identify the plane and crew. Antonov again referred to the King case saying, "there was very definite and fixed proof according to the data and that this man taken on board was an agent of the London Polish Emigre Government." Here was another opportunity to demand that "very definite and fixed proof." It was not done.

In a last outrageous comment Olsen told Antonov that they wished to hold the Court Martial of King as soon as possible and wanted to know how soon they could get air transportation (either April 17 or 18) to bring the necessary personnel to Moscow from Poltava. Antonov said he would let them know no later than the next day. How could Olsen have requested proof of Stalin's accusations, yet before receiving that proof tell the Russians we are going ahead with the Court Martial? It is interesting to know that the recording of this meeting was classified SECRET until declassified on July 26, 1988.[63]

During Admiral Olsen's testimony on April 25 he said that no further proof was received from the Russians.[64] On the following day, after he had completed his testimony, Olsen and Capt. Ware met with Gen. Slavin. Also present was Archer, identified only as British, and with Slavin was a Col. Lebedev. Olsen reviewed the King incident saying, "It was easy to mistake this Pole for the General's interpreter and logical to bring this person on the King plane after the Pole had evidently been left behind when the General's plane took off." He also noted that the King aircraft and the General's C-47 flew together to the same destination. Olsen also said the Americans were not trying to excuse the conduct of the King crew in supplying the Pole with American flying clothes or in hiding him. He said for these offenses King was now being Court Martialed. Olsen insisted the King case did not confirm Stalin's accusation that American air forces were conniving with any political movements in Poland. Slavin remarked characterizing Olsen's explanations as "more than strange," "hard to conceive" and "totally unsatisfactory."[65] The foregoing meeting took place on the second and last day of the King trial. Although some of Olsen's remarks were unfair, he did show better knowledge of the facts than he did at the meeting with Gen. Antonov on April 15.

Olsen had no basis for saying that King's crew supplied Jack Smith with flying clothing or had hidden him. During cross-examination Olsen conceded they had no proof that Jack Smith was a Pole, only statements of the Russians that he was. He was asked if the base at Poltava had ever been closed before, referring to the grounding of all U.S. aircraft. Olsen did not answer directly, saying there were a number of times it had been difficult to obtain Russian clearance for flights. He continued, saying the King incident came at a time when there were a number of complicating factors in their relations with the Soviets and "it appeared" to climax things. The defense asked if one of the groundings happened during the period that the base at Poltava was supposed to serve the Yalta conference during the first week in February, 1945. Admiral Olsen said, "Yes, there was an incident at that time. The exact reason for it, I do not know." He then advised, "I remember the airfield was under considerable snow; that Colonel Hampton had flown in from the Crimea to Poltava and for some reason was told he could not land until cleared by Moscow, and after circling the field several times he landed anyway. Then I believe he was told that he could not take off, but having the responsibilities for arrangements for the conference at Crimea, he felt it was absolutely necessary he get back, and took off without permission." In Chapter 15 Richard I. Lowe, said he believed that this incident was a factor in the decision to Court Martial Lt. King.

Colonel Thomas K. Hampton had been the commander of American forces at Poltava at that time and his counterpart was General Kovalev, commanding the Russian forces there. The Yalta conference, in the Crimea, was held during the first eleven days in February 1945. The defense inquired whether the Hampton incident, and other incidents that displeased the Russians involving Lt. Col. Alexander and Major Kowal, resulted in those officers being relieved of their duties in Russia in April 1945? Olsen admitted: "they were relieved from their duties, but I can't say that it was because of this one incident, although I would say it was a contributing factor." In response to another question, Olsen said he would not respond whether those transfers were "without prejudice" as such would be a violation of Deane's confidence, as he and General Hill were responsible for making the transfers.[66] The Hampton incident was in part explained by a letter from General Hill to Marshal of Aviation S.A. Khudyakov on April 10 which said; "...no instances are known in which Hampton was responsible for friction between the U.S. and Soviet authorities except for the incident where he took off from Poltava to return to Saki in violation of instructions from Gen. Kovalev. It is nevertheless felt that friction exists on that base and I have decided to relieve Hampton and also Alexander because of the inversion in rank with Kowal, a Major, being selected to succeed Hampton."[67] (The airport at Saki in the Crimea was used to reach Yalta some 75 miles to the south.) The Soviets were ready with a reply to Hill's letter.

On April 12 a cable from the USMM to Poltava (Hill to Hampton) said a letter had been received from Gen. Slavin that Major Michael H. Kowal had shown himself to be "inamiable and frequently hostile to Red Air Force officers and was a source of deterioration of relationship at Poltava" and was "absolutely undesirable." The cable further issued instructions to transfer Kowal to the USSTAF.[68] Subsequent communications disclosed that Hampton, Alexander and Kowal all left Poltava April 12 leaving recently promoted Major Roger M. Trimble in command of the few Americans left at Poltava.[69] It seems pretty obvious that the USMM and the Eastern Command were prepared to Court Martial a combat pilot while again protecting another one of their own command who had likewise displeased Soviet officials.

The defense called Olsen's attention to the other incident which Olsen had not mentioned — the Wilmeth case mentioned in the Antonov letter. He was asked, "Do you know what disposition has been made of the displeasure caused to the Russians by this incident in Poland?" Olsen sidestepped the question saying, "I believe the Wilmeth case was incidental to this overall picture; that if there had been anybody else at Lublin at the time it would have made no difference; that the Soviets had merely grounded and immobilized planes and personnel." That response was not an answer to the question making it more obvious that the USMM had protected another of his own, sacrificing two other Americans, Lt. King and Lt. Bridge.

Olsen was then asked if the Russians had a tendency to be vindictive in international matters, and he conceded they tended to take drastic action regarding any infringement upon their rights or rules. The defense pointed out to Olsen that the American Embassy had remonstrated over the delay in permitting the evacuation of seriously ill and wounded American personnel from Poltava. When asked Olsen, admitted the Soviets had not offered a quick remedy to that situation. He was then asked if the charge against King by the Russians was made to put the Americans on the defensive in retaliation for such charges made against the Russians? He said, "No. I wouldn't say that." The Court President, Col. Pettigrew, asked Admiral Olsen for his opinion as to what percentage of the charges made by Stalin would the case against King occupy? He said it is the only case involving a Pole. He went on to say he had received no answer from the Russians to the request he made on April 16 to Antonov for proof. Olsen admitted that this one case had been "inflated". Col. Pettigrew followed this by asking, "In general, were the broad allegations put to the Ambassador by Mr. Stalin, in your opinion, founded or unfounded?" Olsen replied, "My opinion is that they were unfounded completely. You ask for my opinion – I can go no further. I can say the case was misrepresented to Marshal Stalin..." Lt. Col. Crandall asked Olsen if he felt it might have been an accumulation of these events which had (been) brought to the attention of Stalin and they selected one to which they could attach more importance? Olsen responded, "I feel it was an accumulation of these events which brought out the reaction which resulted in the grounding of everybody." Olsen later characterized the case saying, "In my opinion the case was apparently inflated, blown-up, and misrepresented to Marshal Stalin; so that he reacted and caused other reverberations down the line..."[70]

A closing statement by the prosecution, not recorded for the record, followed. At the end of that statement the prosecution rested its case. The defense followed with a motion for a finding of not guilty as to the specification and the charge on the grounds that the prosecution had failed to present sufficient evidence to support a finding of guilty. The Court was then closed to consider this motion. Following their deliberation the Court was reopened to announce that the motion for acquittal was denied.[71] Dolin said he recalls his motion for a finding of not guilty was based on the fact that the only evidence as to what happened was the testimony of fellow crew members who were really accessories before the fact and therefore principals in the case. He said that the 96th Article of War applied to them as it did to King and to convict him on the testimony of co-principals should not be permitted without corroboration.[72]

The defense made an opening statement for its case which was not made a part of the record. The first witness for the defense was the accused, 1st Lieutenant Myron L. King. His direct examination consisted of his very detailed rendition of the events beginning with the bombing of Berlin on February 3, point by point, as was furnished in his story found in Chapter 15 and testified to by his fellow crew members earlier in the trial. There were no contradictions on anything of substance when he testified. Toward the end he stated: "One telegram shows our crew in Kuflevo with nine men, for I gave the Russians a list of nine men and technically they sent that telegram to Moscow. At the next stop, Szczuczyn, we gave the Russians a list of ten men with Jack Smith's name on it. If there had been any intent to take him out of the country, the Russians needed only to wait for us at Poltava. There would have been no way for us to put him over as one of the crew because they already had the first list of the crew when we landed..." After Myron told his story the prosecutor had no questions.

Questions by Court members followed for nine pages with some members at times improperly assuming a prosecutorial role.

Major Conner asked King why they did not turn Jack Smith over to the Russians when they arrived at Szczuczyn? He said there was no way to have turned him over to the Soviets that night since there was no interpreter there then or the next day. He had previously emphasized that no one could speak any English when they arrived at Szczuczyn and they got by using sign language alone. Myron admitted that they did not use Jack Smith as an interpreter at Szczuczyn because they had told him they would take him with them and turn him in at Poltava. Lt. Col. Robb asked: "Why did you keep him with you after you got there? What business was it of yours to show him any hospitality?" King responded: "We did not show him any hospitality." Col. Pettigrew inquired whether he realized he was conniving in the concealment of Jack Smith when they arrived at Szczuczyn? He answered: "No sir, we did not consider it that." In response to Lt. Col. Crandall, King said he did not have any conversations with Jack Smith other than what he had related, and he had no way of knowing that the Russians at Szczuczyn were going to include Jack Smith in their plans for providing mess and billet for the crew.[73]

The next defense witness called was Lt. Col. James D. Wilmeth, the trial judge advocate. It was pointed out by the defense that Admiral Olsen had said that in his opinion this case had been misrepresented and inflated. Wilmeth was asked whether from his recent knowledge, on the occasion of his recent mission to Lublin, if he had formed an opinion as to Russian deception, evasion and prevarication in official quarters? He responded, "...the acts that I was alleged to have committed were out of consonance and exaggerated with those of actual commission." The defense felt this was not a direct reply and asked if he gained a knowledge of Russian evasion and prevarication on his recent trip. Wilmeth said, "I have. But I can state only from my own personal experience that I have the conception that they exaggerated that particular event. The one incident isn't enough for me to state what is the general Soviet temperament." Wilmeth was obviously trying to avoid saying that though there was evasion and prevarication by the Soviets in his case, such also could have existed in the King case. He did admit on further questioning that he had heard evidence of such deviuosness by the Russians from top ranking staff at the Eastern Command. (That information may have been from or about Hampton and Kowal, who were conveniently no longer in Russia.) When no questions were made to Wilmeth by members of the Court the defense rested its case.[74]

Major Taylor was again recalled for further questions to clarify the dates in the Shenderoff case and to pin down the date that American aircraft had been grounded. One interesting exchange took place when Lt. Col. Crandall asked a question about American aircraft having shot down Soviet aircraft as a possible basis for retaliation by the Soviets in grounding American aircraft. Crandall said with respect to the date of the grounding of U.S. aircraft, "I do recall being on night duty about the time I heard of the ban. During the same tour of duty, the same night, I recall hearing – and I unfortunately am unable to say who it was that I heard speaking about it – that a number of Russian planes had been shot down by American Fortresses. And it was my impression that the ban had been imposed for that reason. I would like to know if that incident occurred just before the ban was imposed, or whether it was after?" Taylor said he would have to check the records on this. Apparently no one requested that he do so and he was then excused.[75] That concluded the Court session at 6:30 P.M. April 25, they were then to meet next at a call of the President.

The Court was reconvened at 11:05 A.M. April 26 at which time S/Sgt. Ernest Pavlas was recalled as a witness. He was questioned about his having found Jack Smith aboard their aircraft before leaving Kuflevo and the subsequent comment made to him by Jack Smith about having an uncle in London that he wanted to visit. It will be recalled that the prosecutor failed to ask those questions on direct examination. Other questions to Pavlas related to what King may have said concerning his plans for Jack Smith. Pavlas said King made no statement to him as to what he planned to do with Jack Smith.[76]

After Pavlas was excused Col. Pettigrew had Wilmeth read the testimony of Admiral Olsen.[77] Following this the Court recalled Capt. Ware. The purpose was to determine whether there had been any document or conference which provided an explanation to the Soviets in response to the letter from Antonov. Wilmeth interjected that Ware was present at a meeting when the King case was discussed. Lt. Col. Crandall then asked Capt. Ware, "Has there been to your knowledge any explanation made to the Soviet officials on the King case?" Ware responded, "An explanation? There have been oral conversations between our officials and Soviet officials. I believe it was General Deane, but I don't know exactly which one of our officials discussed the matter on this particular occasion; but there was a definite effort made to convince the Soviet officials that if such an incident took place, it was purely of a local nature and did not represent any change in U.S. policy or the attitude of the U.S. toward areas occupied by the Red Army, and that it was merely due to error and misunderstanding of local U.S. Army officers." He was asked if he understood or could infer that this explanation was acceptable to the Russians? Ware replied, "It was indicated that they did not accept that explanation." Major Conner pursued this a step further asking, "You say an effort was made to convince them that there was not anything more than local significance to this case. What information did they have on the King case to offer? In other words, did they have the results of an investigation of that case at hand, or was it merely, more or less expressed in general terms?" Capt. Ware said: "I understood at the time it was an effort of General Deane to explain to the Russians that everything we do, and all the things that individual American officers do, do not necessarily reflect the national policy – contrary to the policy of the Russians – and that they should not attach undue significance to it." Capt. Ware was then excused and the defense recalled Wilmeth as a witness "to report his recommendations as investigating officer in this case, with his knowledge of it at the time."[78]

Wilmeth explained that there were two separate investigations conducted in the King case, the first of which was the one by Major Nicholson at Poltava. (That investigation, if it can be called that, was merely a report dated March 28 which set forth the joint interrogation of King, Sweeney and Lowe.) Wilmeth said that this first investigation provided evidence "that would substantiate the act itself." He said it did not provide evidence to substantiate "discredit to the military service" nor could he establish that Jack Smith had been "willfully concealed." In light of the foregoing he made to Deane a "personal recommendation and not a legal recommendation" that the charge against King should be withdrawn. He said that after he came to Moscow he made what he called another investigation. (Here Wilmeth refers to the Antonov letter, the testimony of Edward Page and Admiral Olsen in an effort to establish Soviet displeasure as the basis for "discredit to the military service.") Based on this he then recommended to Deane that King be tried by General Court Martial. On redirect examination by the defense, reference was made to the cable Wilmeth sent to Deane which inquired whether the King case should be pushed because real harm had been done or because of political reasons. It will be recalled that Deane hastened to respond that political reasons were not involved. In looking at the case after all these years I believe there must have been a political reason since there does not appear to have been any "real harm." Who other than Jack Smith had been really harmed? Wilmeth was asked if he recalled that statement in his cable. He dodged by repeating himself, claiming that his first recommendation was made without the benefit of the information obtained in the Moscow investigation. He then summarized as follows: "Please appreciate there were two viewpoints involved: my status as an investigating officer, and my status as a subordinate acquaintance of General Deane. Neither of us had the other's viewpoint because I had the unofficial investigation made at the point of an order, which Col. Hampton made and which General Deane did not have. On the other hand, I did not have the evidence concerning the Soviet reaction to the act." The record shows Wilmeth was the investigator at Poltava not Hampton.

Possibly one of the most significant areas of questioning during the trial may have been a thrust by Leon Dolin. He was endeavoring to establish what particular thing started the process which led to King's trial. Dolin pointed out that Col. Hampton had sent a communication to General Deane, possibly the cable of March 21, setting forth that the King crew had been seven weeks behind Russian lines, that no notification was made to Poltava as to their safety, and their attempts to get to Poltava had been obstructed by the Russians. He then said General Deane sent a letter to either Slavin or Antonov requesting an explanation as to why these combat crews behind Russian lines were obstructed. He opined that the letter from Antonov which was Exhibit No. 2 in this trial was the result. The point of this effort by Dolin was to raise a question whether the Antonov letter was in retaliation for Deane's letter requesting an explanation for holding the King crew incommunicado for seven weeks. Much was made of the reason for the delay of the Russians in failing to complain until March 30 about an incident which occurred February 5. Could it be that the Soviets had decided the King incident was much ado about nothing until Deane was critical of their behavior in detaining his crew? If that were so the next logical step in logic would be that Deane himself could have been responsible for the grounding of American aircraft. Despite research efforts to locate Deane's letter to either Slavin or Antonov it could not be found. Dolin's conjecture on this subject did not contain a question for the witness. Wilmeth however, again stated his reason for originally recommending to Deane that the charge against King be withdrawn. In doing so he said, "There was enough evidence to have convicted the accused as a result of my first investigation..." An objection to such a clearly prejudicial conclusion was made. It was the first and only recorded objection by the defense to have been sustained by the law member.[79] Wilmeth was again excused as a witness.

Major Taylor was again recalled and testified that Deane had answered Antonov's letter of March 30 on March 31. It should be noted that Admiral Olsen testified that Deane did not receive Antonov's letter until April 1. Taylor was asked to tell the Court the "gist" of Deane's letter. He said that Deane advised Antonov that he had learned the facts of the King incident on March 29. (The details of Major Nicholson's March 28 report about the stowaway were put in a cable on that day to the USMM.) Taylor said that Deane told Antonov he had ordered King to be tried by Court Martial and commented that he did not think there was any excuse for King's conduct. According to Taylor, Deane's letter "asked the Soviets if they would have a Soviet officer come or be represented in some way during the trial." Major Light of the Court asked if any reply had been received. Taylor responded that he had never seen a written answer. He did say that Deane had met with Slavin April 4th and had then requested Soviet witnesses appear for the trial. Slavin replied that he thought it would be out of order in a purely American case. He also inferred that to require testimony of eye witnesses would be an insult to General Antonov who had outlined the whole thing in his official letter. Taylor was then excused.[80] The Court President had the reporter read the testimony of the accused. Following this both the prosecution and the defense said they had no further testimony; oral arguments which were not recorded for the record were then made by both sides. Dolin has said that in his summation he tried to point out all the problems in the case. He added, "Kingsbury said nothing except for me to shut up and sit down."[81] Also not recorded in the transcript were other motions that Dolin said he made, all of which were denied. Dolin said he viewed the case as lacking in direct evidence and built on poor overall circumstantial evidence. He also noted that the SECRET classification on all documents contributed to the lack of justice.[82]

The transcript discloses that the Court was then recessed until it reconvened at 2:45 P.M. April 26. The findings of the Court were as follows: "With respect to the specification the Court found him guilty except the words 'without proper authority.' Of the excepted words, not guilty. Of the specification after the deletion of the three words 'without proper authority, 'guilty.'" The sentence was recorded was that King be reprimanded and to forfeit $100. per month of his pay for six months. A rough draft letter dated April 26 which included as signatories the names of all members and officers of the court recommended clemency for King based on his youth and his lack of intent to violate regulations and thus cause Soviet displeasure.[83]

Dolin said that after the sentence he felt lousy because King felt lousy. He said that Col. Pettigrew came over to him and thanked him for doing such a good job. He said that Pettigrew told him, "Don't worry. When this gets back to Washington for review, it will be set aside. I am making such a recommendation." Dolin said that he related Pettigrew's comment to King and he seemed to feel better. King said that Pettigrew jokingly told him, "Don't do this again, or if you do, don't get caught because if you do I will have to reprimand you."[84] No such recommendation was found in the King Court Martial file or in the other files reviewed.

Myron said that while they were in Moscow he could not say they were mistreated. He recalled that when they were free they were permitted to come and go at will, but they were always accompanied by a Russian interpreter. He said that their interpreter claimed he had been an American citizen who had returned to Russia during the 1930s. He said this interpreter had shown them a photograph of himself and others on their arrival from the United States publicly tearing up their American passports. He told Myron that was when he was young and foolish. Myron said they did not trust this person and believed that he was assigned to report to the Soviets on their activities and their conversations. Myron said that after the trial Generals Roberts and Ritchie were concerned that the Russians would consider his sentence of a reprimand and forfeiture of pay to be too lenient; they wanted to get him out of the country before he might be snatched by the Russians.[85] There seemed to be some substance to this concern in a cable that was sent by the USMM to the Adjutant General in the War Department in Washington on April 26. The message, intended for Deane who was still there, said that Slavin advised that the Soviets at Poltava would not release the King crew for departure from Russia until Moscow approved. It pointed out that the trial of King would end that day and the USMM wanted to remove the crew to Poltava on April 27 or the following day and thence to Teheran. The cable desired a clearance request for the King crew from Washington. It said that Slavin had commented that there must be some misunderstanding as all aircrews except King's were cleared and that was to be handled separately. The cable continued, "He said you promised to inform Antonov of results of the trial, indicating he would not clear crew until he had that information. Did you promise to tell Antonov verdict (guilty or not guilty) or disclose sentence?" The cable then set forth the sentence given King that day and stated: "Case reviewed here unless you want immediate forwarding to JAG. Feel it better to get them away from Moscow to prevent any possibility of leaks in this case."[86] No reply from Washington was located. During the interview of King in 1992 he said he did not know until then that General Deane was not in Moscow during his trial.

King said after the trial ended on April 26 he met with Generals Roberts and Ritchie who had a typed, minute-by-minute schedule and itinerary to get him out of town the following day. He described their departure as a clandestine operation with he and General Ritchie sneaking out the back door of the Embassy the next day, picking up his crew members along the way to the airport. As they approached the aircraft Ritchie explained he would say good-bye then, instructing Myron to leave the car as soon as it stopped and to board the aircraft immediately. Myron said that as soon as all were aboard the aircraft left.[87] Although Myron does not recall, Leon Dolin was also aboard on the flight to Poltava. With respect to their departure from Moscow Dolin recalls, "The next morning we were put on a C-47 to Poltava. A General came to see us off and swore us to secrecy on all that happened. I asked why and was told that it was sensitive and should remain so until King was in the U.S.A.; then it would be handled." (Actually, the trial record remained classified SECRET until declassified January 11, 1952; other correspondence was not declassified until much later)[88.] Dolin said that some time after the war he read a comment about the King trial in Deane's book. He said that he had not heard any more about the case until he was contacted in 1992 and at that time said: "I believed to this day that the Army had set the decision aside on review after what Pettigrew had told me. The case was so obviously staged for Stalin's benefit that I could see no other result."[89]

Myron King said he believes he received a lenient sentence because there were several other American officers who made flights that were unauthorized by the Soviets and were in trouble. He felt his trial "was covering those folks who had been slipped out of the country." (It will be recalled that Hampton, Alexander and Kowal had left Russia on April 15th ten days before Myron was tried). Myron said, "...we thought we told them everything...we just volunteered all of that information and there would have been no way they could have had a trial had we not volunteered it.[90]

On May 10, four days after Deane's arrival back in Moscow, he signed a document in the King case captioned "ACTION BY REVIEWING AUTHORITY". This very brief statement read: "In the foregoing case of 1st Lieutenant Myron L. King, AC, the sentence is approved and will be duly executed."[91] Also on May 10 he signed the letter of reprimand which was a part of the sentence. It is a particularly strong letter in light of the trial transcript and in consideration of the unanimously signed plea for clemency by the Court Martial members and officers. However, it is not surprising given the General's stated conviction that King was guilty before he was tried. It also raises a serious question whether Deane ever really reviewed the proceedings (read the transcript) before preparing the letter, or whether he personally prepared the latter. That question may in part have been answered by General Deane himself in his book published just two years later.

Speaking of the deterioration of relations between the Americans and the Russians at Poltava, Deane described briefly some of the incidents instigated by the Russians and said, "In fairness it must be said that the situation was not improved by the irresponsible acts of some Americans. For example, one crew attempted to smuggle a discontented Polish citizen out of Poland by disguising him in an American uniform. This was used as evidence that our Air Forces were carrying on subversive activities against the Red Army."[92] These words obviously refer to the King case but the facts are wrong and irresponsible.

Certainly, if Col. Pettigrew had any influence at all as President of that Court and as a subordinate staff officer it is not apparent in the harsh and inaccurate letter of reprimand signed by Deane which read:

"To: 1st Lt. Myron L. King, 401 Bomb Group, 614 Bomb Squadron
"Subject: Reprimand "
1. On 3 February 1945, having sought sanctuary for your aircraft and crew in a foreign country, you came under the jurisdiction of the military forces of an ally. Subsequently you transported an unauthorized foreigner to another airfield within the jurisdiction of this ally. Upon arrival, you failed to check the identity of this unauthorized person and did not report him to the proper authorities. You further aggravated this situation by allowing this person to be associated with your crew and to wear U.S. flying clothing, and by otherwise indicating that he was a member of your crew, thus attempting to deceive the military authorities of our ally, until he was sought out and apprehended by them.

"2. This foreigner, transported and covered by you, was alleged by our ally to be an agent dangerous to their interests. As a result of your misguided and reprehensible actions, our ally assumed that representatives of the U.S. Army were engaged in activities with an ulterior purpose. So seriously were these events received that they were brought to the attention of our Ambassador by the Chief of State of our ally.

"3. Your abuse of the hospitality and sanctuary offered you by our ally is totally inexcusable.

"4. Your actions in this case have demonstrated a deplorable lack of judgement and common sense on your part, and have brought discredit upon your organization and upon the Military Service of the United States.

"5. A copy of this reprimand will be filed with your record.
John R. Deane, Major General,
U.S. Army Commanding General
U.S. Military Mission"[93]

King and his companions arrived back in Poltava on April 27 rejoining the rest of their crew. It was only a one night stopover. Their orders read that they were to be given high priority on the first ATC aircraft departing. Soon they were on their way back to England and the 401st Bombardment Group at Deenethorpe. Their ordeal seemed to be behind them. The outcome of the trial in Moscow did not end the matter for Myron. Further, one member of the crew was left behind in Russia; he was to have his own ordeal and trial in a Soviet Court.

Notes to Chapter 18
1. Telephone interview with Leon Dolin by author July 6, 1992
2. Letter and enclosure, Leon Dolin to author July 21, 1992

3. See 2 above, enclosure
4. See 2 above
5. See 3 above
6. See 1 above
7. See 3 above
8. Cable, Poltava to USMM March 28, 1945
9. See 3 above
10. See 1 above
11. Cable, Poltava to USMM (From Wilmeth to Deane) T-3533 dated April 10, 1945
12. Record of trial of Myron L. King by General Court Martial April 25-26, 1945 at the American Embassy, U.S.S.R. p. 40
13. Deane, John R. _The Strange Alliance_ p. 120-121
14. See 3 Above
15. Ibid.
16. See 12 above p. 2
17. See 12 above p. 5
18. Cable, USMM to Poltava March 29, 1945 M-23527
19. Telephone conversation Myron L. King and author September 27, 1992
20. Cable, AGWAR to Moscow April 16, 1945
21. Maslen, Selwyn V. _614th Squadron: Crews-Missions - Aircraft_ p. 42
22. See 3 above
23. See 1 above
24. See 12 above p. 6-22
25. See 1 above
26. See 12 above p. 14, 18
27. See 12 above, Exhibit No.1, first addendum p. 99
28. See 12 above p. 20
29. See 12 above p. 20-21
30. See 12 above p. 22
31. See 12 above p. 24
32. See 12 above p. 29-34
33. See 12 above, Exhibit No.2, second and third addendum p. 99
34. Letter and enclosures, U.S. Army Legal Services Agency to author June 21, 1991
35. Deane, see 13 above p.196
36. Ibid. p. 301
37. See 12 above p. 37-38
38. See 18 above
39. See 12 above p. 49
40. Cable, USMM to Poltava (Deane to Hampton for Wilmeth) March 31, 1945
41. National Archives Record Group 334, Box 6, USMM Letter, Gen. Deane to Gen. Slavin April 11, 1945.
42. National Archives Record Group 334, Box 6, USMM Recording of meeting, Soviet Foreign Military Liaison Office April 17, 1945
43. USAF Historical Research Center, Maxwell AFB, Al Cable Poltava to USMM (Hampton to Hill) April 6, 1945.
44. USAF Historical Research Center, Maxwell AFB, Al Cable Poltava to USMM (Hampton to Deane) April 9, 1945
45. USAF Historical Research Center, Maxwell AFB, AL Cable Poltava to USMM (Hampton to Deane) April 9, 1945
46. USAF Historical Research Center, Maxwell AFB, AL Cable, USMM to Poltava (Deane to Hill for Wilmeth) April 10, 1945
47. USAF Historical Research Center, Maxwell AFB, Al Cable, Poltava to USMM (Hampton to Deane) April 10, 1945
48. National Archives Record Group 334, USMM Cable, Poltava to USMM (Roberts for Deane from Trimble) Message 104 from Wilmeth T-3637 April 17, 1945
49. See 3 above
50. See 12 above p. 39-43
51. National Archives, Suitland Reference Branch, Record Group 84, Foreign Service Posts, U.S. Department of State, Shenderoff Affair file
52. National Archives Record Group 334, Box 10, Incidents USMM Cable, War Dept. to McNarney and Deane, info Cannon; repeated to AFHQ Caserta and MAAF Caserta
53. See 51 above
54. National Archives, Record Group 334, Box 10, USMM Incidents U. S. and Soviet, "Receipt" for custody of Soviet Engineer Captain M.I. Shenderoff April 12, 1945.
55. Interview of Myron L.King by author at Nashville, TN June 9, 1992
56. See 12 above p. 44-46
57. See 1 and 3 above

58. See 12 above p. 44-48

59. See 12 above p. 83

60. See 12 above p.46-47

61. Harriman, W. Averell & Abel, Elie *Special Envoy to Churchill and Stalin 1941-1946* p. 445-446

62. See 12 above p. 49-50

63. National Archives, Record Group 334, USMM Recording of meeting at Red Army Staff Headquarters April 16, 1945; Subject: operation of United States Aircraft in Soviet Occupied Areas.

64. See 12 above p. 50

65. National Archives Record Group 334, Box 6 USMM Recording of meeting at Soviet Foreign Military Liaison Office April 26, 1945,

66. See 12 above p. 53-54

67. National Archives Record Group 334, Box 63 Adjutant General USMM Letter, General Edmund W. Hill to Marshal of Aviation S.A. Khudyakov April 10, 1945,

68. USAF Historical Research Center, Maxwell AFB, AL Cable USMM to   Poltava (Hill to Hampton) April 12, 1945

69. National Archives Record Group 334 Box 63 Adjutant General USMM Various cables between USMM and Poltava in April, 1945

70. See 12 above p. 55-60

71. See 12 above p. 63

72. See 3 above

73. See 12 above p. 63-81

74. See 12 above p. 82-83

75. See 12 above p. 83-86

76. See 12 above p. 87-89

77. See 12 above p. 89

78. See 12 above p. 89-90

79. See 12 above p.90-95

80. See 12 above p.95-98

81. See 3 above

82. See 1 above

83. See 12 above, fifth addendum p.99

84. See 55 above

85. Ibid.

86. National Archives, Washington, D.C. Record Group 334 USMM Cable, USMM to AGWAR April 26, 1945

87. See 55 above

88. Letter, Lt. Col. John A. Doolan to Judge Advocate General USAF, Subject Myron L. King December 27,1951 and handwritten notes of Col. Doolan

89. See 3 above

90. See 55 above

91. See 12 above, fourth addendum p. 99

92. Deane, see 13 above p. 123

93. National Archives Record Group 334, Box 6, USMM Official letter of reprimand to 1st Lt. Myron L. King from Major General John R. Deane May 10, 1945.

CHAPTER 19 — A TRIAL IN THE UKRAINE...ANOTHER FARCE

Lt. Myron King, Lts. Sweeney and Lowe; and S/Sgt. Pavlas arrived back at Poltava from Moscow on April 27, 1945. They had a very high priority for transportation out of the Soviet Union which meant they had little time for a reunion with the rest of their crew.[1] A cable from Poltava to the USMM on the day of their arrival from Moscow said, "King crew cleared by local Soviets to leave by next ATC transport now scheduled to depart tomorrow morning. Only exception is King crew member Sgt. Atkinson involved in recent traffic accident being held by local authorities until Moscow issues orders on case."[2]

Myron said that because they were only at Poltava overnight he had very little time to visit with his tail gunner, Sgt. George E. Atkinson who was being detained in Russia because of his involvement in a vehicle accident which resulted in the death of a Soviet female. He thought at the time that this was a mere formality and once it was resolved George would be allowed to follow them back to Deenethorpe. He said he did not like leaving a crew member behind in Russia but he had no choice in the matter. Myron was not concerned for George because there were still many Americans at Poltava and he was sure that George would be well taken care of. He also had the impression that although the incident involved a fatality, which was unfortunate, it did not involve any liability on George's part. Myron said he now understands that George felt he was being deserted by his crew. He said he regrets this but was not aware of it at the time. After the war George visited Myron in Nashville. He told Myron, "I didn't know what to think of a fellow who would leave a 19 year old boy in Russia by himself." Myron is sorry that George felt that way but he did not see it the same way.[3]

On the following day, April 28 the King crew, minus Sgt. Atkinson, left the Soviet Union. A TWX was sent from the Headquarters of the 1st Air Division to the 401st Bomb Group which quoted a cable from the Eastern Command received April 28, "Crew from 401 BG left Poltava via ATC for Home station: Lts. King, Sweeney, and Lowe. S/Sgt. Pyne, Pavlas, DeVito; Sgts. Reinoehl and Spellman. Sgt. Atkinson detained as witness to traffic accident."[4]

It took seven days for the King crew to get back to England even with their high priority because ATC flights only flew during daylight hours with many stopovers en route. They stopped at Teheran, Cairo, Athens, Naples, Marseilles and Paris before arriving at London. Myron recalled time permitted some sightseeing and shopping along the way. At each stop they claimed they had not been paid for six months and each of them was able to draw $100 against his pay at a military Finance Office. He said he bought numerous items of value, but due to weight limitations on the aircraft he had to leave some of his purchases behind at each city.[5] Richard Lowe recalled a photograph taken of them in Egypt; included in the picture were camels, with pyramids and the sphinx in the background. Finally, about May 5 the King crew reached Deenethorpe in time to celebrate the German surrender and VE Day on May 7-8, 1945 with the other "Lucky Devils" of the 614th Squadron.[6]

After their arrival Myron and the others went out to visit the "Maiden." To commemorate their return Myron painted the title of the book **Mission to Moscow** on her nose. Richard furnished a photograph taken that day. Myron was decked out wearing a Russian style Persian lamb hat which he said belonged to Bill Sweeney; with him in the picture are DeVito, Lowe, Pavlas and Pyne.

Meanwhile, back in the Soviet Union, George Atkinson found himself in a predicament. Being able to discuss those events with George has been important to me. In July, 1990 Ralph "Rainbow" Trout tipped me off to the fact that George had just joined the 401st Bombardment Group Association and was living in Anchorage, Alaska. I wrote to him in August and within a week he called on the telephone. He has since been a regular caller, preferring long distance calls to writing letters. The information and documents he furnished have been very helpful. George said that after they had arrived at Poltava on March 18 he had become bored with inactivity. He recalled that after Myron and the others went to Moscow April 17 he volunteered to help the Poltava permanent party personnel who were involved in the deactivation of the base. He said instead of shipping equipment and supplies back to the U.S. they were giving most of it to the Russians. He was given the chore of ferrying U.S. Army trucks, from the air base motor pool to the Army depot warehouse, a distance of several miles, where they would be turned over to the Soviets. On April 19 he was assigned to deliver one of these trucks and to tow another which was not in running condition. The Army provided a tow rope for this purpose and the driver, Lt. Martin R. Schlau, was to steer the disabled vehicle. George said Schlau was a also a "downed flyer" or combat transient like himself.[7]

It was shortly after 4:00 P.M. when George, towing the other truck, slowed to cross railroad tracks. Both he and Schlau said they slowed to about ten miles per hour; an Army investigation showed that it would have been difficult to maintain control of the vehicle crossing those tracks at a speed in excess of 15 miles per hour. Just after crossing the tracks George was confronted with a Red Army Model A Ford truck which was parked 45 feet from the tracks at a 30 degree angle to the roadway with about five feet of the vehicle extending out into the road. George turned, going around the Russian truck, clearing it by three or four feet. Schlau was unable to turn his truck short enough to avoid a collision with the Russian vehicle. The right front fender and bumper of Schlau's truck struck the left rear end of the Russian vehicle. Atkinson and Schlau stopped on impact but the Russian vehicle, which was unoccupied without brakes engaged, rolled forward and off the road for about 40 to 50 feet. As it left the road it ran over a Russian female six feet off the roadway, causing her death.[8]

The witnesses to the accident were four Americans, all of whom were Eastern Command

Touring the sights in Egypt en route from Russia to Deenethorpe. 3rd from left is Myron L. King. 4th from left is Richard I. Lowe. 3rd from the right is William J. Sweeney. Far right is Leon Dolin who was King's Ass't Defense Counsel. Courtesy of Richard I. Lowe.

The King crew following their return from Russia had a reunion with "Maiden U.S.A." at Deenethorpe in May 1945. The art work on the "Maiden" was done by King. The Russian hat worn by King was a souvenir of copilot William J. Sweeney. Left to right: Patsy DeVito - radio, Richard I. Lowe - navigator, Myron L. King - pilot, Robert Pyne - togglier, and Ernest Pavlas - engineer. Courtesy of Richard I. Lowe.

personnel who were also engaged in the ferrying of trucks to the depot. S/Sgt. James L. Almond was driving a truck and was towing another disabled one steered by S/Sgt. John F. Skalny. Almond stopped, disconnected his tow rope, put the injured woman in his truck and took her to the hospital close-by. Almond said that although 30 to 40 Russians were standing around only two Russian sergeants offered to help get the injured woman into the truck. After the woman was removed to the hospital Atkinson and Schlau took their trucks to the depot. They then returned to the base motor pool and George immediately reported the incident.[9]

An investigation was conducted by Captain William Fitchen, AC; the same person who conducted the first interrogation of Myron King on March 19. The Fitchen accident investigation consisted of a three-page report, an accident report form, and statements of the four witnesses, Atkinson and Schlau. Also included was an autopsy report dated April 20 by Major Earl Koepke, MC, who had been invited to observe the autopsy conducted by a Russian physician. The file on the accident at the National Archives includes various forms and exhibits in support of a claim for action by the U.S. Claims Commission.[10] The investigative report, the statements of witnesses and the autopsy report were forwarded to General Deane by letter April 25, 1945 (Deane was then in the U.S. and did not return until May 6).

Captain Fitchen's report called attention to discrepancies between his findings and charges made by the Soviet NKVD which also made an investigation of the accident. First, the Soviets claimed the incident occurred at 4:30 P.M. whereas the American witnesses all agreed that it happened at 4:05 P.M. Second, the Soviets claimed that Atkinson crossed the railroad tracks at 30 to 40 kilometers per hour (18 to 20 miles per hour) whereas both Atkinson and Schlau said they were doing about ten miles per hour; further, the Fitchen report said it was impossible for them to maintain a speed of 15 miles per hour and still be able to retain control of the vehicle. Third, the Soviets charged that brakes on both American trucks did not work, yet the American investigators checked the brakes on both trucks and found them to be in good condition.

The tow "chain" which the Army provided was measured and was found to be slightly longer than four meters (a little more than 13 feet). The Soviets charged that this violated their law which required a distance of not less than six meters (more than 19 feet) between towed vehicles. Atkinson was accused by the Soviet investigation with violation of the local speed limit of 20 kilometers per hour (a little more than 12 miles per hour), which limit was unknown to American officials at Poltava who in October, 1944 had set a local speed limit of 25 miles per hour. The speed of the truck driven by Atkinson had to be negligible since the investigation disclosed the collision caused only $5.00 damage to the American vehicle being towed, and the damage to the Soviet truck was so small that no monetary amount was estimated or claimed.[11]

Road conditions were described by the investigation as very poor, rough and filled with ruts. Pedestrian traffic along both sides of the road was described as very heavy.[12] The accident form stated that although Lt. Schlau was the senior officer, Sergeant Atkinson was in command of the operating vehicle and was responsible for the safety of Schlau. The report concluded that the accident would not have occurred if Atkinson had properly signaled his intention to turn so as to insure that Schlau could safely clear the Russian vehicle.[13]

Atkinson recalls that when he went over the railroad tracks the Russian truck was not visible to him until the last minute preventing him from giving a timely signal to Schlau.[14] The American investigation also concluded, contrary to its own facts, that Atkinson was "driving at an excess rate of speed" for the condition of the road even if his rate of speed was within the authorized limit set by Army regulations. They went even further, again contrary to the facts of their own investigation, by saying, "...it is believed Sgt. George E. Atkinson violated Soviet traffic rules..." and by so doing also violated Army regulations which required military personnel to abide by limits set by local law or regulation.[15] The latter logic is flawed since American authorities did not know, and were themselves negligent, in failing to ascertain what the local laws required; they set their own standard which did not comply with the Russian traffic laws. All this aside, the facts did not establish that Atkinson violated any Russian or American laws or regulations except for the use of a tow rope provided by the American base motor pool, which the Soviets complained did not meet Russian requirements.[16]

George said that he and Schlau were detained in American custody and confined to their respective quarters pending a decision on the matter in Moscow.[17] The letter transmitting the accident investigation to Moscow said the Russian Commander at Poltava, General Kovalev, had been contacted in connection with the Atkinson/Schlau case. In this regard the letter said, "He was more or less noncommittal stating that as far as he knew the driver, Sergeant Atkinson, was the only one who should be held. However, he stated that the final decision was up to Moscow."[18] The comments of General Kovalev are patently irrelevant and prejudicial even in a transmittal letter. To have sought his views on the matter gives the impression that Russian officials had some say in the result of the investigation.

On May 2, 1945 the USMM advised Poltava that, "A financial claim for settlement in Atkinson case excepted pending action. A Federal Claims Commission to be set up when and if specific claim is made."[19] On May 9, 1945 Poltava advised the USMM that, "The evidence indicates U.S. Government responsible as a result of faulty judgement of Sgt. Atkins."[20] On May 31, 1945 Major Herbert Hoffheimer, Jr. of the Eastern Command signed a report as the unit claims officer. The report recommended the payment of 23,000 Russian rubles ($1916.67) to the 14 year old daughter of the accident victim. The report indicates that the recommendation was approved and was paid June 4, 1945. The approval bears the signatures of Col. Moses W. Pettigrew, GSC and Major John C. Light, Ord.[21] Interestingly, Pettigrew was the President and Light a member of the Court which in April tried Myron King in Moscow. A cable from Washington to the USMM May 20, 1945 designated Pettigrew and Light as members of Foreign Claims Commission 53, under the supervision of the USMM.[22] It would appear that the commission had been established for the express purpose of providing compensation in this case. Apparently no claims requiring a Commission being established had been made by Russians until then. One must note that the matter was finalized even before Atkinson and

Schlau were tried on any charge. The impression conveyed is that American authorities were admitting guilt on behalf of these two combat airmen, without their consent or knowledge, and paying the victim's daughter in hopes that such would influence the Russian court.

The Hoffheimer report contained a number of exhibits which included a recommendation that no disciplinary action be taken against Atkinson, it being noted he was a combat transient who had volunteered his services to base personnel.[23] Another exhibit however, said the responsibility for the accident lies with Atkinson "who is guilty of faulty judgment and ignorance of local Soviet regulations but is not guilty of careless driving and is not guilty of violating AW-105."[24] Not only do these two exhibits conflict with each other, but they totally ignore the possibility of culpability on the part of Schlau, and the indirect responsibility of the U.S. for its failure to determine the Soviet speed limit and to inform its drivers on that road. These pronouncements show very clearly that the U.S. authorities were ready to throw Atkinson to the wolves to appease the Russians just as they had done in Myron King's case. The latter exhibit recommended, "that the amount awarded to the claimant be held to a minimum as it is believed that local customs do not award damage claims in cases of this kind."[25] This is another reason to believe the "claim" was for appeasement purposes. The daughter of the victim is referred throughout the exhibits as the "claimant" but at no place is there documentation that the daughter made the claim to the U.S. or that one was made in her behalf. Actually, the amount had been approved by the U.S. on May 31, 1945, the daughter and her adult uncle signed a deposition June 4, 1945 taken by Captain William Fitchen, as Acting Adjutant at Poltava. Therein she "hereby claims the sum of 23,000 rubles for her support...and in full satisfaction of her claim."[26] From this it is clear the claim was initiated by the Americans and the deposition prepared after the fact, to serve as a claim supposedly made by the victim's daughter in the hope that it would influence the Soviets.

There are some voids in the rest of the story of the Atkinson/Schlau travail. George Atkinson has contributed his recollection of those events some of which were substantiated in part by several published accounts but could not be verified by official records at the National Archives.

George said that he and Schlau were presented with documents written in Russian. He was told that one of these was an indictment charging them with manslaughter and the other was an order which required them to appear in a Russian court to stand trial on that charge.[27] Until the day of the trial he and Schlau remained in custody in their respective quarters without any counsel representing them or anyone to provide them legal advice.[28]

Back in Moscow, on May 18 a meeting was held at the Foreign Military Liaison Office which was attended by General Deane and Captain Ware. Present on the Soviet side were General Slavin and a Colonel Sinozersky. The subject of the meeting was the "auto accident" at Poltava. Deane wanted to send Pettigrew to Poltava immediately to "help clear up the automobile incident and arrange for settling the claims of the daughter of the deceased Soviet woman." He added that "our people" considered the incident to be a "pure accident."

Deane said that General Ritchie had informed him that General Levandovich indicated our representative would find the local Soviet commander in charge of this case and would work it out with him.[29]

On May 27, 1945 Colonel Pettigrew sent a cable to General Deane from Poltava. Since the message used "teletype language" its complete meaning is somewhat obscure but is furnished in its entirety since it is important as to how the Atkinson/Schlau incident was handled. It said, "Atkinson case is not in hands of military. Case referred by Mr. Gorshenin, prosecuting attorney Moscow to S.V. Rudenko, prosecuting attorney for Poltava for investigation to determine if sufficient grounds for court action against Atkinson or Schlau. Rudenko, high type experienced lawyer who impresses me as friendly and impartial. With one friendly and two hostile assistants he has been in my presence for three days conducting very detailed examination of both American and Russian witnesses; will advise Pettigrew whether A. to permit men to leave U.S.S.R., B. to recommend military court action with trial either civil or Russian military as directed. Hopeful of: Unlikely testimony of Russian witnesses damaging as to speed and differing with ours on several points. Cannot tell what weight Rudenko is giving to Russian testimony but understandable in ability on his part to understand how accident happened if speed was not excessive. Principals are both young and inexperienced showing extreme ignorance Russian traffic regulations, particularly those requiring vehicles to remain in place until investigated. Reference outcome: B-1 I have explained Claims Commission procedure to Rudenko and maybe get him to recommend to Moscow B-1 that such a procedure is accepted in lieu of further court action...view Russian testimony shudder to think what Russian court either civil or military might award as punishment and feel we should in latter case exhaust every argument with Gorshenin to avoid further court action...If Rudenko advises his decision B-2 plan to place Schlau and Atkinson under technical arrest by Trimble in your name with instructions not to release them except on your orders (while we work with Gorshenin) Request information."[30]

On June 2, 1945 George F. Kennan, Charge d'affaires at the U.S. Embassy prepared a note signed "GFK" addressed to "Mr. Ambassador." The note sheds additional light on the Atkinson/Schlau case emphasizing the degree of government involvement and manipulation behind the scenes not known to the principals in the case. The verbatim note follows in light of its importance:

"General Deane came to see me two days ago to tell me about two cases they have recently had in Poltava of motor accidents in which vehicles driven by members of our armed forces caused the death of Soviet citizens. The first of these cases is about to come to trial before a People's Court in Poltava.

"As you know, we never concluded any agreement with the Russians on the legal protection of members of our armed forces in this country and the men involved are, therefore, now at the mercy of the Soviet courts. In both cases it would appear to be quite possible for the courts to find our men guilty of the accidents and give them rather severe sentences.

"General Deane had asked the day before yesterday whether I thought we ought to make representations on the diplomatic level before the cases came to trial, with the view to getting them quashed. He thought that we could say that as long as they hung fire we would not be able to carry to completion the liquidation of the base at Poltava, and this would be an inducement to the Russians to let the fellows go.

"I was at that time inclined to favor this idea; but yesterday Colonel Pettigrew, who has been handling the matter for General Deane, came to see me and said that he had talked to the prosecutor at Poltava who had given him a strong hint that in the first case which is to come to trial, the Americans will be let off with a scolding. Colonel Pettigrew was afraid that if we entered into the case at this time, it might change the situation with respect not only to the first but to the second trial as well and that the court might be more likely to give heavy penalties in order to prove its independence. In view of what Colonel Pettigrew says I agree that it would be better for us to take no action at this time. The cases are surely open to appeal and if the men should be given prison sentences we will still have time later to intercede."

The note was followed by the handwritten comment "I agree" and the initials WAH, for W. Averell Harriman.[31]

By his cable to General Deane on May 31, mentioned above, Pettigrew was quite definite that the U.S. should exhaust every argument to avoid further court action in the Atkinson/Schlau case. Then after Deane suggested diplomatic action to quash the matter Pettigrew on June 1 argued the case should be allowed to go to trial. In five days he did a complete change in point of view. The trial of Schlau and Atkinson was held in a Soviet court presided over by a female judge, a Major in the Red Army. Colonel Pettigrew was present, representing both of the defendants. George said that there were other Americans present as observers and an interpreter,[32] although George did not understand much of what transpired during the trial.[33] Both Atkinson and Schlau were required to testify, as were the other Americans who were witnesses to the accident. George said that the testimony of Schlau and the American witnesses was consistent with what happened. He said that he does not recall Colonel Pettigrew, or any other American, discussing the case with him before trial with respect to developing a defense strategy, nor did he meet Colonel Pettigrew until the day of the trial. He recalls he was able to tell Pettigrew his side of the incident just before the trial began. Pettigrew made no comment, did not question any of the witnesses during the trial, nor address the Court at any time. George said that in addition to the allegation that he had driven at an excessive speed, the Russians during the trial said their laws require a vehicle to sound its horn when passing another vehicle.[34] George's feelings about the experience are probably best described by a comment he made in a 1990 letter to the Department of Veteran Affairs, "I really believed my government would have let this 19 year old hang."[35]

According to George, he and Schlau were both found guilty of manslaughter and were sentenced to two years at hard labor.[36] None of the records reviewed contain an account of the trial or of such a sentence. It should be noted that General Deane's book contains the following comment related to what he called the "irresponsible acts of a few Americans." He said "there were two cases of American reckless driving in Poltava, each of which resulted in the death of a Russian woman."[37] That there were two such cases is confirmed by George Kennan's note to Harriman earlier in this chapter. No record could be found with respect to the disposition of any other accident case involving the death of a Soviet woman. In support of Atkinson's story that he was initially sentenced to two years at hard labor is a comment in the book by Glenn B. Infield relating to the problems of General William L. Ritchie.

General Edmund W. Hill, tired of Soviet harassment, requested he be relieved as head of the Air Division at the USMM and as Commander of the Eastern Command. He was replaced by General Ritchie "well-known in American military circles for his toughness and stubbornness in dealing with the Soviets...Ritchie arrived at Poltava for an inspection on May 30, 1945 and within a matter of hours he realized there was a 'secret war' going on at the air base between the Russians and the Americans about which the outside world knew nothing."[38] It is hard to believe that the serious problems which had existed there from July, 1944 were not even known to a General officer who had been in Moscow since December of 1944 as problems escalated at Poltava. Certainly General Deane had to have been aware of the change in relations at Poltava after the disaster of FRANTIC II in June, 1944. Had there been an American cover-up in the desperate effort to salvage American/Soviet collaboration? At Poltava General Ritchie faced many problems as he proceeded with the deactivation of the Eastern Command. Glenn B. Infield wrote, "One of the most delicate problems the General had to settle was the charge against an American lieutenant who had accidently killed a Russian woman in an automobile accident near Poltava. The lieutenant was not permitted to leave the Soviet Union until he stood trial for the woman's 'murder.' Ritchie was determined that no American officer was going to be left behind when 'Operation FRANTIC' ended. When a Soviet trial board found the lieutenant guilty and sentenced him to two years at hard labor, Ritchie was prepared to load the officer on his C-47 and shoot his way out of the Soviet Union, if necessary. Aware of the General's anger, the Russians reopened the case, suspended the sentence, and handed the lieutenant over to Ritchie who had him aboard the next American plane heading for Cairo."[39] Infield provided no documentation as to the identity of the officer and it is not known whether this incident referred to Lt. Schlau or to the other unidentified accident case referred to in the Kennan note to Harriman. However, the facts appear to coincide with Atkinson's further recollections as to what happened. George Atkinson recently said that he was unaware of any other accident at Poltava which resulted in the death of a Russian female other than that which involved Schlau and himself.

George said that several days after he and Schlau were convicted the case was inexplicably reopened and their sentences were suspended. They were both placed on probation for three years and they were each fined 25 percent of their respective pay for a period of 12 months, which had to be paid before they would be permitted to leave the country. George said he has no idea what caused the Russians to reopen the case. When asked if he knew General Ritchie, George said the name did not mean anything to him. Atkinson's base pay as a sergeant was $78 per month. He had some winnings at poker and had to draw an additional amount from the Army against his future pay in order to pay the fine.[40]

Colonel Pettigrew sent a cable to Deane from Poltava on June 4, 1945 which stated, "After excellent example of showmanship which privately scared the hell out of me, the court found both accused guilty of violating Soviet traffic regulations. Saying it took into consideration government payment and youth of defendants court fined them 25% of their pay for 12 months. Further stated this was the absolute minimum possible under the circumstances. Total fine must be paid before defendants can depart. We have five days to appeal, privately advised against and I concur. Defendants desire to pay fine 2400 rubles for Schlau and 1350 for Atkinson. I plan to offer payment tomorrow and barring complications, defendants will leave next plane. Result of Soviet arrest of second case promised soon."[41]

After their fines were paid their departure from Russia was delayed by an incident involving a Soviet Yak fighter aircraft forcing down an American C-47, this long after the war with Germany had ended.[42] He recalled he was finally able to board an American ATC flight from Poltava on or about June 18 with the priority of a liberated POW. While he was seated on board before takeoff a Red Army officer boarded the aircraft and came to him, produced a scroll, and read something from it in Russian. After the officer left he asked other passengers if they knew what the Soviet read. He said one American responded that it meant, "Get your ass out of Russia and never come back."[43]

The ATC flight took Atkinson on the Mediterranean route with stopovers at Teheran, Cairo, Naples and Paris before reaching London. After George arrived in London he learned that the 401st Bombardment Group had already left for the U.S.[44] It is interesting to know that George got out of Poltava just before it closed. Four days later, on June 22, 1945 the last two aircraft with files and the last of the Americans left Poltava.[45]

George reported to Eighth Air Force Headquarters on June 22 where they took his dog tags to check his identity, telling him that they thought he was dead. He gave a five-page signed sworn statement to officers of the Judge Advocate General's Office in support of a claim for reimbursement of the 1350 rubles he had paid to the Soviet court. He believed that he paid the fine to get out of Russia and was "never so glad to leave a place in his life." However, he believed he was improperly subjected to the jurisdiction of the Soviet court and to be required to pay that fine was unjust.[46] Considerable Army correspondence on the claim followed into September of that year. In Washington D.C the Chief of the Claims Division of the Judge Advocate General's Office said it was prepared to request funds for reimbursement to Atkinson, subject to a receipt of a confirmatory statement from Colonel Pettigrew[47] whom they finally found in Washington, D.C. at the Military Intelligence Service of the War Department. On August 22 Pettigrew responded saying he was thoroughly familiar with the case "having defended Atkinson before a Russian civil court in Poltava U.S.S.R." He said, "I strongly recommend against reimbursing Atkinson." He said the fine was assessed by a court which unquestionably had full jurisdiction and found Atkinson "guilty of driving at a speed faster than circumstances warranted." Pettigrew said he considered the findings and the sentence to be a just verdict. He also said that the fine in rubles was at a rate of five rubles to the dollar. Since the air base had been flooded with rubles acquired at very much less than the official rate, the fine in terms of actual cost to Atkinson was inconsequential.[48] Pettigrew certainly was no F. Lee Bailey! Being questioned about his reaction to Colonel Pettigrew's letter and his general opinion of the adequacy of Pettigrew's counsel at the trial, George Atkinson said the Colonel probably considered him to be a "snotty kid." He added, "I probably was, but Colonel Pettigrew was an "ass———."[49]

On June 25 George left the Eighth Air Force Headquarters for the 70th Reinforcement Depot for processing to return to the United States.[50] By August he was at Fort MacArthur, California and was transferred to the AAF Redistribution Center at Santa Ana, California. Orders on November 7 gave him 20 days temporary duty at his home in Pasadena, California for "rehabilitation, recuperation and recovery."[51] George received an Honorable Discharge from the Army of the United States at the Santa Ana Separation Base December 1, 1945.[52]

In an effort to obtain additional facts and corroboration of the Atkinson/Schlau trial a search was made for Martin R. Schlau. He was located residing in New York State but failed to respond to several letters. When George Atkinson learned this he made three telephone calls in June, 1992 before getting Schlau to talk to him. He said Schlau refused to discuss the trial in Poltava and asked, "Did you ever have a bad experience and put it out of your mind?" George replied that no matter how hard he might try he would never be able to put out of his mind the fact that they had been tried in that Russian court. He asked Schlau, "How could you forget that woman who was a Red Army Major who was our Judge?" Schlau said he remembers being at Poltava but does not remember anything else until he got back to his base.[53]

One final note in the Atkinson trial – a letter was sent by Major Trimble at Poltava to General Deane on June 10 wherein he said, "We are deeply indebted and grateful to Colonel Pettigrew who has given unceasingly of his time and efforts in the handling of the two accident cases involving Eastern Command personnel."[54] There are no accolades from George Edward Atkinson!

Both trials, the American Court Martial of King in Moscow and the Russian trial of Atkinson at Poltava suggest much chicanery. It is also strange that these circumstances befell two members of the same crew after the criminal detention of that crew for seven weeks by the Soviets.

Notes to Chapter 19

1. Interview of Myron L. King by author at Nashville, Tennessee June 9, 1992
2. Cable, Poltava to USMM (Trimble to Deane) April 27, 1945
3. See 1 above
4. Copy of TWX from BMP to DPE April 29, 1945 signed Turner COMAIRDIV ONE furnished author by Richard Mettlen from 614th Squadron records
5. See 1 above
6. See 1 above
7. Telephone conversations, George E. Atkinson and author between August and October, 1990
8. National Archives, Washington, D.C. Record Group 334 USMM Box 63, sub file FRANTIC-Accidents; transmittal letter from Eastern Command to USMM April 25, 1945 re Atkinson/ Schlau accident case. Exhibit A. Investigative Officer's Report.
9. Ibid. see Exhibit G. Statements of Witnesses
10. National Archives, Washington, D.C. Record Group 334, Box 63 sub file FRANTIC-Accidents Report of Claims Officer and action taken May 31, 1945 with enclosures in Atkinson/Schlau accident case.
11. See 8 above Exhibit A. p. 1
12. See 8 above Exhibit C WD39 Accident Report Form
13. See 8 above Exhibit A. p. 2
14. See 7 above
15. See 8 above Exhibit A. p. 2
16. Ibid.
17. See 7 above
18. See 8 above transmittal letter
19. USAF Historical Research Center, Maxwell AFB, Al; cable, USMM to Poltava May 2, 1945
20. National Archives, Washington, D.C. Record Group 334, USMM; cable, Poltava to USMM May 9, 1945
21. See 10 above Report of Unit Claims Officer, Major Herbert Hoffheimer, Jr.
22. Cable, Adjutant General War Department, Foreign Claims Commission to USMM May 20, 1945
23. See 10 above Exhibit N (Recommendations)
24. See 10 above Exhibit 1 to Report of Unit Claims Officer
25. Ibid.
26. See 10 above deposition of Maria Andreevna Tverdochlev dated May 31, 1945.
27. Copy of signed sworn statement of Sergeant George Edward Atkinson given at Eighth Air Force Headquarters June 22, 1945
28. See 7 above
29. National Archives, Washington, D.C. Record Group 334, Box 10 USMM recording of meeting at Soviet Foreign Military Liaison Office, Moscow May 18, 1945
30. National Archives, Washington, D.C. Record Group 334 Cable, Poltava to USMM (to Deane from Pettigrew) May 27, 1945
31. National Archives, Suitland Reference Branch, Foreign Service Posts, U.S. Department of State; U.S. Embassy, Moscow, U.S.S.R.; note GFK (George F. Kennan) to Mr. Ambassdor (W. Averell Harriman) June 2, 1945
32. See 7 above
33. Ibid.
34. Ibid.
35. Copy of letter, George E. Atkinson to Charles Phillips, Department of Veteran Affairs, Anchorage, Alaska May 28, 1990 furnished author by Atkinson, Fall 1990
36. See 7 above

37. Deane, John R. _The Strange Alliance_ p. 123-124
38. Infield, Glenn B. _The Poltava Affair_ p. 220
39. Ibid. p. 222-223
40. See 7 above
41. National Archives, Washington, D.C. Record Group 334 USMM Cable, Poltava to USMM (To Deane from Pettigrew) June 4, 1945
42. See 7 above and 27 above
43. See 7 above
44. Ibid.
45. See 38 above p. 225
46. See 27 above
47. Copy of letter, from HQ.ASF,JAGO to W.D.G.S. Personnel Division and Military Intelligence Division, signed Ralph G. Boyd, Colonel, JAGD, Chief of Claims Division date not readable
48. Copy of Memorandum for Colonel Richards, Subject: Claim of Sgt. George E. Atkinson from M.W. Pettigrew, Colonel, GSC, August 22, 1945
49. See 7 above
50. Copy of memorandum from Bert A. Arnold, LT.Col., AGD, Headquarters Eighth Air Force to Military Attache, U.S. Embassy, London July 1, 1945 concerning George Edward Atkinson
51. Special Orders No. 268, Headquarters, Santa Ana Army Air Base, California November 7, 1945
52. Copy of Honorable Discharge, Army of the United States for George E. Atkinson at AAF Separation Base Santa Ana, California December 1, 1945
53. Telephone conversation, George E. Atkinson and author June 5, 1992
54. National Archives, Washington, D.C. Record Group 334 FRANTIC, letter, Trimble to Deane June 10, 1945

CHAPTER 20 — THE "MAIDEN" GOES HOME...AND LIVES ON!

Myron L. King said the 401st really celebrated VE Day on May 8. He recalled the fireworks in particular. Flying Control log books for the 401st described the celebration on that day: "0001 hrs. - Bloody good fireworks at the Control Tower tonight to celebrate VE Day! About half the base present and not more than 5000 flares, rockets, mortars etc. were fired off as a token of better days to come."[1]

The celebration continued in the afternoon at the Control Tower when all 401st personnel gathered to hear a speech from the C.O., Lieutenant Colonel Seawell. The gathering then broke up for religious services by Chaplain Ward Fellows for the Protestants, Chaplain Joseph E. Burke for the Catholics and Mr. W. Meier of Kettering for those of the Jewish faith. By nightfall there was a beer party with more fireworks.[2]

During the previous month allied armies in Europe were putting the 401st out of business as their strategic targets were overrun. The Group flew only 14 missions in April with the 254th, and the last mission, being one to Brandenburg on April 20.[3] The Eighth flew two other bombing missions and four night leaflet missions as well as other non-bombing operations between April 21 and the 25. The latter date marked the end of combat missions for the Mighty Eighth.[4]

After those combat operations ended Myron King participated in several interesting operational flights. Myron said that with a skeleton crew he was a part of the four flights made to Linz, Austria to evacuate liberated French and British POWs.[5] They flew into the big airfield there which had recently been liberated from the Nazis by the U.S. 3rd Army. Each aircraft brought back 30 of the former prisoners, flying the French to Orleans, near Paris, and the British back to England. Myron also took part in the three observation trips, sightseeing flights at low altitude, down the Ruhr Valley to Frankfurt Am Main, with the ground personnel of the 401st as honored passengers. It was a fitting gesture to those who labored so hard under adverse conditions for almost a year and a half.[6] Roger Freeman speaking of the contribution made by them said:

"For every man in the air there were some 20 on the ground in their air force of assignment...three or four to every bomber crewman. For the combat crews the most important were their ground crews on whose care and diligence their safety could depend...The ground crews literally held the lives of the flight crews in their hands. The skill and dedication of the average ground crew was of high order and it was important that the flight crews trusted them implicitly...It was a matter of pride of many of the ground crew chiefs that their particular charges suffered no mechanical or equipment failures that could cause a pilot to abort - turn back without completing the assigned mission. Many crew chiefs only left their aircraft in order to eat and sleep, devoting the rest of their time to administering to the demanding machine in their care."[7]

Myron said of those "Cook's Tours" that, "one of the more momentous views was that of Cologne and its still standing Cathedral amid the ruins of the city."[8]

However, post VE Day operations soon came to an end. By May 14 military discipline was back! They had bugle calls, drill and calisthenics with reveille at 5:45 A.M. and taps at 10:30 P.M. When orders were received that the Group was to be quickly returned to the United States; the drill and calisthenics ended; there was too much to do in the weeks that followed. As Captain Gordon R. Closway, the Group Public Relations Officer wrote, "everyone had work to do - plenty of work...crews were taken on celestial navigation missions and instrument checks, airplanes were tuned up for the overseas hop, fuel consumption checks were made and they were weighed for balance...There was the usual processing, the physical examinations, checking of equipment and inspections and more inspections...and as usual the medics ordered and dispensed more shots for everyone."[9]

Each Squadron was to send 19 aircraft home, each supposedly with its regular crew and each with ten passengers chosen from ground crew personnel. The rest would return by ship although some, when they got to the Replacement Depot, were sent home on aircraft as passengers. The decision to take those passengers required fitting the aircraft chosen for the overseas flight with extra dinghies and necessitated ditching drills by the aircraft complement which were checked by ATC.[10]

During that very busy month the 401st learned that Colonel Bowman had left USSTAF and returned to Washington, D.C. where he was assigned as the Public Relations Officer for General Arnold. Also, the "Old Man", William T. Seawell, was promoted to Colonel. Imagine, being an old man and bird colonel at 26!

The momentum escalated during May with everyone pitching in as they all prepared for the trip home. The ground personnel were to evacuate the base by June 10.[11] When the word got around the nearby communities that the Yanks were leaving, it was said that crowds of their English friends flocked to the base to say a fond farewell.[12]

The "Maiden" was chosen as one of the 614th aircraft to participate in the trans-Atlantic trip, which project came to be known as "Operation Home Run,"[13] but for some reason the honor of flying her back to the States did not go to Myron King and his crew. For two years efforts to learn the identity of the crew or passengers who flew the "Maiden" home were for naught. Since the crew chief for an aircraft was usually chosen as a passenger, a concerted effort was made to identify the "Maiden's" crew chief. As previously reported in Chapter 13, during the Group reunion at Norfolk, Virginia in September, 1992, Dr. Peter J. Carter, who had been Sisson's engineer, advised that their crew chief had been Edward Nepyjwoda who has resided in Kent, England for many years. Efforts to communicate with him brought no response. This was a disappointment since it was also hoped he could share the experience of that most important flight or at least provide a name or names of others who could. Since he would have known her as well as anyone it was hoped that he could also provide some intimate details concerning his life with the "Maiden." Myron said that he and his crew were shipped to a Replacement Depot near Blackpool and from there the enlisted crew members were sent home by ship. He was chosen to be a passenger on a B-24. They took off and for some reason were to go to another airfield about 30 miles away before heading out over the ocean. The pilot missed the base and before they realized it they were out over water. They turned back and landed at a short runway-fighter base to get their bearings. Then trying to takeoff, the pilot struck a gas vent pipe breaking off about two feet of the wing tip which, of course, had to be repaired before they could leave. That could make a seasoned pilot wonder where the guy won his wings! Finally, they successfully left the UK returning on what seemed a strange route via the Azores; Gander, Newfoundland; landing at Bangor, Maine. Myron took a train to Atlanta where he received his orders for leave which he spent in Chattanooga. After his leave he reported to San Antonio where he was separated from the Army and returned to civilian life.[14] Richard Lowe said that he and Bill Sweeney returned to the States together, also as passengers on a war weary B-24. He said they had about five aborted attempts to takeoff due to some mechanical problems. If they were as superstitious as most flyers, I am sure they were relieved when they finally made it aloft and were safely headed home.[15]

The whole operation, "Home Run" and the evacuation of the base, was one of excitement for all personnel. The complexity of moving all of those people and their equipment after 17 months being entrenched there was confusing and mind boggling. It was like moving a small town across the Atlantic with less than a month of preparation. In several days more than a month after VE Day, they were gone. According to Captain Closway 1440 persons from the 401st came home on "Home Run". Since each B-17 carried a crew of ten and ten passengers this would confirm that there were 72 aircraft departing from Deenethorpe. He also said that 1528 of our comrades came home by ship. Station 128 was left with Major L.P. Davison in charge of 150 men to close the base and turn it over to the Air Ministry to become a training school for RAF pilots.[16] After "Home Run" was scrubbed several times,[17] probably due to unfavorable weather, the green light was finally given and on Memorial Day, May 30 the first aircraft, 42-102468, IY-C of the 615th Squadron lifted off the runway at 11:00 A.M. Special Orders for the project instructed the aircraft to proceed to Valley, Wales and then by "best available air route to Bradley Field, Windsor Locks, Connecticut." Those Orders listed the persons aboard in two sections, the crew and the passengers. The passenger group included Colonel Seawell; Lt. Col. Ralph J. White, the 615th C.O.; Maj. Julius Pickoff, the Group Bombardier; Maj. Harold M. Kennard, the Group Communications Officer; both Chaplains, Maj. Joseph H. Burke and Capt. Ward J. Fellows.[18] Lt. John R. Althoff, was the listed co-pilot. He had served in that capacity on the crew of Allen Aschenbach; they had trained with the Babcock crew at MacDill in Tampa before going to England. John said that although Lt. John D. Gerber was the listed pilot, Colonel Seawell flew in the left seat on that memorable trip and that he was the co-pilot.[19] On this let there be no question; no matter what those Orders said it is a sure bet Colonel Seawell was going to be the pilot, leading his victorious Group home from combat.

Seawell's B-17 was followed that day by 15 other birds in that flock. On June 2 another 20 set forth and on June 4 the remaining 36 of "Operation Home Run" bade farewell to Deenethorpe and to England. They stopped at RAF Valley, Wales and then were out over the north Atlantic with stops at Iceland, Greenland, Goose Bay, Labrador and Gander, Newfoundland before touching down at Bradley Field in the good old U.S. of A.[20]

Unable to locate anyone who made the trip on the "Maiden" and could provide some interesting details it was necessary to turn to others who were a part of that same experience. Lt. Elliott F. Cameron's crew flew their first mission on February 28 to Soest. They went on from there to pile up what Vic Maslen called an "impressive record." Their last mission was to Dresden on April 17 which gave them a total of 23 missions in 48 days.[21] He and his co-pilot, Lt Robert L. Davidson, provided their recollections. Bob said that those non-combat missions after VE Day were interesting. They flew two missions, May 11 and May 12 to Linz, Austria to pick up those liberated French POWs who had been captured at Dunkirk five years before. They also took part in two "sightseeing" flights over Europe for the 401st ground personnel on May 14 and May 15. He said these trips were quite "revealing to our eyes as well as to those of the 'ground pounders' as we used to call them. Even we had no idea of the devastation!" He said their crew departed from Deenethorpe on Monday, June 4 and arrived at Bradley Field on Thursday, June 7 with a total flying time of 21 hours and 50 minutes.[22]

Elliott said that his only recollection of the briefing for "Home Run" was the part played by a young WAAC who sternly warned them that "there would be no fraternizing between officers and enlisted WAACs." Elliott's crew on their first leg home headed for Prestwick, Scotland where they picked up the "radio range" and set course for Iceland. Elliott found it necessary at Iceland to fly down a fjord between high mountains to get to the airfield at Reykjavik. He said the meal there included a dark, stringy stewed meat which he had never tasted before and "often wondered whether it was polar bear, reindeer, walrus or something equally exotic."[23] Bob recalled that there was still a mound of snow in the middle of the airfield left over from a white carpet many feet thick when they had passed through in February on their way to England. Their next stop was Goose Bay, Labrador and on the way they saw the coast of Greenland off to their right. They flew at about 10,000 feet crossing the ocean on top of a solid deck of cloud that persisted until they approached mainland. Since they had the aircraft on autopilot most of the way there was plenty of time to gaze at the sights and eat K rations when they became hungry.[24] Elliott said at Goose Bay the snow had disappeared except for small patches under bushes but they well remembered moving around the base on paths through shoulder high snow on either side in February.[25]

Bob Davidson's "Individual Flight Record" known to pilots as the Form 5, shows that they had four landings en route which would confirm his recollection that they also landed at Bangor, Maine before landing at Bradley Field.[26]

They were back home! Elliott said,"I think I made a pretty good landing when we arrived at Bradley. I hope so because that was the last time I ever saw a B-17."[27] He said that the stay at Bradley was a short one, "...we had our supper and then went through some processing. We were restricted to the base as I recall, but I remember that the cold beer flowed copiously at the Officer's Club that night. At breakfast the next morning there were piled up cases filled with quarts of cold, fresh milk. This was a real welcome from the powdered milk we had to drink in England. I remember everybody drank at least one quart of milk for breakfast. Some

B-17s lined up along the runway at Deenethorpe for Operation "Home Run" — First in line was 42-97478 IW-Q better known to members of the 614th Squadron as "Shade Ruff #2." Courtesy of Robert L. Davidson.

drank two or three. We did some more processing that day and then everybody departed for 30 days R&R at home, to reassemble for shipment to Sioux Falls, South Dakota at the end of our leave."[28]

Bob said they had to go through Customs at Bradley which meant their B-4 bags had to be searched. He said some of them still had their .45 caliber automatics and were nervous about declaring them. He was so concerned that he left his on board the B-17 but now regrets it.[29] Bob Davidson provided a photograph of the 401st "Home Run" B-17s lined up along a runway at Deenethorpe. The first in line, ready to go, was 42-97478, IW-Q, known to many old "Lucky Devils" as "Shade Ruff II."

Although research would not yield any leads to provide an account of the "Maiden's" return, the National Air and Space Museum of the Smithsonian Institution in Washington provided some detail hitherto not recorded. The Individual Aircraft Record Card for B-17G 44-6508 discloses she was manufactured by Douglas at Long Beach, California and accepted by the AAF August 24, 1944. On the same day she was taken to Palm Springs and delivered to the ATC. From Palm Springs she was turned over to the 2nd Air Force at Lincoln, Nebraska on August 26. The "Maiden" was then flown to Grenier Field, Manchester, New Hampshire arriving September 8 from which she left for England on September 12. There is a break in the record here until she arrived back at Bradley Field June 6, 1945. That date may indicate she was in the second contingent to leave Deenethorpe on June 2nd. She left Bradley on June 13 stopping at Newark, New Jersey and another airfield, name illegible, and Dallas, Texas arriving at South Plains AAF, Lubbock, Texas June 18 where she was assigned to storage. On October 26 she was declared excess and was ferried to the Reconstruction Finance Corporation facility at Kingman, Arizona for disposal on November 27, 1945.[30]

The word "disposal" on that government form has a certain finality to it which to some would be construed as the death knell for "Maiden U.S.A." There are those who would find that unacceptable; to those she lives on! I'm sure she lives on in the hearts of those on the crews of Sisson, King, Morton, Ochsenhirt, Seder, St. Aubyn, R.B. Richardson, Wittman, Fondren, White and Hartsock. She took them to war 35 times and returned them without a fatality, not even one recorded Purple Heart. She also lives on with fondness in the imagination of those thousands, both young and old, who have seen her painting at the Air Force Museum, and the hundreds who have a print of that painting in their offices and homes. Though she was only a part of the AAF for one year and three months, during that span she developed a spirit of her own and is "forever aloft"[31] to those who appreciate her. For all of them she is a symbol of the Mighty Eighth; to all my comrades she embodies all those memories of our days as Bowman's Bombers.

Notes for Chapter 20

1. Program for service at the dedication of the Memorial for the 401st Bombardment Group (H), Deenethorpe, Northamptonshire, England September 16, 1989
2. Maslen, Selwyn V. 614th Squadron (H): Squadron History p.161
3. Closway, Gordon R. 614th Squadron History Summary of Events, April, 1945
4. Freeman, Roger A. The Mighty Eighth War Diary p.494-496
5. Maslen, see 2 above
6. Ibid. p.161
7. Freeman, Roger A. Experiences at War: The American Airman in Europe p. 115
8. Interview of Myron L. King by author at Nashville, Tennessee, June 9, 1992
9. Maslen, see 2 above p.161-162
10. Ibid.
11. Bowman, Harold W. & Selwyn V. Maslen Bowman's Bombers p. 75
12. Ibid.
13. Maslen, see 2 above p. 160
14. See 8 above
15. Telephone conversation, Richard I. Lowe and author January 3, 1993
16. Closway, Gordon R. Pictorial Record of the 401st Bomb Group, also known as the Blue Book; unnumbered pages in section captioned History: 401st Bombardment Group (H) and Associated Units
17. Bowman & Maslen see 11 above p. 75
18. Copy of Special Orders Number 1, Headquarters 401st Bombardment Group (H) 24 May 1945 re shipment 10034 - E (A) furnished author by Harold M. Kennard, Jr.
19. Telephone conversation, John R. Althoff and author January 3, 1993
20. Closway, see 16 above
21. Maslen, Selwyn V. 614th Squadron: Crews - Missions -Aircraft p. 8
22. Letter, Robert L. Davidson to author June 17, 1991
23. Letter, Elliott F. Cameron to author June 8, 1991
24. See 22 above
25. See 23 above
26. See 22 above
27. See 23 above
28. Ibid.
29. See 22 above
30. Letter, National Air and Space Museum, Smithsonian Institution enclosing copy of the Individual Aircraft Record Card for B-17G, 44-6508, sent author May 22,1992
31. From the poem "High Flight" by Pilot Officer John Gillespie Magee, Jr. RCAF.

CHAPTER 21 — JUSTICE DELAYED IS JUSTICE DENIED

In 1986 Myron King was reluctant to furnish information concerning his crew and their "Maiden." He did not answer my letter and it took several telephone calls before he would speak to me. Even then he furnished no information. Some weeks later he mailed some 18 pages of William J. Sweeney's testimony from the court martial trial transcript and some cover pages from that record. I read that material and was shocked since I had no knowledge of what happened to the King crew after they left our formation on February 3, 1945. It was obvious from the initial cover sheet to the transcript and handwritten comments that Myron had been tried by General Court Martial in Moscow and had been found guilty of violating the 96th Article of War. My objective at the time was related to the upcoming reunion of the 401st Bombardment Group which was to be held in Savannah in October, 1986. Door prizes for the banquet at the reunion were the last existing prints of the painting of the "Maiden" which had been obtained for that purpose. I was trying to write a short version of the life of the "Maiden" which would add some interest to recipients of the prints and I felt a contribution from Myron would be significant. The material Myron sent, without a note of explanation, conveyed to me a strong impression that this was a sensitive subject, and one involving personal pride. Not wanting to open an old wound I concluded the article with the mission to Berlin and the King crew MIA.

In 1990 my interest was renewed after I had obtained a reprinting of the print of R.G. Smith's painting of that aircraft to provide copies for 401st members, their families and friends. I continued to wonder about all the crews that flew the "Maiden" on 35 missions, as well as our other comrades who flew in formations with her over Europe. I also thought more and more about Sweeney's straightforward testimony which convinced me that Myron had, at the very least, not had a fair trial. In addition to Sweeney's testimony, the initial cover sheet had a handwritten comment which made me anxious to explore the story further:

"This is the worst miscarriage of justice I have ever witnessed. To say that a multitude of ignorant practitioners destroys a court is charity to those involved in this scandal. Under the circumstances of this case it is impossible to determine who voted to condemn Lt. King. The Uniform Code of Military Justice should be amended to provide for a poll of the members of a court on a finding of guilty. At present the cloak of secrecy is a shield for the cowardly. All the members of this court should be forever banned from passing judgement on their fellow man. Let each one of them state how they voted."

(signed) JD[1]

At first I wondered whether the note was written by General John R. Deane. This made little sense because he convened the Court Martial and had expressed the opinion that King was guilty before he was even tried. I later observed that this notation did not appear on the cover of the original copy of the transcript on Myron's case at the National Archives; then later I learned that these were the initials of Lieutenant Colonel John A. Doolan, AFUS, the hero of this chapter.

I was overjoyed when Myron and his wife agreed to lend their assistance to my effort. They had read some of the preliminary material I had prepared which had been given to them by Philip Reinoehl, his ball turret gunner. Philip visits them in Nashville almost each year on his way to or from Florida. King and his wife Eleanor became convinced that I would be sympathetic to Myron's story. They also had sought the advice of their County Sheriff, "Hank" Hillin, an old friend of mine from our FBI days in Washington, D.C. in the 1950s. Hank, a member of Myron and Eleanor's church, urged them to help me tell Myron's side of the story and that of "Maiden U.S.A." So in March, 1991 I became committed to a story which began to unravel. By that time I was convinced that the King trial resulted in an injustice to

Myron King. The facts as they have been reported here were such that, as an attorney by education with 26 years as a law enforcement officer, I would have been too ashamed to present such a lousy circumstantial case to a prosecutor. But, had I done so, I would have expected to have been severely censured for incompetence. It is apparent that Myron's crew also suffered from this miscarriage of justice as well; one of them, George E. Atkinson, suffered even more than the others.

In April 1991 I made the first of four trips to Washington, D.C. to conduct research at the National Archives. I was surprised at the amount of information that I found, but the more I learned the greater my disappointment that King's own countrymen, wearing the same uniform as he, caused him to be dragged off to Moscow for a SECRET trial on the unsubstantiated charges of General Antonov and the unfounded and ridiculous allegations of Marshal Stalin, so bizarre they were not worthy of serious consideration.

All of this made me understand Myron's initial concern over telling his part of this story. The return of the King crew to Deenethorpe must have been awkward for them at the very least. In our long talk at Nashville in June 1992 Myron said that after the trial and what he had learned about the Russians, it became very clear to him "what those SOBs were trying to do to this country" and he couldn't wait to get home to tell everybody. However, he said that everybody thought he was all "flaked up" which in Eighth Air Force parlance meant that he was suffering from the usual mental distress from experiencing too much German flak shot in his direction. Others referred to this condition as being "flak happy" which was usually cured by finishing a combat tour and going home. Myron said that at Deenethorpe and back home there was "sympathy" for him almost without exception, but they didn't try to listen or understand "the gravity of what was going on over there."[2] The U.S.S.R. was an ally; that nation's contributions to the defeat of the Axis Powers were significant. However, the actions of the Soviet Government in international affairs subsequent to 1945 were such that most Americans developed reservations over our relationship with that nation. Among the many contributors to this saga of the "Maiden" and her friends is an interesting one from our Protestant Chaplain, Captain Ward Fellows. Ward said that after the King crew returned to Deenethorpe he received a visit from either Myron or Bill Sweeney. He wrote as follows:

"I was in my office, a separate hut across from the chapel, when this officer came in and said he wanted to talk to me, which I was of course glad to do. It soon developed that he had a new problem, one I had never met before. He needed to talk to someone about his experiences while briefly with the Russians after piloting one of the few planes which flew on to land there.

"I summarize what I can remember of what he said, and what I assumed then and do now, about the problem he had - an unusual but real one. It was obvious that he had been psychologically traumatized by the experience of having been in effect 'interned' by the Russians. While he reported no mistreatment or threats, he was amazed and troubled by the way the Russians regarded and treated him and the rest of the crew. In brief, the Russians were mistrustful and suspicious of them. Where the crew had expected welcome and camaraderie from allies, they had actually been held at arms length. I gather that their hosts were formally correct to their American involuntary guests, but in personal terms they were cold, suspicious and inhospitable. I think that our mens' movements were severely restricted and they were under constant surveillance. I assume that as pilot and thus C.O. of the crew he felt responsibility for them and was frustrated, puzzled, unable to understand why they should be treated in that fashion; yet he was, of course, unable to do anything about it. If you will pardon the graphic vulgarity, it was a classic case of 'a pain in the ___ ': something you can't stand but cannot do anything about it...But it was sure tough on one young, friendly American to come up against it when he thought he was with friendly allies, on the same side. He was troubled enough about it to go talk to the chaplain; perhaps nobody else would listen, or he was afraid it would get him in trouble. I don't know. I hope I helped him by listening, but I never tried to be an amateur psychologist."[3]

Although he said the substance of Ward's letter was correct as far as what they all felt Myron does not recall visiting the Chaplain after they returned from Russia. He speculated that it may have been Sweeney who made that visit.[4] Reading Ward's letter after Myron's comment that no one would listen or try to understand what he and the others learned in the Soviet Union, I had a better appreciation of his feelings. His reaction was understandable, particularly when one considers the backdrop in the Spring of 1945. The King crew arrived back at Deenethorpe just days before VE Day when everyone in the ETO was expecting day after day to hear that the Germans had surrendered. I am sure the only serious thought on the minds of those at Deenethorpe was whether they were going to go directly to the Pacific or if they would get to go home first and regroup. Myron's words about an ally who was hostile and had become an enemy were probably considered by some to be "off the wall;" those who did listen didn't want to believe them! Also those who understood and believed "the gravity of what was going on over there" quickly forgot about it in the euphoria of those weeks in May and June as they all headed home. Myron, too, headed home and there in the bosom of his own family experienced the same lack of understanding of what he had learned about the Russians. He said they were, of course, sympathetic to what he had endured personally, but they could not, or did not want to, accept the idea that the Russian bear was going to be a threat to a hard-won peace in the world.[5]

Myron did what a great number of us did, he tried to put the war behind him and get on with his life. He returned to school, married Eleanor, and went into business. He started as a furniture designer and that evolved into a large and flourishing art gallery in Nashville which bears his middle name, "LYZON". That also had been the name of his father's internationally-known millinery and hat design studio on Long Island. However, Myron never forgot the broken promise of Colonel Pettigrew that his conviction in Moscow would be set aside when it was reviewed in Washington. The answer then for him, in the words of the First Amendment in our Bill of Rights, was to "...petition the Government for a redress of grievances."

To get the attention of Government was almost an impossible task. He was dealing with the military justice system, not our Federal or State courts. It will be recalled that after the related Court Martial of Lt. Donald Bridge in Italy, an effort was made in that case through a United States Congressman to have that case reviewed. The Under Secretary of War in 1945 wrote the Congressman saying, "There is no provision of law under which a valid sentence of a Court Martial when fully executed can be modified or set aside by administrative action."[6] Further, Myron couldn't even get access to Court records for appeal purposes since they were still classified SECRET. The only thing he had was his copy of the trial transcript and his letter of reprimand. As Leon Dolin the assistant defense counsel said recently, the classification of the trial documents contributed to the lack of justice. It appeared that there was little that could be done.

The process following a General Court Martial which results in a conviction requires certain review procedures. It is interesting to follow the paper trail in Myron's case and understand that none of that process was ever made known to Myron. It all took place in 1945 while King was still in uniform, and it is obvious that access to what follows would have been of value to him in his search for justice.

The initial review of the trial was by General Deane who on his return to Moscow from the U.S., gave it his perfunctory approval and signed the letter of reprimand. I am sure the document for that approval and the letter to Myron were prepared for him and were lying on his desk ready for his signature; he probably never read the trial transcript.

Six days prior to Deane's action the Acting Staff Judge Advocate of the USMM, Colonel James C. Crockett, GSC, signed a review of the King Court Martial records. It stated:

"(a) It is the opinion of the Staff Judge Advocate:

(1) The evidence supports the findings and that the sentence is in consonance with the findings
(2) That there were no errors or irregularities in the conduct of the trial which jeopardized the right of the accused

(b) In view of the foregoing reasons it is recommended that the proceedings
   and findings of the court be approved and the sentence duly executed."[7]

It can be assumed that General Deane read the above, signed off on it and probably never thought about it again until he wrote his book several years after the war.

On May 10, the day Deane approved the trial decision and signed the letter of reprimand, both Lieutenant Colonel Wilmeth and Colonel Crockett signed a Court Martial Data Sheet. On May 12 Colonel Crockett signed a letter of transmittal sending all the documents of the trial to the Judge Advocate General's Department (JAGD) in Washington. Among other things the letter said,"...no member of the JAGD was on the court nor was such an officer on duty at that station, and if any deficiencies exist they are not of a material character from the data furnished."

There followed a listing of deficiencies as follows:
"a. Many delays occurred in the case
 b. Accused's act in Poland was not uncovered by U.S. authorities until seven
    weeks later.
 c. Restriction on transportation between Moscow and Poltava delayed trial for
    three weeks from the time charges were served.
 d. Correspondence between Moscow and Poltava for preparation of case was by
    radio. Exchange of messages are not included in record but because of this
    there is some discrepancy in dates of endorsements and forms (earlier than
    actually obtained).
 e. Although sufficient evidence was available at Poltava to influence investigating
    officer to recommend trial bulk of evidence did not come into his hands until
    court reached Moscow.
 f. All delays occurred with knowledge of appointing officer and it is not believed
    any action is warranted under Article of War 70."

The letter then included the following statement, "Although the case from beginning to completion has many exceptions, it is believed that the rights of the accused have been protected and that the ends of justice have been met."[8]

A review of the listed deficiencies can be criticized on several points. Item (c) is not accurate. The record shows the charges were served on April 10th, eight days before the Court moved to Moscow and 15 days before the trial began, so the delay was 15 days rather than three weeks. Item (d) says the messages between Moscow and Poltava were not included with the record without giving a reason. Since a separate file of certified copies of most messages had been compiled for the trial, which still exists, it is strange not to have furnished that along with the rest of the documents.[9] As has been pointed out previously, a review of some of those messages could have been embarrassing to the USMM, and to General Deane in particular. Still, even more strange, is the fact that one message must have been included because it was quoted in an opinion by the Board of Review in Washington, D.C.[10] Item (e) claims sufficient evidence was available at Poltava for the investigating officer to have recommended trial. This is contrary to the testimony of that officer, Lieutenant Colonel Wilmeth, who clearly recommended the charges be withdrawn on the basis of what he learned at Poltava. He said it was only after he arrived at Moscow that he learned of the allegations on which the charges were pursued. Lastly, Colonel Crockett's comment that the case had many exceptions was an understatement, but to say that King's rights had been protected was a gross misstatement. It is interesting to note that General Deane later wrote that Colonel Crockett was a member of the USMM and a friend of long standing.[11]

The record of the King Court Martial apparently reached Washington, D.C. on or about June 11, 1945. On that date Captain Stanley D. Waxberg, JAGD, signed the Court Martial Data Sheet. The trial record was then examined in the Office of the Judge Advocate General under Article of War 50 1/2 and was found "legally insufficient to support the findings and sentence."[12]

Next, it was reviewed by three Judge Advocates sitting as a Board of Review. Two of those Judge Advocates, Colonel Terry A. Lyon, JAGD, and Charles A. Luckie found the record of trial was legally sufficient to support the findings and the sentence.[13] That opinion was 13 pages in length and is only summarized with some observations. It took two and a half pages to say that the "omission of the word 'wrongfully' or words similar are not necessary in this instance especially when the specification contains the words 'bringing discredit on the military service'."[14]

On page four of the opinion the majority wrote that the most obvious question presented by the facts is whether the specification, as amended by the Court, charges an offense.[15] On the ninth page they wrote, "there still remains the question of whether the specification, as amended by the Court, alleges an offense." They then said the allegation is "a statement in simple and concise language of the facts constituting the offense attributed to him."[16]

The Judge Advocates then made a judicial assertion, on the law which prohibits the illegal wearing of the uniform. In a leap of logic they declared that Myron King, "who had flying clothes under his control and knowingly permitted the alien to violate the statute and regulation, also technically, if not actually, offended against the law in violation of Article of War 96."[17] Such reasoning fails to acknowledge that the specification did not state that Myron wrongfully or in other like language allowed Jack Smith to wear that clothing; he was not charged with that offense and could not be found guilty of such. In fact the flying clothes worn by Jack Smith, devoid of any rank or insignia were not a "prescribed uniform" within the meaning of the statute and the intent of Congress.

The majority opinion rambled on, insisting the "specification charged an offense, did not mislead the accused, and the Court was justified in finding the acts of the accused brought discredit on the military service."[18]

They further wrote, "...the accused did not object to the specification as being vague or multifarious and expressly waived the right to make any special pleas or motions.[19] The latter contention was written by military lawyers, well versed in the niceties of justice, military style. King was a 23 year old combat B-17 pilot. He was an innocent who placed his faith and trust in those army superiors with the conviction that he would be justly treated. The majority members of the Court which tried him probably had not fired a shot in the war or been fired at. There was no consideration during the trial as to what the King crew had to tolerate from the Russians when they were MIA for those seven weeks while being unreasonably detained by that ally which initiated the complaint against King.

The Court ascribed to King an understanding of the Manual of Court Martials and precedents thereunder that even his lead defense counsel, Lt. Col. Kingsbury (a medical doctor), clearly did not have. On the other side there were career officers led by the General Staff Corps who were leading Myron King down the primrose path.

Further discourse by the majority was held as to the meaning of the word "discredit", what constituted an "alien" and whether the conversation between Harriman and Stalin and the conversations between General Deane and General Slavin were properly admitted as evidence in the case. Finally, they wrote, "Upon the established and admitted facts in this case and the inferences and presumptions which arise from the facts, the Board of Review holds the record of trial to be legally sufficient to support the findings of guilty and the sentence."[20] It is very interesting to note that just prior to the above pronouncement, the Board referred to the fact that the reviewing authority was not furnished the reprimand, which was separately administered, nor did the General Court Martial Order include a copy of the reprimand. Since the rhetoric of that reprimand contained statements which were not supported by facts on the record it would have been interesting to see what, if any, comment the majority would have made concerning that letter signed by General Deane.

There was a dissent to the majority opinion by the third Judge Advocate, Herman Moyse.[21] Rather than attack the considerable argument by the majority as to the admissibility of the aforementioned conversations, Moyse dismissed the question saying that "it is unnecessary to pass on the admissibility of this evidence."[22]

He zeroed in on the argument that there was a violation of the law which prohibited the illegal wearing of the uniform. He said for this question to be advanced it must be established that the "uniform" must be one prescribed by army regulations.[23] Since such was not established he said no more need be said on that issue.

Moyse then pointed out that when the Court amended the specification by the deletion of words or phrases such as "willful concealment" or "failure to disclose" it removed any offense which would have been against the Soviet Union. In doing so, he said, they completely changed the character of the offense charged. He then said the court eliminated "without proper authority" from the offense on which they went to trial without substituting other words which might convey "carelessness, dereliction of duty or culpable conduct." He said in doing this the Court implicitly found that "in view of the extraordinary situation which confronted the accused, accused acted within the authority vested in him."[24] Thus did Moyse dispose of the first of the acts charged to Myron, in that he did "transport without proper authority, an alien from near Warsaw to Szczuczyn."

The Judge Advocate then said that the eliminated words "without proper authority" related only to that first act, not to the others in the specification. He said he found nothing to indicate that the fact Myron allowed Jack Smith to wear army flying clothes (act two) and to permit him, under an alias to associate with his crew (act three) brought discredit on the military.[25] He said there was not one single suggestion in the record that what Myron did brought discredit on the military service.[26] Herman Moyse concluded by saying he "concurred with the view expressed by the Office of the Judge Advocate General that the record of the trial is legally insufficient to support the finding of guilty and the sentence."[27]

The General Court Martial Order of the USMM bears a stamp which includes the signature of Lieutenant Colonel Lee H. Cope as the Chief Examiner, Military Justice Division of the JAGD. The signature was followed by a statement by Cope that the record of trial was examined by that office and found to legally support the sentence, and that such was done by the Board of Review for the Judge Advocate General. Next to this notation was the handwritten word "defective" with the initials which appeared to be "SDW" (possibly those of Captain Stanley D. Waxberg). The comment of Lt. Col. Cope is interesting. On July 28, 1945 Cope signed the Court Martial Data Sheet beside which is a handwritten notation which said, "record held legally sufficient by B/R with which holding I thoroughly disagree."[28] Apparently, Lt. Col. Cope had a change of heart. Elsewhere in the file was the opinion of Captain Waxberg who concluded that the record was legally insufficient to support the finding and the sentence. Likewise, Colonel R.E. Kunkel, JAGD, said that the record was legally insufficient, but added, "However, in view of the international situation the case be reviewed by Colonel King, Chief, International Law Division, for his comments."[29]

The file strangely contains no further action or comment by the U.S. Army JAGD, and no response from Colonel King. Under the circumstances, with the considerable disagreement as to the majority opinion by the Board of Review at the JAGD, one would certainly have expected some further review of the matter. Did Colonel King's review of the case, with its SECRET classification, label it as too volatile to become public knowledge because of the deterioration of relations between the United States and the Soviet Union? Or was there concern in the War Department about embarrassing those in the USMM who served up Lt. Myron L. King to appease Marshal Stalin? The final dated item in the file was on July 28; then on August 6 and 9 the Atomic bombs were dropped on Japan, and on August 14 the war ended. It is quite logical that the King case may have been lost in the confusion of postwar separations from the military and laid in the file without any conclusive action taken. It is important to know that none of the actions pro or con on his case that were taken up to the end of July were ever made known to Myron.

Additional details of Myron's story were provided by Chester H. Smith, a former journalist, a combat Marine correspondent and a veteran of 30 years on Capitol Hill in Washington, D.C.[30]

Mr. Smith is married to Miriam Fox, a close family friend of Myron and Eleanor King, who served for many years as the secretary to the Chief Counsel to the U.S. Senate Judiciary Committee. She knew of Myron's Court Martial in a cursory way and suggested that he pursue reopening of the matter. It was her idea that the matter be examined by Carlisle Ruddy, a staff attorney on the Judiciary Committee and a close friend. After Mr. Ruddy examined some of Myron's material he turned it over to Lieutenant Colonel John A. Doolan, AFUS. Doolan, an attorney, then attached to the Pentagon and assigned as an Air Force liaison officer to the Senate. Mr. Smith said the function of such officers was to pass out "good cheer" and "take care of", when appropriate, problems from constituents back home for members of the Senate.

Mr. Smith said that Doolan was as entranced with the case as was Carlisle Ruddy. He said that Colonel Doolan apparently put the case in the right office with the right people, that was with Senator Pat McCarran, of Nevada, who then was Chairman of the Judiciary Committee and the senior member of the Appropriations Committee. That, along with Colonel Doolan's ability to open the right doors at the Pentagon, and see that the case did not get hung up in bureaucratic channels, was fortunate for Myron. It was Mr. Smith's guess that these efforts resulted in a decision to review Myron's case in light of the passage of years and the obvious substantive questions involved, and whether "international politics (Stalin versus the U.S.A.) or true military justice" should prevail.[31]

There is no record of exactly how the case was reopened but it can be presumed that it was done through the Office of the Judge Advocate General of the Air Force. Unfortunately, Lieutenant Colonel Doolan is deceased. His observations here would be of value since he is the real hero in Myron's story. Doolan must have assumed representation of Myron in late 1950 and spent a full year working on the case on his own time. Myron's recollection and letters provide some of the story, but the most important is Doolan's work, a 97 page petition directed to the Judge Advocate General of the Air Force. Crucial to King was the fact that in 1947 the United States Air Force was created as a separate establishment no longer a part of the United States Army.[32] Most crucial was Section 12 of the Uniform Code of Military Justice, passed in 1950 as a result of agreements between the armed services. Section 12 provided that Court Martial cases tried subsequent to December 7, 1941, in which the accused was a member of the Army Air Forces, would be considered by the Air Force for review.[33]

In early July, 1951 the nationally-known and controversial syndicated columnist, Westbrook Pegler, wrote a complete column on the Myron King case. Though his journalistic style was often offensive, he did a good job of exposing to the public the fact that a young man named Myron King had been dealt an injustice by the army he had served. The column quoted a "competent authority" who said Myron's Court Martial trial was "probably unparalleled in its violation of procedures and substantive rights of the accused." He said the "authority" reviewed the documents, charging that members of the court testified for the prosecution and said the record is 'replete with hearsay and irrelevant testimony'." The article continued saying the material includes a "wild and erratic deposition by General Antonov who bulldozed the timid American functionaries sent to Russia by Harriman..." The article said that in his book "General Deane describes Antonov as a forceful man." Pegler said that bureaucrats of the Roosevelt regime including generals "were not equipped by knowledge to cope with the Russians and lacked the patriotic manhood to stand up to sycophants such as Harriman..." He referred to the incomplete and inaccurate version of the King story in Deane's book, **The Strange Alliance**, as leaving "important questions unanswered and leaves Deane in no enviable position." Pegler said King was still afraid of the power of the Air Force to persecute him. Pegler continued saying that an appeal was being prepared for review and vindication but "King refuses to talk lest mention of his case will so anger the Air Force that he will never get fair treatment." Pegler concluded by saying, "...the King case has been smothered all this time out of the obsequiousness of certain Americans toward the Russians and later out of a determination for obvious reasons, to conceal the facts from the American public."[34]

The appeal on behalf of Myron King went forward on July 30, 1951 by a cover letter to the Judge Advocate General of the Air Force, Lt. Col. Doolan enclosing his petition on the King case.[35] In the preparation of this document Doolan did not have access to the Army file which contained the majority opinion of the Board of Review and, more importantly, the dissent of Moyse and the other Army JAGD officers who concluded the record of the Court Martial was legally insufficient to support a finding of guilty and the sentence Myron received. He included a request that the Air Force obtain "deficient parts of the record" for the petitioner, although I do not believe Doolan, in his wildest dreams, would have guessed the amount of support for Myron King that he would have found there.[36] From all the data reviewed concerning Doolan's effort in 1950 and 1951 it is apparent that the only thing he had to work with was Myron's copy of the trial transcript. Even though it was then a classified document, under law it was required that a copy had to be furnished the accused. This had been mailed to Myron at Deenethorpe on May 12, 1945.[37]

Doolan listed as a specification of errors, ten errors which occurred in the trial which he said were prejudicial to Myron King's substantive rights. Each of these errors was followed by lengthy and strong legal arguments to buttress Doolan's position; they consumed 85 of the 97 page petition. The following is not an attempt to summarize all of Doolan's arguments but to provide one or more significant points that were made with respect to each of the errors.

1. The accused was not adequately and fairly apprised of the nature of the offense intended to be charged against him. Doolan's point was that the deletion of certain words and phrases by the court left the specification defective, vague and indefinite.[38]

2. The specification is fatally defective in that it alleges more than one offense. The specification sought to join the violation of Army Regulations regarding the Illegal Wearing of the Uniform and unauthorized flights as well as a provision of the Manual of Court Martials. To join more than one offense by the word "and" makes a specification either conjunctively or in the alternative substantially defective.[39]

3. The facts under the circumstances alleged in the specification are in insufficient to constitute conduct to the prejudice of good order and military discipline or to the discredit of the military services of the United States. Doolan wrote that acts which allege such prohibited conduct must **directly offend against our Government and military discipline** and not do so indirectly or remotely.[40]

4. The specification as found proved by the court fails to allege facts sufficient to support the charge. Doolan said the court by deleting the words "without proper authority" removed the gist of the offense leaving the specification without words which constituted an unlawful offense.[41]

5. The findings are based on an error at law prejudicial to the substantive rights of the accused. The admission of the Antonov letter as evidence without proof of the allegations made therein was an error of law by the court. To admit that letter violated King's Sixth Amendment right to be confronted with the witnesses against him. Also the error led to the introduction of acts by others extraneous to the scope of the trial which had no bearing on the guilt or the innocence of the accused.[42]

6. The evidence is insufficient to support the findings of guilty of the charge and specification. Doolan said the acts of the accused did not constitute a crime and Soviet displeasure disclosed by the evidence did not make it so.[43]

7. The findings of the court were contrary to the weight of the evidence. The weight of the evidence was provided by the testimony of King and three members of his crew. It was contrary to unsupported allegations which lacked credible proof.[44]

8. The accused has been, by the deficiency of the record, deprived of the right to have the complete proceedings of his trial reviewed in an appellate capacity as provided by the Articles of War. The trial transcript did not include substantial portions of the trial proceedings including the closing statements by each side which Doolan said are essential features of a General Court Martial trial.[45]

9. The unanimous recommendation by members of the court for clemency constitutes a finding that the accused is not guilty of the charge preferred. Doolan said that proof of mere acts without proof of unlawful intent is insufficient for a finding of guilty. He said the clemency recommendation specifically said that King did not have such intent.[46]

10. Members of the court by their conduct failed to render to the accused a fair and impartial trial. Doolan pointed out that the court permitted the introduction of improper testimony prejudicial to the defense, allowed improper questioning of witnesses on legal points, allowed court members to assume the adversarial role reserved for the prosecutor, allowed them to improperly cross-examine and harass witnesses and permitted them to express opinions, impressions, conclusions and deductions.[47]

After the points of errors Doolan provided a conclusion to the petition which included the following five items:

1. The proceedings failed to exhibit an offense to any person or thing connected with the military service..
2. The accused acted from necessity and was wholly free from wrong or blame in occasioning or producing the necessity which required his action.
3. Conditions under which the trial was held created a mental atmosphere in which reason could not function.
4. Error of law were so plainly violative of fundamental principle of military law and justice that it cannot be said accused had a fair trial.
5. Irrespective of the question whether accused's guilt was established he ought not stand convicted of and be punished as a result of a trial conducted as was the one under consideration.[48]

Doolan followed with the following Prayer for Relief, or request, to the Judge Advocate General of the Air Force:

1. That the Judge Advocate of the Air Force allow oral argument upon this petition.
2. That the Judge Advocate of the Air Force cause such additional investigation be made and such additional evidence be secured as he may deem appropriate.
3. It is requested that the Judge Advocate General obtain such deficient parts of the record and furnish copies thereof to the Petitioner in order that he might have a complete copy of the record as provided by the Articles of War in order to adequately present his case on oral argument upon this matter.
4. That the Judge Advocate General of the Air Force grant a new trial or vacate the sentence adjudged in Petitioner's general Court Martial trial and restore all rights, privileges and property affected by the sentence.[49]

It is readily apparent that Lieutenant Colonel Doolan attacked the trial record from many different angles and in a much broader way than the Board of Review dissent by Herman Moyse. Moyse, primarily, confined himself to the question whether the record was "legally insufficient to support the finding of guilty and the sentence." Doolan, bless him, tore the trial transcript apart in a way which might be considered overkill. It appears that he hoped to provide overwhelming legal justification for vacating the conviction and the sentence without having to subject Myron to another trial.

There is nothing in the Army Court Martial file which constitutes any of the deficiencies referred to by Doolan, nor is there anything which would indicate a request was made to correct the deficiencies noted. The file contains only those documents forwarded to the JAGD by the USMM in 1945. Further, there is no indication that a copy of Doolan's petition was ever furnished for the completion of that file much less the final disposition of the case.

Doolan, and especially Myron King, had an anxious wait for months for a response to the petition. On December 18, 1951 Doolan received a letter from Lieutenant Colonel Charles E. Wainwright in the office of the Judge Advocate General of the Air Force, Major General Reginald C. Harmon. The letter, making reference to Doolan's petition, advised that arrangements had been made for an oral hearing of the case before a New Trial Board at the Pentagon on January 8, 1952. At the bottom of this letter are the handwritten comments of Doolan, which are as follows: "Called Gen. Kiddner. Informed him that I did not request a hearing before the New Trial Board. That if I didn't get a personal hearing before the Judge Advocate General - Harmon I was not interested. Also I asked Gen. Kiddner for a copy of any memo or brief that the New Trial Board was submitting to Gen. Harmon. Gen. Kiddner was disturbed by this request. Also I requested copy of closing arguments."[50]

The note was written with an obvious degree of irritation on the part of Doolan. I think it can be fairly assumed that the petition, when received around the first of August was forwarded to the New Trial Board for review and decision as to whether a oral hearing should be granted to King. Doolan's irritation may have been that someone in General Harmon's office made the decision for a New trial Board hearing although Doolan understood that he had a prior personal commitment that Harmon would hear the case personally. Doolan did not want the case to be heard by the New Trial Board for some reason. Myron said Doolan believed General Kiddner wanted a New Trial Board hear the oral presentation on January 8 and then possibly refuse to grant a new trial.[51] Since nothing more is known about this, it is probably a good bet that General Kiddner took the course of least resistance to let Harmon handle the case personally.

Doolan pressed on with a letter to General Harmon on December 27 which requested the record of proceedings in Myron's case, classified SECRET, be declassified. He said, "The authority for making the original classification no longer exists. The information and the matter contained therein would not now endanger National Security, cause injury to the interests or prestige of the Nation, or be of any advantage to a foreign nation, except, that the evidence adduced in the trial of subject officer indicates that officials of the Soviet Union summarily executed a combatant of Great Britain in a combat area, clothed in an English uniform. The presumption being that in time of war one who wears the uniform of a particular country in a combat area owes allegiance to that country...The record of proceedings is of a personal and disciplinary nature the knowledge of which it is no longer desirable to safeguard. It has been common knowledge in civil and military circles that subject named officer was Court Martialed during World War II. Failure to disclose the nature of his offense and surrounding facts has caused and is causing him irreparable harm."[52] Had he known, Doolan could have added more fire if he had been aware that we forcibly returned Captain Morris Shenderoff to Moscow from Italy, to his certain death by execution, without carefully checking his claim of American citizenship. The request for declassification of the trial proceedings was forwarded to the Army JAGD on January 9 with a response that there was no objection to declassification. On January 11 the record was regraded to unclassified, signed by Lt. Col. G.J. Freeman, AGO, for the Chief of the Security Classification Review Branch. That was prompt action; the chips seemed to be falling Myron's way.[53] However, many documents directly related to the King case were not declassified until many years later.

Then came the good news that Myron had waited for so long, that he had been cleared of the charges for which he had been Court Martialed. General Harmon's Memorandum Opinion was dated January 11, 1952; ironically Myron first learned of it on a radio show on Sunday January 13.[54]

General Harmon restated the facts of the King incident. He then said, "There is no admissible evidence in the record of trial tending to show that accused intended to fly the interpreter to England; that the interpreter was a Pole, a terrorist, or a saboteur; or that the accused flew into Soviet controlled territory to drop supplies, wireless sets, or to contact the Polish underground. On the contrary, the evidence discloses the accused landed in Poland because of aircraft damage caused by enemy gunfire while bombing Berlin; that he had good reason to believe the interpreter to be a member of the Russian General's staff; that he did not know of the stowaway's presence until it was too late to place him on the Russian aircraft; that he was 5,000 feet in the air where the temperature was 53 degrees below zero before learning the interpreter wore American flying clothes and was not a member of the general's staff; that he told fellow Americans of his intention to surrender the interpreter to American authority at Poltava; and accused's impropriety, if any, was motivated by a sincere desire to return his crew and plane to his home base in England without any undue delay."[55] Gen. Harmon then provided the legal basis for his decision which succinctly followed the Herman Moyse dissent, in a number of places quoting passages word for word.

General Harmon said that "an injustice has resulted from the findings and the sentence and that there is good cause for granting relief." He concluded his opinion with the following, "Therefore, good cause for relief having been established, the findings of guilty and the sentence are vacated, and all rights privileges and property of which accused has been deprived by virtue of the findings and the sentence so vacated will be restored."[56] While the decision which overturned the Court Martial verdict was a just one long overdue, one can question whether the Army JAGD would have seriously considered Doolan's petition and, even if it did review and grant an oral hearing that it would render a decision to vacate the sentence. It is almost a certainty that the specter of the General Staff Corps would have hung over the process with the usual condescension toward those whose service had been with the USAAF.

Myron's family friend, Miriam Fox, who got the ball rolling for him, wrote him an airmail special delivery letter on Friday, January 11. She said Doolan informed Carlisle Ruddy that Myron should listen to a radio program on Sunday night, June 13 for "some good news." She said that Doolan cautioned Myron not to make any comments until he had been officially notified and had an opportunity to read the opinion, and suggested that Myron say that such a response was on the advice of his attorney.[57] On January 17 the Department of Defense issued a press release on the King case with the caption "Former Bomber Pilot Cleared of Wartime Russian Charge." That caption was the first admission that the Army brought Court Martial charges against King on behalf of the Soviet Union. The release mentioned that the Russians claimed King had carried on his aircraft a "Polish saboteur" but no mention was made of Stalin's wild charges.[58] On that same date Lt. Col. Doolan wrote to Myron. He said that in addition to the errors set forth in his petition he was prepared, upon oral hearing before Gen. Harmon, to submit, among additional specification of errors, that Myron was denied a fair trial because the record shows that Major Taylor was called as a witness and testified in effect that General Deane, who ordered the Court Martial trial and acted as the reviewing authority, was of the opinion that King was guilty. This denied King a fair and impartial review as required by the Articles of War. Colonel Doolan continued saying, "I wish to state that I was never under any apprehension in this case, because I knew under the provisions of the new Uniform Code of Military Justice, Major General Reginald C. Harmon, the Judge Advocate General of the Air Force, would grant a hearing before him personally. I requested such a hearing and General Harmon stated that he would personally hear the oral argument. Prior to such a hearing, General Harmon informed me that it would not be necessary to bring you and other witnesses from Tennessee to Washington, D.C. to attend an oral hearing because he would vacate the findings and sentence on the petition, without the necessity of oral hearing."[59]

By January 18 the King victory was public knowledge. On that date, "The Evening Star" in Washington, D.C. carried an article on the decision of General Harmon with the caption, "Air Force Clears Former Pilot of Soviet Charge After 7 Years."[60] The news reached the "The Chatanooga News- Free Press", in Myron's hometown on January 24. It was a long article under a caption, "Army Clears Lt. M.L. King: Was Court Martialed On Russian Complaint."[61] Of course it was not the Army but the Air Force that cleared Myron; the Army should have agreed that it wronged him but it never has. Doolan didn't leave any loose ends; on March 11 he prepared a letter for Myron's signature addressed to the Air Force Finance Center which resulted in recovering the fine which had been imposed by the sentence.[62] Doolan suggested that Myron come to Washington to discuss the whole thing with him. He and Carlisle Ruddy thought Myron should write a book or at least some magazine articles.[63] Westbrook Pegler finally got around to writing a sequel article on the outcome of the King case in a column on June 6, 1952 with the caption "Exoneration of U.S. Flier Court Martialed in Russia." Pegler wrote, "after more than seven years a disgraceful injustice to an American bomber pilot inflicted by a Court Martial in Moscow has been corrected by Maj. Gen. Reginald C. Harmon, Judge Advocate General of the Air Force. The case of an American soldier's ill treatment by an American court sitting in the American Embassy about 200 yards from the Kremlin was brought to public notice in these pieces last July 9. It had been suppressed under orders that conceal nobody knows how many other outrages." With reference to General John R. Deane's postwar book, **The Strange Alliance**, Pegler said that Deane himself had the sense to perceive that the United States was being betrayed. Nevertheless, Deane wrote a reprimand to be entered as a lasting blemish on the record of a young compatriot. The trial was, in the words of a competent authority, 'probably unparalleled in its violations of procedures and the rights of the accused.'"[64]

Notes to Chapter 21

1. *Record of trial of Myron L. King by general Court Martial April 25-26, 1945 at American Embassy, Moscow, U.S.S.R. unnumbered cover page to transcript*
2. *Interview of Myron L. King by author at Nashville, Tennessee June 9, 1992*
3. *Letter, Ward J. Fellows to author December 3, 1991*
4. *See 2 above*
5. *Ibid.*
6. *Letter, and enclosure, Office of the Clerk of Court, Department of the Army, U.S. Army Legal Services Agency to author June 21, 1991 re Lt. Donald Bridge*
7. *Court Martial File of Myron L. King, Office of the Clerk of Court, Department of the Army, U.S. Army Legal Services Agency, reviewed at the National Archives, Suitland, Md. April 22, 1991*
8. *Ibid.*
9. *National Archives, Washington, D.C. Record Group 334, Box 10 Cable File in King case*
10. *Copy of dissenting opinion of Judge Advocate Herman Moyse, Board of Review, JAGD July 17, 1945 in King case p. 7*
11. *Deane, John R. The Strange Alliance p. 255*
12. *See 7 above*
13. *Copy of memorandum for General Cramer in the King case with majority opinion of Judge Advocates, Colonel Terry A. Lyon and Charles A. Luckie July 17, 1945*
14. *Ibid. p. 6*
15. *Ibid. p. 4, 9*
16. *Ibid. p. 10*
17. *Ibid.*
18. *Ibid.*
19. *ibid. p. 11*
20. *Ibid. p. 13*
21. *See 10 above*
22. *Ibid. p. 5*
23. *Ibid. p. 6*
24. *Ibid. p. 8*
25. *Ibid. p. 9*
26. *Ibid. p. 11*
27. *Ibid.*
28. *See 7 above*
29. *Ibid.*
30. *Letter, Chester H. Smith to author September 22, 1992*
31. *Ibid.*
32. *Copy of letter of transmittal, Lieutenant Colonel John A. Doolan to Judge Advocate General, Department of the Air Force; enclosure Petition for a new trial on behalf of Myron L. King furnished author by King June 9, 1992*
33. *Copy of press release by the Department of Defense, Office of Public Information No. 63-52 January 17, 1952 captioned "Former Bomber Pilot Cleared of Wartime Russian Charge"*
34. *Column "As Pegler Sees It" by Westbrook Pegler Savannah Morning News July 6, 1951*
35. *See 32 above*
36. *Ibid. p. 96*
37. *See 1 above, unnumbered cover page captioned "RECORD OF TRIAL BY GENERAL COURT MARTIAL"*
38. *See 32 above p. 9-16*
39. *Ibid. p. 17-18*
40. *Ibid. p. 19-20*
41. *Ibid. p. 21-24*
42. *Ibid. p. 25-34*
43. *Ibid. p. 35-49*
44. *Ibid. p. 50-78*
45. *Ibid. p. 79-84*
46. *Ibid. p. 85-87*
47. *Ibid. p. 88-94*
48. *Ibid. p. 95*
49. *Ibid. p. 96*
50. *Copy of letter, Lieutenant Colonel John A. Doolan from Lieutenant Colonel Charles E. Wainwright, USAF, Office of the Judge Advocate General USAF December 18, 1951*
51. *Telephone conversation Myron L. King and author January 20, 1993*
52. *Copy of letter, Lieutenant Colonel John A. Doolan to the Judge Advocate General, Department of the Air Force December 27, 1951*
53. *Copy of letter to Adjutant General's Office, Department of the Army from JAGD, Department of the Army*

January 9, 1952 with endorsement from the Adjutant General's Office January 11, 1952

54. Copy of Memorandum Opinion of Major General Reginald C. Harmon, Judge Advocate General, USAF on Petition of Myron L. King January 11, 1952

55. *Ibid.* p. 3-4

56. *Ibid.*

57. Copy of letter, Miriam Fox to Myron and Eleanor King, January 11, 1952

58. See 33 above

59. Copy of letter, Lieutenant Colonel John A. Doolan to Myron L. King January 17, 1952

60. <u>The Evening Star</u> Washington, D.C. news article January 18, 1952 captioned "Air Force Clears Former Pilot Of Soviet Charge After 7 Years"

61. <u>Chattanooga News - Free Press</u> January 24, 1952 news article captioned "Army Clears Lt. M.L. King: Was Court Martialed On Russian Complaint"

62. Copy of letter, to Army Finance Center, Denver, Colorado March 11, 1952 from Myron L. King

63. Copy of three page note on stationary "U.S. Senate" to Dear Eleanor and Myron" March 11, 1952 signed "Miriam"

64. Column "As Pegler Sees It" by Westbrook Pegler <u>Savannah Morning News</u>, Savannah, Georgia on June 6, 1952

EPILOGUE

As the story of "Maiden U.S.A." began to unfold it was obvious that there would be stories within the story. As early as 1986 when I first read those photocopied pages of Bill Sweeney's testimony, sent without comment by Myron L. King, I had a gut feeling that Myron had been dealt a serious injustice and had been abused by his own country. As that part of the "Maiden's" life began to evolve I came to realize that the entire crew was also hurt by the conviction of their aircraft commander, as well as the prosecution of their tail gunner, George E. Atkinson. The latter forced to endure a trial before a Soviet tribunal, and suffered additional indignities while American military officers sat on their hands, failing to stand up to the bullying of the Russians, even to the extent of bribing a Russian court.

The saga of the King portion of the "Maiden's" story leaves unanswered questions on why the Soviets pressed charges. The recent political upheaval that brought an end to the Soviet Union might someday uncover answers to some of these questions.

Some of the questions that remain are: Who was Jack Smith? Was he a Pole? Was he a part of the Polish underground Army? Was he dropped into Poland by the Polish Government in London under the auspices of the British? If in fact he was a Polish saboteur and terrorist of the London Poles, why were the Russians reluctant to provide the proof they claimed to have? Or were they afraid of further criticism by the allies for their barbaric decision to allow the "tragedy of Warsaw"? Since Jack Smith was presumably executed by the Russians why did they not, at least, present the nameless Russian General who escorted King to Szczuczyn to testify? Or would that General have created a bigger problem? It is an accepted fact that Jack Smith appeared at the side of the General on his arrival at Kuflevo. The King crew have said that after three days at Kuflevo it was the first time any of them had seen Jack Smith. When Jack Smith acted as an interpreter could he have already been in the custody of the General, who in the confusion was able to escape when he stowed away on the "Maiden"? Any other conclusion is improbable; a member of the Polish underground would not have been so stupid as to attach himself voluntarily to a Russian General or wear even a part of a British uniform. Why then would the Russians not produce the General for the trial, if only to take the heat off General Antonov?

The Antonov letter produces some significant questions. Did Antonov write that letter in response to one from General Deane because he found it difficult to defend his country on charges of obstructing Myron King's crew ot those 50 American aircraft crews who had been shot down behind Russian lines? Why was a copy of General Deane's letter to General Antonov not produced during the trial? Was it not produced because it might have been the real reason for the grounding of all American aircraft in the Soviet Union? Why is that letter not to be found in the file of the National Archives? Why did General Antonov settle for the Court Martial of Lt. Donald Bridge and Lt. Myron L. King and ignore the complaint he made in the same letter about Lieutenant Colonel James D. Wilmeth? Did General Deane interject himself or make a deal with the Russians to save Wilmeth from charges that may have included his possible violation of the 96th Article of War? Why, when the King case was discussed with Antonov by USMM "brass," did Antonov orally add the Shenderoff affair to his complaint but ignore the Wilmeth complaint which he had included in his letter? Why was the Wilmeth episode not brought up by the Americans during their meeting with Antonov? After Wilmeth arrived back at Poltava from Lublin, en route to Moscow, why was he chosen to investigate the King incident? And why was Wilmeth named prosecutor of King, particularly since he too was a subject of the same complaint in the Antonov letter?

Was Morris Shenderoff born in the United States? Did anyone conduct a full investigation in the United States of the many leads on Shenderoff which were available from his interrogation? Was the decision to return Shenderoff to Moscow from Italy, as demanded by the Russians, and to certain death, part of a deal to permit Harriman's aircraft to leave Russia for the United Nations Conference in San Francisco when all American aircraft in the Soviet Union were still grounded?

Why were vital matters not included in the trial transcript such as the prosecution's closing statement, the opening statement by the defense, and oral arguments by both sides at the end of the trial? Also why were the motions and objections made during the trial by assistant defense counsel not included in the record?

Why was Lt. Col. Kingsbury, a medical officer, who was obviously inept, chosen to be the defense counsel? Why did he not rely on the legal expertise of Leon Dolin, the assistant defense counsel, and why did he interfere with with efforts of Dolin during the trial? Cable messages establish that Kingsbury was the third name submitted to be defense counsel, and was a colleague of Wilmeth in Lublin; who submitted his name and why? What were the reasons for other names being rejected for service on the Court; particularly combat transient officers of the USAAF? Why did Kingsbury not review the Embassy file on King even after he was advised of its contents by Dolin? Why did Kingsbury not counsel King before trial? What disposition was made of some of the items in that file seen by Dolin which are not now in the Court Martial file or the USMM files? Were Wilmeth and Kingsbury intelligence officers? If not, were they performing a secondary intelligence assignment in Lublin? What primary assignment did Kingsbury have if he was not an intelligence officer?

Why was General Deane so determined to move the trial to Moscow? Why did General Roberts and General Deane tell General Slavin two completely different reasons for changing the trial venue to Moscow? Since the facts of the case reveal both stories to be false, what was the intent of the USMM?

The cable file for the King trial confirms that Colonel Moses W. Pettigrew, was a second choice to serve as President of the Court? Did that assignment have anything to do with his subsequently being chosen to serve as the counsel for George E. Atkinson when he was tried by a Soviet court at Poltava? Why did Pettigrew not meet with Atkinson until the day of his trial? Why did Pettigrew not discuss any trial strategy with Atkinson or take any active part in the trial? Why did Pettigrew interfere with George Kennan's decision to take positive diplomatic steps to have the case against Atkinson dismissed? And why was Pettigrew listening to Russian prosecutors and not providing positive representation for his client?

Why was it decided that the King trial would be held at Spaso House rather than at the Embassy? Was it significant that both Harriman and General Deane left Moscow to return to the United States before the King trial? Why wasn't the trial held prior to their departures so as to eliminate hearsay and inaccurate testimony by subordinates? As for Deane, was his departure so urgent that he could not have remained until the trial was concluded? Or would his personal involvement in the case been such that it would have caused him serious embarrassment?

Why were the arrangements to move King and the others out of Moscow under clandestine circumstances necessary? Why were all parties at the Moscow airport told that they could not divulge what had occurred during the King trial? Why then were all documents related to the King trial classified SECRET? Did the classification SECRET have anything to do with the deterioration of American-Soviet relations or was it a device to protect those Americans, assigned to the USMM and involved in the trial, from embarrassment?

One of the biggest question of all is who masterminded the Russian complaint against Myron King? Many who served in Moscow during those war years would have said the accusation would not have gone forward without the approval and direction of Joseph Stalin. Although Stalin had a close grip on everything, it seems more likely that the nitty-gritty was handled by those lower down in the Soviet heirarchy. Hands on responsibility probably began with General A.E. Antonov, the Red Army Chief of Staff. He was, almost without question, the head of the conspiracy to end all collaboration with the United States, and in particular get the U.S. military out of Poltava. General Kovalev, a later Russian commander at Poltava, was involved but was probably a lower level participant. It was he who initiated the problems at Poltava which resulted in Colonel Hampton, his American counterpart, and others at Poltava, being thrown out of Russia the same month as the King trial. Wilmeth believed General Kovalev was responsible for his being thrown out of Lublin and probably suggested the idea of including him in the complaints listed in the Antonov letter. Kovalev also knew the reason why the King crew was detained at Poltava and not permitted to leave Russia before Americans at Poltava; or even those in Moscow, knew. Kovalev, when interviewed in the George Atkinson case, expressed his personal judgement to American investigators that George was guilty. However, the strong anti-American activity went back to June, 1944. A major player in the Poltava exercise who was involved from the beginning and remained involved right up to the end in June, 1945 was General N.V. Slavin, Antonov's deputy. He was always the obstructionist, seeming to take pleasure in being the messenger of bad tidings. He sat in on almost every meeting that Antonov had with Americans and didn't mind saying nyet to everything proposed by the Americans. Even after the King trial ended he attempted to interfere with the departure of the crew from the Soviet Union. The use of the expression "Slavinism" becomes clear.

The King case was, from the point of view of the USMM and the American Embassy in Moscow, one example of a continuing effort to salvage U.S. policy of collaboration with the Soviet Union. The decision was to sacrifice a young man's reputation, without regard for his service to his country in combat, by a trial to placate the Russian ego. It was not the only such decision; to declare persona non grata Colonel Thomas K. Hampton and Major Kowal are examples which came out during the King trial. Also the Court Martial of Lt. Donald Bridge was an example which grew out of the same Russian complaint involving Myron King. How many more like George E. Atkinson were also sacrificed as an expedient in American efforts to kowtow to the Russians to save a policy which was doomed before it began? It cost seven years of injury to Myron and his family. Those decisions of expediency remind me of a quote from the late Michigan Senator, Arthur H. Vandenberg, who said "Expedience and Justice frequently are not on speaking terms."[1] And what is justice? One definition is, "Justice is usually understood as including such social virtues as fairness, equality and correct and impartial treatment."[2] There was no justice in the King trial as expediency got in the way on April 26, 1945. The decision of General Reginald Harmon in 1952 helped the cause of justice in righting a wrong but "Justice delayed is justice denied!"[3] Myron King has said that some of his crew would like to have a crew reunion and he thought this is now an appropriate idea. It would be fitting for them to hold it in Dayton, Ohio. There at Kettering Hall of the USAF Museum on the grounds of the Wright-Patterson AFB they could gather under that painting, the portrait of their "Maiden U.S.A." What a special reunion that would be!

Notes to Epilogue

. Spinrad, Leonard and Thelma _Speaker's Lifetime Library_ p. 140
2. _The New York Public Library Desk Reference_ p. 222
3. Henry, Lewis C. Ed. _Five Thousand Quotations For All Occasions_ p. 141

The 401st Bomb Group (H). Their motto: Caelum Arena Nostra (Heaven is Our Arena)

Photograph from the USAF Collection courtesy of the NASM of the Smithsonian.

GLOSSARY
Acronyms - Abbreviations

AAB – Army Air Base

AAF – Army Air Force (1940 - 1947), also Army Air Field

Abort – Aircraft turned back from mission due to mechanical failures

AC – Air Corps also known as (aka) Army Air Corps (ACC) until 1940; also Aviation Cadet and see Flying Cadet

Ace – Five or more confirmed kills (aircraft shot down) by fighter pilots

AGWAR – Adjutant General, War Department

APO – Army Post Office

ARCADIA – Code name for Combined Chiefs Of Staff (CCS) conference Washington, D.C. December 20, 1941 to January 14, 1942

ARGUMENT – Code name for final campaign to destroy German Luftwaffe and aircraft industry by May 1, 1944 in accordance with plan for OVERLORD

A-2 – Leather flying jacket popular for casual uniform wear on base for flying personnel

ATC – Air Transport Command

AWPD-1 – Air War Plans Division-1; a strategy for U.S. air war before U.S. entry into World War II

AWPD-42 – Revised Air War Plans Division strategy in 1942

Bandits – Enemy fighter aircraft

B-17 – U.S. four engine heavy bomber aka the Flying Fortress, the Fort, etc. by Boeing

BG – Bomb Group

Box – Unit formation; a concentrated formation of aircraft projecting the formation as an invisible box shape for primarily defensive purposes

Brig. Gen – Brigadier General

B-24 – U.S. four engine heavy bomber aka the Liberator by Consolidated

Capt. – Captain

Casablanca Conference – Conference of CCS January 1943 (also see CBO)

CBW – Combat Bombardment Wing or Combat Wing

Col. – Colonel

CBO – Combined Bomber Offensive set by Casablanca Directive at CCS Conference January 1943

Chaff – Metalic foil strips dropped to confuse German radar

CCS – Combined Chiefs of Staff (American and British)

C.O. – Commanding Officer

DR – Dead reckoning navigation; the determination of position or a "fix" of a aircraft using compass, speed, distance from known point allowing for wind and drift

Ditch – Emergency wheels up landing on land or water

Do 17 – Dornier German light bomber also used as an intruder or night fighter

drop tanks – Expendable fuel tanks carried on exterior of fighter aircraft to extend their range; when empty or when enemy was engaged they were jettisoned

Engine numbers – four engine heavy bombers identified their engines by numbering them beginning with the outboard engine on the port side #1 through #4 and the last being the outboard engine on the starboard side.

Eighth Bomber Command – Usually referred to as the VIII Bomber Command; in England from January 1942 until January 1944

ETA – Estimated Time of Arrival or ETR Estimated Time of Return

ETO – European Theater of Operations in World War II

Feathering propeller – On engine failure propeller blades must be angled, or feathered, with leading edge forward to stop propeller spin. Unless feathered vibration could endanger aircraft

1st or 2nd Lt. – First or Second Lieutenant

FG – Fighter Group

Fix – position of aircraft by navigation

Flak – Shrapnel from exploding antiaircraft shells

Flak happy – Symptoms of stress and strain on members of air crews from regular exposure to aerial combat

Flak house – a facility run by the American Red Cross for members of air crews for relief from combat stress

Flying Cadet – Designation for those individuals in Army flight training in the 1920s and 1930s (designation later changed to Aviation Cadet)

FW 190 – Focke-Wulf German single engine fighter aircraft

Frags – Fragmentation bombs; anti personnel bombs which on explosion scattered pieces of metal (shrapnel) in all directions

FRANTIC – Code name for shuttle bombing missions by 15th and 8th Air Forces to bases in Russia; initial code name was BASEBALL

Gee – British navigation aid which enabled aircraft to obtain a fix from three ground stations which provided transmissions received on a radar scope

Gee-H or G-H – British adapted Gee for use in blind bombing

GSC – General Staff Corps, U.S. Army

GP – General purpose demolition bombs

G.I. – Government Issue; also slang for a member of the armed services, especially enlisted personnel

G-2 – Army military Intelligence

Groesbeck – Mission in support of airborne invasion of Netherlands; also see MARKET GARDEN

GYMNAST – Code name for projected invasion of North Africa aka SUPER GYMNAST and see TORCH

He 111 – Heinkel German two engine bomber

H2S – British airborne radar for blind bombing 1943

H2X – American modification of H2S aka Pathfinder Force, PFF, Mickey Mouse, Mickey

IP – Initial Point; the start of the bomb run.

IB – Incendiary bomb

JAGD – Judge Advocate General's Department, U.S. Army or U.S. Air Force

Jerry – Name for German military personnel, particularly those of the Luftwaffe

Ju 87 – Junker German aircraft known as "Sturkampfflugzeug" or Stuka Dive Bomber also used as a tank destroyer and a night ground attack bomber

Ju 88 – Junker German aircraft designed as a dive bomber with success as a night fighter

KGB – Komitet Gosudarstvennoy Bezopasnosti, Soviet internal security police, previously known as the NKVD

KIA – Killed in Action

Let down – Coordinated formation decrease in altitude

Lt. – Lieutenant

Lt. Col. – Lieutenant Colonel

Luftwaffe – German Air Force

Maj. – Major

Maj. Gen. – Major General

MARKET GARDEN – Code name for British airborne attack in the area of Arnhem, Netherlands 1944

MAAF – Mediterranean Allied Air Forces

Milk run – An easy combat mission with little or no enemy fighter attacks or flak

MIA – Missing In Action

ME – Maximum effort

Me 109 – Messerschmitt German single engine fighter aka Bf109

Me 110 – Messerschmitt German two engine fighter aka Bf 110

Mickey Mouse or Mickey – See H2X, Pathfinder Force, PFF

MPI – Mean Point of Impact; Target for bomb impact

NKVD – Narodnyi Kommissariat Vnutrennykl Del, the Soviet internal security police replaced by the KGB

NOBALL – Code name for V-1 and V-2 targets

OVERLORD – Code name for invasion of Europe June 6, 1944

O.V.S – Soviet Foreign Military Liaison Office, Moscow

Oxygen checks – Checks by radio requiring response of each crew member to insure system had not failed and to protect against death from anoxia

PFF – Pathfinder Force; see H2X, Mickey Mouse

P-51 – U.S. single engine fighter by North American aka the Mustang

P-47 – U.S. single engine fighter by Republic aka the Thunderbolt

POINTBLANK – Code name for June 1943 amendment of Casablanca Directive making top priority for CBO the destruction of the Luftwaffe and the German aircraft industry

POW – Prisoner of War

P-38 – U.S. Lockheed two engine fighter aka the Lightning

QUADRANT – Code name for CCS conference at Quebec August 14- 24, 1943

RAF – Royal Air Force

RCAF – Royal Canadian Air Force

ROTC – Reserve Officer Training Corps

SAP – Semi armour piercing bombs

Sgt. – Sergeant

SEXTANT – Code name for CCS conference at Cairo, Egypt andTeheran, Iran November and December 1943

SHAEF – Supreme Headquarters Allied Expeditionary Forces,Europe 1944-1945

Spares – Extra bombers taking off and assembling with Group for mission to fill vacancies if aircraft abort

S/Sgt. – Staff Sergeant

SUPER GYMNAST – See GYMNAST

T/Sgt. – Technical Sergeant

Toggelier – aka Toggleer or Bomb dropper. An aerial gunner replacing officer bombardiers to toggle or salvo bombs on bomb release by the lead aircraft

TORCH – Code name for the North African invasion 1942

Triangle First – Name for the 8th Air Force 1st Bomb Division later called the 1st Air Division

TRIDENT – Code name for CCS meeting Washington, D.C. May 1943

U.K. – United Kingdom; England, Scotland, Wales and Northern Ireland

USA – United States Army also United States of America

USAF – United Sates Air Force (since 1947)

USAAF – United States Army Air Forces (1940-1947)

USMA – United States Military Academy, West Point, New York

USMM – U.S. Military Mission, Moscow aka MILMIS, Moscow

USSTAF – United States Strategic and Tactical Air Forces,Europe

USO – United Service Organizations providing all types of services to military personnel

VE Day – Victory in Europe May 8, 1945

VELVET – Code name for Anglo-American air force project in Russian Caucuses 1942

V-1 – German unmaned missile aka "buzz bomb"

V-2 – German unmaned rocket weapon

West Point – See USMA

WW II – World War II

YAK – Russian fighter aircraft

Yalta – Conference of CCS in the Crimea February 1-10, 1945

BIBLIOGRAPHY
Books - Periodicals - Correspondence - Documents - Interviews

BOOKS

Andrews, Paul M., William H. Adams & John H. Woolnough. Bits and Pieces of the Mighty Eighth, Eighth Air Force Memorial Museum Foundation, 1991.

Bowman, Harold W., Selwyn V. Maslen. Bowman's Bombers, privately printed at Tampa, Fl, date unknown.

Bowman, Harold W., Selwyn V. Maslen. 401st B.G. Casualties in WW II, privately printed at Tampa, Fl, date unknown.

Bowman, Martin W. Castles in the Air: The Story of the B-17 Flying Fortress Crews of the Eighth Air Force, Patrick Stephens Ltd. Wellingborough, Northamptonshire, England, 1984.

Churchill, Sir Winston S. The Second World War, Vol. 5, Closing the Ring, Houghton Mifflin, Boston, MA, 1951.

Closway, Gordon R. 614th Squadron History, unpublished record of events 1943-1945, Richard Mettlen, McPherson, KS.

Closway, Gordon R. (Editor) Pictorial Record of the 401st Bomb Group, also known as the "Blue Book," Newsphoto Publishing Co., San Angelo, TX, 1946.

Deane, John R. The Strange Alliance: The Story of Our Efforts at Wartime Cooperation With Russia, Viking Press, New York, NY, 1947.

Deighton, Len Goodbye, Mickey Mouse, Alfred A. Knopf, New York, NY, 1983.

Denny, Robert. Aces: A Novel of World War II, Donald I. Fine, Inc., New York, NY, 1990.

Eveland, I. Wayne. Memories and Reflections: A Personal Story of World War II, Before and After, privately printed, 1988.

Freeman, Roger A. B-17 Fortress at War, Ian Allan Ltd. Shepperton, Surrey, England, 1990

Freeman, Roger A. B-17G Flying Fortress in World War 2, Ian Allan Ltd. Shepperton, Surrey, England, 1990

Freeman, Roger A. with Selwyn Vic Maslen & Alan Crouchman The Mighty Eighth War Diary, Janes Publishing Co. Ltd., London, England, 1981.

Freeman, Roger A. The Mighty Eighth War Manual, Janes Publishing Co. Ltd. London, England, 1984.

Freeman, Roger A. The Mighty Eighth: Units, Men and Machines (A Story of the Eighth Air Force), Janes Publishing Co. Ltd. London, England, 1970.

Freeman, Roger A. Experiences of War: The American Airman in Europe, Motorbooks International, Osceola, WI, 1991.

Harriman, W. Averell, Elie Abel. Special Envoy to Churchill and Stalin 1941-1946, Random House, New York, NY, 1975.

Henry, Lewis C. (Editor) Five Thousand Quotations For All Occasions, Doubleday Co. Inc., Garden City, NY, 1945.

Howard, James H. Roar of the Tiger, Orion Books, New York, NY, 1991.

Infield, Glenn B. Big Week, Pinnacle Books, New York, NY, 1974.

Infield, Glenn B. The Poltava Affair: A Russian Warning - An American Tragedy, Macmillan Publishing Co., New York, NY 1973.

Julian, Dr. Thomas A. Operation FRANTIC: And the Search for American - Soviet Military Collaboration 1941-1944, An unpublished dissertation, Syracuse University 1968, printed by UMI Dissertation Service, Ann Arbor, MI, 1990.

Kaplan, Philip, Rex Alan Smith. One Last Look, Abbeville Press Inc., New York, NY, 1983.

Kennan, George F. Memoirs 1925-1950, Little Brown and Co., Boston, MA, 1967.

Koger, Fred. Countdown!, Algonquin Books of Chapel Hill, Chapel Hill, NC, 1990.

Maslen, Selwyn V. 614th Squadron: Crews - Missions - Aircraft privately printed at Tampa, FL, date unknown.

Maslen, Selwyn V. 614th Bombardment Squadron (H): Squadron History, privately printed at Tampa, FL, date unknown.

New York Public Library Desk Reference, New York Public Library and Stonesong Press, Inc., Simon and Shuster, Inc. 1989.

Parton, James. Air Force Spoken Here: General Ira Eaker and Command of the Air, Adler and Adler Publishers, Inc. Bethesda, MD. 1986.

Rust, Kenn C. Eighth Air Force Story, Sun Shine House, Inc., Terra Haute, IN. 1978.

Schnatz, Helmut. Aerial Warfare in the Region of Koblenz 1944-45: A Description of its Course, Its effects and its Background, Publisher, Harald Boldt, Boppard on the Rhine, Germany, date unknown.

Spinrad, Leonard and Thelma. Speakers Lifetime Library, Prentice Hall, Englewood Cliffs, NJ, 1979.

Strong, Russell A. Biographical Directory of the Eighth Air Force, 1942-1945 (Command and Staff Officers), Sunflower University Press, Manhattan, KS, 1985.

Sunderman, Col. James F. (Editor) World War II in the Air: Europe, Van Nostrand Rheinhold Co. New York, NY, 1963.

Toland, John. The Last 100 Days, Random House, New York, NY, 1966.

Werrell, Kenneth P., Robin Higham (Editor). Eighth Air Force Bibliography: An Extended Essay and Unpublished Materials, Sunflower University Press, Manhattan, KS, 1981.

Who's Who in America 1990-1991

Woolnough, John H. The 8th Air Force Album, 8th Air Force News, Hollywood, FL, 6th printing, 1989.

NEWSPAPER AND PERIODICAL ARTICLES

The Advocate, Brown, Danny "Fatal Mission Recalled," Baton Rouge, LA, October 22, 1989

Aero Art Magazine "The Art of R.G. Smith: The Man and the Legend," Vol.1, No.1, Summer 1988, Society of Aviation Artists.

Air Britain Digest Gibson, Michael "401st Bomb Group," March- April 1980.

Arizona Daily Star "Slain Banker's Marana Friends Sad and Angry," Tucson, AZ January 9, 1982 (re death of Kenneth J. Hartsock)

Chattanooga News-Free Press, "Air Force Clears Lt. M.L. King: Was Court Martialed on Russian Complaint," Chattanooga, TN January 24. 1952.

Department of Defense Press Release No.63-52, "Former Bomber Pilot Cleared of Wartime Russian Charge," January 17, 1952.

The Evening Star "Air Force Clears Former Pilot of Soviet Charge After 7 Years," Washington, D.C. January 18, 1952.

Poop From Group, Quarterly publication of the 401st Bombardment Group (H) Association, Inc., Tampa, FL:
   March, July and December 1979 issues - biographies of
   General officers who served in the 401st.
   December 1984 issue - Trout, Ralph W. "Forever Aloft: Joseph L. Cromer August 27, 1919 - October 13, 1984"
   December 1991 issue - Sismey, Ron "A Tribute to Vic Maslen."

The Savannah Morning News, Pegler, Westbrook "As Pegler Sees It," Savannah, GA June 6, 1951.

The Savannah Morning News, Pegler, Westbrook "As Pegler Sees It," Savannah, GA July 6, 1952.

Stars and Stripes, "Eighth's Blow Sets Berlin Ablaze," published in England February 4, 1945 furnished by Donald S. Anderson as enclosure to his letter to author August 14, 1991.

Various news articles, from unidentified English publications dates of publication unknown from personal scrapbook of Allen H. Crawford loaned to the author during 1992.

Various news articles, from unidentified English publications dates of publication unknown in England from Jack Healy furnished the author by letter from Norman L. Sisson February 1992.

Various news articles from unidentified publications at Topeka, KS on unknown dates and news articles from unidentified English publications dates of publication unknown; furnished author by Norman L. Sisson as an enclosure to his letter February 13, 1991.

LETTERS

Anderson, Donald S. to author August 14, 1991.

Atkinson, George E. to Charles Phillips, Department of Veterans Affairs, Anchorage, AK May 28, 1990 furnished the author Fall 1990

Aufrance, Russell L. with enclosure to author February 27, 1991.

Browne, Mrs. Carolyn C. to author January 27, 1991.

Cameron, Elliott F. to author June 8, 1991.

Chapman, Alvah H. Jr. to author June 3, 1992.

Cranz, Edwin R. to author April 15, 1991.

Crawford, Allen H. with enclosure to author March 30, 1992.

Daves, Edward H. to author March 25, 1991.

Davidson, Robert L. to author June 17, 1991.

Dennis, Mary B., Office of the Clerk of Court, U.S. Army Legal Services Agency with enclosure re Lt. Donald Bridge to author June 21, 1991.

Doolan, Lt. Col. John A. to Myron L. King January 17, 1952 furnished to author by Myron King.

Dolin, Leon with enclosure to author July 21, 1992.

Fellows, Dr. Ward J. to author December 3, 1991.

Fox, Miriam to Myron and Eleanor King January 11, 1952 furnished author by Myron King.

Fox, Miriam to Eleanor and Myron King March 11, 1952 furnished author by Myron King.

Freeman, Roger A. to author September 24, 1990.

Gaskins, Col. Leslie E. to author May 10, 1992.

Gray, D'Wayne, Chief Benefits Director, Department of Veterans Affairs to Senator Ted Stevens August 14, 1990 re claim of George E. Atkinson furnished author by Atkinson.

Hope, John to author February 23, 1991.

Klefisch, Theodore H. to author May 4, 1992.

Lowe, Richard I. to author September 16, 1991.

Menzel, George H. V-Mail letter to Mrs, H.G. Menzel February 3, 1945

Picker, Nathan to author March 29, 1991.

Pink, Brig. Gen. Jack to author May 31, 1991.

Rundell, Col. Francis E. to author February 9, 1991.

Rundell, Col. Francis E. to author November 4, 1991.

Rundell, Col. Francis E. with enclosure to author November 12, 1991.

Schiefer, William F. with enclosure to author June 19, 1991.

Seder, Arthur R. to author January 27, 1991.

Sisson, Norman L. with enclosures to author February 13, 1991.

Sisson, Norman L. to author March 29, 1991.

Sisson, Norman L. with enclosure January 17, 1992.

Sisson, Norman L. with enclosure February 12, 1992.

Smith, Chester H. to author September 22, 1992.

Speelman, K. Hampton with enclosure to author Fall 1990.

Stauffer, Dr. David H. with enclosures to author February 5, 1991.

Stauffer, Dr. David H. to author April 2, 1991.

Stauffer, Dr. David H. with enclosure to author June 22, 1991.

Stelzer, Robert L. to author January 19, 1992.

Stehman, Robert M. to author June 27, 1992.

Trout, Ralph M. to author October 20, 1990.

Utter, Charles W. with enclosures January 25, 1991.

Zaborsky, Stephen A. to author March 5, 1991.

DOCUMENTS

Atkinson, George E. – Honorable Discharge from the Army of the United States at Santa Ana, California December 1, 1945, furnished by Atkinson.

Atkinson, George E. – Signed sworn statement at Eighth Air Force Headquarters June 22, 1945 furnished by Atkinson.

Babcock, Capt. Frederick H. – official 614th Squadron mission record card furnished author as enclosure to letter November 26, 1990.

Babcock, Capt. Frederick H. – "Individual Flight Record" known as Form 5 furnished author as enclosure to letter November 26, 1990.

Chapman, Capt. Alvah H. Jr., Acting Squadron Commander – Letter of Commendation to "All concerned" November 23, 1944.

Chapman, Major Alvah H. Jr., dated December 29, 1944 commendation to crews (614th Squadron) participating in operations between December 19-26, 1944.

Doolan, Lt. Col. John A. – Letter to Judge Advocate General USAF bearing handwritten notes of Doolan, subject: Myron L. King dated December 27, 1951 furnished author by Myron King.

Doolan, Lt. Col. John A. - letter to Judge Advocate General, Department of the Air Force transmitting a Petition for a New Trial on behalf of Myron L. King, furnished the author by Myron King (including the above petition).

Healy, Jack - Portions of personal log furnished the author as an enclosure to a letter from Norman L. Sisson February 1992.

Magee, Pilot Officer John Gillespie, Jr. - Poem "High Flight."

National Air and Space Museum, Smithsonian Institution - Letter to author dated May 22, 1992 enclosing Aircraft Record Card for B-17G serial number 44-6508.

National Archives, Suitland, MD Reference Branch - Record Group 18, Mission Reports of 401st Bombardment Group (H).

National Archives, Suitland MD Branch – Record Group 92, Microfilm No. 4474, MPCR No. 12213.

National Archives, Suitland MD Branch – Record Group 84 Foreign Service Posts, U.S. Department of State; U.S Embassy Moscow, typewritten note from GFK (George F. Kennan) to Mr. Ambassador (W. Averell Harriman) June 2, 1945.

National Archives, Suitland MD Branch – Record Branch 84 Foreign Service Posts, U. S. Department of State; U.S. Embassy Moscow, "Shenderoff Affair" file.

National Archives, Washington, D.C. – Record Group 334 Interservice Agencies, U.S. Military Mission to Moscow as follows:

Box 10, Cable file in the case of Myron L. King.

Box 10, note captioned "receipt" for custody of Soviet Engineer Captain M.I. Shenderoff.

Box 18, biographic information concerning Lt. Col. James D. Wilmeth..

Box 6, letter Gen. John R. Deane to Gen. N.V. Slavin April 11, 1945.

Box 6, Memorandum described as a recording of meeting at O.V.S. (Soviet Military Liaison Headquarters, Moscow) April 17, 1945.

Box 6, Memorandum described as a recording of a meeting at Red Army Staff Headquarters, Moscow April 16, 1945 subject: Operation of United States Aircraft in Soviet Occupied Territories.

Box 6, Memorandum described as a recording of a meeting at O.V.S. April 26, 1945.

Box 6, Letter of Reprimand from Major General John R. Deane to Myron L. King May 10, 1945.

Box 63, sub file: Adjutant General - letter Gen Edmund W. Hill to Marshal of Aviation S.A. Khudyakov.

Box 63, sub file: Adjutant General - miscellaneous cables between USMM and Eastern Command at Poltava during April 1945.

Box 63, sub file: FRANTIC Accidents - Following items related to fatal vehicular accident involving Sgt. George E. Atkinson:

1. Letter of transmittal from Captain George Fincher AC Adjutant, Eastern Command to Commanding General USMM on April 25, 1945 setting forth results of Investigation and enclosing Exhibit A Investigating Officer's Report, Exhibit C Accident Report Form WD 39 and Exhibit G Individual statements of six witnesses.

2. Report of Claims Officer, U.S. Claims Commission U.S.S.R. and action taken May 31, 1945 and numerous enclosures including: Exhibit N Recommendations for Disciplinary Action, Exhibit 1 to Par.8 of report on deposition of Maria Andreevna Tverdochev.

All of the following sub files in Record Group 334:

Courts-Martial
Downed aircraft
Flight clearances
Meetings with the Soviets
      Office memoranda
      Personnel:
            (1) General
            (2) Military Mission
      Poland
      Yalta Conference
      Closing

Picker, Nathan – Personal log furnished the author as an enclosure to letter from Norman L. Sisson February 13, 1991.

Sisson, Norman L. – Personal log and Bomb fuse tag collection furnished author as enclosure to Sisson's letter February 13, 1991.

Sisson, Norman L. – "Captains of Aircraft Map" for briefed mission to Berlin August 27, 1944 as an enclosure to letter Norman L. Sisson to the author February 13, 1991.

U.S. Army TWX communication BMP (Brampton Grange) to DPE (Deenethorpe) April 29, 1945 signed TURNER COMAIRDIV ONE furnished author from 614th Squadron memorabilia by Richard Mettlen.

U.S. Army – Memorandum from Lt. Col. Bert A. Arnold AGD to Military Attache, U.S. Embassy, London July 1, 1945; subject reimbursement for Sgt. George Edward Atkinson furnished author by Atkinson.

U.S. Army – Letter from JAGD, Department of the Army to Adjutant General's Office, Department of the Army January 9, 1952 with endorsement of the Adjutant General's Office January 11, 1952 to declassify documents in the Court Martial case of Myron L. King furnished author by Myron L. King.

U.S. Army – Memorandum from Col. M.W. Pettigrew GSC to Col. Richards, subject: Claim of Sgt. George E. Atkinson August 22, 1945 furnished to author by Atkinson.

U.S. Army – Letter from HQ.ASF, JAGO, Washington, D.C. to WDGS (1) Personnel Division G-1 and (2) Military Intelligence G-2 signed Col. Ralph G. Boyd JAGD Chief of Claims Division. Date stamp in 1945 unreadable; subject: claim by Sgt. George E. Atkinson and furnished author by Atkinson.

U.S. Army Air Forces – Movement Orders 370.5-1008 (198-20) July 7, 1944 Headquarters, 271st Staging Base, Kearney AAF, Nebraska. Furnished by Norman L. Sisson as enclosure to his letter to the author February 13, 1991.

U.S. Army Air Forces – General Orders 114 Headquarters 1st Air Division, Eighth Air Force February 7, 1945 conferring Distinguished Flying Cross on Lt. Norman L. Sisson furnished as an enclosure to Sisson's letter February 13, 1991.

U.S. Army Air Forces – Special Orders No.1, Headquarters, 401st Bombardment Group (H) May 24, 1945 re Shipment 10034-D (A) furnished author by Harold M. Kennard, Jr.

U.S. Army Air Forces - Special Orders No.1, Headquarters, 401st Bombardment Group (H) re Shipment 10034-E (A) furnished the author by Robert L. Davidson.

U.S. Army Air Forces – Special Orders No. 268, Headquarters Santa Ana AAB CA November 7, 1945 furnished the author by George E. Atkinson.

U.S. Air Force – Letter from Lt. Col. Charles E. Wainwright, USAF, Office of the Judge Advocate General to Lt. Col. John A. Doolan December 18, 1951 including hand written notes of Doolan furnished author by Myron L. King.

U.S. Air Force Historical Research Center, Reference Division, Maxwell AFB, AL as follows: Microfilm records of the 401st Bombardment Group (H) including rolls BO488, BO489 and AO647 furnished the author June 13, 1991 and October 19, 1991.

Various cables between USMM and Eastern Command at Poltava February to June 1945.

U.S. Army Legal Services Agency – The Court Martial File in the case of Lt. Myron L. King made available for review by Mary B. Dennis, Office of the Clerk of Court on June 22,

1991. With particular interest are the following documents from that file:

Report of Captain William Fitchen AC dated March 19, 1945 in the investigation of the case involving Myron L. King. (A copy of this report was also a part of the Cable File in the King case.)

Report of Major Donald S. Nicholson AC dated March 28, 1945 in the investigation of the incident which involved Myron L. King and crew.(A copy of this report was also found as a part of the Cable File in the King case.)

Record of Trial of Myron L. King by General Court Martial, April 25-26, 1945 at the American Embassy, Moscow U.S.S.R. (Spaso House). Copy of this trial transcript was made available to the author by King.

Copy of the dissenting opinion of Judge Advocate Herman Moyse, on the Board of Review for the JAGD dated July 17, 1945 in the Myron King case.

Copy of Memorandum for Gen. Cramer incorporating the majority opinion of the Board of Review by Judge Advocates Col. Terry A. Lyon and Charles A. Luckie of the JAGD dated July 17, 1945, in the Myron King case.

Copy of "Memorandum Opinion" by Major General Reginald C. Harmon Judge Advocate General USAF, on the Petition of Myron L. King dated January 11, 1952.

U. S. Army Legal Services Agency – Letter and enclosures setting forth the details of the trial by General Court Martial of Lt. Donald R. Bridge in Italy on April 25, 1945. Letter from Mary B. Dennis, Office of the Clerk of Court to the author June 21, 1991.

Veterans Administration Form 21-4138 "Statement in Support of Claim signed by George E. Atkinson September 27, 1990 furnished the author by Atkinson.

INTERVIEWS

Althoff, John R. – telephone inquiry January 3, 1993.

Atkinson, George E. – numerous telephone inquiries between August and October 1990 and June 5, 1992.

De Vito, Mrs. Rosemary – telephone inquiry October 2, 1990.

Dolin, Leon – telephone inquiry July 6, 1992.

King, Myron L. – Interview at Nashville, TE June 9, 1992 and telephone inquiries September 22, 1992 and January 20, 1993.

Lowe, Richard I. – telephone inquiry January 3, 1993.

Pink, Brig. Gen. Jack – telephone inquiry June 3, 1991.

Reinoehl, Philip A. – telephone inquiry October 4, 1990.

Rostrom, C. Richard – telephone inquiry February 17, 1993.

Rundell, Francis E. – telephone inquiry April 4, 1992.

Smith, R.G. – telephone inquiries on several dates in 1990.

Speelman, K. Hampton – telephone inquiry August 26, 1990.

Stauffer, Dr. David H. – telephone inquiry July 14, 1992.

Veterans Affairs, Department of – telephone inquiry to Regional Office, Atlanta, GA September 4, 1991 for information concerning Robert E. Pyne.

APPENDIX

The following pages are items of interest to this story which are listed below arranged in the order in which they are mentioned specifically or alluded to.

1. Certificate of combat service with the 401st Bombardment Group. Preface
2. Commendation letter, Captain Alvah H. Chapman, Jr. dated November 23, 1944 to crews on the Merseburg mission on November 21, 1944. Chapter 10.
3. Commendation letter, Major Alvah H. Chapman, Jr. dated December 29,1944 to crews participating in operations between December 19-26, 1944. Chapter11.
4. Three page DR Navigation Certificate, Eighth Air Force. Chapter 12.
5. Author's V-Mail letter to his mother dated February 3, 1945. Chapter 14.
6. Three formation charts of the lead, high and low squadrons for mission to Berlin on February 3, 1945. Chapter 14.
7. Special Orders #46 Eastern Command; travel orders March 29, 1945 for King crew to leave Poltava for England later rescinded. Chapter 17.
8. Copy of statement of Lt. W. J. Sweeney dictated by Lt. Col. James D. Wilmeth used as Exhibit #1 during King court martial trial. Chapter 18.
9. Copy of certified translated two page letter to General John R. Deane dated March 30, 1945 from General Antonov, Chief of the Red Army General Staff used as Exhibit #2 during King court martial trial. Chapter 18.

401st Bomb Gp. H

Certificate of Combat Service

This is to certify that

1st Lt GEORGE H. MENZEL, O-782938, 614th Bomb Squadron, 401st Bomb Group (H)

completed an operational tour of duty in the European Theater of Operations as of the

31st   *day of*   March 1945.

Operational Record

OPERATIONAL MISSIONS: Completed thirty-five (35) actual missions.
DEMONSTRATED PROFICIENCY: Excellent.
RECOMMENDED DUTY: Instructional Duties in Zone of Interior.
AWARDS & DECORATIONS: Air Medal per GO#524, Hq 1st Bomb Div, 14 Nov 44.
    1st Oak Leaf Cluster to AM per GO#612, Hq 1st Bomb Div, 11 Dec 44.
    2nd Oak Leaf Cluster to AM per GO#20, Hq 1st Air Div, 8 Jan 45.
    3rd Oak Leaf Cluster to AM per GO#214, Hq 1st Air Div, 11 Mar 45.
    4th Oak Leaf Cluster to AM per GO#260, Hq 1st Air Div, 3 Apr 45.
    5th Oak Leaf Cluster to AM per GO#272, Hq 1st Air Div, 1 Apr 45.
BRONZE SERVICE STAR, Ltr Hq ETO, AG 200.6 OpCA, 5 Feb 45 - "Germany."
BRONZE SERVICE STAR, GO-40 WD 45 - "Ardennes"
BRONZE SERVICE STAR, GO-40 WD 45 - "Central Europe"
BRONZE SERVICE STAR, GO-40 WD 45 - "Rhineland"

SIGNATURE OF COMMANDING OFFICER

WILLIA. T. SEAWELL, Lt Col., Air Corps.

Certificate of Combat Service with the 401st Bombardment Group (H) Preface

SUBJECT: Commendation   23 November 1944

TO: All Concerned

    1. On Tuesday, the 21st of November, the 401st Group with the 614th leading, gave the German Air and Ground Defenses all the odds in their favor and still bored in and put bombs in the target area of one of their most vital targets, the oil refinery at Merseburg.

    2. The determination to make a difficult bomb run, shown by every crew that participated in the mission, does credit to the past traditions of the Squadron and justifies the long hours and tedious work done by our ground crews. It is the desire of the Squadron Commander to commend every man of the air echelon who participated in the mission, as well as every man of the ground echelon, who put the ships over the target.

    3. The Squadron suffered the loss of one of the finest crews ever to be a member of the outfit. Lt. Rundell and his crew had an excellent record and were destined to become a lead team of excellent capabilities.

    4. The work of the two new crews which were flying the mission is especially deserving of praise. Lt. White's crew with Lt. Hoeman as co-pilot, and Lt. Thompson's crew with Lt. Hosley as co-pilot, performed their duties splendidly under fire.

    5. (a) Lt. Mays and Lt. Wittman did excellent jobs of getting their ships over the target and keeping formation on the withdrawal despite the handicap of flying formation on instruments with only three engines.

    (b) Lt. Gaskins, Lt. Aufrance and S/Sgt. Grasela were all wounded in action, and each man remained calm and unexcited and attempted to perform their duties in spite of their wounds. Lt.Gaskins' work was especially commendable in that he returned to the waist from the nose, after being wounded himself, in order to treat the wounds of Sgt. Grasela.

    (c) It is desired to commend:

    1. Captain Charles M. Smith, for an excellent job of navigating the formation during the entire mission in that no flak was encountered except in the target area while preceding and following formations in the column lost aircraft both on the flight to the target and on the withdrawal. This excellent navigation was performed in spite of the fact that the nose of the lead aircraft was without sufficient oxygen.

    2. Lt. Mercer, whose excellent job of flying the lead ship on instruments manually, on the bomb run and on the withdrawal, enabled the formation to keep as many ships together as possible under the instrument conditions.

    3. T/Sgt. Fowler, who remained in his upper turret despite a shattered glass which caused him to suffer immensely from the cold.

    5. The excellent airmanship demonstrated by the following pilots and their crews, and their determination to go after a rough target at an unfavorable altitude, is worthy of commendation by the Squadron Commander: Lt. Mercer, Lt. Rundell, Lt. White, Lt. Hoeman, Lt. Mays, Lt. Wittman, Lt. Richardson, Lt. Muesel, Lt. Sisson, Lt. Babcock, Lt. Thompson, Lt. Hosley.

    6. The Hun has many "rough" targets but he will find that they don't come too rough for "Heaven's Hellions."

    Alvah H. Chapman Jr., Captain, Air Corps, Actg. Sq. Commander.

Commendation for 614th Squadron crews on the November 21, 1944 mission to Merseburg. Chapter 10

614th Bombardment Squadron (H)
401st Bombardment Group (K)
AAF Station #128
APO 557, U.S. Army

SUBJECT: Commendation   29 December 1944

TO: All Concerned

1. It is the desire of the undersigned to commend each man on the combat crews mentioned below for outstanding devotion to duty during the period from the 19th to the 26th of December.

2. The majority of the crews were away from the base from the 19th to the 26th of December. During this time, most of these crews flew one mission from a base other than their home base. The hardships usually associated with a diversion were present, to a degree not usually found and, in addition, it was the coldest week in 76 years of English cold. Handicapped by lack of proper facilities for food, warmth and sleep, the spirit displayed by all these men was nevertheless indomitable. The desire to help the ground forces in Europe at a time when our help was urgently needed was predominant and overcame all physical handicaps.

3. The Squadron Commander has no words to express his appreciation for the sight that greeted him on Christmas morning at Loverham when crews, six days away from home, some having to go to war in battle-damaged and improperly serviced ships, with not a gripe to be heard. Their only concern was that they might lose their chance to help the boys on the other side. Such spirit deserves the highest of commendations.

4. Lt. Spuhler's, Lt. St. Aubyn's and Lt. Babcock's crews were alerted on the night of the 23rd and spent the entire night servicing their own ships at other fields in order to take off and join the Group for the mission.

5. The crews it is desired to commend are: Lt. Spuhler's entire crew, Lt. St. Aubyn's entire crew, Lt. Babcock's entire crew, Lt. R. Thompson's entire crew, Capt. Seder's entire crew, Lt. White's entire crew, Lt. Moran's entire crew, Lt.Crozier's entire crew, Lt. Richardson's entire crew, Lt. Uttor's entire crew, Lt. Fondron's entire crew, Lt. Morton's entire crew, Lt. King's entire crew, Lt. H.L. Thompson's entire crew, Lt. Mercer's entire crew.

6. It is desired that a copy of this letter be given to each man concerned.

Alvah H. Chapman Jr., Major, Air Corps, Acting Sq. Commander

Commendation for 614th Squadron crews which participated in operations between December 19th and December 26th, 1944. Chapter 11.

D. R. NAVIGATION   CERTIFICATE

DR Navigation Certification Certificate, Chapter 12.

HEADQUARTERS EIGHTH AIR FORCE
Officer of the Commanding General
APO 634

Certificate

Date: 24 March 1945

1. This is to certify that 2nd Lt. G.H. Menzel, Bombardier, having satisfactorily completed a course of instruction in accordance with Eighth Air Force Memorandum 50-7, is qualified to act as NAVIGATOR on flights involving the use of dead reckoning navigation, pilotage, and the use of radio aids.

2. The course of instruction has included the following:

    a. Ground Training

        (1) Dead Reckoning Navigation

            (a) Basic Principles

            (b) Air Plot and its Value in This Theater

            (c) Methods of Obtaining Winds

            (d) Log Book Procedure

            (e) Maps and Projections used operationally in This Theater

            (f) Navigational Aids Obtained Through VHF on Operational Flights

        (2) Pin-Point Navigation

            (a) The Most Reliable Check Points to be Used in This Theater

            (b) Correct Procedure in Doing Pin-Point Navigation

            (c) Advantages of Pin-Point Navigation as Compared to Pilotage

        (3) Signals, Aids and Equipment

            (a) Radio Aids in the United Kingdom

                1. Theory of GEE and its Operation

                2. Radio, Compass and Beacons

                3. Radio Flimsies and Their Use

            (b) Code: Aural - 8 words per minute

                Visual - 6 words per minute

            (c) Navigational Aids That Are Obtained Through the Radio Operator

            (d) Emergency Procedure

        (4) Night Flying Procedure

            (a) Navigational Aids Available to Night Fying

            (b) "Q" Sites

          (5) Instruments and Equipment
               (a) Use of the E6-B Computer
               (b) Compasses
                   <u>1.</u> Theory of Magnetism
                   <u>2.</u> Advantages of Remote Indicating Compasses
                   <u>3.</u> Gyro-Fluxgate Remote Indicating Compass or,
                   <u>3.</u> Magnesyn Remote Indicating Compass
               (c) B-5 Driftmeter
               (d) Astro-Compass
               (e) Care of Navigation Equipment
               (f) Calibration of Airspeed Indicator and Altimeter
               (g) Use of the Bomb Sight and the A.B. Computer as a
                    Navigational Aid

b. Flying Training. A minimum of 15 hours flying as navigator on which the following have been accomplished:

          (1) One fix taken by use of the radio compass and plotted every 30 minutes
          (2) Air-plot kept and winds determined every 30 minutes of flight
          (3) Complete log-book kept with all navigational data entered
          (4) Demonstrated ability to pin-point by map-reading
          (5) Demonstrated ability to take and plot fixes by GEE, selecting proper chain of stations
          (6) Demonstrated crew co-operation in duties required of a navigator

c. Examination. Satisfactory grade of 80 percent on the Navigation Exam, pages 2-3 through 2-7 in the *Eighth Air Force Group Navigator's Handbook* and the Quiz on Signals, Aids and Equipment, pages 4-12 through 4-14, also from the *Group Navigator's Handbook*.

By command of Lieutenant General Doolittle:

William T. Seawell
Commanding Officer
401st Bombardment Group

James F. Eagan
Group Navigator

William A. Sherwin
Lt. Colonel, A.C.
Executive to Deputy C/S Operations

Frederick Stugard Jr.
Major, Air Corps
Air Force Navigator

Enlargement of V-Mail letter to author's mother after February 3, 1945 mission to Berlin. Chapter 14.

LEAD SQUADRON, 94TH "B" GROUP

CAPT. LOCHER

CAPT. STELZER   3 FEB. 1945

CAPT. STELZER

613

RIEGLER (LOCHER)

401ST FORMATION AT TAKE-OFF
449 PFF   CRUISE, AND OVER TARGET

SPEER (MALONEY)   TAUSIG (STELZER)

132   550 PFF

613   614

SCHELLER   BABCOCK

113   596

CAREY   COX   RICHARDSON   MORAN

862   607   012   677

CURRAN

072

KELSO   HART

791   706

NIELSON

588 (SPARE RETURNED)

Lead squadron formation February 3, 1945; mission to Berlin. Chapter 14.

HIGH SQUADRON, 94TH "B" GROUP

LT. HASKETT

3 FEB. 1945

LT. TURK

CAPT. STELZER

613

HASKETT

608 PFF

CALLAHAN
425

TURK
077

615

614

JONES
669

THOMPSON, R.
646

MAIRE
779

JORDAN
551

KING
508

HARTSOCK
458

DJERNES
468

SMITH
730

CRACRAFT
983

STEPHENS

113 (SPARE RETURNED)

High Squadron formation February 3, 1945; mission to Berlin. Chapter 14.

LOW SQUADRON, 94TH "B" GROUP

LT. SCHAUNAMAN

3 FEB. 1945

LT. ASCHENBACH

CAPT. STELZER

612

SCHAUNAMAN

153 PFF

LOVELL   ASCHENBACH

788 (ABORT RETURNED)   993

612   614

ROADMAN   ST. AUBYN

662   738

FRENCH   COMER   WHITE   STAUFFER

506   341   478   602

SCHLIEMANN

059

SMITH   HUDNALL

628   680

HOWARD

393

Low squadron formation February 3, 1945; mission to Berlin. Chapter 14.

Headquarters, Eastern Command
U.S. Strategic Air Forces in Europe
APO 790   U.S. Army

Special Orders   AAF Station 559
Number 46   Extract   29 March 1945

3. Fol pers will proceed to London, England, reporting upon arrival thereat to Escape Officer, Headquarters, Eighth Air Force. Travel by rail, surface vessel, belligerent vessel, and/or air in mil or commercial acft atzd. O atzd per diem alws of seven dollars ($7.00) per day while traveling and while absent fr perm sta in accordance with existing laws and regulations. Eld atzd per diem alws of seven dollars ($7.00) per day while traveling by air. At such times as Eld are not traveling by air and govt qrs or billets and messing facilities are not available, monetary alws in lieu of rations and qrs as prescribed by Sec II, Change 5, AR 35-4520, 21 January 1944, atzd. Air priority authorization will be alloted by the Air Priorities O, Persian Gulf Command, APO 523, U.S. Army, TCNT. TDN. 60-137 P 431-02, 03,04, 07, 08 A 212/50425.

Capt. J. Ernst, 0763979, AC	1st Lt. M.E. Jensen, 0779877, AC
1st Lt. M.L. King, 0828453, AC	1st Lt. A.S. Rothstein, 0832017, AC
2nd Lt. J.R. Bogardus, 0835132, AC	2nd Lt. J. Adromomitz, 02069899, AC
2nd Lt. J. Cassels, 0780517, AC	2nd Lt. C.E. Lavkin, 0783791, AC
2nd Lt. W.J. Sweeney, 0829101, AC	2nd Lt. R.I. Lowe, 02065794, AC
2nd Lt. L.W. Clark, 02072418, AC	F/O C.L. Kemp, T5214
F/O R.R. Scroizan, T133964	F/O R.P. Geyser, T132266
2nd Lt. R.J. Kofroticz, 0835221, AC	2nd Lt. S.G. Elkins, 0757166, AC
F/O D.V.Dryson, T134538	T/Sgt. P.T. Dempsey, 12135037
S/Sgt. William T. Fraser, 14101397	S/Sgt. J. Brown, 13099869
S/Sgt. L.R. Genoway, 18077498	S/Sgt. T.L. Gallagher, 37672375
S/Sgt. J.T. Palmer, 17118282	S/Sgt. C.F. Friel, 33792888
S/Sgt. R.E. Pyne, 19087650	S/Sgt. E.S. Ravlas, 38461292
S/Sgt. P.A. DeVito, 12211585	S/Sgt. A.T. Kester, 19181843
Sgt. J.F. Rahrer, 16056763	Sgt. R. Winfrey, 37105423
Sgt. R. Sass, 33508655	Sgt. J.F. Kohl, 35050200
Sgt. M. Griffith, 39575287	Sgt. C.L. Kivero, 16099002
Sgt. S. Wojcick, 36875557	Sgt. N.C. Schemdri, 19111942
Sgt. H.B. Hodges, 34816725	Sgt. J.F. Mason, 33631254
Sgt. E.C. Porter, 31323441	Sgt. J.E. Phillips, 14177028
Sgt. G.O. Dragon, 13179779	Sgt. C.E. Atkinson, 39720163
Sgt. D.G. Plaut, 14154552	Sgt. K.H. Speedman, 35296011
Sgt. P.A. Reinokhl, 35896310	Sgt. J.J. Murphy, 19215713
Sgt. U.B. Melton, 6346768	

By order of Colonel Hampton: Official, George Fischer, Captain, AC, Adjutant. Distribution C,

Charges against Lt. King were ordered on March 27th yet two days later these orders were issued for the crew to leave the Soviet Union. They were unable to leave until late April. These orders were referred to in Chapter 17.

Summary of Evidence
in case of

614 Bomb Sqdn.
King, Myron L.   0-828453   1st Lt.   401 Bomb Group

Expected Testimony

"The accused is senior pilot in aircraft of which I am co-pilot. On February 5, 1945, he allowed an alien, whom he discovered in our plane before take-off, to travel in the plane, flying in formation with a Russian airplane which carried a Russian General directing our flight, between an airdrome near Warsaw, Poland to Szczuzyn, Poland. Upon completion of flight and until the afternoon of February 6, 1945, he permitted this alien to wear an American flyer's clothes and to be associated with ourselves and other crew members and to call himself 'Jack Smith,' a name known not to be his own."

W.J. Sweeney, 2nd Lt., 0-829101,AC.

The above statement was dictated by Lt. Col. Wilmeth and signed by Lt. Sweeney. It was admitted as an exhibit during the King trial over defense objections described in Chapter 18.

Major General John R. Deane
Chief, United States Military
Mission in U.S.S.R.

Dear General Deane:

This is to bring to your attention that the Soviet Command, on the basis of an Allied relationship, is giving the necessary help to the American crews and planes making forced landings on territory occupied by the Red Army. However, we have a number of instances when crews of American airplanes and individual military personnel of the American Army rudely violate the order established by the Command of the Red Army in territory occupied by the Soviet troops, and do not live up to elementary rules of a relationship between friendly nations. For instance:

1. On 5 February 1945, an American B-17 airplane, Lieutenant Myron King, commander of the plane, made a landing at Kuflevo (Poland) where, without the knowledge of the Soviet military command, he took a civilian in the plane for the purpose of taking him to England.

After this, Lieutenant Myron King's plane made a second landing at the Shchuchin Airdrome, where the person taken on the plane gave himself first of all as a member of the crew of the plane, with the name Jack Smith, and the crew covered him. And only after interference by the Soviet Command, Lieutenant King announced that this was not a member of the crew but a stranger whom they did not know and took on board the airplane to take him away to England.

On further questioning, this civilian person admitted that the name Jack Smith was fictitious and that actually he was a Pole. According to our information he is a terrorist-saboteur brought into Poland from London.

2. On 22 March 1945, on the airdrome occupied by the Soviet air force at the city of Meletc, an American Liberator plane made a landing, supposedly for lack of fuel. The crew of the plane, 10 people. Commander of the plane, Donald Bridge. The plane was placed under guard. The crew was fed and put up for the night, and the plane refueled. The senior Soviet Chief on this airdrome, Colonel Kozhemykin, personally, through an interpreter, at 1000 hours, 24th of March, forbid the commander of the Liberator ship to fly the plane away from the airdrome before receiving proper permission.

At 1500 hours, 24 March 1945, the crew asked for permission to check the plane for their belongings, which was granted. The crew, on going into the plane, started up the engines and regardless of the signals given from the place of start forbidding the flight, took off from the place where it was parked.

In this manner, regardless of the fact that the crew was afforded friendly assistance and

Certified copy of two page letter to General Deane from General Antonov March 30, 1945. This letter was the controversial exhibit admitted as an exhibit during the King trial. It was the contention of the prosecutor that the letter was a complaint which brought discredit on the military service of the United States. Lt. Bridge, par. 2 was also Court Martialed but no action was taken against Lt. Col. Wilmeth, par. 3. Chapter 18 hospitality, the American crew rudely violated military discipline and, through deception, took off from the airdrome.

These actions of the American crew called forth extreme indignation and perplexity on the part of the personnel of the Red Army air force. A Soviet engineer, Captain Melamedov, who accepted Donald Bridge's crew, was so indignant and put out by this instance that on the very same day he shot himself.

3. Lieutenant Colonel Wilmeth, of the American Army, was permitted to make the trip from Moscow to Lublin to get acquainted on the spot with the situation of the former prisoners of war-Americans. The period for Lieutenant Colonel Wilmeth's stay in Lublin was established as up to the 11th of March 1945. At the end of the established period of Lieutenant Colonel Wilmeth's visit in Lublin, an airplane was made available for him to return to the place of his permanent work in Moscow. However, Lieutenant Colonel Wilmeth refused to leave for Moscow, with the excuse that he did not have instructions from General Deane to return to Moscow, and that he did not consider it necessary for him to hold to the established time of the visit in Lublin.

The facts listed are a rude violation of the elementary rights of our friendly mutual relationship.

I am obliged to remind you that the obligation assumed by you on a strict observance by American military personnel of the order established by the Command of the Red Army on territory occupied by Soviet troops, with regrets, is not being carried out.

I request you to take the necessary measures to keep us from a repetition of such instances of rude violation of the order established by the Command of the Red Army on territory occupied by Soviet troops.

Please inform me on the measures taken by you.

Sincerely yours,
/s/ ANTONOV
General of the Army
Chief of the Red Army General Staff

I certify that the original letter in Russian is in the files of the U.S. Military Mission, Moscow: *Howard R. Taylor, Major, AUS, Official Custodian. Translated by Henry H. Ware, Captain, AUS.*

INDEX

The book relates to stories of the life of a B-17 Flying Fortress, its crews, and those other crews which flew with them in combat. Since that aircraft was a part of the 614th Squadron in the 401st Bomb Group no effort has been made to index the extensive mention of those two units. The Author also apologizes to those whose military rank herein is of a lesser grade than they earned during or after WWII.

Printed in the USA
CPSIA information can be obtained
at www.ICGtesting.com
JSHW022215140824
68134JS00018B/1069

9 781681 623528